The Jurisprudential Foundations of Corporate and Commercial Law

This collection brings together new essays by some of the most prominent scholars currently writing in commercial law theory. The essays address the foundations of efficiency analysis as the dominant theoretical paradigm in contemporary corporate and commercial law scholarship.

Some of the questions addressed in the volume are: What are the historical roots of efficiency analysis in contract, sales, and corporate law? Is moral theory irrelevant to efficiency analysis in these areas? If moral theory is relevant, are morality and efficiency compatible? Even if efficiency is otherwise reasonable as a normative goal in corporate and commercial law, does the complexity of efficiency make it practical to administer in adjudication? What role should custom play in contract interpretation? Do efficiency concerns favor plain meaning or incorporationist methods of contract intepretation? What is the best way of pursuing efficiency in corporate and commercial law?

The volume reflects the most exciting work being done in contemporary legal theory. It will be of interest to professionals and students in law and philosophy of law.

Jody S. Kraus is Professor of Law and E. James Kelly, Jr., Research Professor of Law at the University of Virginia School of Law. He is author of *The Limits of Hobbesian Contractarianism* (1994).

Steven D. Walt is Professor of Law and Nicholas E. Chimicles Research Professor of Business Law and Regulation at the University of Virginia School of Law. He is the author (with Clayton P. Gillette) of *Sales Law: Domestic and International* (1999).

Cambridge Studies in Philosophy and Law

Other books in the series:

Jeffrie G. Murphy and Jean Hampton: *Forgiveness and Mercy*
Stephen R. Munzer: *A Theory of Property*
R. G. Frey and Christopher W. Morris (eds.): *Liability and Responsibility: Essays in Law and Morals*
Robert F. Schopp: *Automatism, Insanity, and the Psychology of Criminal Responsibility*
Steven J. Burton: *Judging in Good Faith*
Jules Coleman: *Risks and Wrongs*
Suzanne Uniacke: *Permissible Killing: The Self-Defense Justification of Homicide*
Jules Coleman and Allen Buchanan (eds.): *In Harm's Way: Essays in Honor of Joel Feinberg*
Warren F. Schwartz (ed.): *Justice in Immigration*
John Fischer and Mark Ravizza: *Responsibility and Control*
R. A. Duff (ed.): *Philosophy and the Criminal Law*
Larry Alexander (ed.): *Constitutionalism*
Robert F. Schopp: *Legal Positivism in American Jurisprudence*
William Edmundson: *Three Anarchical Fallacies: An Essay on Political Authority*
Arthur Ripstein: *Equality, Responsibility, and the Law*
Heidi M. Hurd: *Moral Combat*
Steven J. Burton: The Path of the Law *and Its Influence*

The Jurisprudential Foundations of Corporate and Commercial Law

Edited by

Jody S. Kraus

University of Virginia School of Law

Steven D. Walt

University of Virginia School of Law

CAMBRIDGE
UNIVERSITY PRESS

CAMBRIDGE UNIVERSITY PRESS
Cambridge, New York, Melbourne, Madrid, Cape Town, Singapore, São Paulo

Cambridge University Press
The Edinburgh Building, Cambridge CB2 8RU, UK

Published in the United States of America by Cambridge University Press, New York

www.cambridge.org
Information on this title: www.cambridge.org/9780521591577

First published 2000
This digitally printed version 2007

A catalogue record for this publication is available from the British Library

Library of Congress Cataloguing in Publication data

The jurisprudential foundations of corporate and commercial law / edited by Jody S.
Kraus, Steven D. Walt
p. cm. – (Cambridge studies in philosophy and law)
Includes bibliographical references.
ISBN 0-521-59157-0 (hb)
1. Commercial law – Philosophy. 2. Corporation law – Philosophy. I. Kraus, Jody S. II.
Walt, Steven D. III. Series.
K1005 .J87 2000
346.07′01–dc21 99-053684

ISBN 978-0-521-59157-7 hardback
ISBN 978-0-521-03876-8 paperback

Contents

Contributors

RICHARD CRASWELL, Professor of Law, Stanford Law School

DANIEL A. FARBER, Henry J. Fletcher Professor of Law and Associate Dean for Faculty, University of Minnesota

LEWIS A. KORNHAUSER, Alfred and Gail Engelberg Professor of Law, New York University

JODY S. KRAUS, Professor of Law and E. James Kelly, Jr., Research Professor of Law, University of Virginia

ALAN SCHWARTZ, Sterling Professor of Law, Yale University

ROBERT E. SCOTT, Dean and Lewis F. Powell, Jr., Professor of Law, University of Virginia

STEVEN D. WALT, Professor of Law and Nicholas E. Chimicles Research Professor of Business Law and Regulation, University of Virginia

Introduction

Efficiency is the dominant theoretical paradigm in contemporary corporate and commercial law scholarship. The jurisprudential foundations of corporate and commercial law, then, are the foundations of efficiency analysis. They present a mix of historical, moral, and methodological questions, as well as issues of institutional design. What are the historical roots of efficiency analysis in contract, sales, and corporate law? Is moral theory irrelevant to efficiency analysis in these areas? If moral theory is relevant, are morality and efficiency compatible? Even if efficiency is otherwise reasonable as a normative goal in corporate and commercial law, does the complexity of efficiency make it practical to administer in adjudication? What is the best way of pursuing efficiency in corporate and commercial law? The essays in this volume address one or more of these jurisprudential questions.

The historical roots of efficiency analysis. In Chapter 1, "Karl Llewellyn and the Origins of Contract Theory," Alan Schwartz argues that Llewellyn was an important proponent of the modern law and economics approach to regulating contracts. The received view of Llewellyn depicts him as a rule-sceptic who sometimes advocated the regulation of sales contracts by standards other than economic efficiency. Schwartz rejects the received view, based on a critical evaluation of Llewellyn's writings on sales law between 1925 and 1940. Llewellyn's proposals, as efforts at law reform, assumed the existence and efficacy of legal rules regulating sales contracts, and only sought to replace bad rules with better ones. According to Schwartz, Llewellyn argued that the state should reduce contracting costs and create default rules, and used economic considerations to understand parties' contracting behavior. Llewellyn simply made mistakes in the efficiency analyses upon which he based his recommended rules. These mistakes, Schwartz suggests, were due to the immature state of the economics of Llewellyn's day, not to a concern to promote values other than efficiency. Some of Llewellyn's recommended rules are outdated because the economic theory of his time was too primitive to offer policy analysts much help. When devising rules to regulate contracts, analysts today can draw on advances in the economics of information, finance theory, and transaction cost economics. These results were unavailable to efficiency-minded contract theorists in the first half of the century.

Schwartz's rejection of the received view is novel and promising. It allows a range of reassessments of Llewellyn that fall between rule-scepticism and a hostility to law reform proposals based on efficiency. Schwartz's depiction of Llewellyn's position, for instance, describes one of a number of possibilities. Another position would diagnose Llewellyn's shortcomings as simple failures to use then-current research techniques and results. This is because some of Llewellyn's proposed rules are inadequate even by the standards and knowledge available to Llewellyn. Llewellyn's defense of both the mailbox rule for when acceptance becomes effective as well as his notion of substantive unconscionability rely on the reasonable expectations of a party. The defense rests on a circularity in reasoning, as Schwartz notes. The current state of law partly grounds expectations it is reasonable to have. Thus, to justify the law by those expectations presupposes the law which they are to justify. This is a straightforward failure in analysis, which was apparent to David Hume in the somewhat similar context of promise-keeping and should have been familar to Llewellyn. Theoretical considerations were not needed to show him the circularity. There is also the failure to abide by research and sampling techniques known to Llewellyn's contemporaries. Llewellyn, and some other legal realists, generated proposed rules on the basis of unsystematic samplings of appellate caselaw. Restricting a survey to caselaw exposes one to selection effects exhibited by litigated cases, and the further restriction to appellate cases can exacerbate them. Llewellyn's methodological mistake was avoidable even by the analytic standards or sampling techniques of his day. Of course, it is possible that some of Llewellyn's proposals were marred by a failure to take into account then-contemporary learning, while other proposals were marred by the then-primitive state of economic theory.

Efficiency and morality. Daniel Farber assumes that commercial transactions implicate morality and argues that morality underwrites the use of efficiency principles in commercial law. In Chapter 2, "Economic Efficiency and the Ex Ante Perspective," he finds that the application of the efficiency principle to commercial law can derive from a moral theory. Farber uses Rawlsian hypothetical consent to justify a suitably constrained principle of Pareto efficiency as a principle of adjudication. His analysis relies on conclusions of the classic debate over the normative foundations of the economic analysis of law. According to Farber, the debate justifies four propositions: (1) Economic efficiency cannot be the sole principle of justice, (2) the ex ante perspective produces an economic efficiency rule only in the absence of risk aversion, (3) prospective legislation can properly use an ex ante perspective in selecting rules, and (4) economic efficiency requires a prior decision about the initial allocation of resources. Farber follows Rawls in assuming that Rawls' principles of justice apply to the basic structure of society, not to detailed questions of institutional design. He acknowledges that principles of adjudication, like all principles of nonbasic institutional design, are subordinate to the principles of justice. Subject to this constraint, Farber maintains that the original position can be used as a device for selecting an impartial principle of adjudication.

Farber adopts Rawls' suggestion that ideally just legislation is the legislation ideal legislators would agree to behind a thin veil of ignorance that allows them to know the general facts about their particular society. He argues that this "second stage" Rawlsian inquiry can be modified to justify a principle of adjudication. Ideal legislators, according to Farber, would agree to a limited principle of efficiency for adjudication if they were not risk-averse or did not have to undergo shifts in preferences dramatic enough to constitute a change in personal identity. Farber concludes that such a principle is both fair to litigants and, at least in a limited domain, reasonably administrable by judges. It is fair because the common law process embeds the practice of finding new principles, such as the efficiency principle, in past cases. An efficiency principle is administrable by judges because they will sometimes be able to rely on established economic theory to decide cases and mitigate the effects of error by limiting the principle's application to default rules.

Farber's argument raises a large question about the applicability of morality to commercial transactions. Simply put, does morality apply to commercial contexts to restrict the principles that properly regulate private ordering in commercial transactions? Three positions can be taken on the relation between morality and commercial contexts: (1) Some aspects of morality such as distributive justice are inapplicable to commercial transactions and the rules governing them[1]; (2) distributive justice is applicable to such transactions and rules but wrong as a substantive moral matter to use to evaluate them; and (3) distributive justice is applicable to commercial transactions and rules but itself allows other principles to be used to evaluate them. Position (1) is implausible. Distributive justice seems to apply in commercial settings. After all, whatever elses it involves, distributive justice involves the distribution of benefits and burdens to individuals.[2] What it requires, of course, is another matter. Whether morality requires that commercial transactions be tested by principles of distributive justice is a question of substantive moral truth. That distributive justice applies in commercial contexts does not guarantee that morality gives priority to distributive justice over all other moral values. Thus, the implausibility of position (1), the "inapplicability" position, still leaves both positions (2) and (3) possible. Although a discussion of the details of the positions is beyond this introduction's scope, Farber's argument for the moral permissibility of efficiency principles illustrates the difficulty of offering a compelling argument for either position.

Farber follows Rawls in assuming that distributive justice applies only to what Rawls describes as the basic structure, not to commercial transactions occurring within it. The assumption is a version of position (1). In fact, however, Farber's argument for the use of an efficiency principle in adjudication can be understood as based on either position (1) or (3). According to Farber, parties in a variant of the original position would prefer courts to select legal rules to govern routine contractual transactions that maximize joint satisfaction of contracting parties. They would do so because basic institutions are assumed to satisfy Rawls' principles, and routine transactions do not affect individual rights or mandated wealth distributions. Farber therefore proposes that distributive justice would not condemn the use of efficiency principles to evaluate commercial transactions. The proposal does not evaluate routine transactions by principles of distributive justice.

Now the proposal faces the following dilemma: It either restricts distributive justice to basic institutions or it does not guarantee the parties' selection of satisfaction-maximizing rules. For the order in which the parties select principles is crucial to the argument and needs to be justified. Farber supposes that parties first select principles of justice to govern the basic institutions and then select principles to govern routine contractual transactions. This order of approach is justified if distributive justice is restricted to the basic institutions. In that case, distributive justice has nothing to say about routine transactions because it is inapplicable to them. Given this justification, Farber's argument therefore supports position (1), not position (3). But the prima facie applicability of distributive justice to commercial settings again makes position (1), "inapplicability," independently implausible.

Alternatively, distributive justice applies to both basic institutions and routine transactions. The exercise is to select principles to govern both environments. In that case, there is nothing inevitable about Farber's preferred order of selection – first select principles of justice to govern the basic structure and then select principles that govern routine transactions within it. Another order for choosing principles could result in different principles selected. For instance, under a "basic structure first" approach, principles P could be selected for the basic structure and principles P' for routine transactions. But under a simultaneous selection of principles, principles R might be selected, where R applies to both sorts of items. Or different principles, R and R', might be selected for application to different items. And R (and R') might be cast in terms of distributive justice, not preference satisfaction. Neither Rawls nor Farber provides a reason to prefer one approach over the other. Thus, parties might choose rules that evaluate routine transactions from a distributive perspective.[3]

An illustration of the importance of order in rule selection is helpful. Bankruptcy law largely consists of rules allocating the cost of the debtor's financial distress. Assuming that the choice of rule is partly a matter of justice, and that justice turns on the hypothetical choices of affected parties under suitably specified conditions, the rule chosen will depend on other rules in effect. If other rules already in effect guarantee debtors, creditors, or third parties a level of welfare, for instance, they might select bankruptcy rules that maximize their expected utility. Without that guarantee, they might be risk-averse and select a rule that assures them a minimum level of welfare.[4] Parties, for instance, in the circumstances might prefer a bankruptcy discharge because it assures them of control over the postpetition returns on their human capital. Given the discharge, affected parties might be risk-neutral and select corporate bankruptcy rules that maximize expected wealth. Crucial to the choice of a bankruptcy rule is the attitude toward risk associated with each rule, and the attitude therefore can vary depending on other rules in effect. The order in which rules are selected is not inevitable. To impose a particular order on the selection of rules – for example, by assuming that the basic structure satisfies certain principles and then asking about the choice of a bankruptcy rule – requires defense.

The complexity of efficiency-based adjudication. Lewis Kornhauser is less optimistic than Farber about the use of efficiency principles in adjudication. Complexity in the notion of efficiency is a barrier to its application. Kornhauser assumes that efficiency concerns predominate in corporate and commercial law, where well-informed, profit-maximizing parties typically engage in arm's-length transactions. But the pursuit of efficiency, according to Kornhauser in Chapter 3, "Constrained Optimization: Corporate Law and the Maximization of Social Welfare," is far more complex than is typically recognized in the law and economics literature. Kornhauser first demonstrates how legal rules influence a large number decisions made by corporate and commercial actors, even though the rule that is best with respect to one decision need not be best with respect to another decision. Developing and segregating rules that are efficient for each decision is difficult. Because the information possessed by courts and commercial actors is likely to be both imperfect and distributed asymmetrically, only second- and third-best legal rules may be available. Kornhauser further argues that it may be impossible to specify an appropriate maximand under uncertainty. If actors must act without knowledge of the satisfaction of all decision-relevant factors, the evaluation of a legal rule will depend on an appropriate probabilistic weighting of potential outcomes. Probabilistic assessments based on both actors' and policymakers' beliefs create either problems of consistency or objectionable policy prescriptions. Kornhauser concludes that both actor- and policymaker-assessed conceptions of social welfare are not completely satisfactory.

Kornhauser argues for a more modest role for efficiency in commercial and corporate law. In a complex commercial world, judges cannot plausibly achieve efficiency or wealth maximization by consciously aiming to do so. Kornhauser therefore questions the wisdom of courts directly pursuing efficiency or wealth maximization. Judges, he speculates, nonetheless might indirectly pursue efficiency by pursuing it only within a particular doctrinal domain.

Whether Kornhauser's doubts about the use of efficiency criteria are justified obviously depends on the purpose for which such criteria are being used. Are they used to measure social welfare or are they used only as rough but reliable enough proxies for social welfare? Objections to the former sort of use need not be telling against the latter sort of use. Both uses raise questions of morality, but they are different questions. This point is illustrated by Kornhauser's criticism of cost/benefit analysis (CBA). One of Kornhauser's concerns is that CBA appears to require that different affected parties' beliefs about social states be aggregated by summation. His objection is that the summation of individual valuations of social states involves the summation of beliefs about the likelihood of their realization. Roughly, CBA assesses a social state by the maximum amount of money parties will pay, or the minimum amount they will demand, to have that state realized. These amounts depend on parties' beliefs about likelihoods, and with incomplete information, parties (and policymakers) can have different beliefs. Thus, in evaluating social states by summing amounts affected parties will pay or demand, CBA seems to be summing beliefs across individuals. This is at least conceptually odd and, even if possible, almost certainly very often morally undesirable.

Whether Kornhauser's argument marks a failing in CBA depends on how CBA itself is understood. CBA could be taken as either as a *direct test* of aggregate well-being or as a *justified decision procedure* in which there is potential conflict.[5] As a direct test, CBA measures well-being by the amount of money a person is willing to pay or accept, and the amount depends on his or her beliefs about the likelihood of an eventuality occurring. Summing monetary amounts to test aggregate well-being therefore arguably requires the summation of beliefs. This demand is conceptually questionable. If Peter believes that x and Paul believes that *not-x,* summing their conflicting beliefs is incoherent. Even if the summation were coherent, if welfare is being measured directly, and welfare depends on beliefs about the likelihood of social states, then some way is needed to select among beliefs to resolve the conflict. Kornhauser is right that summation of conflicting beliefs is not the most attractive way to proceed. Summation is too unreliable as part of a test of well-being in a social state.

Summation of belief, however, is unnecessary if CBA is understood only as a justifiable decision procedure. Here there is no assumption that beliefs must be aggregated in any way. Monetary amounts associated with each social state are offered or demanded by affected parties, and these amounts are summed. (CBA presumably is committed to holding that the amounts indirectly test individual, subjective welfare.) How individual parties arrive at these amounts is irrelevant for CBA because CBA is not directly testing well-being. The analysis is only being offered as a justified way of making social decisions, including decisions where parties have conflicting beliefs about the likelihood of social states. Thus, CBA can proceed by taking conflicting beliefs as given and assessing social states only by a willingness to pay or be compensated. After all, CBA is a way of implementing a criterion of social choice based on potential Pareto improvements, and potential Pareto improvements do not require that all affected parties' well-being in fact is left unchanged or improved. CBA need not therefore directly test well-being, including the resolution of conflicting beliefs via any sort of aggregation.

Understood as a justified decision procedure, CBA avoids other difficulties. Kornhauser correctly observes that if policymakers want to maximize social welfare, based in part on the beliefs of affected parties, they can do so by altering those beliefs. This seems undesirable if one's concern is for well-being, not a party's expectations about well-being. As a decision procedure, however, CBA need not endorse the engineering of belief as a policy prescription. In general, a justified decision procedure is one thing; when and how it is properly used are other matters. Although each turns on moral concerns, the relevant moral concerns can be different. Even if CBA is a justified procedure, this does not mean that policymakers properly can arrange things to influence the result of the procedure's application by engineering beliefs, for instance. Doing so raises moral concerns other than the justification of CBA as a decision procedure, and CBA's decision procedure says nothing about these matters. Of course, for all of this, CBA still might be a bad decision procedure to use.

Implementing efficiency through the incorporation strategy. The complexity of implementing an efficiency-based adjudication principle suggests that judges might be ill-suited to create efficient rules, even in corporate and commercial law contexts. But it may be possible to determine a relatively efficient legal solution to corporate and commercial law problems without attempting to design such solutions. If commercial actors follow commercial norms, and these norms themselves are likely to be efficient, judges might create efficient legal rules simply by incorporating the norms into substantive legal rules. A growing literature asks whether commercial norms are likely to provide a suitable source for efficient commercial default rules.[6] There is also a separate question whether they are likely to provide an appropriate basis for interpreting the express and implied terms in commercial contracts. The remaining contributions to the volume consider the case for and against incorporating commercial practice through the judicial interpretative process.

In Chapter 4, "Do Trade Customs Exist?," Richard Craswell considers Karl Llewellyn's incorporation strategy for default rules and judicial interpretation. Craswell rejects the view that trade customs can be identified independently of the goals and beliefs of the person who attempts to identify such customs. Thus, trade custom cannot plausibly be viewed as merely a pattern or regularity in merchants' behavior or beliefs held subjectively by industry members in the form of bright-line rules. Because a pattern of behavior is subject to many different interpretations, it does not alone determine a unique custom. Similarly, because subjective beliefs by industry members are case-specific, many different interpretations of a trade custom might account for them. Craswell makes the point by relying on the philosophy of language. Custom, like linguistic meaning, cannot plausibly be viewed as taking the form of bright-line rules. Just as meaning is determined by contextual cues, through what philosophers call "pragmatic implication," custom has a context-specific character rather than a clear semantic meaning. Thus, Craswell maintains that custom consists in industry members' own case-by-case judgments about proper behavior, the judgments taking a form that often cannot be reduced to bright-line rules. Because custom turns on judgment rather than simple empirical fact, Craswell argues that the judgment of courts, expert economists, and philosophers might be equally reliable bases for determining custom as the judgment of merchants. After examining a range of appellate decisions, Craswell concludes that courts often exercise their own judgments in determining the content of commercial custom.

It is fair to ask about the implications of Craswell's characterization of custom for the incorporation strategy. Craswell acknowledges that standards of behavior in an industry often exist, even though they might be difficult to identify and frequently are not statable as bright-line rules. Contrary to the title of his chapter (and as he acknowledges), Craswell does not deny that trade usage exists. The question therefore is how, and whether, contract terms should be interpreted by custom. There is an infinite number of true descriptions of any pattern of behavior, and selecting among them to identify custom can be difficult. The selection of a description also can involve normative evaluation of the behavior, here as with any piece of behavior. This does not by itself impugn the use of custom to interpret contract terms. Certainly there are ways of implementing the incorporation strategy that are inconsistent with the judgment-based notion of custom described by Craswell. For instance, simple frequency requirements for behavioral regularities fail to distinguish mere regularities from the prescriptive standards of custom. The judgment-based nature of custom also makes some allocations of fact finding between judge and jury more defensible than others. For instance, given the vagueness of much custom, allocating the finding of custom to a lay jury risks a higher rate of interpretive error than allocating it to a judge. Both examples show that there are better and worse ways of incorporating custom into contracts, not that incorporation is not a good idea. The incorporation strategy is unjustified only if it either produces inefficient equilibria or cannot be feasibly implemented.

In Chapter 5, "Rethinking the Uniformity Norm in Commercial Law," Robert Scott focuses on the incorporation strategy in Article 2 of the Uniform Commercial Code. Scott views the principal task of sales law to be the efficient regulation of incomplete contracts. Courts must both accurately interpret parties' contracts and provide both standardized, "predefined" meanings for contract terms as well as default terms to fill in gaps in incomplete contracts. Scott argues that accurate interpretation and efficient standardization are inconsistent goals. No single interpretive regime can pursue both without constraint. Scott suggests that the common law, which largely prohibits the use of commercial custom to interpret the meaning of express terms, provides a far superior compromise to Article 2's incorporation strategy, which requires express terms to be interpreted in light of commercial custom. He concludes that Article 2 combines the worst of both worlds: uncertainty and thus unpredictability of contractual interpretation, few predefined express terms, and inefficient default rules. According to Scott, Article 2's failure is that it is too much of a "true" code. Because Article 2 encourages courts to ignore precedent and look to the code itself for the interpretation of express terms and for gap-filling, it undermines its own objective of incorporating commercial practice effectively. In contrast, the common law "plain-meaning" regime, Scott argues, has generated clear and predictable meaning while facilitating the development of predefined terms and relatively efficient default terms.

Central to Scott's argument is a speculation about the source of Article 2's failure to defensibly incorporate commercial practice. Since accurate interpretation and supplying standardized meanings are inconsistent goals, neither common law or statutory schemes can pursue both without constraint. The question therefore is whether common law interpretive schemes produce more accurate and efficient standardized meanings than are produced by Article 2. This is an empirical question, and Scott's speculation has testable implications. The trouble is, however, that the implications are difficult to specify with any precision. If Scott is right that Article 2's nature of a "true" code inhibits the updating of commercial practice, changes in industry practice are less likely to induce judicial reexamination of the meaning of trade terms. Thus, other things being equal, less judicial reinterpretation of trade terms would be expected under Article 2 than at common law. For the same reason, less reinterpretation would be expected under Article 2 than under codes that are not "true" codes, or less so. Scott's speculation predicts that there is less reinterpretation of custom under Article 2 than under the Uniform Sales Act. However, other things might not be equal. Common law doctrines about trade usage and its admissibility could operate to inhibit the rate at which custom is judicially updated.[7] In general, doctrinal and evidentiary matters can produce the same treatment of custom as is produced by a relatively self-contained statute such as Article 2. The potential equivalence in result makes Scott's hypothesis hard to evaluate.

In Chapter 6, "In Defense of the Incorporation Strategy," Jody Kraus and Steven Walt agree with Scott's central observation: All interpretive regimes face a trade-off between minimizing the costs parties incur to specify their most desired terms and minimizing the probability of judicial error in interpreting the express and implied terms of their contracts. Thus, in their view, any optimizing solution requires the minimization of the sum of specification and interpretive error costs. Speculation of the size of these costs must be made at the margin. This does not condemn the incorporation strategy. Acknowledging the complexity of interpreting custom and the inherent difficulties in creating a code that effectively incorporates commercial practice, Kraus and Walt suggest that the incorporation strategy nonetheless is likely to create lower aggregate specification and error costs than alternative regimes for interpreting contracts among heterogenous contracting parties. Kraus and Walt offer a two-stage argument in support. First, anti-incorporationists overlook or underestimate the magnitude of the specification cost savings that can be achieved under an effective incorporation regime. Second, they presume that the defects of Article 2's implementation of the incorporation strategy provide strong evidence of the failure of the incorporation strategy generally. But because the incorporation strategy can be implemented in many ways, criticism of Article 2 only serves to suggest revisions that would reduce or eliminate defects; it does not undermine the incorporation strategy. Kraus and Walt consider three different critiques of Article 2's incorporation strategy and argue that each overestimates the magnitude of interpretive error costs and underestimates the magnitude of specification costs compared to "plain-meaning" interpretive regimes. They also suggest possible amendments or alternatives to Article 2 that could reduce its relative interpretive error rates and lower specification costs even further.

As Kraus and Walt acknowledge, their analysis is incomplete. Specification costs and interpretive error costs are only two of a number of variables relevant to the efficiency of an interpretive regime. Intrepretive regimes also affect the frequency and sort of contracts entered into, as well as their performance. Contract formation and performance therefore are endogenous variables that require estimation. For example, if parties' performance over the course of the contract is deemed relevant to the contract's terms, the cost of deviating from express terms is increased. The expected stream of benefits from entering into a contract with that possibility might be low enough to dissuade parties from contracting in the first place. A full assessment of efficiency of an interpretive regime must estimate its effect on contracting and performance, not just on the ex ante costs of formulating contract terms and ex post enforcement costs. Such an assessment is difficult to make, not only because reliable information about the values of all of the variables is hard to come by and intuitions must suffice. More serious is the problem flagged by Kornhauser, that a complete efficiency analysis requires comparing costs associated with competing legal rules across all variables. This requires gauging all of the potential contracting parties affected by a legal rule, identifying affected decisions, and estimating the impact of the rule on the different decisions of potential contracting parties. Kraus and Walt's analysis, as well as the analysis of antiincorporationists, must be modest because it considers only a small subset of variables relevant to the efficiency of an interpretive regime.

Notes

1. See F. A. Hayek, 2 *Law, Legislation and Liberty: The Mirage of Social Justice* 33, 70, 78 (1976), H. B. Acton, *The Morals of the Market and Related Essays* 104 (1993). Karl Marx arguably held the position in the case of societies in the final stage of communism; see Karl Marx, "The Critique of the Gotha Program," *The Marx-Engels Reader* 525 (2d ed., R. Tucker, ed., 1978).
2. See G. A. Cohen, *Where the Action Is: On the Site of Distributive Justice,* 26 Phil. & Pub. Aff. 3, 12 (1997). For a critical assessment of default rules based on fairness to the contracting parties, see Alan Schwartz, *The Default Rule Paradigm and the Limits of Contract Law,* 3 S. Cal. Inter. L. J. 389, 402 (1993).
3. For an early paper that recognizes the point, see Anthony T. Kronman, *Contract law and Distributive Justice,* 89 Yale L. J. 472, 501 (1980).
4. For an example of an exercise in which the order of rule selection is simply assumed, see Donald R. Korobkin, *Contractarianism and the Normative Foundations of Bankruptcy Law,* 71 Tex. L. Rev. 541 (1993); for an example of the choice of products liability rule that recognizes the point in the text, see Alan Schwartz, *Proposals for Products Liability Reform: A Theoretical Synthesis,* 97 Yale L. J. 353, 359–60 (1988).
5. David Brink makes a similar distinction between criteria of right-making and a decision procedure. See David O. Brink, *Moral Realism and the Foundations of Ethics* 256–9 (1989); cf. Matthew Adler, *Incommensurability and Cost-Benefit Analysis,* 146 U. Pa. L. Rev. 1371, 1373, 1407–8 (1998).
6. See, e.g., Jody S. Kraus, *Legal Design and the Evolution of Commercial Norms,* 26 J. Leg. Stud. 377 (1997); Eric A. Posner, *Law, Economics, and Efficient Norms,* 144 U. Pa. L. Rev. 1765 (1996); Michael Klausner, *Corporations, Corporate Law, and Network Externalities,* 81 Va. L. Rev. 767 (1995).
7. See *Brandao v. Barnett* (1846) 12 Cl. & Fin. 748 (Lord Campbell) (usage established by prior decisions need not be supported by new evidence).

1

Karl Llewellyn and the Origins of Contract Theory

ALAN SCHWARTZ[†]

I. Introduction

Karl Llewellyn was America's leading legal realist, academic law reformer, and contract law theorist. There are extensive analyses of Llewellyn's performance as a realist and reformer, but his contracts scholarship, written between 1925 and 1940, has not been seriously analyzed.[1] As an example, William Twining's famous study answered the question of what of Llewellyn should be read today as follows: "A number of essays on specific topics are still of value, and this is particularly the case with most of the articles on contract and commercial law of the middle period." But Twining did not analyze any of these articles in detail in a 533-page book.[2] Similarly, a recent major collection of readings on legal realism has a single chapter on contracts that is twenty-one pages long and has only a two-page excerpt from one Llewellyn contracts article – (3) – that does not set out his views on any contract issue.[3] Modern scholars commonly infer Llewellyn's views on contract theory from early drafts of the Uniform Commercial Code, from the Code itself, or from Llewellyn's later jurisprudential writings.[4]

The attention that modern scholars pay to Llewellyn and a citation analysis of his work confirm that Llewellyn's contract theory has current relevance.[5] This chapter evaluates the theory through an analysis of the contracts articles themselves. Turning to the sources sometimes is unnecessary for a figure who is as well known as Llewellyn, but is necessary here because the usual references are not illuminating. UCC drafts, especially those after 1941, reflected the work of several authors as well as what it was politically acceptable to say.[6] There also are marked differences between the Llewellyn to whom modern scholars commonly refer and the Llewellyn who created the theory (or perhaps differences between the earlier and later Llewellyns).[7]

That Llewellyn's contracts scholarship is largely unread is unsurprising: The articles are opaque to nonspecialists and difficult even for experts. The readability problem should be stressed at the outset because it renders tentative any conclusions about what Llewellyn actually believed. The problem does not stem from Llewellyn's inability to write an English sentence or his colorful prose. Llewellyn could write lucidly, but the papers are difficult because Llewellyn pursued multiple objectives when writing them, and overestimated the typical reader's knowledge. A discussion of warranty, for example, will also be a discussion about why warranty doctrine was often confused and how sales law should be regulated generally. Llewellyn commonly expressed views on such issues interstitially, in the context of historical discussions of the law and of business practice (as Llewellyn conceived it) that ranged over a century and covered England and the United States. The papers also assume an audience who had read everything Llewellyn had read, and who had it as clearly in mind when reading as Llewellyn had when writing. Thus the warranty articles cite over a hundred cases but give the facts of a handful; readers apparently are expected to know the facts and holdings of the other cases. A criticism of the rules respecting a buyer's rights when receiving a defective tender assumes that readers know the nineteenth and twentieth century law on conditions, waiver, and damages. Nonspecialists quickly get lost and specialists have problems. These difficulties and others detailed below imply that no interpretation can be definitive, and this one attempts to be cautious.

Before turning to Llewellyn's theory, a few remarks should be made about this chapter's nature and scope. The chapter treats Llewellyn's contracts articles as if they were chapters in the same book. This ahistorical approach to Llewellyn's thought is taken for two reasons. First, ten of the thirteen works were written between 1936 and 1940, and so were contemporaneous in fact. Second, while his analysis grew richer in the period analyzed here, Llewellyn's basic views did not change.

Turning to issues of scope, to understand a theoretical contribution fully requires at least these inquiries: (1) What was the state of theory when the contribution was made? (2) What led up to that state and what changed later? (3) What was the context of discovery for the scholar himself (what did he personally know, read, and so forth)? (4) What was the social setting in the profession (how were new ideas received)? (5) What cultural and ideological factors outside the field of study were influential? (6) What epistemological and thematic notions (*i.e.*, what would a good theory be like?) did the scholar hold? There has been little scholarship concerning questions (1), (3), (4), and (6) in connection with Llewellyn's contract theory, and not a great deal on (2) and (5). No chapter-length treatment can fill this gap. This chapter's contribution rather is to set out the theory itself in a preliminary way, to evaluate this tentative rendering, and to make a few speculations concerning the second and sixth inquiries.

Part II below sets out Llewellyn's theory as a whole and without citation to the work. Documentation, illustration, and critique follow. This part attempts to do what Llewellyn did not – to set the theory out in one place. As said above,

Llewellyn scattered his theoretical ideas interstitially throughout his writings. Turning directly to the articles thus would be confusing. Part III begins with an illustration of Llewellyn's approach to resolving sales issues, then shows how he thought custom could illuminate adjudication and rule making, and finally elaborates the institutional aspect of the theory – what legal rules could do, who should make them, and what form they should take. Part IV illustrates how Llewellyn found what he believed were the real legal rules (as contrasted with the rules that were taught in law schools), and then analyzes typical Llewellyn law reform proposals. The object here is to see how Llewellyn attempted to solve concrete problems. Part V next examines the freedom of contract aspect of Llewellyn's theory, which has the greatest contemporary relevance. Part VI is a conclusion.

An essay about Llewellyn's contract theory could have two sets of addressees: scholars working today on contract or sales issues who may look to the theory for illumination; and scholars interested in Llewellyn's other work or in legal realism, who may want to know what light Llewellyn's contract theory throws on these broader matters. This essay is addressed primarily to the former group. It argues that Llewellyn's general approach to the legal regulation of contracts remains valuable but his solutions to specific legal problems often are unhelpful. This partly is because many of the economic techniques needed to analyze these problems had not been developed when Llewellyn wrote. Llewellyn's limited knowledge of actual commercial behavior and his failure to pursue his ideas systematically also flawed the work. Regarding this chapter's broader implications, many of the notes below form a subtext that argues that there are important inconsistencies between what Llewellyn and other realists are said to believe and the ideas expressed in Llewellyn's contract articles. This subtext is briefly developed in the conclusion.

II. The Theory

Llewellyn's contract theory was meant to tell decisionmakers how to regulate sales transactions. The decisionmakers in the theory were courts and law reform organizations such as the National Conference of Commissioners on Uniform State Laws; legislatures played a minor role. The theory had a substantive aspect (what the legal rules should be) and an institutional aspect (which legal institutions should make the rules and what form the rules should take). Both aspects of the theory implied views that would be regarded as conventional in today's law and economics world.

A theory directed to decisionmakers should identify and motivate its norms. Law reformers then were concerned with efficiency and redistribution. Llewellyn believed that distributional goals had no place in a contract theory because the commercial actors in the theory commonly occupied the two relevant roles of buyer and seller. This multiplicity of roles would vitiate the pursuit of distributional ends, for what a party would gain when wearing her seller hat she would lose when wearing her buyer hat. The regnant norm in Llewellyn's contract theory thus was efficiency, as then understood. Llewellyn never explicitly justified the pursuit of efficiency. Rather, he believed that American society had accepted the efficiency norm and he did as well.

A. The Substantive Aspect

The substantive aspect of Llewellyn's contract theory followed from four premises:

1. Courts should interpret contracts in light of the parties' commercial objectives and the context in which they dealt.
2. Decisionmakers should complete incomplete contracts with rules that reflect the deal typical parties would make in the circumstances.
3. A court should not enforce a contract without an independent inquiry into its substantive fairness if one party's consent to the contract was unconscionably procured.
4. Decisionmakers should reduce the transaction costs of doing deals.

Versions of these premises (except perhaps the fourth) were held by others when Llewellyn wrote. Llewellyn took the first two premises more seriously than his contemporaries did, however. He believed that the typical court or law reformer viewed the commercial world through the distorting lens of taught legal doctrine. This produced the incorrect interpretations and flawed rules that much of his work sought to correct. Llewellyn also was more concerned than other scholars of his time with the question of when the state should restrict private contract. The most original aspect of Llewellyn's work, however, lay not in his recognition of the relevance of these four premises, but rather in the many provocative substantive and institutional implications he drew from them.

Law and economics scholars today commonly attempt to develop contract rules by identifying the cost-minimizing solution to a contracting problem. Thus, an analyst will develop a model to show what contract term respecting damages would be efficient for a particular transaction type. The scholar then will recommend that the law adopt this term as the default solution when the parties' contract is silent concerning damages. Llewellyn seldom worked in this way because the economics of his time were too primitive. Continuing with the example, optimal contract terms respecting damages today are derived as the equilibria of asymmetric information contracting games.[8] Game theory had not been developed when Llewellyn wrote, so he could not identify game theoretic solutions to the particular contracting problems his theory had to solve.

Llewellyn thus worked "indirectly": He used commercial practice as the best evidence of the efficient transaction. Parties, he believed, pursued their self-interest when contracting (maximized their expected utility). Hence, the parties' consent to a deal was good evidence that the deal was efficient. It was this method of analysis that made Llewellyn sensitive to freedom of contract issues. When one party dictated the contract terms, an analyst could infer only that those terms maximized the utility of the powerful party, not that the deal was globally efficient. Dictation would occur, in Llewellyn's view, if one party had structural market power or was more knowledgeable or sophisticated than the other. Such "fiat contracts" lacked the epistemological relevance of "bargained for" contracts. Consequently, courts must make an independent inquiry into a contract's normative suitability when a party's consent to the contract was not conscionably procured. To use practice as evidence of efficiency, that is, requires a theory of unconscionability.[9]

Llewellyn also interestingly pursued several implications of his epistemological view that common practice commonly is efficient. The typical judge, he thought, seldom could discern the parties' commercial goals, but a judge could become sophisticated by repeated acquaintance with the facts. Thus Llewellyn was ambivalent regarding the ability of courts to develop good commercial law rules. Judges of unusual ability with an interest in commerce could do well, as could judges on courts that saw many commercial cases. But the ordinary judge needed help. Such judges could find help from three sources: arbitrators, custom, and trade association rules. Arbitrators were helpful, in Llewellyn's view, because they had the expertise to identify the deal the parties actually made.

Llewellyn had a nuanced view of custom and trade associations. He believed that trade custom could be good evidence of the efficient arrangement, but also that the existence of a custom often was irrelevant to adjudication. Custom commonly is challenged in law suits: The party against whom the custom is asserted claims that the custom does not exist or does not apply to the case at bar. Llewellyn was sympathetic to these challenges. Customs, he thought, reflected the solutions to normal business problems, but the disputes that came to court often were caused by exogenous economic shocks. A custom meant to govern in normal times could shed no light on the efficient resolution of unusual – "trouble" – cases. Rather, the court or law reformer must develop the best solution directly.

Llewellyn was similarly cautious regarding the epistemological relevance of trade association rules. If all parties whom a rule affects are represented in the trade association, the rule is a contract between parties of equal bargaining power, and as such is good evidence of the efficient arrangement. Trade associations, however, often imposed rules on outsiders such as unorganized consumers, and these rules were like contracts between parties of unequal bargaining power; one could not conclude that such a rule was efficient just because the sophisticated side of the market liked it.

To summarize the substantive aspect of Llewellyn's thought, Llewellyn believed that decisionmakers should enforce, facilitate, and enact efficient commercial arrangements. The decisionmaker could infer the efficient solution from what parties commonly did. Llewellyn's frequent references to the parties' goals, their deals, custom, and rules of the trade thus were epistemological in intention. What is out there is evidence, but not always reliable evidence, of what maximizes social welfare. Contrary to Llewellyn's reputation among some modern scholars, he did not believe that decisionmakers could infer values from facts, nor did he think that the state should delegate lawmaking power to private groups.

When practice did not supply reliable evidence of efficiency, Llewellyn sometimes would derive the transaction cost-minimizing solution directly. For example, he argued that sellers should be permitted to sue for the price when buyers rejected in distant markets. After rejection, either the buyer or the seller could mitigate damages by reselling the goods. A successful price action would force the buyer to resell because the buyer would become the owner. It is efficient to make distant rejecting buyers resell because these buyers have a comparative advantage at maximizing resale revenue: The goods are in the buyer's market, and the buyer commonly knows that market well.

B. The Institutional Aspect

Contract law rules performed three functions in Llewellyn's theory: to fill gaps in incomplete contracts; to develop and apply appropriate constraints on the parties' freedom to contract; and to direct or "channel" the adjudicator's fact-finding function. Creating rules to perform these functions requires expertise, and the rules themselves must be clear. The need for expertise underlay Llewellyn's view that commercial law rules are best created by administrative agencies or specialized law reform organizations. Llewellyn's stress on rule clarity presupposed the ability of rules to guide parties and constrain courts, and Llewellyn accepted this presupposition. Rule scepticism played no role in his theory. Legal rules, he thought, also should ask courts to find facts – which party had possession of the goods when the fire struck? – rather than require conceptual analysis – which party had title when the fire struck? Llewellyn, however, rejected conceptual analysis only at the level of rule application. Otherwise, he admired this form of analysis and sometimes did it.

Llewellyn's thought about rules written for commercial codes was a major exception to these views. Llewellyn believed that codes were difficult to amend, and so would have to be applied in quite varied commercial circumstances. As a consequence, code rules should not reflect solutions to specific contracting problems, but rather should constitute normative premises for reasoning or channel the courts' fact-finding function. Llewellyn's position concerning the appropriate level of abstraction for UCC rules thus did not reflect his thought on rules generally.

C. Critique

Llewellyn's general substantive and institutional approaches to sales and contract law rules remain relevant. Modern law and economics scholars believe, with Llewellyn, that the state should pursue efficiency in the contract area because efficiency is the only implementable goal. And efficiency should be pursued, by and large, in the ways that Llewellyn advocated: Courts should enforce the deals that parties make, which requires courts to understand the economics of commercial transactions; and doctrine or statute should attempt to reduce the costs to parties of making deals by choosing as the default solution the efficient contract term. Llewellyn's major achievement was to develop this general approach to the legal analysis of contract.

Many of Llewellyn's specific analyses, however, rest on errors and it is therefore a mistake to rely on his recommendations for what should be done in concrete cases. Without the concepts and tools of modern economic analysis, Llewellyn could not understand how market power is acquired and exercised, and so his unconscionability theories are too primitive. He did have perceptive insights respecting when rules should be mandatory or defaults and which transaction costs the state likely could reduce. But because Llewellyn could not understand these concepts as moderns do, his work often is unhelpful. It must also be said, however, that Llewellyn sometimes did not satisfy the standards of his time. Other realists recognized that more can be learned about the world by studying it directly than can be learned from Llewellyn's method of reading appellate opinions with particular attention to the facts. And consistency in thought has always been a virtue. A perhaps illuminating way to summarize this chapter's critique is to remark that Newton's theory remains true over much of the domain it was created to explain, but a fair amount of Llewellyn's work is not true in this sense because it never was true.

III. Norms, Rules and Institutions

A. Norms and the Basic Approach

Llewellyn believed that distributional goals played no role in a contract theory. He explained that "most of the Sales Field is uncolored as most other law is not by the clash of class and passion," because "the same parties, and the same types of party, can tomorrow be occupying each the other end of similar disputes."[10] Rather, sales law had to solve "practical" problems: "law and legal rules are practical tools for practical men, and have as their job to center on practical issues. And most conflicts of doctrine do just that."[11] Turning to these practical issues, Llewellyn asked, "What, then, are the problems with which it is the business of the mercantile law of Sales to cope? They turn chiefly about occasional hitches in the process known to economists as distribution (which includes assembling), to business-schools as marketing, . . . to lawyers as formation and performance of contract. . . ."[12]

Decisionmakers need a source of policy to resolve even practical issues. Llewellyn sought to increase efficiency by enforcing the parties' deal: Parties should be permitted to make "any contract they please" because "the animals probably knew their own business better than their keeper did – a theory which has not only charm but virtue, *most* of the time."[13] On a slightly more abstract level, "business has been the biggest single man-made fact in our living."[14] Courts therefore have not "failed to reflect the sound American point of view that it is business which makes the wheels go round" and thus "have felt it good to favor" commerce.[15] In a similar vein, Llewellyn observed that Americans live "in a bargain economy," and that if courts are to enforce contracts, "Benefit of the bargain is the sane standard for a court to enforce by." This also is the law: "Our policy is fixed in most cases in terms of purporting to award Benefit of the Bargain. I think the choice is wise."[16]

Llewellyn's adoption of premise (1), that courts should implement the parties' goals, is nicely illustrated by his view of warranty law. He approved of the Uniform Sales Act warranty and presumption rules because these "*seek* less to lay down controlling rules than to standardize, on the basis of the most general practice discernable, the probable meaning of the acts or words concerned to most bargainers concerned, and to give effect to that meaning. . . . And this, in my view, is the sound basic approach to regulative law about socially unobjectionable transactions which can be reasonably standardized, and where bargaining power is moderately balanced or fair dealing is the practice."[17] The parties' meaning is reflected in their contract. Thus, warranty law should be put "on a *contract* basis"[18]: ". . . in the normal modern case the first measure of the parties' rights is not the seller's conduct but the seller's contract. . . . Every problem of modern sales law splits into two major lines of inquiry: according to whether the seller's action does or does not conform with that contract. . . ."[19]

When a contract was incomplete, the court should ask what quality risk the typical seller would assume (this is premise (2)). In the early part of the nineteenth century, that seller was a wholesaler or factor who purchased goods in sealed packages from a distant merchant. The factor thus "sells wares of whose origin, growth, manufacture, handling, packaging, he can have no personal knowledge and may not have even hearsay. Is such a seller to be held to quality responsibility unless he [explicitly] warrants?"[20] Because sellers would not warrant without knowledge of product quality and buyers would know this, the typical deal would reflect the rule of caveat emptor.

A counter-rule grew "out of factorage, but out of busier factorage." Under caveat emptor, the buyer must make a "full examination of the wares" before acceptance. A seller who warrants that the sample he or she exhibits fairly represents the bulk will "speed turnover" because the warranty substitutes for buyer inspection. The warranty also would increase seller costs, but (the exogenously caused) growth in nineteenth century American commerce would have permitted such a seller to "cover with increased commissions any seller's responsibilities assumed." Therefore, courts who recognized a trade usage that samples are taken to represent the bulk, and who "'imposed' implied warranties . . . are creating merchants' law for merchants, where farmers' law has ceased visibly to cover merchants' needs."[21] Many courts, however, took a long time to understand that they should imply the sample warranty because "*either* view [of the quality obligation the seller must assume] is a view for the passionate furtherance of trade."

The warranty example illustrates the creativity of Llewellyn's approach to creating sales law rules. Llewellyn did not ask what rule sellers and buyers in general would want, but rather what rule parties would agree to given their *particular* circumstances. This focus on context implied the conclusion that caveat emptor was once the better rule for allocating the risk of nonconforming goods. When commercial circumstances changed, the parties' rule preferences should change as well. Thus, when the volume of trade increased, the increased costs to sellers of making warranties would be more than offset by the gain from additional business. Sellers in this new circumstance would want to warrant. Hence, the law should change so that sellers are taken to make an implied sample warranty when the contract is silent. As also is typical, the economics of Llewellyn's argument are a little off: The volume of trade is irrelevant to the question of which quality risk allocation is efficient; rather, the question is whether factors or retailers could infer the nature of the bulk from the sample more cheaply. For if the costs to factors of learning what the bulk is like are higher than the costs to their buyers of learning this, then a factor could not recover the higher inspection cost attributable to the warranty by selling more goods.[22]

B. The Relevance of Custom

It is a commonplace that custom played an important role in Llewellyn's theory, but a disagreement exists as to what that role was. The claim here is that custom had epistemological relevance. The first two premises in Llewellyn's theory held that courts should interpret contracts to achieve the parties' goals, and that decisionmakers should complete contracts with rules that typical parties would accept. Custom is relevant to decisionmakers, then, to the extent that it evidences what commercial parties want.[23] In contrast, modern scholars hold that realists, in particular Llewellyn, urged courts to find in commercial practice the norms with which to resolve business disputes.[24] The articles analyzed here contradict this view.

There are two reasons for custom not to be an independent source of norms for decisionmakers. First, custom often is unhelpful. The law resolves troubled cases, and in troubled cases custom can run out.[25] Llewellyn explained:

> "Business understanding" of what an agreement means, and indeed of whether an agreement exists, is by no means unambiguous and not always adjustable. It is not alone wilful default, but honest difference of opinion, which leads to disputes, and which leaves some proper room for law officials. Both ways and norms of business practice may be firm at the center, but they are hazy at the edge; they offer little sureness to guide in dealing with the outside or unusual case.[26]

The accompanying footnote added:

> Practice is, however, rarely marked definitely enough to set a clear standard for judging unusual cases. . . . A given trade may recognize unlimited cancellation as of right, in the ordinary course. But in the ordinary course cancellations of given orders do not pile up. Is the freedom to cancel to be regarded as holding equally in a cataclysmic market? One main business of law is to set, to *create,* norms for such cases of conflicting or uncertain expectation.[27]

Second, to let custom control is to make the cognitive mistake of suppressing a moral premise. If the law is to enforce right conduct, then it cannot direct a result just because it is the result many parties would reach. Rather, while practice is relevant to decision, it is a separate question whether the usual result is the normatively correct result. To decide cases only according to custom thus is implicitly to assume that what is customary is also right.

Llewellyn did not make this assumption, but rather explicitly denied the normativity of the actual. It was false to assert that the realist has "no interest on his part for better law." The error of critics is to assume "that anyone conceives that all law has to do is to *follow* society because in a *particular* instance under discussion the following of society is urged to be the adjustment needed."[28] Llewellyn gives as an example that "banking practice" should determine how much time a holder needs to present a check, but there remain "certain regular abuses in the affiliate practices of the same banks" that the state should curb.[29] In a later analysis, he argued that buyers received too much protection under the nineteenth century factors acts, and added, ". . . I hope the doubts I have raised as to the wisdom of this full range of his protection under the . . . [statutes] may guard me from any misinterpretation that I am urging the protection of interests simply because they are, or of the market as it is because it is."[30] When doing contract theory, Llewellyn did not attempt to deduce *ought* from *is,* but rather sought to learn from and improve the *is.*[31]

C. The Nature, Function and Creation of Legal Rules

Llewellyn's substantive theory as applied to contract rules followed from premises (2) and (4) above – that the rules should be defaults that either reflect the terms that typical parties would adopt or reduce transactions costs. Rules that achieve these functions have to constrain decisionmakers, who are required to apply the appropriate legal default, and guide parties, who need to know what legal result will obtain unless they change the default. Rules that can constrain courts and guide parties must be stated on a low level of generality. A rule that requires parties to behave "reasonably" thus is unsatisfactory relative to a rule that imposes a particular risk on the seller if certain facts are found to exist. Rules that impose commercial risks, in turn, are best created by persons well informed about commerce. Llewellyn's substantive theory thus had these institutional implications: Rules should be concrete; concrete rules can constrain decisionmakers and guide parties; and the rules preferably should be created by experts.

1. **RULE FORM.** Llewellyn believed that commercial law rules should be concrete: "Nor can they [prevent disputes] if, when found, they are vague: 'do right'; 'do not perpetrate a combination in restraint of trade. . . . The specific character of administrative rules on those technical points which ethics and even custom hardly touch, or touch with no uniformity, is an engineering device of rare value."[32] Llewellyn later softened this view, conceding that a rule may be useful though "rather indeterminate in form"; such rules should be "issue-pointing rules which marshall the relevant factors around the vital criterion."[33] Llewellyn's views on such concepts as "title" and "property in the goods," however, illustrate his preference for the concrete.

This preference followed from his view of what questions a good legal rule should require the decisionmaker to answer, not from a distaste for broad analytical categories or conceptual analysis.[34] Llewellyn disliked rules that required courts to address questions to the facts that the facts could not directly answer. Thus, the facts could tell who did what and when but could not tell where "title" to the goods was because title is a legal concept. To be sure, a rule holding that title was in party S if facts x and y were found, but otherwise was in party B, could be applied intelligently. Where title was, however, determined legal consequences, such as who bore the risk that the goods would be destroyed before the contract was performed. As a consequence, a legal rule could simply state that party S bore the risk of such a loss if facts x and y were found but otherwise party B bore the risk. Title is "a wholly unnecessary major premise."[35] Making the application of a rule turn on legal concepts such as title is unwise as well as unnecessary. A rule meant to tell courts what questions to address to the facts is more likely to be applied correctly if the rule requires an explicit factual inquiry – did fact x exist? – rather than a conceptual inquiry – where was title? As Llewellyn said in another context, meaningful rules are defined by "operative fact" rather than "legal consequence."[36] A meaningful rule thus is specific, not abstract.[37]

Llewellyn's preference for precision in rule statement was not an objection to the width of analytical categories in legal analysis or to the use of conceptual analysis in general. Llewellyn disliked bad concepts, not concepts per se.[38] Indeed, Llewellyn sometimes urged a widening of the then-regnant categories of legal analysis. Thus, he argued that warranties and remedies should be considered together because whether or not a warranty is found has meaning only in so far as legal consequences flow.[39] Llewellyn also considered warranties in connection with other doctrines. For example, some nineteenth century courts in his view correctly expanded the scope of the seller's quality obligation but then vitiated the expansion in face-to-face sales by taking the buyer to waive defects when he or she accepted the goods: "no damage remedy survived your accord and satisfaction."[40] The courts' mistake was to treat the connected issues of substantive liability and waiver as if they were separate.[41] In accident law, the appropriate category for analysis was not food but rather the uninformed consumer purchase of potentially dangerous products.[42] Finally, the field of contract law itself is too narrow an analytic category: The appropriate category is "transactions," which should include corporate law and property.[43]

In Llewellyn's theory, wide analytical categories, conceptual analysis, and concrete rules thus easily coexist. The former two modes of thought help the scholar or decisionmaker to choose the appropriate rule, which in turn will constrain courts and guide parties if cast in concrete form. Llewellyn departed from these views only when considering rules that were to appear in a code. In Llewellyn's view, codes differed from ordinary statutes along the dimension of amendability: "a codificatory Act" is not "ordinary legislation" because "it is not legislation capable of easy or frequent amendment; errors in it . . . are rather to be suffered . . . over very considerable periods."[44] Uniform laws meant to codify fields had not been amended frequently when Llewellyn wrote, but he provides only a mystical explanation: "The Code of a Field builds itself into the life and work of men; it cannot be lightly altered."[45] In any event, such a code cannot "long answer the needs of a whole field. It therefore makes judicial *development* (not mere 'interpretation') a necessity."[46] A good code should facilitate judicial development by stating principles and directing courts to reason by analogy from them: Courts should be made to realize that "the act is a freshly stated take-off from explicit, true common-law principle into the common-law type of development of true common-law principle."[47] There is little or no evidence in these articles, however, indicating a Llewellyn belief that a code is the best lawmaking vehicle.

2. THE ABILITY OF RULES TO GUIDE AND CONSTRAIN. Llewellyn held that doctrine is "a convenient and fairly accurate summation of past decisions and of apparent trends, one which makes possible the intelligent decision of a new case in the light of its bearing on doctrine and on life."[48] Llewellyn thus told students "that the examination gives no room at all for policy discussion except *after* the positive rules prevailing have been brought into play upon the problem; that policy discussion *after* the question is decided and the relevant authorities considered will be welcome; otherwise disregarded."[49] That rules can decide cases implied for Llewellyn that, "Rules must be framed to hold up – and hold down – judges who are not supermen."[50] And also, "judges are by no means free to be 'arbitrary', and must be held down and directed."[51] This is a common theme.[52]

Llewellyn at least once sought to demonstrate that rules could reduce disputes. He analyzed two negotiable instruments principles, one dealing with bona fide purchasers of commercial paper and the other requiring notice to conditional obligors. The former principle "is expressed in the Negotiable Instruments Law in rather broad language setting up standards"; the latter "is expressed in a multitude of detailed rules." The former approach, Llewellyn observed, generated far more litigation than the latter. Hence, "I conclude that, along with principle, rules have their realm of service."[53]

Other evidence suggests that the Llewellyn of these articles did not believe that law was best made by drafting statutes stating broad principles and then letting courts apply the principles. Llewellyn remarked that judges "sit as laymen groping to solve a controversy [in this case, chattel security law, but the point was general] they cannot understand."[54] A softer version of this view pervades Llewellyn's early work, in which a constant theme held that the law was often confused or wrong because courts did not understand commercial situations. This failing could not be cured by giving courts vaguely worded statutes to enforce. Llewellyn gave this example: Sellers financed sales early in the nineteenth century, but by the 1870s, bank financing had become prominent. The courts never perceived this switch, and so failed to read the Factors Acts to facilitate bank financing.[55] The early Acts, he concluded, were later "mutilated in American seaboard courts . . . when the main fact picture which the judge sees, knows . . . has come to change."[56] Only statutes that tell courts what questions to address to the facts can prevent such disasters.

Though Llewellyn believed that rules could constrain courts, it is too simple to say that he defined law merely as a set of predictions of what the courts will do.[57] To be sure, he believed that, "If it is moderately clear how future cases will come out, then a statement of that clarity is the Rule of Case-Law . . . irrespective of whether it is a nice rule or a wise one or a just one."[58] Statutes also are controlling rules in this sense, whether the statutes are nice, wise, or just. Llewellyn went further, though, to distinguish between rules for lawyers and rules for courts. One could "challenge the title of rules for counselors to be called rules of law at all; for such rules are not normative; they command nothing. . . . They are of the nature of a weather forecast. . . ."[59] In contrast, the judge is to choose the "wise" or "just" rule.[60] Rules for counselors can be called rules, however, because the function of a rule is to guide conduct, and counselors' rules do that. Nevertheless, the distinction between rules for lawyers and rules for judges should always be kept clear.

3. RULE CREATION. Implementing the results of Llewellyn's contract theory requires expertise. A court could develop expertise if it were presented with a line of cases that repeatedly raised the same issues: "fact-pressures, if they can be canalized and kept moderately repetitive, give us some fair quantum of wise case-results." But whether courts get repetitive cases is a matter of chance,[61] and having the cases is only a necessary condition for getting efficient rules: Also needed are "a prophet and a suitable doctrine."[62] Prophets, however, are unusual: Holmes and Mansfield "stand out because of rarity."[63] The rules therefore should come at least in part from outside the common law system.

Llewellyn thus repeatedly expressed a preference for specialized decisionmakers. These were desirable both because of their expertise and because they could develop specific rules. Llewellyn's preference for expert decisionmakers was expressed early: "legislatures . . . though better adopted for general policy-shaping than courts, are by both size and membership hampered in doing the legal engineering. . . . Legislators, too, are only men, and in technical fields, laymen." An administrative tribunal is best: "It offers means of developing experts specialized in their fields, of getting quick decisions, and, above all, of getting a wealth of *detailed specific* rulings."[64] Similarly, public or quasi-public bodies could best effect law reform: It would be good to have "the creation of some agency which serves in private law as the cop serves in public law: an appointed person who will do what it has been discovered George will not." Examples include the National Conference of Commissioners on Uniform State Laws and the New York Law Revision Commission.[65]

Courts played a residual but significant role in the theory. Society faces a scarcity of regulatory resources, but parties always can sue. In a discussion of standard form contracts, Llewellyn said "administrative supervision . . . is to be welcomed" but "new fields" emerge and agencies are hard to create. Consequently, we need "a judicial technique built to face the problem in its always new forms."[66] And when public regulation of product quality waned, "then private remedy on private agreement became the law's one immediate hope."[67]

Private parties also can fill the regulatory gap. After noting that juries may not reliably understand commercial custom, he remarked, "This is one point at which commercial arbitrators have a tremendous advantage over lawyers," and he added that "for the mercantile man," the remedy for bad law lay in good drafting and arbitration.[68] Trade associations also could substitute for bad or absent law. A trade association could best develop "the working rules of a technical activity"[69] because, "In the self-government of sub-groups contract provides an original framework, a constitution, a source of ultimate sanction in dispute or breakdown."[70] More precisely, trade associations reduce disputes by specifying the quality obligation that sellers must meet and by providing the parties with better decisionmakers than courts. Llewellyn, however, would uphold trade association rules only when all affected parties participated effectively in the trade association. The rules emerging from such a process would be balanced, and thus as deserving of enforcement as ordinary contracts.[71]

IV. Illustrative Substantive Views

Llewellyn described himself as a "Contract theorist", and defined the role: "the theorists . . . have as their *first* objective to state accurately and neatly what the courts have been doing" and "to do criticism only *after* stating accurately and neatly what it is that they are criticizing."[72] Part IV first focuses on how Llewellyn stated the law and then illustrates his mode of criticism. The object is to give a richer statement of Llewellyn's theory by analyzing two of his major concerns.

A. Stating the Law

The taught doctrine and the words of statutes, Llewellyn thought, differed substantially from the law that courts applied. This theme pervades the articles, but appears most clearly in the offer and acceptance papers. The first began with the claim that the taught doctrine differed from the living law, and stated the thesis that one can work up from the cases "a rather coherent and workable body and moderately simple body of case-principle and even often clean case-law about the formation of business agreements. . . ."[73]

Llewellyn used the method of normal science to state the law – induction from good data. An analyst using the inductive method states a preliminary hypothesis, gathers the data, sometimes refines the hypothesis, and then tests it. Llewellyn self-consciously worked in this way. He said, "The emphasis on rules and, in our own case law, the particular emphasis on the derivation of rules from case-to-case decision focuses particular attention on the *problem of induction.*"[74] He then cautioned:

> without a hypothesis which *unambiguously* means *one* thing, attempted observation or research into new data or old is somewhere between 90 and 95 per cent waste motion. Granted . . . that the hypothesis conditions observation. . . . Granted . . . that the shaping and fixing (partly by the hypothesis) of the multicolored data in turn conditions the conclusion. . . . The fact remains. Without the unambiguous hypothesis, no advance.[75]

In the offer and acceptance articles (and generally), Llewellyn's preliminary hypothesis held that "case-law doctrine in Contract . . . is likely both to reflect life-conditions and to stay moderately close to them."[76] The taught doctrine then distinguished between bilateral and unilateral contracts. Under the former, the offeror wanted a return promise as the acceptance so the offeree could accept by promising. Under the latter, the taught doctrine took the offeror to want a return performance as both an expression of acceptance and as the consideration for the offeror's promise. Hence, the offeree could not accept an offer to make a unilateral contract merely by saying that she would perform it. This taught doctrine, Llewellyn thought, was inconsistent with practice: "in life, expressed agreement does operate as a commitment. It just does."[77] Typical parties thus would assume that both were bound when the offeree said she would perform; the distinction between unilateral and bilateral contracts "represents doctrine divorced from life."[78] This led to the refined hypothesis: "This [assumption by parties that there was a deal] is business; it is sense; it will be surprising if it does not prove to be at least majority case-law."[79] Llewellyn's admittedly nonexhaustive survey then showed that American caselaw did not distinguish between bilateral and unilateral contracts; rather, a seriously meant expression of assent commonly was held to bind the offeror.

Llewellyn's use of the inductive method was not unique. Arthur Corbin also sought to infer the actual law from case data. The novelty in Llewellyn's method was to assume that courts did (as well as should) further business goals, and thus to derive his hypotheses respecting what the law was by asking what rules would advance these goals. The weakness in Llewellyn's use of the method also derived from its novelty: The method cannot be used correctly if the analyst does not know what business practice is and why. As is well known, Llewellyn took much of his knowledge of practice from appellate court opinions. In a typical treatment, he once remarked that certain warranty contracts had attracted so much attention from nineteenth century courts that one "is forced to believe" that the contracts were "becoming familiar in practice."[80] It is preferable to look directly at the practice. Llewellyn also sampled cases rather than collected them exhaustively.[81] Llewellyn's views about what the living law then was thus should be regarded as hypotheses, not facts.

B. *Criticism and Reform*

Llewellyn as a law reformer sought to implement the second and fourth premises of his theory. These held that the state should create efficient default rules (2) and enact transaction cost reducing rules (4). Llewellyn thus said of the realist enterprise, "There is a strong tendency [of realists] to approach most legal problems as problems in allocation of risks, and so far as possible, as problems of their reduction. . . . To approach . . . business matters, in a word, as matters of *general* policy."[82] Llewellyn explicitly applied this approach to commercial law. The introduction to his sales law casebook stated, "the book . . . views the contract as a device for allocating various business risks; it takes up the presumptions [*i.e.*, defaults] of Sales Law as a device for allocating risks which parties have not expressly covered."[83] The law could allocate risks with default rules (he called them "yielding rules") or with mandatory rules ("rules of iron").[84] A fault of the Uniform Sales Act was to be unclear about which of its sections were mandatory and which were not.[85] This section of the chapter examines three Llewellyn proposals to reform the law of sales. These proposals illustrate a thesis of this essay: The premises of Llewellyn's theory were sound but he often implemented those premises imperfectly because he lacked the right economic tools.

1. SELLER'S ACTION FOR THE PRICE. Llewellyn sometimes pursued transaction cost reduction explicitly when recommending specific reforms: The applicable "general policy reasoning" is to have "speed and cheapness of adjustment."[86] In particular, the question of when the seller should get the price should be answered on the basis of "a careful canvass of the business and economic bearings of the competing choices."[87] Llewellyn used this canvass to conclude that the seller should be limited to damages if breach occurred when the seller had the goods: "To force such goods on the buyer, when they are reasonably marketable by the seller, is social waste. . . ." Making the vendor resell when the buyer breaches *after* delivery, however, has two disadvantages: The duty to resell would be "burdensome" for the seller and thus imposing this burden on the seller would give the buyer excessive power in a renegotiation; and the seller does not know the local market as well as the buyer does. "This presents a case that tips the balance of social utility in favor of forcing title on the buyer."[88] This analysis remains apt in many markets today.[89]

2. COVER. The law when Llewellyn wrote permitted a disappointed promisee to recover market damages – the difference between the contract and market prices measured at the time of breach. Llewellyn argued that the promisee in the alternative should be permitted to seek cover damages – the difference between the contract price and the price of a substitute transaction. The availability of cover damages would permit parties to avoid expensive actions to prove a market price. Cover also would facilitate renegotiation, which reduces the costs of resolving disputes.[90] When only market damages were available, Llewellyn argued, a breached-against buyer would make a substitute purchase at once; for if the buyer waited and the market rose, market damages would not make the buyer whole: The buyer would have bought at a high price but will have his damages measured by the lower price prevailing at breach time. The market damage rule thus discouraged a buyer from attempting to salvage the deal privately. The buyer, however, would negotiate with his seller for a reasonable time after breach if he could have his damages measured by the cost of a substitute purchase should the negotiations break down. "Given such a provision [for cover], a buyer can negotiate with his defaulting seller with no more fear of the market than afflicts any business man. . . ."[91]

As with many of Llewellyn's specific substantive claims, the economics of the argument are not exactly correct. The modern view holds that market prices incorporate all publicly available information. As a consequence, market participants perceive new price-affecting information as generated by a random process. This implies that the next period's price for goods is today's price plus interest plus an error term with positive variance and mean zero. Put less technically, a commercial actor with rational expectations and no inside information will assign an equal probability to market increases and decreases. Applying this theory to the problem at hand, a buyer who could get only market damages would face conflicting incentives. Contrary to Llewellyn's argument, the buyer has a reason not to make a substitute transaction immediately. If the market fell after breach, a buyer who waited to repurchase would profit from default: He would have bought at a low price but have his damages measured by the high price that existed on the date of breach. And as Llewellyn recognized, the possibility of a price rise after breach creates an incentive for the buyer to repurchase at once. Since the buyer would believe that a fall is as likely as a rise, the buyer would assume that the price will not change.[92] Such a buyer would negotiate with the breaching seller if that seemed helpful and otherwise purchase on the market. Giving a buyer only market damages thus will not discourage renegotiation.

In addition, adding cover damages to the remedies a disappointed buyer can assert would produce overcompensation. To see why, recall that when cover becomes available, the buyer is permitted to measure damages at the more favorable of two dates: breach or cover time. The buyer thus is given a free option to speculate after breach. Because options are valuable, adding a free option to the buyer's damage remedies overcompensates him.[93] Llewellyn's advocacy of a cover remedy thus was flawed in three ways: First, making cover available will not increase the likelihood of renegotiation; second, it was contradictory of Llewellyn to argue that the law should protect the expectation interest and also permit a buyer to cover (because cover overcompensates); and third, Llewellyn never analyzed the decisionmaker's real choice, which is whether to facilitate deals by reducing the promisee's costs of proving damages or to impede deals by adding a supra compensatory remedy.[94] The primitive state of financial economics in Llewellyn's time likely would have caused any analyst to make these errors.[95]

3. **SUBSTANTIAL PERFORMANCE.** Llewellyn's views on the perfect tender rule illustrate well the strengths and weaknesses of his substantive analyses. A strength is attention to context. He perceptively argued that perfect tender ("recision for minor defects") is appropriate for consumers and for buyers of machines for use. In the former case, the rule "fits the case of the wallpaper which is just enough off-color, or the radio which is just enough off true, to edge the nerves." In the latter case, perfect tender is appropriate because "a

machine even slightly defective can disrupt processes." Perfect tender is not appropriate for manufacturing buyers of such inputs as "print-paper, chemicals, leather, or wool" unless these are to be used in "the choicest manufactured product." Perfect tender never is appropriate for mercantile buyers.

Llewellyn objected to a perfect tender rule in mercantile transactions because the rule would encourage what today is called strategic behavior: "It [the rule] is an invitation to throw back the risk of any dropping market upon a seller who has performed as a reasonable seller should perform."[96] Buyers would "throw back the risk" by rejecting on the basis of defects that would not have produced rejection had the market gone their way. Such rejections are breaches of the real contract that the parties thought they had made (which imposed the risk of price increases on the seller and of declines on the buyer). To enforce the real contract thus is to preclude rejection, but the real contract also did not require the buyer to pay the full price for defective goods. When the goods were "gradable . . . or moderately gradable," the custom, Llewellyn believed, was to have price allowances. A decisionmaker would enforce the true deal – premise (1) of Llewellyn's theory – by following this custom.[97]

Llewellyn's reform proposal was to generalize the custom by having the legal default permit courts to bar rejection but order price allowances in mercantile transactions. In 1940, he urged an amendment to the proposed Federal Sales Act that would have banned rejection in sales between merchants if "the delivery offered in no material manner increases the risk resting on the buyer, and is of such character as to reasonably meet the buyer's operating requirements, so that an appropriate reduction of the price can serve as adequate compensation for failure of exact performance."[98] An analysis of this suggestion shows that Llewellyn did not appreciate the parties' contracting concerns as well as a modern scholar would, and also did not study business practice seriously. Llewellyn's proposed rule conditions on information that courts will not have. The rule requires a court (i) to cost out "the risk resting on the buyer" in order to decide whether the defective tender increased that risk in a "material manner"; (ii) to know the buyer's production function in order to decide whether the defective tender nevertheless "reasonably meets the buyer's operating requirements"; and (iii) to trace the financial consequences to the buyer of a "failure of exact performance." Information respecting these issues commonly is unverifiable. That is, it seldom would be cost-justified for parties to ascertain the actual risks the promisee faced, her production costs, and her expected profits, and so to verify to a court data respecting these.

Default rules that condition on unverifiable information are objectionable because they produce moral hazard.[99] Here, a seller may attempt to force the buyer to take a defective tender because, the seller may plausibly think, the buyer could not rebut the seller's claim that the tender "reasonably met the buyer's operating requirements." In addition, there seldom is a market price for every quality level of a product, from the perfect to the almost worthless. Thus, establishing an "appropriate reduction of the price" for a defective tender also may cost parties more in litigation expenses than they are willing to pay. The evidence unsurprisingly suggests that merchants respond to the strategic rejection concern with rules more precise than this proposed law.[100]

Llewellyn's advocacy of substantial performance probably was consistent with his advocacy of expert decisionmakers because there is some evidence that he wanted the issue decided by a merchant jury.[101] The availability of an expert trier of fact, however, would not respond fully to the difficulty raised here, for that difficulty goes less to a decisionmaker's lack of expertise than to the decisionmaker's inability to access the relevant information (because the parties will not provide it). Once again, an analyst writing when Llewellyn did could easily miss this point because the economics of his time missed it.

In sum, Llewellyn encouraged the state to adopt efficient defaults and to reduce transaction costs.[102] This approach is now conventional. Llewellyn, however, seldom could apply this approach productively because he lacked modern tools of economic analysis. The approach requires the analyst to understand commerce at the level of the individual transaction. This understanding is hard to acquire without a knowledge of game theory, transaction cost economics, and finance. None of these economic specialities were well developed when Llewellyn worked.[103]

V. Freedom of Contract

Llewellyn paid considerable attention to freedom of contract issues – see premise (3) – because of the epistemological role that actual contracting played in his theory. When parties contracted under ideal conditions, the deal would maximize the utility of both. However, "free contract presupposes free bargain, and . . . free bargain presupposes free bargaining."[104] Hence, "where bargaining power, and legal skill and experience as well, are concentrated on one side of the type-transaction," the transaction is not necessarily efficient but rather "is a form of contract which, in the measure of the importance of the particular deal in the other party's life, amounts to the exercise of unofficial government of some by others via private law."[105] In such cases, judicial review or regulation is necessary to ensure fairness: "When drafting [by the powerful] began to gain ground, it thus became not only an enterpriser's measure, but a social menace. . . . The menace calls for 'public' measures of control and cure."[106]

Llewellyn believed that there was less free bargaining in his time than previously because of the increasing use of standard form contracts and the growth of powerful trade associations and companies. As he said, "once . . . [the] process of agreeing" involved the freedom to choose and "choice with some inkling of consequence." But at the time when he was writing, there were standard form contracts and "differential knowledge, power and bargaining skill. . . . This means need for control, lest old rules based on Adam Smithian postulates be made tools of outrage."[107]

These views were the premise to Llewellyn's unconscionability thesis: Contracts that are substantively objectionable ("lop-sided") should not be enforced when the bargaining process that produced them was procedurally defective. An unconscionable term commonly withdrew something that the weaker party valued. A disclaimer, for example, eliminated warranty protection. Thus to hold disclaimers unconscionable is to make the warranty term mandatory, and this is what Llewellyn believed should be done: "so far as . . . rules of *implied* warranty are intended to *control* contractors, they must be rules of Iron nature, and must therefore not be subjected to contracting out."[108] When the structural factors that support a finding of unconscionability would continue to exist, Llewellyn believed, the state thus should require the results that it desires. Default rules are appropriate when bargaining power is roughly equal. Otherwise, to permit contracting out of the law would result in "*penalizing little men* while bigger outfits bargain out."[109]

These perceptive views helped to organize the unconscionability debate that began in the 1960s and continues.[110] The views, however, were general. A workable theory of unconscionability should provide criteria specifying when a contract is too lop-sided to enforce and when a contracting process is importantly defective. Llewellyn was unable to develop these criteria. In their place, he developed questionable concepts whose implication was that procedural defects were ubiquitous. These concepts led him to be more interventionist than his general theory otherwise would support. Part V thus continues a theme of Part IV: Llewellyn helped to develop what is today the basic approach to regulating contracts for fairness but could not apply this approach productively, in considerable part because he lacked the requisite economic tools.[111]

A. Substantive Unconscionability and Remedies

On Llewellyn's view, a contract is substantively unfair if it is "lop-sided," not "balanced."[112] A lop-sided contract imposes too many risks on one party. The law is balanced – "*Bodies* of yielding rules [i.e., defaults] have grown some *balance* in their allocation of risks and rights"[113] – but strong parties create imbalance when they contract out.

Llewellyn could not say how much imbalance was too much. He remarked: "the policy of leaving . . . yielding rules free to change by individuated bargain does not involve commitment to a policy of allowing displacement of the whole set of yielding rules at once, and without individuation"; "there must be decent *balance* in the *frame* of contracting which is to hold for all points not individuated by the parties."[114] These views only restate the question.[115] Llewellyn did claim that a contract which shifted the quality risk entirely to the buyer was lop-sided,[116] and advocated "legislative intervention, prohibiting certain clauses and prescribing others. . . ."[117] Apart from outlawing warranty disclaimers, however, he never clearly said what legislatures were to do.

Llewellyn's unembellished directive to decisionmakers to achieve "balance" in contracting thus seems inconsistent with his belief that a good commercial law rule will address to the courts factual questions that courts are capable of answering. Llewellyn attempted unsuccessfully to resolve this tension in his thought by developing methods of analysis to guide judicial inquiry. Initially, he rejected the standard judicial technique of construing the language in unfair contracts against the drafter. Ignoring the drafter's intent would create too much uncertainty. "No man is safe when language is to be read in the teeth of its intent."[118] Also, when a court strikes a term, firms using it respond by drafting a substantively identical but linguistically different term. As a consequence, the process of construing contracts against drafters is often wasted effort.[119]

Llewellyn recommended two other judicial techniques. First, a court should read the contract to contain what the weaker party would expect the contract to contain. His earliest major article thus advocated giving "the insured . . . the protection he might decently believe he was buying, without too close regard to the exceptions of the policy."[120] Fourteen years later, he argued that, "when bargaining is absent in fact," courts should "read into" a form contract the terms "which a sane man might reasonably expect to find on that paper."[121] One of the drafts of the Article 2 revision adopts this technique.[122]

The "reasonable expectations" standard on which the technique rests can be either factual – courts should ask what terms a buyer actually should expect to have purchased – or normative – courts should ask what terms a buyer would expect the seller to offer if the seller were behaving fairly. Llewellyn apparently wanted courts to employ the technique in both of its senses. Thus he said that courts should strike terms that are inconsistent with trade practice.[123] This view implies a factual standard: Buyers actually would expect their seller to use the industry term unless the seller said otherwise, so courts should read contracts to contain industry terms. A substantive unconscionability inquiry would be relatively predictable if the standard for the legally permissible were the widely acceptable.

Llewellyn, however, did not want to limit the inquiry in this way. As said previously, he rejected the idea that the law should follow a custom just because the custom existed. Relevant here, Llewellyn believed that buyers should be taken to expect terms that corresponded to the holdings in the cases[124] because the common law contained a set of balanced default rules. Also, the common law refines notions of fairness in the course of deciding new cases. A buyer thus could reasonably expect his seller to offer terms that corresponded to current conceptions of fairness. Therefore, Llewellyn is plausibly read as arguing that courts should use both the factual and the normative aspects of the reasonable expectations test when deciding whether a contract term is substantively conscionable.

The difficulty here is that the normative aspect yields unclear rules. To see why, realize that Llewellyn's use of a normative test is circular: He holds that courts should give buyers what buyers expect, which is balanced clauses, and that buyers expect what courts give them, which is balanced clauses. This circularity exemplifies a general problem: A normative reasonable expectations standard necessarily collapses into some other substantive test. Under the standard, courts should give the buyer what he is morally entitled to expect, and he or she is morally entitled to expect substantively conscionable terms. Thus, the normative reasonable expectations test merely restates the inquiry, for the test reduces to a directive to courts to strike substantively unfair terms and add substantively fair terms.[125] Since Llewellyn devised the reasonable expectations test because he was unable to distinguish what was fair from what was not, his thought here is unhelpful.

Llewellyn's second proposed technique for guiding a substantive unconscionability inquiry directed courts to focus on transaction types. "The proper judicial aim seems to me to be here the fixing . . . of a basic minimum which the bargain carries merely by virtue of being a bargain of that type. But that would imply a limitation on contractual capacity. . . ."[126] Llewellyn also referred approvingly to the English idea that "the quality obligation . . . is something inherent in the deal: a basic minimum from which Contract may spring-board but which Contract will not be allowed to undermine."[127] And again, courts should not enforce a standard term that is "repugnant to the balanced nature of the *type* of *transaction* which the parties have obviously entered on."[128]

Llewellyn appears to claim that sales transactions come in types that private parties cannot alter. This claim could rest on the view that sales are natural kinds whose essence is that sellers bear certain risks, such as the risk that the goods will not perform in the described manner. Words in a contract could not alter a particular transaction type's essence any more than calling a lion a sheep will make the lion docile. If Llewellyn held this view, he would have made a category mistake. The question for the state is not what a "sale" is, but what terms in sales contracts should be legally enforceable. This is a normative question. Thus directing a court's attention to a transaction's "type" also is unhelpful.[129]

To summarize, Llewellyn's theory held that when true consent to a contract was lacking, the state should instead enforce the contract that would be fair. Llewellyn, however, could not develop criteria specifying when a contract was fair – that is, substantively conscionable. This failure led him into inconsistency. According to Llewellyn, courts should resolve questions of contractual fairness by reference to a party's "reasonable" expectations, to a transaction's "type" or to whether a contract was appropriately "balanced." These tests do not identify the facts that should tell a court whether to find for the seller or the buyer. Llewellyn, however, justified his rejection of the title concept by arguing against rules that did not call for clear factual inquiries. Recall Llewellyn's claim that a court should allocate the risk of loss of the goods by asking which party had possession of them when the loss occurred, not by asking which party had title to them then. A consistent Llewellyn would also claim that a court should decide whether to enforce a disclaimer by asking (for example) which party had a comparative advantage at reducing the defect risk, not by asking whether a disclaimer was consistent with a buyer's "reasonable" expectation or a particular "transaction type." It is a puzzle why Llewellyn rejected unhelpful concepts for some legal areas but not others.

B. Procedural Unconscionability

1. THE STANDARD APPROACH. Llewellyn was an important originator of what has become the standard approach to procedural unconscionability. He believed that bona fide consent to a contract term was absent when one side had market power, or when one side was more sophisticated or knowledgeable than the other.[130] Llewellyn also believed that competition among sellers sometimes would protect buyers,[131] but competition by "the contract-dodger" more commonly will degrade "standards of performance generally." Apparently in consequence of this latter phenomenon, the commercial "tendency" has been to have "seller-protective instead of consumer-protective clauses."[132]

These views also were held on a high level of generality. The related imperfect information and market power concerns are illustrative. A buyer would be uninformed if he (i) was unaware of what the contract said or of the legal consequences of the words used; (ii) could not evaluate the risks he understood the contract to impose on him; or (iii) understood the deal offered to him but did not know what offers competing sellers would make or were making. Llewellyn never distinguished among these senses of the imperfect information concept. These distinctions are important to make because the law should, and now often does, respond to these forms of imperfect information in different ways. Plain language laws respond to form (i), requiring firms to quote contract terms in a standard fashion responds to form (iii) (by reducing search costs), while no policy response to form (ii) is today generally considered to be efficacious.

Llewellyn also believed that market failure existed when all firms in a market used the same terms. This assumes that the relevant unit of analysis, in consumer markets, is the individual transaction. As Llewellyn recognized in other contexts, however, mass transactions occur in these markets and it would be inefficient to alter standard form contracts to suit the preferences of individual buyers. Therefore, buyers do best when the market itself is competitive, for then every firm prices at cost and buyers receive the entire surplus that sales create. That all firms charge very similar prices or use very similar terms is consistent with either a monopoly or a competitive equilibrium.[133] In the former case, consumers engage in little search about market alternatives because information acquisition costs are high. Firms commonly respond by charging supra competitive prices. In the latter case, consumers engage in considerable search, in consequence of which all firms are compelled to price at the cost of the low cost producer.[134] Thus nothing normative follows from the similarity of prices or contracts alone. Rather, the decisionmaker must evaluate the competitive state of the market in which the contract was made.

Llewellyn therefore deserves considerable credit for helping to invent the conceptual vocabulary in which unconscionability discussions have been held since he wrote, and to have introduced the useful distinction between procedural and substantive unconscionability. Llewellyn, however, deployed this apparatus in a primitive way. Again, this largely is due to the primitive state of the economic analysis of his time.[135]

2. AN EXTENSION OF THE STANDARD APPROACH. Llewellyn advocated banning warranty disclaimers without direct evidence of defects in the bargaining process. He argued that in the nineteenth century, "mercantile-mindedness of any court leads towards widening seller's obligation, whether implicit or constructive," and, "also to giving a decent buyer some remedy in the case in hand."[136] The doctrine that governed how different warranties related to each other had become confused. Llewellyn thus proposed an amendment to the Uniform Sales Act stating that courts should construe warranties as consistent with each other, but if this could not be done the "order of preference" should be that blueprints should control samples that should control merchantability warranties that "arise without words." Llewellyn added a substantive proviso to this interpretative section:

> Provided, however, that any express clause negating or modifying warranties, conditions or remedies provided by this [Sales] Act for the buyer is presumptively void; and provided further that any party setting up such a clause shall carry the burden of alleging and proving, first that the party against whom the clause is invoked has freely agreed thereto; and second, that the clause lies within the reasonable region of self-regulation by parties.[137]

Thus, a disclaimer could be unenforceable although the buyer has "freely agreed thereto," if the disclaimer falls outside the "reasonable region of self-regulation by parties." In line with this view, Llewellyn later suggested adding to the warranty section of a proposed Federal Sales Act the words, "The warranty herein is not subject to negation."[138]

Llewellyn recognized that disclaimers were widely used. Given his view that widespread contractual practices likely are efficient, a disclaimer thus for him should lie within the "reasonable region of self-regulation by parties." Excluding disclaimers from this region thus seems inconsistent with Llewellyn's more general views. Llewellyn did not perceive an inconsistency, however, because he thought that the usual warranty clause was the product of procedural defects.

Llewellyn came to this questionable view because he took an ex post approach to the subject. To see what is meant, suppose the buyer purchased goods that turned out to be worthless and the seller had disclaimed warranties. Llewellyn reasoned backward from the buyer's unfortunate position to the contracting stage. A well-informed buyer would not consent to a deal that left him with worthless goods. Hence, he said of cases that sought to help the weaker party, "The lop-sidedness of bargain-result is thus taken as the mark of lop-sidedness of bargain making,"[139] and later that, "A bargain . . . shows itself not to be a bargain, when lop-sidedness begins to scream."[140] Procedural defects were even more likely when the price was substantial. Llewellyn thus approved of an alleged older practice under which, "In merchants' sales of wares a sound price warrants a sound article, merchantable and proper to pass as a sound ware under the designation. . . ."[141] It followed that a seller behaved wrongfully if she assumed no obligation respecting quality but charged a sound price.[142] The link between this conclusion and the existence of procedural defects is found in Llewellyn's approval of "Holmes' observation that the price paid for a contract commonly negates expectation of unusual risk."[143] In sum, the coexistence of broad exculpatory language with a high price almost conclusively evidences defects in the contracting process.

The mistake here was to neglect the parties' contracting problem. A warranty is an insurance policy that protects a buyer against losses attributable to the goods. A full warranty – complete insurance – would create moral hazard: The marginal cost to the buyer of reducing the probability of a loss would be positive while the marginal gain from buyer investments in prevention would be zero because the full warranty would already have protected the buyer against any loss. Hence, the buyer would be careless. A common remedy for moral hazard is coinsurance: The insurer – the seller – bears some risks, and the insured – the buyer – bears others. The more risk the insured bears, the more careful he will be. Therefore, both full warranties and complete disclaimers are rare. Under the usual practice, the seller warrants against harms that she was likely to have caused or which she could repair most cheaply, but does not warrant against harms that commonly result from buyer misuse or against which the buyer could best insure.[144] Because informed buyers would agree to bear some product risks, it is incorrect to infer bargaining failure from the presence of uncovered risks alone. Rather, the analyst must either identify bargaining failure directly or show that an efficient warranty contract would have imposed on the seller the risk that the buyer was made to bear.

Llewellyn's argument that high prices imply the existence of warranties is similarly flawed. The argument can be illustrated in this way: Let a buyer purchase a stereo system for \$1,000. If the system were defective, it would be worth nothing. When the seller charges \$1,000, then, she is affirming that the stereo is worth that much. Buyers expect to have remedies when seller affirmations turn out to be untrue. Hence, the buyer who pays the \$1,000 price expects that the seller agrees to bear the quality risk – that the seller has made a warranty. The error in this reasoning is to analyze the problem after sale. Then the stereo is worth either \$1,000 or zero. Buyer inferences respecting the contract's risk allocation must be drawn at the time of sale, however, and the stereo then is worthless only with a particular probability. If that probability is low, then the product is worth a lot without a warranty, and will sell for an appropriately high price. Hence, the contract price *alone* cannot support a plausible buyer inference that the seller has made a warranty. This point perhaps is clarified with an example.

Assume that a firm sells a stereo that is produced at a constant marginal cost of c. The probability of a defect is π, and a defect makes the stereo worthless. The firm makes a warranty that requires it to replace worthless units. The firm thus must produce more units than it makes sales in order to be able to replace nonconforming units, and the replacement units also could be defective. Solving this problem, a firm that warrants would have to produce $1/(1 - \pi)$ units to "support" each sale. If the firm sells x stereos in a period, its total variable cost is $cx/(1 - \pi)$, and the marginal cost is $c/(1 - \pi)$. When the firm prices at the minimum of its average cost curve (*i.e.* the market is competitive), the fixed cost that each sale recovers is f. The stereo's price with a warranty thus is $p_w = f + c/(1 - \pi)$. The stereo's price without a warranty would be $p_{nw} = f + c$. Suppose that f = \$100, c = \$1,000, and $\pi = .01$. The transaction price when the firm warrants would be \$1,110.10, and the price when it disclaims would be approximately 1% lower, \$1,100. This example shows that rational buyers would pay almost as much for products with disclaimers as for products with warranties. It thus is incorrect to claim that whenever the price is nontrivial, buyers expect their sellers to have made warranties.[145]

To summarize, Llewellyn's advocacy of a disclaimer ban in merchant markets is formally consistent with his views on freedom of contract generally because he believed that buyers did not consent to disclaimers freely. Llewellyn, however, inferred this lack of consent from the property of disclaimers to impose risks on buyers and the penchant of sellers to charge prices that, given product failure, seemed high. This inference was mistaken. When it is rejected, the inconsistency in Llewellyn's thought is restored. Llewellyn's error here is understandable given the limited economic knowledge of his time. He helped to develop what is now called the exploitation theory of warranty, under which sellers disclaim warranties to exploit buyers. A modern treatment of the subject concluded, "The exploitation theory . . .

does not provide any explanation of the existence of warranties. Therefore, it is unclear why warranties can serve exploitative ends."[146] Explanations for the existence of warranties, in turn, emerge out of the recent literatures on moral hazard and adverse selection.

Again, Llewellyn had an intelligent approach to freedom of contract issues. He recognized the epistemological relevance of the buyer's consent and the need to develop substantive criteria of contract enforcement when free consent is lacking. On a methodological level, he correctly held that procedural and substantive unconscionability were jointly necessary and sufficient conditions for nonenforcement. He also recognized that many equilibria in consumer markets were (and remain) normatively suspect because information is costly to acquire, structural market power sometimes exists, and consumers tend to be less sophisticated than firms. However, he could not progress with the concrete questions of when and how the state should intervene in consumer markets given the economic tools available to him. And even on his own terms, his freedom-of-contract views sometimes were inconsistent with his more general views on how commercial law rules should be written and on the relevance of widespread practice to efficiency assessment.

VI. Conclusion

Karl Llewellyn's contract theory can be analyzed on two levels of abstraction. On the high level, Llewellyn's general approach to the legal regulation of contracting behavior is powerful and current. Llewellyn understood that the law had three tasks: to enforce the parties' deal when the deal was discernable, to create default rules to complete incomplete contracts, and to mark the limits of freedom of contract. Llewellyn justified the law's performance of the first task on efficiency grounds and used the efficiency norm to help the law perform the second task. Llewellyn's commitment to efficiency also informed his analysis of freedom of contract, for he thought that efficiency was unlikely when the bargaining process was conducted under much less than ideal conditions, and the results of such flawed processes therefore were not entitled to the law's deference. On the lower level of application of the approach, Llewellyn seldom is relevant to us. Llewellyn could only work with the tools he had, and those tools were too primitive for the task he set himself. It is difficult to make much progress on the creation of good default rules or on developing criteria for efficient interventions in markets without a knowledge of game theory, transaction cost economics, and the economics of information. Because these bodies of knowledge were created after Llewellyn worked, many of his particular applications were mistaken. In addition, Llewellyn was a poor empiricist (at least in economic areas), and he was not always consistent in his thinking. Nevertheless, Llewellyn's general approach easily accommodated itself to the use of new economic tools and indeed facilitated their introduction. In this significant sense, he was the major founder.

Before turning to more general themes, it is worth remarking of the danger, when doing interpretation, of finding what one is looking for. Llewellyn also wrote in jurisprudence, sociology, and legal anthropology, and he has been variously identified as a jurisprudent, sociologist, and anthropologist. He is described here as a lawyer economist. This new description should not be taken as an implicit rejection of the others. The different interpretation developed above is partly explained by the use of a different data set – the contracts scholarship – but the difference has a deeper cause. Llewellyn did applied normative analysis in these papers: His central question concerned how the law should best regulate sales transactions between merchants. There are today protests against economic imperialism – can economic analysis explain sex?– but it is becoming a consensus that economics has much to say about markets. This essay's description of Llewellyn thus should not surprise, for its claim is only that when Llewellyn wrote in contracts, he took an intellectual approach that was appropriate to the subject.

As for the relevance of the papers discussed here to broader jurisprudential issues, it will be helpful to set out briefly what have become the standard views of realism:

1. Realists believed that the law inevitably is and should be instrumental; legal rules should self-consciously implement policies.
2. Realists had an anticonceptual bias, which led them to reject broad analytical categories, such as "title" and "property," because these obscured what was at stake when choosing rules.
3. Realists, however, were vague respecting what policies the state actually should pursue. They tended to call for policy analysis rather than do it, and many of them were ethical relativists.
4. Realists held a philosophically indefensible view of law, as being only a set of predictions of what courts will do.
5. Realists were rule sceptics, who believed that precise rules could not bind courts, and perhaps could not confine a decisionmaker's discretion very much.
6. In consequence of (4) and (5), realists believed that there was no separation between law and politics.
7. Realism was not a jurisprudence of the modern regulatory state, but rather was court-centered – more so than the situation of American society would warrant.

Llewellyn has been associated with all of these positions, and has been defended against only (5).[147] The first view does apply to Llewellyn, who described himself as a legal reformer. There is little support in the contract articles for associating Llewellyn with the other positions. These articles show that Llewellyn did not reject conceptual analysis or broad analytical categories, but rather rejected legal concepts that directed to courts questions that courts could not answer; he explicitly believed that the state should promote efficiency by reducing transaction costs and by enforcing business contracts, subject to a fairness constraint that he worked hard (though unsuccessfully) to make precise; he rejected the view that the law was no more than a set of predictions of official behavior; and he believed that rules could seriously constrain a decisionmaker's discretion. Llewellyn did spend much of his time with the law in courts, but out of a sense of necessity. He believed in the superiority of regulatory solutions to many of the problems he discussed, but also thought that there was a scarcity of lawmaking resources so that the ability of parties to sue each other implied that the residual role of courts would remain large in the contract field. Llewellyn did not address the relation between law and politics in these papers because he believed he was addressing problems that did not deeply divide people morally: The American ethos implied the pursuit of efficiency in the contexts he considered, so for him sales law raised technical rather than political issues.

This disjunction between Llewellyn as a contracts scholar and the views that realists generally are perceived to hold raises a methodological point. Realism on the ground may have differed from realism in the air. Perhaps the substantive work of other realists should be read to see whether this distinction holds generally.

Notes

† This chapter benefited from workshops at Georgetown, Harvard and Yale Law Schools, and a seminar at the Haas School of Business, Berkeley. Helpful comments also were made by Bruce Ackerman, Ian Ayres, Jack Balkin, Richard Craswell, Hanoch Dagan, Dan Kahan, Alvin Klevorick, Brian Leiter, Stephen Morse, Eric Posner, George Triantis, Richard Posner, Steven Walt, and James Whitman.

1. The terms "contract theory" and "contracts scholarship" are meant here to include Llewellyn's work on sales law. The scholarship is found in (1) *The Effect of Legal Institutions Upon Economics,* 15 Am. Econ. Rev. 665 (1925); (2) *Introduction to Cases and Materials on Sales* (1929); (3) *What Price Contract? An Essay In Perspective,* 40 Yale L. J. 704 (1931); (4) *On Warranty of Quality and Society I,* 36 Colum. L. Rev. 699 (1936); (5) *On Warranty of Quality and Society II,* 37 Colum. L. Rev. 341 (1937); (6) *Through Title to Contract and a Bit Beyond,* 15 N.Y.U. L. Rev. 159 (1938); (7) *The Rule of Law in Our Case-Law of Contract,* 47 Yale L. J. 1243 (1938); (8) *On Our Case-Law of Offer and Acceptance I,* 48 Yale L. J. 1 (1938); (9) *On Our Case-Law of Offer and Acceptance II,* 48 Yale L. J. 779 (1939); (10) *Across Sales, on Horseback,* 52 Harv. L. Rev. 725 (1939); (11) *The First Struggle to Unhorse Sales,* 52 Harv. L. Rev. 873 (1939); (12) *Book Review,* 52 Harv. L. Rev. 700 (1939); (13) *The Needed Federal Sales Act,* 26 Va. L. Rev. 558 (1940). Citations to these works are by integer, as in 3 at 705. Llewellyn

wrote several articles advocating the adoption of the Uniform Commercial Code after 1940, but did no further work in contract theory.

2. William Twining, *Karl Llewellyn and the Realist Movement* 368 (1973). Twining also does not discuss these papers in *The Ideal of Juristic Method: A Tribute to Karl Llewellyn,* 48 U. Miami L. Rev. 119 (1993).
3. *American Legal Realism,* W. W. Fisher, M. Horowitz, and T. W. Reed, eds. (1993). See also, e.g., Laura Kalman, *Legal Realism at Yale* (1986) (extensive discussions of Llewellyn, but none of his contract work).
4. E.g., Brian Leiter, *Rethinking Legal Realism: Toward a Naturalized Jurisprudence,* 76 Tex. L. Rev. 267 (1997); Lisa Bernstein, *Merchant Law in a Merchant Court: Rethinking the Code's Search for Immanent Business Norms,* 144 U. Pa. L. Rev. 1765 (1996); Dennis M. Patterson, *Good Faith, Lender Liability, and Discretionary Acceleration: Of Llewellyn, Wittgenstein, and the Uniform Commercial Code,* 68 Tex. L. Rev. 169 (1989); Zipporah B. Wiseman, *The Limits of Vision: Karl Llewellyn and the Merchant Rules,* 100 Harv. L. Rev. 465 (1987); Ingrid M. Hillinger, *The Article 2 Merchant Rules: Karl Llewellyn's Attempt to Achieve the Good, the True, the Beautiful in Commercial Law,* 73 Geo. L. J. 1141 (1985).
5. The twelve articles that appeared in law reviews were cited 426 times between 1972 and January of 1999. This would be a large number of citations for a modern set of private law articles. The third article, *What Price Contract?,* was twenty-eighth on the list of the thirty most-cited articles in the *Yale Law Journal* as of 1991, and was the oldest article on the list. See Fred R. Shapiro, *The Most-Cited Articles from* The Yale Law Journal, 100 Yale L. J. 1449, 1462–3 (1991). The citation figures for each article are (1) 16; (3) 130; (4) 36; (5) 44; (6) 27; (7) 14; (8) 20: (9) 17; (10) 24; (11) 20; (12) 67; (13) 11.
6. The political constraints under which uniform law drafters work are analyzed in Alan Schwartz and Robert E. Scott, *The Political Economy of Private Legislatures,* 143 U. Pa. L. Rev. 595 (1995).
7. Anthony Kronman argues that Llewellyn's later thought on issues of method differed substantially from his views in the period analyzed here. Anthony T. Kronman, *The Lost Lawyer* 196–201 (1993). For similar views, see William C. Heffernan, *Two Stages of Karl Llewellyn's Thought,* 11 Int'l J. Soc. L. 134 (1983); Wilfrid E. Rumble, Jr., *American Legal Realism* 147–54 (1968).
8. See, e.g., Aaron Edlin, *Cadillac Contracts and Up-Front Payments: Efficient Investment under Expectation Damages,* 12 J. Law, Econ. & Org. 98 (1996); Benjamin E. Hermalin and Michael Katz, *Judicial Modification of Contracts Between Sophisticated Parties: A More Complete View of Incomplete Contracts and Their Breach,* 9 J. Law, Econ. & Org. 230 (1993).
9. Llewellyn's theory sometimes collapsed the difference between substantive and procedural unfairness. A "lop sided" contract, he often said, is unfair because knowledgeable parties would not voluntarily agree to it. Such a claim offers the substantive defect as sufficient evidence of the procedural defect. Part V. A below pursues the implications of this type of claim.
10. 10 at 725–6.
11. 8, n. 55 at 27.
12. 6 at 164.
13. 5 at 403. Llewellyn later said: "Almost any particular clause included in a deal represents

the parties' joint judgment . . . and this alone is good enough for letting it . . . displace and replace the general law." 12 at 700–1.

14. 10 at 725.
15. Ibid. at 734.
16. 6 at 175–6. Llewellyn's view presupposed "mercantile outfits who have bargained *on a moderately equal footing*." Id.
17. Ibid. n. 72 at 197.
18. 4 at 701. Llewellyn praised Mansfield because he "had laid down the root of the whole mercantile approach to 'warranty': that it rests in contract." 4 at 719. Mansfield's warranty theory is thoughtfully analyzed in James Oldham, *Reinterpretations of 18th-Century English Contract Theory: The View from Lord Mansfield's Notes,* 76 Geo. L. J. 1949, 1969–79 (1988).
19. 2 at xiv. Again, "Dealers' obligations can be reckoned in terms of . . . what the dealer has *engaged* to deliver, rather than what in semi-tort he should be held accountable for not delivering. . . ." 4 at 728.
20. 11 at 885.
21. Ibid. at 836. The sample warranty is express today but was implied in the nineteenth century. For readers unfamiliar with Commercial Law, an implied warranty arises without words. For example, when the contract is silent, a merchant seller is taken to guarantee product quality; the seller makes an implied warranty of merchantability. An express warranty is in effect a promise relating to quality – that the goods are machined to a certain tolerance. The seller makes an express warranty by using words: The seller must say that the goods are machined in a certain way.
22. The volume of trade would be relevant to risk allocation if there were economies of scale to making warranties. Whether scale economies regarding the sample warranty existed in the nineteenth century seems unknown, and Llewellyn did not consider the point.
23. Llewellyn saw, "'pictures in judges' heads of what trade looked like, and what trade meant, as going far to determine what type of quality obligation they read into the dicker of the parties . . . . Common to all [the nineteenth century cases] is a picture of the way in which dickers of this kind typically happen, and so of how the parties *ought* to have understood what was said and done." 4 at 719, 722. Courts who hold correct pictures of what business parties want to do thus will construe commercial contracts correctly. This is said in 11 at 880–1 and implied often, and is consistent with the modern notion that "commercial norms will develop only if they provide merchants with a more cost-effective method of adopting commercial practices on average than the alternative of each merchant starting from scratch." Jody S. Kraus, *Legal Design and the Evolution of Commercial Norms,* 26 J. Legal Stud. 377–8 (1997).
24. Articles claiming Llewellyn believed that dispute-resolving norms were immanent in practice, and that courts thus should discover and implement these norms, include Richard Danzig, *A Comment on the Jurisprudence of the Uniform Commercial Code,* 27 Stan. L. Rev. 621 (1975); Kenneth Casebeer, *Escape from Liberalism: Fact and Value in Karl Llewellyn,* 1977 Duke L. J. 671; Alexander M. Meiklejohn, *Castles in the Air: Blanket Assent and the Revision of Article 2,* 51 Wash. & Lee L. Rev. 599 (1994); Allen R. Kamp, *Between-the-Wars Social Thought: Karl Llewellyn, Legal Realism, and the Uniform Commercial Code in Context,* 59 Albany L. Rev. 325 (1995).
25. Llewellyn held that, "Disputes are the eternal heart and core of law. They do not mark its

circumference, but they will always mark its center. . . . when two people are in a dispute . . . not otherwise settled, . . . law shows its first societal value: the cleaning up of the matter. . . ." *Legal Tradition and Social Science Method – A Realist's Critique,* in Brookings Institution, *Essays on Research in the Social Sciences* 89, 91 (1931). Llewellyn's general thought respecting law and the troubled case is described in Twining, supra note 2, at 160–1.

26. 3 at 722.
27. Ibid., n. 45 at 723. Practice nevertheless remains relevant because the decisionmaker must act "in the light of the standing practices to which the new norm will be added, or on which it places a limiting definition." Ibid. Modern scholars argue that appeals to custom as a source of norms can be mistaken because norms can conflict, be vague, or were not meant to apply to the type of case that gets litigated. See Paul Gewirtz's Editor's Introduction to Karl Llewellyn, *The Case Law System in America* xx (1933, 1989); Jay Feinman, *Promissory Estoppel and Judicial Method,* 97 Harv. L. Rev. 678 (1984); Chris Williams, *The Search for Bases of Decision in Commercial Law: Llewellyn Redux,* 97 Harv. L. Rev. 1495 (1984). Llewellyn anticipated these views.
28. 6 at 162.
29. Ibid. n. 5 at 162.
30. 10 at 903. This was the second such disclaimer in these articles. In an earlier discussion of how a counselor would be a little at sea when the decisions were inconsistent, Llewellyn remarked, "This does not mean that I think that without practice there is no law, nor that I think law must follow custom, even when custom is silly or wrong." 7, n. 39 at 1257. Llewellyn's thought here is consistent with the view that decisionmakers can materially improve commercial norms with selective interventions. See Kraus, supra n. 23.
31. Modern scholars sometimes claim that Llewellyn wanted courts to resolve commercial cases according to the court's "situation sense." It is unclear what this would mean precisely – see Twining, supra n. 2 at 217–25, for a statement of the ambiguities – but seems to mean roughly that a court which had a proper understanding of the facts could infer the regnant norm and should follow it. A recent attempt to use the situation sense notion to solve a concrete problem – when there should be a substantial performance rule – is Todd Rakoff, *The Implied Terms of Contract: Of 'Default Rules' and 'Situation Sense,'* in *Good Faith and Fault in Contract Law* 191 (J. Beatson and D. Friedmann, eds., 1995). Llewellyn used neither the phrase "situation sense" nor the concept in the articles analyzed here, and appears not to have done so in anything he wrote before 1941. Rather, the "early Llewellyn" rejected the method of finding norms in practice.
32. 1 at 671–2. Recall Llewellyn's view that sales law raised mainly technical issues.
33. 8 n. 22 at 10.
34. William W. Fisher III included Llewellyn in his claim, "the Realists argued that most extent legal concepts had to be disaggregated if they were to be of any use. . . . Concepts like 'title', 'property right' . . . were hopelessly general." William W. Fisher III, *The Development of Modern American Legal Theory and the Judicial Interpretation of the Bill of Rights,* in M. Lacey and K. Haakonssen, eds., *The Bill of Rights* (1994). The text next argues that Llewellyn's dislike of the concepts Fisher mentions did not rest on their generality.
35. 2 at xiv. See also 6 at 169–70; 10 at 728–36.

36. 8 at 28.
37. Meaningful rules are "understandable and clear about what action it is which is to be guided, and how . . . [and] must state clearly how to deal with the raw facts as they arise." 8 at 12.
38. As another example of Llewellyn's views, he said of George Gardner's *An Inquiry into the Principles of the Law of Contract,* 46 Harv. L. Rev. 1 (1932): "He attempted a restatement of Principles in Hierarchy; a beautiful and (for our modern case-law) a novel idea; both method and substance deserve attention which they have not received. The method not only of carefully formulating a principle, but of carefully formulating not a single one *ad hoc,* but a number of competing principles, in the light of a whole picture; and then not of simply posing them in competition, but trying to arrange machinery for choice among them: this is almost as fine a contribution to juristic method as is Corbin's relentless and unremitting search for and of the cases and his insistence on making any theory square with them." 7 at 1267. Llewellyn added that he wrote (7) "in sudden worry that some folk might think an attack on pseudo-rules, of case-law . . . to be an Attack on Rules, or on Concepts at large." Id. at 1269. In the same vein, see Karl N. Llewellyn, *A Realistic Jurisprudence – The Next Step,* 30 Colum. L. Rev. 431 (1930).
39. 2 at xiii–xiv.
40. 10 at 887.
41. 4 at 726 makes the same point.
42. 5 at 404.
43. 3 at 748. See also 7 at 1266–7.
44. 13 at 561.
45. Ibid. at 564.
46. 5 at 381.
47. 13 at 563.
48. 2 at ix–x. Llewellyn later added

    "A rule which states accurately the outcome of the cases, seen as *cases,* incorporates *pro tanto* such wisdom on the cases as prior courts have shown, and such similarity of reaction as courts are likely to continue to show. . . . [The rule] gives some guidance (to the judge) about wherein his more personal judgments on such matters may be wisely tempered. It further sets . . . the picture of how far he is or is not really free to move unimpeded, and shows where the penumbra of his honest freedom lies to make further use of the given multiple case-law techniques."

    7 at 1257.
49. 2 at xx.
50. 8 at 19.
51. Karl Llewellyn, *On Reading and Using the Newer Jurisprudence,* 40 Colum. L. Rev. 581, 587 (1940)
52. For example, "rules in the proper sense always have as their office to *guide* action." 8 at 11. In an earlier treatment, Llewellyn said an ideal caselaw rule would fit a consistent line of caselaw, be announced in the cases as the rule, and would "appeal today as leading to a just result." Such ideal rules would guide courts "with some sureness" and afford "a counselor a moderately accurate prediction, and an advocate a solid base of case-planning." 7 at 1256. Brian Leiter, supra n. 4, argues that the "Realists' Core Claim" is

that caselaw results are predictable not because rules facilitate predictability but rather because "psycho-social facts about judges" heavily influence decisions, and these factors "are not idiosyncratic but characteristic of significant portions of the judiciary." Ibid. at 284. Llewellyn did not deny the relevance of "psycho-social facts" in the articles reviewed here, but did believe that courts decided according to rules, so that knowing the actual rules (rather than the doctrinal rules) would permit moderately accurate predictions.

53. 8 n. 25 at 12. Llewellyn's belief that rules can be clearly put also is evidenced by his view that "certainty is of the essence of mercantile law; business could not proceed without it." 10 at 733–4.
54. 1 at 670.
55. 11 at 901–2.
56. Ibid. at 900–1.
57. Since H. L. A. Hart, realists, including Llewellyn, commonly are read to define law in this way. See, e.g., David Luban, *Lawyers and Justice: An Ethical Study* 20–4 (1988); Thomas W. Bechtler, *The Background of Legal Realism,* in *Law in a Social Context* 12 (1978); H. L. A. Hart, *The Concept of Law,* Ch. VII (1961).
58. 7 at 1248.
59. 8 at 10.
60. Ibid., n. 21. Llewellyn often distinguished the functions of lawyer and judge. In an earlier paper, he stated that "prediction, not critique of wisdom, is the base-line job of the counselor; whereas the judge has as one of his two base-line jobs to get a wise and just result." 7 at 1256. And in a later paper, Llewellyn added: "For a counselor at work on counseling, what the courts *do* is thus the most important part of law; whether, I repeat, the doing is right or not. But *judges* (trial judges or appellate) cannot see law that way. . . . the branch of Jurisprudence which deals with the judge and his function must center no less upon the 'just' solution than upon the solution which other courts will reach. . . ." Karl N. Llewellyn, *On Reading and Using the Newer Jurisprudence,* 40 Colum. L. Rev. 581, 593 (1940). Llewellyn also argued that Holmes' statement that the law is only what courts will do was not meant to be taken literally, and was inconsistent with much of Holmes' thought. See 8 at 13.
61. Some European states had set up "specialized tribunals" that were "built for canvassing . . . trade practice. . . . But our own history shows that such specialized machinery is not an essential condition to the coming about of such [good legal] results. Given time enough. And given just a little luck." 11 at 874. The time is needed for cases to come, and the luck is needed to ensure that the cases present repetitive fact patterns.
62. 11 at 876. See also 877, 879.
63. 8 n. 44 at 21.
64. 1 at 671–2.
65. 5 at 380.
66. 12 at 705.
67. 4 at 718.
68. 5, n. 132 at 392, 394.
69. 1 at 672.
70. 3 at 730.
71. That the contribution of trade associations at creating rules lay more in their expertise

regarding commerce than regarding morals may be inferred from Llewellyn's view that association rules sometimes "have carried lop-sided manipulation into the game of Sales Law – and especially as against the ultimate-consumer buyer"; the state should check this tendency. 5 at 394. Llewellyn earlier argued that trade association rules "may threaten the unorganized consumer. . . . Until counter-organization of consumers develops, the only help for such a case lies along lines of government action." 1 at 677. Modern scholars extend Llewellyn's view to argue that the norms operative within private groups may themselves be inefficient. See Eric A. Posner, *Law, Economics, and Inefficient Norms,* 144 U. Pa. L. Rev. 1697 (1996), and Avery Katz, *Taking Private Ordering Seriously,* 144 U. Pa. L. Rev. 1745 (1996).

72. 7 at 1259, 1269.
73. 8 at 1. Llewellyn previously remarked, "There is often enough very considerable implicit and silent consistency in actual decision even when announced rules are at odds." 7 at 1252.
74. Karl Llewellyn, *Legal Tradition and Social Science Method – A Realist's Critique,* reprinted in Karl N. Llewellyn, *Jurisprudence: Realism in Theory and Practice* 92 (1962).
75. Ibid. at 94.
76. 9 at 779.
77. Ibid. at 804.
78. 8 at 36.
79. 9 at 796.
80. 5 at 352.
81. Useful modern examples of inducting actual contract rules from exhaustive case surveys are Douglas Laycock, *The Death of the Irreparable Injury Rule,* 103 Harv. L. Rev. 687 (1990), and Edward Yorio and Steve Thel, *The Promissory Basis of Section 90,* 101 Yale L. J. 111 (1991).
82. Karl Llewellyn, *Some Realism About Realism – Responding to Dean Pound,* 44 Harv. L. Rev. 1222, 1255 (1931).
83. 2 at xv.
84. 8 at 728–30; 12 at 704.
85. 5 at 384–5.
86. 6, n. 63 at 193. Llewellyn's acceptance of the efficiency norm has been remarked previously. Twining, supra n. 2 at 126 (Llewellyn was "a pragmatic, old fashioned American liberal, whose most important operative values were equality of opportunity, individual responsibility and efficiency."); Allan R. Kamp, *Uptown Act: A History of the Uniform Commercial Code: 1940–49",* 51 S. Methodist L. Rev. 275, 283 (1998) ("There are three themes that constantly recur in Llewellyn's thought: the primacy of trade usages; the goal of modernistic efficiency; and the need for balanced trade rules.").
87. Ibid., n. 29 at 178.
88. Ibid. at 177. See also 10 at 735. The gulf between Llewellyn's method and that of earlier scholars is illustrated by comparing Llewellyn's treatment of the seller's price action to the doctrinal article, John Barker Waite, *The Seller's Action for the Price,* 17 Mich. L. Rev. 282 (1919).
89. Another example of this mode of thought is Llewellyn's defense of the mailbox rule, which holds that the acceptance of an offer becomes effective when the acceptance is

mailed rather than when it is received. According to Llewellyn, the typical offeree believes the deal is on when he mails his acceptance and so will begin to engage in reliance. The typical offeror, on the other hand, will not think the deal is on until she receives the acceptance, and so she will delay reliance until then. Therefore, holding that the deal is on – the acceptance is effective – when the offeree mails it ensures that "we can protect the offerees in *all* these deals at the expense of hardship on offerors in very few of them." 9 at 795. This is a standard Kaldor-Hicks justification for a legal rule. The justification may risk circularity, however, without an explanation of how the parties' beliefs are formed. If the offeree believes that his acceptance binds because the law so provides, then the offeree's belief cannot be urged as a justification for the law. Thus Llewellyn's views respecting the mailbox rule are sketched only to illustrate his commitment to reducing transaction costs.

90. 3 at 737–8; 6 at 180–2, 204; 13 at 568.

91. 6 at 209. Llewellyn recognized that parties could create a cover remedy for themselves but argued that the law should provide the remedy to protect small, unsophisticated firms: "But why should sane rules be limited to the use of the careful and informed who can afford to pay counsel who are also skillful and informed?" Ibid., n. 39 at 182. Llewellyn commonly justified the need for default rules on this ground. See, e.g., 5 at 393.

92. To make this point clear, put interest to one side, denote the current period as period t and the next period as t + 1, and assume that the market price can rise by ten or fall by ten. Then if today's price is p_t, a buyer will assume that the next period price is $p_{t+1} = p_t + .5(10) + .5(-10) = p_t$.

93. This is an "other things equal" result for which limitations on recovering damages may sometimes produce undercompensation, for which a free option would be a partial remedy. In any event, the result may be clarified by an example. Assume that the market and contract prices when the deal was made were 10 and the buyer valued performance at 15. The buyer's expected profit thus is 5. The seller breaches when the market price is 12. Suppose that the legally reasonable time for cover would expire three days after breach. Let the buyer in this example have the ability to cover when the seller breached or any time thereafter. The buyer would wait until the third day. If the buyer covered at breach time, he would pay 12, get damages of 2, and earn his expected profit of 5 (the 2 in damages plus the difference between his valuation – 15 – and the cover price – 12.). If the buyer waited three days to cover and the day three market price is 12 or more, the buyer would sue for cover damages and also earn his expected profit. For example, if the market price on the third day is 14, the buyer earns 14 – 10 (damages) + 15 – 14 (profit on purchase) = 5. If the market price on day three is less than it was at breach time, the buyer also will cover but sue for *market* damages, and thus will be overcompensated. For example, let the market price on day three be 11. The buyer who waits to cover but sues for market damages then will earn 12 – 10 (market damages) + 15 – 11 (profit on purchase) = 6. The value to the buyer of the free option that the cover remedy creates – the value of waiting until the third day to cover – is positive because the buyer can profit from a downward market movement but cannot lose from an upward one. In this example, when the market is as likely to rise as to fall, the option is worth .50 (.5(0) + .5(1) = .50). Making cover available thus ensures the buyer an expected payoff in the event of breach that exceeds his expectation: this payoff here is 5 (expected profit) + .50

(value of option) = 5.50. A court using the good faith standard perhaps could require the buyer to sue for the cover price rather than market damages when the buyer makes one purchase, as in this example. However, plaintiff buyers usually are dealers who make many transactions. A court seldom could restrict such a buyer to measuring damages by any particular post-breach purchase. Dealer buyers thus could speculate in the fashion described.

94. Parties prefer remedies that do not overcompensate. See Lars A. Stole, *The Economics of Liquidated Damage Clauses in Contractual Environments with Private Information,* 8 J. Law, Econ. & Org. 582 (1992); Alan Schwartz, *The Myth That Promisees Prefer Supra Compensatory Remedies: An Analysis of Contracting for Damage Measures,* 100 Yale L. J. 369 (1990).
95. Modern examples of applying option theory to explain breach decisions and contract remedies include Alexander J. Triantis and George G. Triantis, *Timing Problems in Contract Breach Decisions,* 26 J. Legal Stud. (1997), and Paul G. Mahoney, *Contract Remedies and Options Pricing,* 24 J. Legal Stud. 139 (1995).
96. See 5 at 388, 389.
97. Ibid.; 4 n. 118 at 731; 6 n. 86 at 205.
98. 13 at 566–7.
99. See Alan Schwartz, *The Default Rule Paradigm and the Limits of Contract Law,* 3 So. Cal. Interdisc. L. J. 389 (1994).
100. See Bernstein, supra n. 4; Alan Schwartz, *Cure and Revocation for Quality Defects: The Utility of Bargains,* 16 B. Coll. Ind. & Comm. L. Rev. 543 (1975) (rules of commodities exchanges regulate breach more explicitly than the UCC rules). Regarding the influence of the three Llewellyn proposals discussed here, the UCC does not require buyers who reject after delivery to resell, but the acceptance rules of § 2–606 sometimes can be manipulated to reach this result; the Code adopts cover rules for buyers and sellers in §§ 2–706 and 2–712; and the UCC rejects a substantial performance rule – see § 2–601 – but prevents a buyer who accepts from revoking acceptance unless the defects substantially impair the value of the contract. See § 2–608. This rule raises some of the concerns discussed above, and parties routinely contract out by using repair and replacement clauses.
101. A comment to § II-A of the Revised Uniform Sales Act (1941) (a version that Llewellyn primarily wrote) advocated a merchant jury, explaining, "a court is rarely, and a jury almost never, equipped to pass with sound mercantile judgment on such a question as substantiality of a defect in performance in a particular trade."
102. Llewellyn's sensitivity to context also led him to recognize that relational contracts may require different legal treatment than other contracts. There are, he reported, a set of transactions that "lie half-way between mere reliance on the general spot market . . . and property-wise assurance of either outlet or supply by vertical integration." These deals include "output and requirements contracts, maximum and minimum contracts . . . sliding scale price arrangements – these are symptomatic of an economy stabilizing itself along new lines." In these arrangements, "long-range buyer seller *relations* come to seem more important than exact definition of the risks to be shifted by the particular dicker. . . ." 3 at 727. He later observed, "Our contract-law has as yet built no tools to really cope with this vexing and puzzling situation of fact," and that, in "standing relations," there is needed "a less-than-full contract damage type of sanction, for which

no rules of damage have yet been evolved." 5 at 375 and 378. Llewellyn wisely did not attempt to solve relational contract problems; the economics requisite to understanding them are being created today.

103. As evidence for this claim, the American Economics Association once commissioned Kenneth Boulding and George Stigler to identify the canon. See *Readings in Price Theory* (K. E. Boulding and G. J. Stigler, eds., 1952). The editors focused on articles "of general theoretical interest. We have followed the policy of not confining ourselves to the most recent literature but have taken a comprehensive view of the economic literature of the past forty years." vi. Of the twenty-five reprinted articles, only one article, by Leonid Hurwicz, concerned game theory, and it was published in 1945. Of the fifteen articles published before 1940, only Ronald Coase's article on the firm was relevant to some of Llewellyn's concerns, but economists themselves did not appreciate this relevance until many years later. A vivid description of the informal way in which economics was done when Llewellyn worked is Robert M. Solow, *How Did Economics Get That Way and What Way Did It Get?,* 126 Daedalus 39 (1997). Oliver W. Williamson also has observed of realists generally that their program was hindered by an inability to do the relevant economics. See Oliver W. Williamson, "Revisiting Legal Realism: The Law, Economics and Organization Perspective," Working Paper No. 95–12, Program in Law and Economics, School of Law, Berkeley (1996).

104. 12 at 704. See also 5 at 403.

105. 3 at 731.

106. 5 at 371.

107. 6, n. 25 at 175. Earlier Llewellyn observed "the most perplexing development of Anglo-American sales practice: to wit, the spread of clauses of indecently broad limitation of buyer's remedies, and even of total exemption of seller from responsibility." 4 at 731.

108. 5 at 386. Llewellyn did not use the phrases "procedural unconscionability" and "substantive unconscionability." They are used here because they are a useful way to describe his thinking and because that thinking made possible the modern unconscionability vocabulary.

109. 6, n. 47 at 185. The insight that default rules cannot remedy unfairness completely because the powerful party can avoid them apparently is reinvented in each generation – see Schwartz, supra n. 99, at 402–03 – and then ignored.

110. Llewellyn's 1939 book review (11) dealt almost exclusively with unconscionability issues and was cited sixty-seven times between 1972 and today. Llewellyn's two warranty articles (4 and 5) also had extensive discussions of unconscionability; these two articles were cited eighty times in the same period.

111. Unconscionability problems usually concern mass transactions (large firms and individual consumers). These transactions cannot be well understood without some competence in the economics of information, a field that George Stigler began in 1961. See George J. Stigler, *The Economics of Information,* 69 J. Pol. Econ. 213 (1961). For a modern review, see Alan Schwartz, *Legal Implications of Imperfect Information in Consumer Markets,* 151 J. of Inst. and Theor. Econ. 31 (1995). The discussion in Part V omits Llewellyn's products liability thought. Prior commentators observed that Llewellyn was among the earliest American scholars to advocate enterprise liability. See James R. Hackney, Jr., *The Intellectual Origins of American Strict Products Liability: A Case Study in American Pragmatic Instrumentalism,* 39 Am. J. Legal Hist.

443, 482–7 (1995); Note, *Karl Llewellyn and the Intellectual Foundations of Enterprise Liability Theory,* 97 Yale L. J. 1131 (1988).

112. 1 at 673. He thus identified with approval "the equivalency-idea," allegedly held by many courts, that bargains should be balanced. 3 at 745.
113. 12 at 704. See also Ibid. at 700–3.
114. Ibid. at 704. In discussing courts, Llewellyn added that the goal is "the marking out of the limits of the permissible." Thus courts should strike "utterly unreasonable clauses." 12 at 704.
115. For an interesting analysis of the difficulties involved in defining substantive unconscionability, see Richard Craswell, *Property Rules and Liability Rules in Unconscionability and Related Doctrines,* 60 U. Chi. L. Rev. 1, 20–9 (1993).
116. E.g., 4 at 712, 718; 5.
117. 3 at 734.
118. 3 at 732. Dennis Patterson, supra n. 4 at 175, argues, "The new conception engineered by Llewellyn [for interpreting contracts] presupposes that the meaning of the agreement of the parties does not depend exclusively or even primarily on the written terms of one or another document." Patterson does not refer to the contracts articles to demonstrate this view. Llewellyn agreed that custom and practice can illuminate the written word, but the Llewellyn of those articles would apply contract language unless it directed an unfair result.
119. Ibid. and 12 at 702.
120. 1 at 673. Llewellyn thus anticipated Fredrich Kessler, who many years later advocated this approach for courts exercising judicial oversight of insurance contracts. See Friedrich Kessler, *Contracts of Adhesion – Some Thoughts About Freedom of Contract,* 43 Colum. L. Rev. 629 (1943).
121. 12 at 704.
122. See Draft Uniform Commercial Code (1996) § 2–206(b): "A term in a . . . standard form . . . to which a consumer has manifested assent by a signature or other conduct is not part of the contract if the consumer could not reasonably have expected it unless the consumer expressly agrees to the term."
123. 12 at 704.
124. Ibid.
125. This criticism of a normative reasonable expectations test for identifying and responding to unconscionable terms has been made by numerous authors. See, e.g., Craswell, supra n. 116; Alan Schwartz, *Proposals for Products Liability Reform: A Theoretical Synthesis,* 97 Yale L. J. 353 (1988); Kenneth S. Abraham, *Judge-Made Law and Judge-Made Insurance: Honoring the Reasonable Expectations of the Insured,* 67 Va. L. Rev. 1151 (1981).
126. 3 n. 62 at 733. A court enforcing the "basic minimum," in this particular discussion, would override a disclaimer in order to permit the buyer to reject if the seller delivered goods different from those ordered. Llewellyn probably would permit the court to enforce the disclaimer in so far as it banned a suit for any consequential damages that the erroneous tender caused. Ibid. at 732–3. The same idea respecting disclaimers appears in 5 at 387.
127. 5 at 399–400.
128. 12 at 705; and also ibid. at 703 (courts will insist upon the "*minimum decencies*" that are

"essential to an enforceable bargain of a given type, or as being inherent in a bargain of that type") Traces of this position survive in comment 4 to UCC § 2–313, which recites that "a contract is normally a contract for a sale of something describable and described. A clause generally disclaiming 'all warranties, express or implied', cannot reduce the seller's obligation with respect to such description and therefore cannot be given literal effect. . . ."

129. That a transaction type exists may be relevant to a finding of procedural unconscionability. For example, if sellers routinely accompany the sale of a particular product with a warranty, then a contract to sell that product with a disclaimer might surprise the buyer. This analysis would not make the warranty an "iron" term that sellers could not disclaim, but it would require a seller who uses a nonstandard disclaimer to bear a heightened disclosure burden.
130. See, e.g., 1 at 673; 3 at 731.
131. 1 at 678.
132. 3, n. 47 at 725 and 734.
133. A monopoly equilibrium exists when there are many firms but each charges the price that a single monopolist would have charged.
134. See Alan Schwartz and Louis Wilde, *Imperfect Information in Markets for Contract Terms: The Examples of Warranties and Security Interests,* 69 Va. L. Rev. 1387 (1983).
135. Modern views respecting procedural unconscionability and related doctrines are summarized in Richard Craswell and Alan Schwartz, *Foundations of Contract Law* 287–341 (1994).
136. 5 at 358.
137. Ibid., n. 58, 364–5.
138. 6 at 207. Llewellyn later justified the need for sales law reform in part because some courts failed to read the Uniform Sales Act to obtain just results. "An instance is found in the whole series of difficulties over implied warranty, and over the degree to which or manner in which various warranty-responsibilities can be avoided in transactions in which they should be present." 13 at 560. See also the earlier statement in 5 at 384–5: "the one thing which should never be allowed to be negated – at least as a *condition,* . . . is a description when taken seriously. . . . Surely a case is to be made for [Uniform Sales Act] Section 14 . . . being an iron section whose effect no agreement can upset. . . ." Llewellyn meant here that if the seller described the goods as grade A but the contract recited that the buyer bears the risk that the goods might turn out to be another grade, the buyer "at least" should be permitted to reject grade B goods, and perhaps should be permitted to assert the other buyer remedies.
139. 3 at 744.
140. 5 at 402.
141. 10 at 743; also at 726 and 741. In eighteenth century England, a warranty of quality may have been implied on the basis of a sound price only when the seller was aware of the defect at the time of sale. See Oldham, supra n. 18, at 1977–8.
142. 5 at 400–1.
143. 12 at 702. This idea also appears in comment 4 to UCC § 2–313, where courts are advised to give "consideration . . . to the fact that the probability is small that a real price is intended to be exchanged for a pseudo-obligation."
144. See Alan Schwartz and Robert E. Scott, *Commercial Law: Principles and Policies*

204–7 (2d ed., 1991). Llewellyn thus mistakenly said of what is now the standard warranty for manufactured goods, under which the seller agrees to repair or replace defective parts for a limited period but precludes rejection for minor defects and excludes recovery for consequential damages, "that precious commodity Justice must be viewed as being as scarce as the scarce economic goods." 5 at 400–1.

145. The driving force in this example apparently is the low failure probability. If the failure probability were 3%, however, the disclaimer price would be 97.3% of the warranty price. Failure probabilities above 3% for standard manufactured products seem uncommon. Also, if the ratio of fixed to variable costs were higher, the price difference would be smaller. In the example above, if the seller's fixed cost were $300 per unit and her variable cost $800, a disclaimer would reduce the price by $8 on an $1,100 item. The UCC permits sellers to disclaim implied warranties – see § 2–316(2) – but also permits courts to strike these disclaimers under § 2–302 if they are unconscionable.

146. Winand Emons, *The Theory of Warranty Contracts,* 3 J. Econ. Surveys 43, 54 (1989).

147. Neil Duxbury observed that Llewellyn, "far from being a typecast rule-sceptic, was adamant that rules 'guide' judicial decision-making." See *The Reinvention of American Legal Realism,* 12 Legal Stud. 137, 143 (1992) (footnote omitted). Fisher also noted Llewellyn's belief that rules could confine decisionmakers. On the other hand, Bechtler, supra n. 57 at 25, Leiter, supra n. 4, Fisher, and others associate Llewellyn with rule scepticism. Twining frequently suggests that Llewellyn was an ethical relativist. Llewellyn has been associated with the position that legal realists were not interested in policy on the basis of his view, expressed in *Some Realism about Realism – Responding to Dean Pound,* 44 Harv. L. Rev. 1222 (1931), that scholars should put the normative aside for a time in order to study how the legal system actually works. Fisher associates Llewellyn, among others, with having undermined democratic theory, a part of view (6), by allegedly showing that "judges deciding individual controversies often derive little guidance if any from statutes (enacted by elected representatives of the people) or from common law rules (implicitly democratically ratified through the legislature's inaction). . . ." Fisher, supra n. 34, at 284. The preceding notes show that Llewellyn has been identified with the other positions. One could add to the list that realists believed scholars should do empirical research about how law affects society. Llewellyn was sympathetic to this project, but was not an empiricist when wearing his contract scholar (as contrasted with his sociologist) hat.

2

Economic Efficiency and The Ex Ante Perspective

DANIEL A. FARBER†

I. Introduction

In 1985, Frank Easterbrook received the prestigious invitation to write the foreword to the *Harvard Law Review*'s annual issue on the Supreme Court. Unlike most of his illustrious fellow foreword authors, he chose to consider a broad range of Supreme Court decisions, not just the comparatively few rulings on major constitutional issues. Easterbrook – then a professor, now a federal appeals judge – argued that a major change had taken place in the Court's legal reasoning: a switch from looking back to the past to looking ahead to the future.

As Easterbrook pointed out, the traditional judicial function was resolving disputes. "For a long time," he said, "courts portrayed rule creation as a by-product of dispute resolution. The court had to decide a case, and in order to show that its decision was not capricious it often had to announce a rule to govern future cases." But dispute resolution is "backward looking," based on the "equities" of the dispute. It revolves around fairness, "an equitable division of the gains or losses among existing parties given that certain events have come to pass." In short, "[f]airness arguments are ex post arguments," and lawyers find it hard to argue about cases without invoking the ideal of fairness.[1]

This retrospective approach is understandable, Easterbrook says. By the time of a judicial decision, the positions of the parties may be essentially fixed: An accident has already happened, or the plaintiff has already created the invention that the defendant seeks to copy, or the hostile takeover bid has already been made. By taking the positions of the parties as fixed, however, judges lose the "opportunity to create gains through the formulation of the legal rule," for the "principles laid down today will influence whether similar parties *will be* in similar situations tomorrow." In this respect, the judge has the capacity to represent the future: prospective consumers, producers, and others who may be affected by the decision.[2]

Easterbrook argued that the Supreme Court was moving toward a forward-looking perspective, which focuses more on a rule's future impact than on fairness. "Today," he said, "cases often are just excuses for the creation or alteration of rules." For example, according to Easterbrook, the Supreme Court no longer looked at securities cases in moralistic terms, but instead focused on consequences. He found the same trend in intellectual property cases, and across a broad range of other economic issues.[3] Although no rigorous empirical study of this question exists, the trend identified by Easterbrook has probably continued. Certainly, the elevation of Easterbrook and his fellow Chicagoan Richard Posner to the appellate bench can only have helped to promote the trend. In the area of commercial law, in particular, some of the most important recent scholarship has also adopted the ex ante perspective.[4]

And yet, there is obvious ground for concern about this shift in perspective. It is one thing for a legislature to make rules for the future. When a court announces a new legal rule, however, it must do so in the course of deciding a particular case. The parties to the case pay the price for the new rule, but they may or may not ever themselves reap the future benefits. In short, the court is erecting its new rule on the backs of the litigants, whose dispute serves only as a convenient occasion for judicial legislation. Is this fair to the litigants? Or, on the contrary, does the ex ante perspective treat them unjustly by overriding their rights solely to benefit others?[5] Even if the application of existing legal rules to the case is not clear-cut, Ronald Dworkin has argued, the parties are entitled to a decision based on the best possible interpretation of existing legal rules, precedents, and principles, not on "social engineering" for the future.[6]

Easterbrook is well known as a practitioner of the economic analysis of law, and it is no coincidence that he was attuned to the shift to the ex ante perspective. Economic analysis is at heart prospective and forward-looking. Not surprisingly, given the historic links of economics to utilitarianism, the economist's motto is to concentrate on future effects and let bygones be bygones.[7] In applying economic analysis to law, Easterbrook and other scholars have asked whether a given legal rule maximizes social wealth. But this goal of economic efficiency was highly controversial in the years just before Easterbrook's foreword.

The most vocal defender of economic efficiency at that time was Posner. Among his battery of arguments in favor of efficiency, the most notable attempted to finesse the ex post/ex ante distinction. Posner's argument was a twist on the standard "social contract" idea that justice can be defined in terms of a hypothetical bargain. He argued that, if it had been practical to do so, the parties to the dispute would have agreed in advance to having the efficient rule apply to any future dispute. So, in some sense, they can be said to have consented to the use of the efficient rule in their case, even though the rule's justification relates to its future effects rather than its past fairness. To the extent it is successful, Posner's argument brings fairness and future utility together, by making the ex ante perspective a standard for ex post decisions.[8]

This argument (as well as Posner's other claims) was vigorously attacked, most notably by Guido Calabresi, Jules Coleman, and Ronald Dworkin.[9] The conventional wisdom is that the attack was successful.[10]

In this essay, I will revisit the debate over Posner's argument. My thesis is that the critics were right about Posner's failure to establish economic efficiency as a universal, let alone supreme, moral norm. Nevertheless, Posner's argument is well worth careful consideration because it actually turns out to be valid, under *some* circumstances, as an argument for judicial use of the economist's ex ante perspective. Specifically, a modified form of his argument works in situations where wealth distribution, risk aversion, and preference shifts are insignificant, and where fundamental rights are not at stake. My argument proceeds from a version of John Rawls' concept of the "original position."[11] I will argue that a limited principle of economic efficiency would be adopted behind a Rawlsian veil of ignorance, subject to higher ranking principles of justice governing basic rights and wealth distribution.

In order to deal with the points raised by Posner's critics, my analysis is necessarily more complex than his in three respects. First, the hypothetical consent that is being used to judge the efficiency standard needs to be separated from the actual transaction itself, and the hypothetical conditions need to be specified and defended as morally relevant. Second, because the law and economics approach is essentially consequentialist, we need to consider the efficiency effects of the rule announced by the judge on *later* transactions, not the hypothetical effect that it would have had on the transaction in the case at issue if it had been agreed to earlier. (Consider, for example, a unique transaction that will never recur – for example, filling a gap under a statute that has been prospectively repealed. Why worry about what rule would have had economically efficient consequences when the court's decision will have distributional consequences but no efficiency effects?) Finally, we need to be more careful about defining efficiency itself than was true during the earlier debate over Posner's argument.

Even if the concept of economic efficiency can be upheld under this kind of Rawlsian analysis, obviously many problems would remain. The concept of the original position as means of gauging fairness has been controversial, and Rawls has to some extent reconceptualized his theory of justice in more recent work.[12] Nevertheless, this Rawlsian argument for efficiency is significant for three reasons. First, Rawls and Posner are by no means natural allies, so drawing a connection between their views is intriguing. Second, there can be no doubt that *A Theory of Justice* is a signal contribution to modern political theory, and the efficiency concept gains a certain amount of credibility if it can be brought within that framework. Third, this hybrid of Rawls and Posner also has some payoff in guiding analysis of specific legal rules. It provides a clear signal of when the efficiency norm is a useful guideline for judges and when it becomes more problematic. As it happens, the cases governed by the norm constitute the core of commercial law.[13]

Briefly, I will proceed along the following lines. Part II recounts the fierce debate between Posner and his critics. Part III considers whether Posner's argument can be rehabilitated in some specific contexts along the Rawlsian lines sketched above, or whether it is utterly bankrupt (as Dworkin in particular would argue). Part IV works through some of the implications of the argument. In particular, I consider whether courts can legitimately and competently apply the ex ante approach. I also discuss how and why the ex ante approach breaks down – usually in just those cases where the law and economics approach seems intuitively troublesome. The range of cases where efficiency is the decisive consideration turns out to be narrow, though significant.

II. The Debate over Wealth Maximization

Before we examine Posner's argument in detail, it may be useful to be more concrete about the difference between the ex ante and ex post approaches. Consider a classic contracts case. The buyer, a woman living on welfare, had purchased furniture on credit. The financing agreement provided that every piece of furniture she had purchased would be treated as collateral whenever she made a new purchase on credit. More specifically, all payments were applied in proportion to the outstanding debt on a particular piece of furniture. Consequently, no piece was ever fully paid off until all of the furniture had been paid for. In the meantime, a default would result in repossession of all the furniture, even though she had paid more than enough to cover the debt on the pieces she had purchased earlier. Thus, although she owed only trivial amounts on some of her earlier purchases, she lost everything she owned when she fell behind in her payments. Applying the doctrine of unconscionability, Judge Skelly Wright – a liberal luminary of the Warren Court era – refused to enforce the cross-collateral provision of the finance agreement.[14] This is a classic application of the ex post, fairness-based approach.

Under the ex ante approach, however, the court's decision is troubling. The future effect of the decision is to reduce a seller's collateral and the buyer's incentive to scrape up the payments. Consequently, the debt becomes more risky. To counter this increased risk, sellers will either have to raise interest rates or refuse to lend to the riskier buyers. So the cost of taking this particular buyer off the hook is that similar individuals in the future will be hurt in one of two ways: They may be unable to buy furniture at all, which seems a doubtful contribution to their well-being, or they may have to pay higher interest. At best, we have forced them to exchange a package of lower interest but strict collection practices, for another package with higher rates but less repossession.[15] Either way, the effect of the decision is to harm future buyers by preventing them from buying the furniture they want on the terms they prefer. From this ex ante perspective, the court's decision is not only inefficient but perverse, because it harms the very group it is intended to help.[16]

My present purpose is not to debate the result in this specific case, but to demonstrate the fundamental change in perspective represented by the ex ante approach. Note, however, that the supposed benefits of the ex ante approach will mostly accrue to other people – the future parties whom Easterbrook says the judge is charged with representing. But this may be little consolation to the buyer in the specific case before the court, who is about to lose all her possessions because of a harsh and obscurely phrased contract clause. If the result is seriously unfair to her, is the court entitled to sacrifice her interests to benefit unknown future buyers? Posner's argument was designed to eliminate this issue by showing that, for the same reasons that enforcing the clause has beneficial future effects, it is also fair to presume that buyers in the past have consented to enforcement. Fairness and economic efficiency, if this argument is valid, turn out to be one and the same.

The relationship between judicial fairness and efficiency is not simply an issue for students of jurisprudence. It also relates to one of the liveliest current disputes in the area of commercial law. This dispute concerns how courts should craft default rules – that is, rules that apply when the parties themselves have failed to say anything about a question in their contract. (One example is a statute providing that if the parties to a sales contract fail to specify a price, the court must determine a "reasonable" price.) This is a central issue in contemporary contract scholarship – indeed, one leading scholar has recently defined contract law as the study of default rules.[17] One school insists that default rules should be chosen on the basis of efficiency: a court should pick the rule that produces the greatest net gains for the parties (even if it hurts one of them). Others argue strenuously against the fairness of this approach. To the extent that we conceive of the parties as knowing about and actually consenting to specific default rules, the fairness problem is obviated in this setting. Realistically, however, the parties will often be ignorant on the subject (or the default rule may be crafted only after the fact), so the fairness of applying the ex ante approach cannot be taken for granted.[18] Posner's argument then becomes relevant.

A. *Posner's Argument*

Before delving into Posner's argument, it may be useful to recall some standard economic terminology. One state of affairs is a Pareto improvement over another if at least one person benefits from the change and no one is hurt. Essentially, no one would have any reason to vote against a Pareto improvement. A situation is Pareto optimum if no other situation is a Pareto improvement over it, or in other words, if any possible change would harm at least one person. There may be many possible Pareto optimal allocations of resources with different distributions of wealth.

Pareto improvements are not easy to come by. A less demanding standard is called Kaldor-Hicks efficiency.[19] Economists often use the term "efficiency" without defining whether they are invoking Pareto or Kaldor-Hicks. In law and economics, economic efficiency usually means Kaldor-Hicks, and the term will be used in that sense in this chapter. One situation is superior to another in the Kaldor-Hicks sense if the gains of the winners exceed the losses of the losers, or more precisely, if after a hypothetical transfer from the winners to the losers, the resulting situation would be a Pareto improvement over the status quo. More simply, the winners benefit enough that they could afford to bribe the losers into going along with the change. In some general sense, Kaldor-Hicks tells us that the total benefits of a change outweigh the total costs, although some people may win and others may lose. Thus, a Kaldor-Hicks improvement would pass a cost/benefit analysis.

Posner's thesis, in more ordinary terms, is that judges should use cost/benefit analysis to make decisions. He caused some confusion by using the term "wealth maximization," which seems to imply that the goal is maximize the value of financial assets. Neither Pareto nor Kaldor-Hicks efficiency is, however, limited to goods that are traded on markets. For example, one situation might be a Pareto improvement over another because one person gains more leisure, which he values, and no one else loses anything.

With these definitions in mind, we turn to Posner's effort to defend economic efficiency as a norm for common law judges. His fullest discussion of the subject is found in a 1980 article, written after he had already exchanged initial shots with some of his critics. The crux of the argument is as follows. Because there is no way of determining whether individuals actually consent to legal rules, the best we can do is to look for implied consent. One way of doing this is to ask whether, if transaction costs were zero, the parties would have agreed to the legal rule in advance. This procedure, he says, "resembles a judge's imputing the intent of parties to a contract that fails to provide expressly for some contingency." Thus, he says, "an institution predicated on wealth maximization may be justifiable by reference to the consent of those affected by it even though the institution authorizes certain takings, such as the taking of life, health, or property of an individual injured in an accident in which neither party is negligent, without requiring compensation ex post."[20]

Posner distinguishes his approach from that taken by Rawls in that he does not assume that the parties are ignorant about their positions in society. His argument against Rawls is not, to my mind, an appealing one:

> In [Rawls'] original position, no one know whether he has productive capabilities, so choices made in that position will presumably reflect some probability that the individual making the choice will turn out not to be endowed with any such capabilities. In

> effect, the choices of the unproductive are weighted equally with those of the productive. . . . I prefer therefore to imagine actual people, deploying actual endowments of skill and energy and character, making choices under uncertainty. I prefer, that is, to imagine choice under conditions of natural ignorance to choice under the artificial ignorance of the original position.[21]

Thus, as Posner explains, his rejection of Rawls is based on the premise that "those who have no productive assets have no ethical claim on the assets of others."[22]

Nevertheless, Posner did recognize some moral limits to the principle of wealth maximization. First, he acknowledged that it is difficult to impute actual consent when a legal rule results in a substantial redistribution of wealth. When it is easy to identify in advance who will lose from a policy, it is hardly realistic to assume that they would consent to adoption of that policy.[23]

Second, Posner admitted that the principle runs into problems when we are considering the initial allocation of rights rather than some incremental adjustment. In general, the concept of economic efficiency becomes problematic when legal changes are large enough to affect prices substantially. It is hard to say whether social wealth has been increased by a shift in resources when the prices used to measure output have also changed. Even in this situation, however, Posner argues that we can make guesses about relative social wealth. For instance, he argues, "if we started with a society where one person owned all the others, soon most of the others would have bought their freedom from that person because their output would be greater as free individuals than as slaves, enabling them to pay more for the right to their labor than that right was worth to the slave owner."[24]

B. *Three Critics of the Ex Ante Perspective*

In retrospect, it is easy to see why Posner's argument sparked such a hostile response. There was first of all his assertion that those who cannot work – the very young, the very old, and the handicapped – have no moral claim whatsoever on society, even for the minimum needed to survive. Then there was his use of the term "wealth maximization" rather than standard economic terminology, which seems to imply that a rising national product is the one and only social goal. Finally, philosophers could not fail to be offended by his analytical nonchalance, such as the way his argument meandered between reliance on some form of implicit but real consent, and claims about purely hypothetical transactions between potential slaves and potential owners. Given the timing of the debate, just at the start of the Reagan Administration, liberals may also have been alarmed by this seeming rationale for the conservative agenda of unregulated markets and government cost/benefit analysis. Whatever the reasons, Posner attracted a vigorous and distinguished array of critics, who took issue, among other points, with his ex ante argument.[25]

Ronald Dworkin made three telling arguments against Posner's ex ante position. First, he argued that Posner could not be talking about actual consent, because it is clear that people do not in any realistic sense give individualized consent to the operation of the rules of the legal system. Thus, we are talking about imputed or, to be more blunt, fictional consent rather than any form of actual consent.[26]

Second, Dworkin pointed out that arguments about hypothetical choice gain their strength from the careful construction of the circumstances in which the hypothetical choice is supposed to take place. These circumstances must be designed to capture the morally relevant aspects of the issue, and must be supported by some argument about why other aspects of actual choice have been suppressed as morally irrelevant. Posner does not lay this groundwork for his ex ante argument (a gap I will try to fill later in this chapter).[27]

Finally, Dworkin criticized Posner's reliance on assertions about what choices most people would make under situations of realistic ignorance. Dworkin saw two flaws in this effort. First, Posner had no way of specifying the relevant point in time at which this ignorance was to be assessed. If he were talking about an actual act of consent, the timing of that act would provide the date for assessing ignorance, but this is not true for hypothetical consent, so Posner needed some independent moral argument for choosing the appropriate time. Second, by abandoning the need for unanimous improvement in welfare, Posner dropped Pareto in favor of what is essentially a utilitarian standard. But of course, under a utilitarian standard, the losses of a single individual or small group might outweigh gains to everyone else, depending on the relative gains and losses in utility.[28] So the "almost everyone" test does not necessarily work for the utilitarian.

Dworkin then considered whether a more attractive form of Posner's argument could be made to work. He offered what he calls the "alpha" principle: "in a hard case judges should choose and apply that rule, if any, that is in the then antecedent interests of the vast bulk of people though not in the interests of the party who then loses." It might be plausibly argued, he said, that alpha itself is in the antecedent interest of everyone, but as a safeguard, Dworkin suggested amending the rule to exclude results that are "against the interests of the worst-off economic group or any other group that would be generally and antecedently disadvantaged."[29] But Dworkin argued that this rule would not, in fact, be adopted by the parties in the Rawlsian original position because of risk aversion: "it works against those who in one way or another have very bad luck."[30] Dworkin seemed to concede that this amended version of alpha might form a wise guide for legislation, but he believed that it would be unfair to apply alpha in adjudication.[31]

Posner's argument was also attacked by Jules Coleman, along lines similar to Dworkin. Like Dworkin, Coleman argued that Posner was confused about the significant distinction between real and imputed consent. He then turned to an argument which he said that Posner did not make, but which would have been more plausible: "Risk-neutral, rational persons facing economic choice under uncertainty would choose to pursue wealth through Kaldor-Hicks institutions." The problem, he said, is that Posner failed to justify the assumption that they would pursue wealth above all other goods, or to put it another way, that they would elevate wealth maximization over alternatives such as utilitarianism or Rawls' theory of justice.[32] Coleman himself was dubious that a rational person would place primary importance on maximizing his wealth, which Coleman defined in the terms of market prices. He was also dubious that a rational person who valued other things would aim for wealth maximization as a strategy for ultimately getting more of those other things.[33]

The final critic whose views I will discuss is Guido Calabresi. Despite having been one of the founding figures of law and economics, Calabresi found the idea of wealth maximization as a social goal absurd. Wealth can be defined only given an initial assignment of rights, which provides the basis for establishing market prices, but the function of law is to make that initial assignment. So the legal system cannot be based on wealth because wealth is based in important ways on the legal system instead.[34]

Calabresi then turned to the argument that "an efficiency improvement – a bigger pie – involves no distributional judgments if at the time of the change subsequent winners and subsequent losers have an equal chance to be gainers or losers." In this situation, he asked, "cannot one assume that all parties would, if they were asked, consent to the change since their *expected* returns would be greater?"[35]

Calabresi found this argument unpersuasive for three reasons. First, in reality, the impact of legal rules on different individuals is not random. Second, different groups may have different levels of risk aversion, so that some groups actually gain relative to others even though their expected returns are the same.[36] Thus, we must always take into account the distributional effects of legal rules, not just their efficiency.[37] Third, he worried that individual preferences may change over the time, so that even if a rule would receive universal consent ex ante, individuals would find ex post that the rule was unacceptable given their later preferences, and would have a valid ground to regret consenting to the rule.[38] This point about preference change is an important one, to which I will return in Part III.

C. The Upshot of the Debate

The debate over wealth maximization seemed at the time to generate at least as much heat as light. In retrospect, however, the clamor of the debate concealed the emergence of some substantial areas of agreement. For simplicity, I will list four propositions that either Posner (then or later) or his opponents seemed to concede.

1. *Economic efficiency cannot possibly be the sole principle of justice.* According to Posner, this has always been his position; it is clear at any rate that it is his current position. For example, he now believes that the moral case against slavery is based on liberty rather than efficiency.[39]
2. *The ex ante perspective produces an economical efficiency standard only in the absence of risk aversion.* Posner now concedes this point, though he believes that private and social insurance can make risk aversion irrelevant.[40]
3. *The ex ante perspective is justifiable in the case of a legislature passing prospective legislation.* As we saw, Dworkin conceded this point.
4. *Economic efficiency requires a prior decision about the initial allocation of resources.* Another Posner concession related to the initial allocation, though he still attempted to minimize the significance of the point.[41]

All of these propositions seem quite plausible, and I will take them as a basis for further discussion. I also believe that the criticisms of Posner established a couple of key weaknesses in his argument. First, although he relied ultimately on hypothetical consent, he failed to sufficiently justify the parameters of the hypothetical situation in which consent is given. Rather than attempt to create such a hypothetical from scratch, I will use a version of Rawls' original position. I will also assume that Rawls is correct that persons in the original position would pick two principles of justice, one protecting basic human rights and another protecting the disadvantaged. (Specifically, Rawls argues for a principle of justice guaranteeing that the choice of basic social institutions should guarantee the highest possible levels of well-being for the most disadvantaged members of society. To put the principle another way, we must favor the society with the highest possible safety net.)

Second, the notion of "wealth maximization" seems unhelpful. It suggests the existence of some measurable entity called wealth which can be used to provide a numerical measure of all possible social states. No such entity exists in economic theory. Moreover, the term is also misleading in its suggestion that financial assets are somehow the paradigmatic form of individual welfare. To avoid confusion, I will simply refer to economic efficiency as a goal of the legal system. The problem to be considered, then, can be stated as follows: "Under what circumstances, if any, would parties in the original position agree that courts should adopt economically efficient rules of law?"

An additional argument would be required to establish that the original position provides a valid method for determining the justice of social arrangements, but a great deal has been written on that subject, and I have nothing to add to that debate. I will say only that, although I am dubious of foundational moral theories, it does seem to me that Rawls has provided a useful heuristic with which to judge the fairness of social arrangements.

III. Hypothetical Bargains and Actual Fairness

In this section, I will consider the status of efficiency as a moral norm, evaluated from a Rawlsian ex ante perspective. I will defer until Part IV any consideration of whether, assuming the principle is valid, judges are under some special disability that blocks legitimate use of the principle in litigation.

A. Is Efficiency a Value?

Ronald Dworkin has questioned whether economic efficiency is a value which judges should consider in reaching decisions. Indeed, Dworkin has argued that social wealth is not a value at all, let alone one which should be the primary guide for judicial decisions.[42]

His argument goes like this: Suppose Derek has a book Amartya wants; Derek would be willing to sell the book for two dollars, and Amartya would be willing to pay three. Assume, for some reason, that a voluntary sale is impractical. A forced transfer from Amartya to Derek is economically efficient (in the Kaldor-Hicks sense) because Amartya would be willing to pay Derek enough to compensate him for his loss. But, Dworkin says, make the example more specific: "Derek is poor and sick and miserable, and the book is one of his few comforts. He is willing to sell it for $2 only because he needs medicine. Amartya is rich and content. He is willing to spend $3 for the book, which is a very small part of his wealth, on the odd chance that he might someday read it, although he knows that he probably will not." Hence, Dworkin concludes, "that goods are in the hands of those who would be willing to pay more to have them is as morally irrelevant as the book's being in the hands of the alphabetically prior party."[43] Dworkin minces no words about his conclusion:

> I did not argue that maximizing social wealth is only one among a number of plausible social goals, or is a mean, unattractive, or unpopular social goal. I argued that it makes no sense as a social goal, even as one among others. It is preposterous to suppose that social wealth is a component of social value, and implausible that social wealth is strongly instrumental towards a social goal. . . .[44]

Put baldly, Dworkin seems to be arguing that economic efficiency cannot be a social value because we can imagine a situation in which economic efficiency has improved but the ultimate outcome is clearly worse than the original situation. Dworkin is clearly correct that economic efficiency flunks this test. Economic efficiency is an aggregate value, but aggregate improvement may be offset by distributive inequities. But Dworkin's implicit criteria for what constitutes a social value is too stringent. For example, under this criterion, improved life expectancy does not qualify as a social value. We can imagine a situation in which average life expectancy has been improved but only at the cost of worsening inequities. Perhaps Amartya, being desperately poor, is unlikely to live long, whereas transplanting his liver to Derek will allow Derek to add many years to his life expectancy – yet an involuntary transfer of Amartya's liver has even less to recommend it than a transfer of his book. So, following Dworkin's argument, we would conclude that raising life expectancy is not a component of social value. But if neither life expectancy nor wealth are components of social value, then it is a mistake for people in Bangladesh to think it would be better if their society had the same levels of wealth and life expectancy as Sweden. Something seems a bit amiss in Dworkin's argument.

The argument is, in fact, seriously flawed.[45] If we want to know whether something is a morally relevant feature of the world, we need to know whether two otherwise identical situations differ morally because of a difference in this quality. We cannot show that X is irrelevant by taking two states of the world, and triumphantly pointing out that one of them has more of quality X but is morally inferior, when it also differs in other morally relevant respects. Dworkin posits a change (the transfer of the book) which is both economically efficient and distributionally retrogressive. If the change is undesirable, this may prove only that the distributional consequences matter more than the efficiency effect. Dworkin also seems to object to the involuntary and uncompensated nature of the transfer, but again, even if he is right, that shows only that we recognize some side constraints against uncompensated transfers.

To see whether efficiency is a reasonable candidate to be a component of social value, we really need to compare two situations which differ only in their economic efficiency. So assume that Amartya and Derek have equal wealth, and that Amartya puts a greater monetary value on the book than Derek. On the face of things, it is not implausible to prefer a state of the world where Amartya has the book over one in where Derek has it. One might well be inclined to criticize a society which systematically allocated items to people who would not have been willing to outbid other people for them at an auction. Even if Amartya is willing to pay more for the book only because of greater wealth, this should not be a concern provided that Amartya has a just claim to his greater wealth, and thus a just claim to possessing a greater ability to obtain material goods.

In short, if we had to decide whether to allot the book to Derek or Amartya, an auction seems like an eminently fair way to do so, and remains fair even if Amartya is wealthier, so long as he has a just claim to his greater wealth.[46] The reason for this is not that giving the book to Amartya maximizes utility. Even if Derek and Amartya have the same wealth, we cannot be sure that Amartya will derive greater happiness from the book than Derek would, just because he chooses to pay more. Perhaps Amartya is a drone and Derek is keenly sensitive, so that Amartya always derives lesser feelings of pleasure from any particular good than Derek does.

Rather, the auction is fair for much the same reason that it is fair for one group to win an election because it has more votes. Like electoral rules, economic institutions are ways of allocating power (in this case, the power to claim certain goods for private consumption). One of the rules of the game is that people who bid higher get to own things even if other people would like to own them. As with majority rule, it is possible to question whether the game as a whole is fair, and it is also quite possible to maintain that the game should be limited in scope, so that some issues cannot be decided either by election or by auction. But in saying that the distribution of wealth between Derek and Amartya is fair, we are implicitly assuming that it is fair for them to own wealth in the first place – which is to say, we have accepted a particular way of voting with money on the allocation of economic output, and we have also agreed that the relative division of "voting" power between them is appropriate. So unless the ownership of a book is, for some reason, a decision that should be placed entirely outside of this particular decisionmaking game – as might be true, for example, with human body parts – we cannot argue against the justice of having the book go to the highest bidder. Thus, to justify the allocation of the book in a particular case, we need to begin with the assumption that certain kinds of institutions and a given allocation of wealth are appropriate. Given these assumptions, however, we can say that it is more just to allocate the book to Amartya than Derek.

Notice, however, that this argument does not tell us how the basic institutional arrangements are justified. Let us suppose, with Rawls, that the question is what institutions rational people would find to be in their advantage in the original position. Now, we can at least say that they would adopt the Pareto principle (subject to the constraint of respecting basic rights, which Rawls puts before any distributional issues). As Lawrence Sager has said, a "Pareto-superior move gives persons in the original position an opportunity for improvement of their lot at no cost; it is a free lottery ticket."[47] Indeed, Rawls himself seems to agree that the Pareto principle would be satisfied in his scheme.[48] But if this is true, it means that satisfying individual preferences (the heart of the economist's concept of welfare) does actually count as a valid social goal. Thus, we are entitled to design institutions that will most effectively satisfy individual preferences, subject to overriding principles of justice.

What this means is that (again subject to higher priority principles of justice), the Pareto principle can be viewed as an acceptable feature of just institutions. Whether Kaldor-Hicks efficiency is an acceptable principle is less clear. That will be the subject of later discussion. But to the extent that it would be accepted in the original position as a subordinate rule for some social decisions, then (on Rawlsian principles at least) economic efficiency counts as a valid goal of a just society.

B. Why Rawls?

In what follows, I will make use of a generally Rawlsian perspective, though perhaps making somewhat free with the details of his analysis. Before turning to the details of the argument about efficiency, some preliminaries about the general strategy may be helpful.

Rawls' method has several features that makes it attractive for present purposes. First, unlike utilitarianism, it provides a framework in which it makes sense to ask the fairness question. Under at least some circumstances, it might be plausibly argued that the efficiency standard improves social utility. Like the utilitarian, we might find this to be a desirable effect. But utilitarianism offers no way of asking whether it is fair to impose a loss on an individual litigant in order to establish a legal rule which will improve social utility in the future. With its Kantian roots, Rawls' framework necessarily requires us to address the morality of using the individual litigant as a means to a future social end.

Second, by positing a suitable hypothetical bargaining situation, Rawls' goal is to investigate whether a disinterested person would endorse a social arrangement. The losing litigant is necessarily unhappy with the application of the efficiency standard and would have preferred some other ground for decision. What we need is some way of considering whether this litigant has a just complaint. We would like to ask whether, apart from the fact that his own ox is being gored, he has any objection that he could put forward as disinterested. The Rawlsian framework seems to be designed to address just this kind of question.

Third, Rawls' use of a hypothetical bargain is especially pertinent. As we have seen, Posner attempted unsuccessfully to invoke such a hypothetical bargain in support of the efficiency principle. Rawls offers a much more fully developed apparatus for constructing such an argument. Because Rawls uses a hypothetical prior bargain to assess the justice of existing social institutions, he provides an opening for the ex ante perspective in more mundane situations.

Not all of the details of Rawls' solution to his hypothetical are relevant.[49] The exact content of the basic rights or of his chosen principle regarding wealth inequalities need not concern us. What we do need is the idea that the parties in the original position will begin by establishing some set of basic rights and some principle of wealth distribution which will then be the foundation for social institutions. Again, this corresponds with some important features of the efficiency argument, for we have already seen that the efficiency principle is unlikely to be defensible without some prior understandings regarding entitlements. Of course, if it turns out that these prior understandings are so detailed and encompassing that they would decide all legal cases, then the efficiency principle would have no room to operate. But this seems unlikely.

In reality, these background conditions of justice are unlikely to be satisfied fully, and at least some readers may believe that they are far from being satisfied in contemporary society. Although this is a serious concern, it can be dealt with by bracketing off cases in which either individual rights or wealth distribution are potentially affected by a judicial decision. Recall that we are not in the position of designing basic institutions but of settling routine disputes. It seems plausible to adopt the principle of deciding such cases as we would in a just society, when the decision of the case will not affect any of society's existing injustices. Again, it is possible that we are left with only a small set of decisions in which to apply the efficiency principle, but this set does not seem to be insignificant. For example, it is hard to see how any judicial decision regarding commercial letters of credit could do anything to dismantle racism or sexism, fight world hunger, or advance free speech.[50]

The upshot is that my argument for ex ante efficiency is modest, not only in its conclusions but in its premises. By turning to Rawls, with the implicit assumption that he has some relevance to our society, I am necessarily turning away from more radical visions of the world. I am also necessarily adopting what is in at least broad outlines a liberal view that affirms individual freedom but worries seriously about social inequality. I will not attempt to defend that viewpoint here. In any event, the primary critics of economic efficiency, such as Dworkin, Calabresi, and Coleman, are themselves broadly aligned with this type of political liberalism. The burden of my argument is that economic efficiency is defensible not only within the libertarian version of liberalism favored by Posner, but within the broader liberal tradition. For those who reject that tradition entirely, this conclusion may only confirm their worst suspicions. Within the limits of the liberal tradition, however, I hope to delineate a place for economic efficiency.

C. Defining the Bargaining Situation

With this background in mind, we return to the task of assessing the efficiency norm in a Rawlsian framework. The crux of the ex ante argument is as follows. Suppose that, behind a veil of ignorance, individuals are seeking to decide what principles should control judicial decisions. We are following Rawls in assuming that they will want basic social institutions that first of all protect individual rights, and then provide the maximum possible level of well-being for the most disadvantaged members of society. But once those issues of basic social design are solved, we must expect many details of the legal system to remain unresolved. It would be fantastic to suppose that the basic principles of justice would directly address issues such as the proper method of allocating liability among joint tortfeasors or the priority of creditors in bankruptcy. Many of those issues will presumably be resolved legislatively, but again, we cannot assume that this legislation will be comprehensive, with courts needing only to implement statutory rules. The issue is whether, knowing that Rawlsian principles are in place but nothing about their own economic position, individuals would agree to the following as a subsidiary principle of fairness:

> In some defined category of cases, when a court is faced with a problem that cannot be resolved by Rawls' two principles and which has not been settled by the legislature, the court should decide the case by applying the rule of law that is most economically efficient in terms of its effects on similar future transactions.[51]

Posner's claim, modified in this way, places economic efficiency third in the hierarchy of principles, below basic human rights and the core principle of equality.[52] With respect to basic human rights, Posner now seems to agree with this ranking – for example, he views the right not to be a slave as trumping any efficiency arguments. He clearly would not accept Rawls' vision of equality, but on the other hand, it is plain that economic efficiency cannot be defined without *some* prior judgment about how to distribute initial allotments, so in some sense distribution issues simply have to be resolved prior to applying the efficiency criterion. Thus, although Posner would not necessarily agree with Rawls' scheme, the general picture of how efficiency relates to basic rights and distributional norms seems sound.

Because we are assuming that Rawls' basic principles are already in place, we are no longer dealing with the original position in the strictest sense, although I have used that term for convenience because it is a familiar part of Rawls' vocabulary. In his scheme, there is actually more than one stage of hypothetical agreement. In the original position, the most fundamental principles of justice are agreed upon, and the profound ignorance which is forced upon the parties is designed to ensure that the resulting principles are fair in the broadest range of circumstances. Our project, however, concerns how to adjust the legal system at the margins, and it seems unnecessary to impose such a thick veil of ignorance on the parties. Instead, I would suggest, we might do well to think of Rawls' second stage, in which a society is called upon to pick a just constitution, which will provide political and legal mechanisms for deciding disagreements about the requirements of justice. At this stage, the individuals still have no information about their own particular positions in society, but they do know relevant general facts about their society. Rawls says that they are to "choose the most effective just constitution, the constitution that satisfies the principles of justice and is best calculated to lead to just and effective legislation."[53] Although Rawls speaks of legislation, sometimes courts will establish legal rules. So it would not be unreasonable for the delegates to establish standards in advance for how courts should decide hard common law cases or fill gaps in statutes.

D. Choosing a Rule of Decision

Suppose, then, that a delegate places the modified efficiency criterion before the convention as a proposed rule for judicial decisions. What objections can be made to the principle? It cannot be opposed on the ground that it violates the basic principles of justice previously adopted in the original position, because it comes into play only when those principles are satisfied. Thus, it cannot be opposed as violating basic rights or undercutting the interests of the disadvantaged, because it is always subject to those principles. (Indeed, the efficiency principle is quite compatible with a Rawlsian strategy of maximizing the welfare of the disadvantaged – society can use the efficiency principle to increase the amount of social wealth, and then take advantage of this increased social wealth via taxing and spending policies to improve the lot of the disadvantaged.[54]) Nor can the efficiency principle be attacked for violating the democratic prerogatives of the legislature, because it applies only when courts lack any clear legislative mandate.

Conceivably, while the principle of ex ante efficiency might be otherwise just, it could nevertheless be incompatible with some special attributes of the judicial role. Perhaps there is some special quality of adjudication that makes it wrong for courts to adopt a forward-looking perspective, perhaps because it is impractical or illegitimate for judges to consider the future consequences of their decisions. I will take up the viability of a consequentialist judicial orientation in Part IV. For the moment, however, I would like to focus on two difficulties that do not relate specifically to the judicial role. One difficulty is that in some circumstances the efficiency principle would not receive ex ante agreement. The other is that in some circumstances ex ante agreement may not be enough.

To understand these difficulties, consider a delegate who is considering whether to adopt the efficiency principle. For simplicity, let's focus on cases where the stakes can be measured in dollars. The efficiency principle says that future legal rules should maximize the net value of the gains and losses from transactions. The delegate has no way of knowing whether he will be on balance a winner or loser from these future rules, but he knows on average that the rules will produce net gains. He may, however, be unwilling to take the risk of being among the net losers. A more subtle problem is that the efficiency of the rule is determined before the transaction, which means it is based on how the outcomes are valued by the parties at that time. But if the delegate expects his values to change during the transaction, he could end up regretting adoption of the efficient rule (judged ex ante). Both of these problems deserve closer examination.

1. RISK AVERSION. The most obvious problem with the qualified efficiency principle is risk aversion. Economic efficiency (unlike the Pareto principle) assumes that total social gains will be increased by a given rule, but says nothing about how those gains are distributed. This means that some parties may well end up in a worse position in any specific case than they would have without the rule, although on average the rule results in improved welfare. But

if individuals are risk averse, they may be unwilling to take the risk of losing out even though on average everyone can expect to be better off under the efficient rule. More precisely, risk-averse individuals might not agree ex ante to the efficiency principle, because they fear that, when new legal rules are announced pursuant to the principle they may sometimes suffer large losses.[55]

Risk aversion is not always a factor, however. In some situations, individuals may have eliminated risk through diversifying their investment portfolios, or insurance may be available without any significant distortion in incentives. Or perhaps the amount at stake is too small for risk aversion to play a significant role. In any event, the ex ante argument for efficiency will not work unless risk aversion toward new rules can be eliminated as a factor.

2. THE ISSUE OF PERSONHOOD. The problem of risk aversion relates to a kind of ex ante assessment of potential regret. The risk-averse person examines the possible outcomes and concludes that the satisfaction produced by the beneficial outcomes is outweighed – from the perspective of the person making the ex ante assessment – by the regret produced by the negative outcomes. This assessment assumes that the individual's preferences are going to remain stable throughout the relevant time period. If preferences shift dramatically, then the calculation of how these satisfactions and regrets compare will be quite different when it is made ex post. Given this later set of preferences, the person would never have agreed to enter the arrangement in the first place, even if it was a good bet given her prior preferences.[56]

Thomas Schelling has proposed a particularly dramatic way of describing the problem of radically changed preferences. Rather than speak of one person with two different sets of preferences, he speaks of two persons in chronological succession, so that the person with the later shifted preferences is considered not to be identical to the earlier person.[57] For example, he recalls the story of Ahab, who first agreed to have his leg cauterized but then had to be held down during the cauterization; Schelling suggests that in some sense the person who agreed to the operation was not the same as either the one who had to undergo it, or the one who would be grateful afterward that it had been performed.[58] Notably, this concept has now received support from Posner. In a study of the economics of aging, he has argued that age is best modeled as involving a series of successive selves:

> When age-related changes in the individual, as distinct from changes in the location of an unchanging individual on the continuum between birth and death, are brought into the economic analysis of aging, one of the most elementary assumptions of conventional economic analysis becomes problematic. This is the assumption that a person is a single economic decision-maker throughout his lifetime. The idea that the individual can be modeled as a locus of competing selves (simultaneous or successive) is not new, but it remains esoteric and is disregarded in most economic analysis.[59]

As he explains, the principal applications of this multiple-selves model have been to issues of addiction, self-control, regret, self-deception, and voluntary euthanasia. But, he believes, "[a]ging brings about such large changes in the individual that there may well come a point at which it is more illuminating to think of two or more persons 'time-sharing' the same identity than of one person having different preferences, let alone one person having the same preferences, over the entire life cycle."[60]

The recondite philosophical literature on personal identity goes well beyond the scope of this article.[61] Nevertheless, using the idea of multiple selves as at least a metaphor seems useful in this context. On the one hand, it highlights the difficulties posed by the concept of self-interested choice in situations where substantial changes in preferences occur. On the other hand, it reminds us that these preference changes ought to be substantial indeed before we start to worry about them – substantial enough that we feel able to say that in some sense we're dealing with a different person.

In situations where the multiple-selves model begins to seem appropriate, the ex ante argument becomes quite problematic, especially when the identity of the selves depends on how events turn out. Suppose that a person agrees to a transaction which carries a high risk, but a risk that is worth bearing given the preferences of the person at that time. But when the transaction goes sour, it produces a person whose preferences are quite different, and in particular, who is much more risk averse. That person would never have agreed to take the risk of entering the transaction. It becomes quite unclear whether we would want to say that this later person is bound by the consent given by an earlier incarnation. If we take the multiple-selves idea seriously, we might want to consider the harm to this possible later incarnation to be an externality – a harm imposed on a third party.

We might conceptualize the consideration of this problem at the constitutional convention in two different ways. We might say that the delegates represent only the earlier selves who enter into transactions, so their consent is meaningless as applied to the different, later selves. Or we could say that the delegates are ignorant about whether, when the partial veil of ignorance is lifted, they will turn out to be selves who are entering into transactions or selves who have been created through earlier transactions, so they have no reason to favor the ex ante perspective. In either event, it is obvious that the ex ante argument is left in a state of disarray.[62]

It is not surprising that the use of a hypothetical agreement breaks down here. The whole point of using the hypothetical agreement is to work out the demands of justice from an impartial perspective. But when personal preferences shift radically, we are in essence being asked to arbitrate a dispute between a person's earlier and later selves. It is not at all clear what it would mean to take a disinterested perspective on such an internal conflict, and we are at something of a loss to posit an appropriate hypothetical bargaining situation.

When risk aversion and preference shifts are not involved, however, the Rawlsian argument for the efficiency principle is quite strong. It seems immune from any obvious objection:

- It cannot be argued that the principle violates basic human rights, because it comes into play only when they are not at issue.
- It cannot be argued that the principle results in an unjust distribution of wealth, because it comes into play only when entitlements have been distributed consistently with the principles of justice.
- It cannot be argued that advance commitment to the principle is against anyone's interest. Because the principle increases expected wealth and is applied only when risk aversion is not a factor, the delegates each know that agreeing to the efficiency principle in advance increases their own expected utility after the convention.
- Nor can it be argued that the efficiency principle unfairly gives binding effect to earlier preferences over later (perhaps better-founded) preferences, because the principle is applied only when preferences are reasonably stable.

Of course, it is impossible to be sure that we have cataloged all the possible objections, and some further objections might require additional limitations, or perhaps even the abandonment of the principle. But no other objections immediately present themselves.[63] At the very least, the efficiency principle seems to be a respectable candidate for adoption at the convention. The final section considers some of the implications of adopting the qualified efficiency principle as a method for decision by judges. But first, I would like to restate the argument somewhat more explicitly by teasing out some of the complexities concealed in the idea of the "ex ante."

E. Unpacking the Ex Ante Perspective

The basic situation with which we have been concerned as is follows. Assume that the parties have entered into a transaction under existing legal precedents. The dispute comes before a judge (say Easterbrook himself) who proposes to decide it based on economic efficiency (judged ex ante). The question is simply whether this is unfair to the parties. I am addressing this question through a variant of Posner's argument. Rather than deciding whether the parties would have agreed in advance to the new legal rule adopted by the judge, I am asking whether they would have agreed (somewhat further in advance) to a meta-rule of ex ante economic efficiency. The answer turns out to be yes, but only for certain kinds of disputes.

Posner employed an analysis based on two time periods. In the first, the parties enter into their transaction. In the second, the court resolves a resulting dispute. His argument is that the court should apply the economically efficient rule of law because the parties themselves implicitly agreed to this at time 1. But this two-phase analysis is too simple in several respects. To begin with, the reason that a rule is efficient may be that it induces efficient bargaining, rather than being the actual result that the parties would then have bargained for. By assuming that the rule is agreed to at the same time as the rest of the transaction, Posner ignores the possibility that the rule could shape bargaining. (Moreover, the rule may be efficient because, once announced by the court, it will induce efficient conduct during a later transaction – but the mere expectation that the court may announce some efficient (but not yet known) rule may not itself be to anyone's advantage.) Thus, in thinking of the efficiency of a legal rule, it is not useful to think of its hypothetical existence as part of the very transaction before the court. Instead, we need to think of its efficiency in terms of future transactions. So rather than looking at only the single transaction before the court, we need to consider future transactions after the court's decision.

It is also morally unilluminating to think about whether the parties would have consented to the rule in the specific case, in the absence of transaction costs. The possibility that two particular people would have agreed to something in circumstances that did not exist has no binding moral authority. It gains such authority only if the hypothetical circumstances are those that we find particularly meaningful in moral terms. These conditions may not hold for an actual bargain,[64] even if we are prepared to enforce the explicit terms of that bargain. For this reason, we need to separate the actual consent that may be involved in a transaction from the hypothetical consent to particular legal rules, and design a separate choice scenario to isolate the morally relevant features of this hypothetical consent.

Consequently, we need to have three basic stages. The first is the hypothetical consent phase, in which the parties look forward to decide what principles judges should use in selecting legal rules. The second is the case itself, including both the underlying transaction and the judge's decision. The third consists of the future transactions governed by the newly announced legal rule.

Essentially, I am asking the reader to consider the following scenario. Beginning with the "veil of ignorance" under which people know little about their society and nothing about their own social positions, assume that something like Rawls' two principles of justice have been adopted. Now assume that the parties are to decide on basic jurisprudential principles, still acting in ignorance of their own societal positions but with an awareness of the essential facts about their own society. This is something close to Rawls' view of the position of the drafters of a specific constitution for a society. The question then is whether, at this quasi-constitutional moment, the parties would adopt as a general principle that courts should apply the ex ante perspective to future disputes. We are thus assuming the following time line:

Phase I: The (Hypothetical) Choice of Legal Ground Rules

Time 1. In the original position, the parties adopt basic principles of justice.

Time 2. In adopting a basic framework of legal principles, the parties decide whether future courts (at time 4) will apply the ex ante perspective. Note that here the parties are choosing metaprinciples to guide future courts, such as the efficiency criteria; they are not designing specific legal rules applicable to particular transactions.

Phase II: The Actual Case

Time 3. The parties enter into an actual transaction, which gives rise to a legal dispute. At this point, existing precedent embodies a legal rule that may or may not be economically efficient.[65]

Time 4. The court decides the resulting legal dispute. If it applies the ex ante perspective, it does so by choosing whatever legal rule will be economically efficient at time 5.[66]

Phase III: Prospective Effects

Time 5. New transactions take place, in which future parties are guided by the new legal rule. As assessed by the preferences of the parties at time 5, the rule is economically efficient – that is, no other rule would be preferred by one party without the other objecting. Thus, even if allowed to do so, future parties will not contract out of the rule chosen by the court.

Time 6. New disputes arise and are resolved on the basis of the rule chosen at time 4.

The question, then, is rather complex: whether people would agree in advance (at time 2) to a general legal principle that future disputes (at time 4) will be decided under the ex ante perspective.

The argument in favor of adopting the ex ante perspective as a legal principle at the "constitutional convention" is Posner's: Doing so will increase the size of the "pie," making society collectively better off. But some limitations on Posner's argument now become apparent. First, the ex ante principle can be adopted only when it would be consistent with the prior commitment, made in the original position, to the basic principles of justice. Thus, economic efficiency (viewed ex ante) cannot on this view be applied when doing so would infringe on fundamental autonomy or produce an unjust distribution of wealth. Second, although the ex ante principle may make society collectively better off than it would be otherwise, it also adds an element of uncertainty, because the parties do not know whether the court will follow existing precedent or will instead adopt a new rule for economic reasons. If individuals are risk averse, they may decide at the constitutional convention that they prefer in the future to have the certainty of existing precedent to the chance of future economic gains created by an improved legal rule. This problem basically involves the forecast at time 2 about what situation parties will prefer when they enter into transactions and litigate disputes at times 3 and 4. Third, they may decide at time 2 against the ex ante approach for other reasons. Suppose they anticipate that between times 5 and 6 their preferences may change in some radical way. Then their future selves at time 5 can no longer be relied upon to act as proxies for the even later selves at time 6, who will actually experience the effects of the new rule. More fundamentally, the concept of economic efficiency breaks down because there is no stable set of preferences to which it can be applied. In particular, the delegates at the constitutional convention (at time 2) have no reason to favor the preferences of those entering into transactions at time 5 over the preferences of those affected by the transactions in time 6, and hence no reason to choose the ex ante perspective.

All of this may seem rather laborious. The complication is due to the effort to tease out the various temporal perspectives involved in asking whether retroactive application of a rule, adopted because its prospective effects, is fundamentally unfair – defining fairness in terms of what people would reasonably have agreed to in advance, under hypothetical circumstances in which their decision would be particularly worthy of respect. Thus, the multiple time stages represent the various phases of this complex and partly hypothetical series of events.

Although in one sense the complexity of this scheme is regrettable, it is also significant. The notion of the "ex ante perspective" is actually much more complicated than it might seem, because there are several different relevant temporal stances involved. The most obvious is the judge's "ex ante" look toward future transactions. Within those transactions themselves, there is the "ex ante" determination at the beginning of the transaction that a particular rule will prove to be economically efficient. And lurking in the background is the hypothetical before-the-fact judgment that the principle of efficiency is itself fair. One of the problems of Posner's original analysis is that he ran all of these "ex ante" perspectives together.

IV. The Ex Ante Perspective in Adjudication

The previous section focused on whether the qualified efficiency principle would win the support of impartial individuals deciding on basic legal ground rules for their society. There is a considerable gap between accepting the principle at this level, however tentatively, and showing that it would work in the hands of the judiciary. In this section, I will consider two concerns. The first relates to the judicial role. We began the discussion with a worry about whether it is fair for a judge to choose a rule from an ex ante perspective but then apply it ex post to the parties in the case before the court. We need to be sure that this worry has been adequately addressed. We also need to consider whether judges have the practical ability to use the ex ante perspective effectively. A second concern does not relate to the special attributes of the judicial role. One possible difficulty with the efficiency principle is that we may have trouble knowing when it is appropriate to apply it. By this, I don't mean that the principle will be incorrectly used to reach the wrong result, but that it will be used in circumstances when it should have been left on the shelf. So, we need to clarify the boundary conditions governing the principle.

A. Judicial Competence and Legitimacy

We began with a concern about the fairness of the ex ante perspective in adjudication. Plainly, it is this worry that drove much of the criticism of Posner. Coleman says that a primary difference between proponents of economic analysis and critics such as Dworkin and himself is that "we have different theories of institutional competence generally, and of adjudication generally." In particular, he says, the "question is whether judges have the authority to seize upon a private dispute framed by and in terms of the litigants' interests as an opportunity to promote desirable social policies, for example, efficiency and distributional justice."[67]

Dworkin makes a similar point, although he is characteristically less cautious in his language. Dworkin attacks a position he labels as pragmatism (apparently in the popular sense of the term rather than in the technical philosophical sense). Pragmatists, he says, fail to take rights seriously. More generally, pragmatism fails to take seriously the obligation to decide disputes based on existing law rather than engaging in social engineering for the future:

> Pragmatism does not rule out any theory about what makes a community better. But it does not take legal rights seriously. It rejects what other conceptions of law accept: that people can have distinctly legal rights as trumps over what would otherwise be the best future properly understood. According to pragmatism what we call legal rights are only the servants of the best future: they are instruments we construct for that purpose and have no independent force or ground.[68]

The qualified efficiency principle is not pragmatic in Dworkin's sense. The judge seeks an economically efficient rule (in appropriate cases) not merely in order to engineer the best possible future, but because economic efficiency provides an impartial standard that, under suitable circumstances, should be accepted as fair by all.

Coleman concedes that under some circumstances economic efficiency might already be incorporated into some legal standard. The judge's responsibility is to determine which litigant has the legal right to prevail, but this decision may sometimes include a reference to economic efficiency, as in Judge Learned Hand's famous use of economic concepts to define the concept of negligence in tort law.[69] Unless he wants to argue that large areas of existing law, such as antitrust,[70] somehow fundamentally violate the basic principles of justice, Dworkin would seem to have no choice but to make a similar concession that legal principles may sometimes incorporate the concept of economic efficiency. Thus, neither Coleman nor Dworkin seems to have any valid objection to judicial use of the modified efficiency principle except where the principle is legally novel. But they do have an argument that a judge should not invoke a principle – even one that might incorporate the best impartial view of justice as applied to the transaction in question – when that principle is not part of the existing legal structure under which the parties have acted. The questions then, is whether shifting to an efficiency-based rule is the sort of legal change that judges must leave to legislators.

The answer depends at least in part on the severity of the change. The efficiency principle is not a longstanding legal rule in the sense of having been articulated by judges as a generally applicable standard. That should not be decisive, however, as to whether it can be legitimately adopted by judges. In the common law tradition, judges have an acknowledged role in reshaping the principles of law. So the question is not merely whether the efficiency canon is already recognized by law, but whether a move toward adopting the efficiency canon exceeds the legitimate bounds of judicial innovation. Clearly, a judge may not follow the efficiency principle at the expense of legislative or constitutional mandates; indeed, that restriction is built into my earlier statement of the principle itself. For similar reasons, we might think it wrong for the judge to do so if the result were to overrule well-settled precedents. Although the difference is sometimes subtle, judges in our tradition have the authority to remold the law but not to perform radical surgery.

But, at least within substantial areas of the law, a judge could properly argue that recognizing the efficiency principle is well within the domain of permissible judicial innovation. First, many existing precedents can arguably be justified on the basis of efficiency – Posner devoted the initial part of his career to making this argument in area after area of legal doctrine.[71] It is a time-honored method of legal innovation to rationalize the results of prior cases on a different basis than the courts originally articulated, and then to apply the new rationalization to the case at hand. Second, although efficiency was not recognized by name in prior judicial decisions except in limited areas of the law, judges often have used related concepts. For example, in tort law, they have worried about deterrence of unreasonably risky conduct, while in contract law they have based decisions on what they believe the parties to a contract would have intended if they had considered an issue in advance. Both concepts can be reformulated without too much difficulty in terms of economic efficiency. So the efficiency-minded judge can legitimately claim, at least in many areas of the law, to be operating squarely within the common law tradition.

The judge may, in fact, be able to appeal to Dworkin himself for authority in invoking the modified efficiency principle in hard cases. To illustrate his vision of "law as integrity," Dworkin discusses how Hercules (his hypothetical ideal judge) would decide a hard case involving nuisance law. Hercules might discover that the leading precedents in this area of the law disclaim any economic analysis in favor of the concept of protecting the traditional use of land. But Hercules finds incoherent the distinction between nuisance law and negligence law where an economic analysis is already used. So, Dworkin says, if Hercules "thought the 'natural use' test was silly, and the economic cost test much more just, he would argue that the negligence and nuisance precedents should be seen as one body of law, and that the economic cost test is a superior interpretation of that unified body."[72] This illustrates the ways in which a common law judge can accommodate the efficiency principle without doing violence to the fabric of the law, and thus without overstepping the legitimate bounds of judicial authority.

B. Economic Efficiency and the Boundaries of Commercial Law

The efficiency principle has four limitations, each of which restricts the appropriate domain for applying the principle. Because the principle is trumped by basic rights, constitutional issues generally fall outside its domain. Because it is also trumped by principles of just distribution, we must also be hesitant in applying the principle where the result is a large, downward shift in individual wealth, especially if the individual is thrown all the way to the bottom economically. Thus, for example, the unconscionability case discussed earlier, involving the purchase of furniture on credit by someone on welfare, has to be carefully examined to see whether the efficient result has unacceptable distributional implications.

Risk aversion is another limit on the application of the efficiency principle. It is not necessarily true that both parties would prefer ex ante that the court apply a rule of law that maximizes their combined wealth, if the amount at issue is large relative to individual wealth and one of the parties is risk averse. Besides desiring optimal incentives, that individual will also want insurance against the risk of adverse legal rules, and the two desires may be at odds. This may be a serious problem in personal injury law. On the other hand, in ordinary consumer transactions, the amounts at stake are too small to trigger risk aversion. The same is true in routine commercial transactions involving amounts that are small relative to the net worth of the business. Moreover, in transactions involving only corporations, risk-aversion is not a factor even when large amounts are at stake, because risk averse stockholders can protect themselves by diversifying their portfolios.[73]

A final built-in limitation to the efficiency principle involves preference shifts. Consider the problem of surrogate motherhood. If a woman enters a contract to be a surrogate mother, should a court enforce the contract if she changes her mind after the birth? One argument is that her preferences may have shifted so much that it is unfair to hold her to a bargain based on her prior preferences. Using the more dramatic language of the multiple-selves theory, we might say that post partum, confronted with the actual baby, she is a different person than she was when she signed the contract prior to the pregnancy. To the extent we take this concept seriously, we cannot comfortably utilize the efficiency principle or its ex ante perspective, because the parties who are before the court are in an important sense not the same people as those whose ex ante preferences are considered.

In addition to these inherent limits on the efficiency principle, there are also some practical barriers to its application. Even if judges have the authority to pursue the efficiency principle, one might well question whether they have the competence. Clearly, a formal cost/benefit analysis of a particular legal rule runs far beyond judicial competence (probably even with the assistance of expert witnesses). But at least in some situations, judges may be able to rely on well-established economic theories rather than making their own empirical determinations of efficiency. These theories are most likely to be available in the area best studied by economists – that of market transactions. In some other cases, the correct resolution of the efficiency issue may also be obvious. But this is most likely to be true in situations where it is fairly easy to monetize the stakes on both sides, which again will be most true in connection with discrete market transactions.

Finally, a judge may feel more comfortable in making an assessment of efficiency in situations where he or she is creating only a default rule. If the judge is wrong, then he or she has decided the case incorrectly, to the detriment of the parties, and he has also imposed on others the burden of opting out of the rule in the future. Still, if the rule is seriously erroneous, the ill-effects will be blunted by opt-outs, and if opting out becomes widespread, future judges may take that as a signal that the decision should be corrected. It is best, of course, for a judge never to make mistakes, but at least it is somewhat better to make them in situations where they can be corrected at relatively low cost. Thus, the efficiency principle seems particularly well suited for use in determining default rules.

This combination of traits is most evident in business transactions. Basic rights or income distribution are rarely at stake; risk aversion is less likely to be a controlling factor than in non-business transactions; and preference shifts are less likely than in more personal spheres of life. Also, the stakes are often likely to be easily monetizable; economic theory may have much to say about the transaction in question; and the issue often relates to the choice of a particular default rule. In short, the core of commercial law is particularly well suited to use of the efficiency principle. The farther we move away from that commercial core, the more careful we need to be before choosing efficiency as the basis for decision.

Some readers may find this match-up between economic efficiency and commercial law less than startling. It is important, however, to identify exactly the reasons that this is such a good match, so that we can understand why other fields of law are more problematic arenas for economic efficiency.

Notes

† Dan Gifford, John Stick, and Steven Walt provided helpful comments.

1. Frank Easterbrook, *The Supreme Court, 1983 Term – Foreword: The Court and the Economic System,* 98 Harv. L. Rev. 4, 5–6, 11 (1984).
2. Ibid. at 11–2.
3. Ibid. at 11, 19–33, 59.
4. See, e.g., Thomas H. Jackson, *The Logic and Limits of Bankruptcy Law* (1986); *The Economics of Contract Law,* Anthony T. Kronman and Richard Posner, eds. (1979); *Readings in the Economics of Contract Law,* Victor G. Goldberg, ed. (1989).
5. The possible tension between moral rights and consequentialism is nicely described in Randy E. Barnett, *Foreword: Of Chickens and Eggs – The Compatibility of Moral Rights and Consequentalist Analysis,* 12 Harv. J. L. & Pub. Pol'y 611, 617–20 (1989).
6. See text accompanying n. 65, infra.
7. Robert D. Cooter, *The Best Right Laws: Value Foundations of the Economic Analysis of Law,* 64 Notre Dame L. Rev. 817, 824 (1989).
8. A more fully elaborated version of the argument can be considered ex ante "squared:" The judge (at T_1) is justified in using an ex ante perspective that focuses the future effects of his decision (at T_2) because this is the judicial perspective that the parties themselves would have favored ex ante, looking forward from an earlier time (T_0) before the transaction.
9. For other critiques, then and more recently, see Russell Hardin, *Magic on the Frontier: The Norm of Efficiency,* 144 U. Pa. L. Rev. 1987 (1996); Jane B. Baron and Jeffrey L. Dunoff, *Against Market Rationality: Moral Critiques of Economic Analysis in Legal Theory,* 17 Cardozo L. Rev. 431 (1996); Donald Keenan, *Value Maximization and Welfare Theory,* 10 J. Leg. Stud. 4098 (1981); Izhak Englard, Book Review, 95 Harv. L. Rev. 1162 (1982); Anthony T. Kronman, *Wealth Maximization as a Normative Principle,* 9 J. Leg. Stud. 227 (1980).
10. For an excellent recent overview of the debate, see Neil Duxbury, *Patterns of American Jurisprudence* 397–406 (1995).
11. In Rawls' theory, individuals choose the principles of justice from behind a "veil of ignorance," which means that they do not know their own positions in society, their own personal goals in life, or even very much about their society. The idea behind using this original position of ignorance as a basis for considering principles of justice is that it requires individuals to make a completely impartial judgment. John Rawls, *A Theory of Justice* (1971).
12. John Rawls, *Political Liberalism* (1993). For a good survey of the literature on Rawls and the law, plus a thoughtful review of *Political Liberalism,* see Lawrence B. Solum, *Situating Political Liberalism,* 69 Chi.-Kent L. Rev. 549 (1994).
13. The debate on Posner's argument in the early 1980s also turns out to be relevant to an ongoing debate in commercial law about what "default rules" a court should apply when a contract is silent on a particular issue. See text accompanying n. 17 infra.

14. *Williams v. Walker-Thomas Furniture Co.*, 350 F.2d 445 (D.C. Cir. 1965).
15. If buyers actually preferred the second package, it would have been worthwhile for sellers to offer it to them, at least as an option.
16. For discussions of the problems raised by unconscionability doctrine from an ex ante perspective, see Richard Epstein, *Unconscionability: A Critical Reappraisal,* 18 J. L. & Econ. 293 (1975); Alan Schwartz, *A Reexamination of Nonsubstantive Unconscionability,* 63 Va. L. Rev. 1053 (1977); Arthur Alan Leff, *Contract as Thing,* 19 Am. U. L. Rev. 131 (1970).
17. Ian Ayres, *Empire or Residue: Competing Visions of the Contractual Canon,* in Jack Balkin and Sanford Levinson, eds., *The Legal Canon* (forthcoming).
18. For an excellent collection of the work of leading participants in this debate, see the *Symposium on Default Rules and Contractual Consent.* 3 So. Cal. Interdisc. L. J. (1993). For a survey of the earlier literature, see Jean Braucher, *Contract Versus Contractorianism: The Regulatory Role of Contract Law,* 47 Wash. & Lee L. Rev. 697, 730–8 (1990).
19. For a discussion of the distinction and its significance for legal policy, see Jim Chen and Daniel Gifford, *Law as Industrial Policy,* 25 Memphis L. Rev. 1315–16 (1995).
20. Richard A. Posner, *The Ethical and Political Basis of the Efficiency Norm in Common Law Adjudication,* 8 Hofstra L. Rev. 487, 492–3 (1980). Of course, he says, only a fanatic would demand unanimous consent; apparently, it is good enough if almost everyone would agree to the rule ex ante. Ibid. at 495.
21. Ibid. at 498. As Posner's critics were quick to point out, his decision to imply actual individual consent rather than hypothetical consent leads to some conceptual difficulties.
22. Ibid. at 497.
23. Ibid. at 500. Any politician would agree without hesitation to this proposition.
24. Ibid. at 501. See also Richard J. Posner, *Law and Economics* Is *Moral,* 24 Val. U. L. Rev. 163 (1990).
25. For a good recent synthesis of the critiques, see Eric Rakowski, *Equal Justice* 199–226 (1991). Posner responded to the critics in two essays, Richard A. Posner, *A Reply to Some Recent Criticisms of the Efficiency Theory of the Common Law,* 9 Hofstra L. Rev. 775 (1981); Richard A. Posner, *The Value of Wealth: A Comment on Dworkin and Kronman,* 9 J. Legal Stud. 243 (1980). Posner's replies focus on criticisms unrelated to the conceptual difficulties of the ex ante argument and are not relevant to the present discussion.
26. Ronald Dworkin, *Why Efficiency? A Response to Professor Calabresi and Posner,* 8 Hofstra L. Rev. 563, 577–8 (1981).
27. Ibid. at 578.
28. Ibid. at 583.
29. Ibid. at 584–5.
30. Ibid. at 585.
31. Ibid. at 588.
32. Jules L. Coleman, *Markets, Morals and the Law* 121–2 (1988).
33. Ibid. at 108–22.
34. Guido Calabresi, *The New Economic Analysis of Law: Scholarship, Sophistry, or Self-Indulgence?,* 68 Proc. of the Brit. Acad. 85, 94 (1981).
35. Ibid. at 94.
36. Ibid. at 94–6.

37. Ibid. at 97.
38. Guido Calabresi, *The Pointlessness of Pareto: Carrying Coase Further,* 100 Yale L.J. 1211 (1991).
39. Richard A. Posner, *The Problems of Jurisprudence* 379 (1990). See also Richard A. Posner, *The Ethics of Wealth Maximization: Reply to Malloy,* 36 Kan. L. Rev. 262–64 (1988).
40. Posner, supra n. 39, at 390. The risk aversion point is also made in connection with the ex ante argument in Robert D. Cooter and Thomas S. Ulen, *An Economic Case for Comparative Negligence,* 61 N.Y.U. L. Rev. 1067, 1098:–100 (1986).
41. Posner, supra n. 39 at 375–6.
42. I discuss some of the other arguments which have been made against recognizing economic efficiency as a social value in Daniel A. Farber, *Eco-Pragmatism: Making Sensible Environmental Decisions in an Uncertain World,* Ch. 2 (1999).
43. Ronald Dworkin, *Is Wealth a Value?,* 9 J. Legal Stud. 191 (1980).
44. Ibid. at 220.
45. Dworkin made the same argument again in a later book. See Ronald Dworkin, *Law's Empire* 286–8 (1986).
46. Obviously, it is crucial that the original assignment of rights be just. See Cento G. Veljanovski, *Wealth Maximization, Law and Ethics – On the Limits of Economic Efficiency,* 1 Int'l Rev. of L. & Econ. 5, 19 (1981).
47. Lawrence Sager, *Pareto Superiority, Consent, and Justice,* 8 Hofstra L. Rev. 913, 922 (1980).
48. Rawls, supra n. 11 at 79: "But it should be noted that the difference principle is compatible with the principle of efficiency. For when the former is fully satisfied, it is indeed impossible to make any one representative man better off without making another worse off, namely, the least advantaged representative man whose expectations we are to maximize."
49. Because of his desire to remain agnostic about conceptions of the good and to eschew any hint of utilitarianism, Rawls posits a set of primary social goods which individuals seek in order to pursue their own life plans. This creates obvious problems about how to balance the various primary goods, but it may be appropriate when considering a hypothetical bargain over the most basic social institutions, where the fine grain of individual preferences may well be irrelevant. We are concerned, however, with legal rules that will govern routine transactions, in which individuals are making only tactical decisions about how best to pursue their ends. Here, it is plausible to assume that they are able to put their goals into the form of some coherent set of preferences.
50. Of course, there is always the option of deciding that current institutions are so evil that only civil disobedience or revolution is morally possible, so that participating in the legal system on any terms except to undermine it is wrong. If so, the efficiency norm would have to wait for judicial implementation until after the Revolution!
51. Apart from legislative rules, judicial precedent might also settle a legal issue so firmly that judicial resort to the efficiency principle would be foreclosed.
52. To establish this claim, it would be necessary to show that there are no intermediate principles of justice between economic efficiency and Rawls' two principles. Although I do not see any particularly appealing candidates for such an intermediate principle

(particularly in the context of commercial transactions), I will not attempt to prove their nonexistence. Thus, what the argument will actually establish, I hope, is that economic efficiency belongs somewhere on the list below Rawls' two principles. The existence of such intermediate principles would clearly limit further the scope for applying the efficiency norm.

53. Rawls, supra n. 11, at 197. Readers who find Rawls' original position too heroically counterfactual and abstract may find the constitutional convention more congenial: The parties are assumed to know the facts about their society and only to be ignorant of their individual identities, which is to say that they must be impartial and are not allowed to pick rules simply to favor their own interests.
54. See A. Mitchell Polinsky, *An Introduction to Law and Economics,* 105–10 (1983). Because of the inevitable inefficiencies of the taxing and spending mechanisms, however, this approach is not a panacea for all conflicts between efficiency and distributive norms.
55. Posner recognizes that risk aversion is a problem for the efficiency principle, but seems to think that the problem can be cured through insurance. But this is not necessarily so, because providing insurance may produce incentives that are incompatible with efficient behavior. For example, suppose we are dealing with liability for fires. If individuals are risk averse, they might not be willing to agree in advance to the liability rule that is most efficient in the sense of providing optimal incentives to take precautions against fire. But if they carry full insurance, they may not take optimal precautions despite an otherwise efficient liability rule, because the insurance company will be unable to condition coverage on their taking the correct level of precautions. This effect of insurance is well known to economists under the name of moral hazard. It derives from the inability of insurance companies to write contracts covering every contingency and to monitor completely the conduct of the insured.
56. See Anthony T. Kronman, *Paternalism and the Law of Contracts,* 92 Yale L.J. 763, 780–4 (1983).
57. Thomas C. Schelling, *Choice and Consequence: Perspectives of an Errant Economist* 57–112 (1984). See also Jon Elster, *Sour Grapes: Studies in the Subversion of Rationality* (1983), for an alternate approach to the problem of changed preferences.
58. Schelling, supra n. 57, at 83–4.
59. Richard A. Posner, *Aging and Old Age* 84 (1996).
60. Ibid. at 86.
61. See Derek Parfit, *Reasons and Persons* (1984); Robert Nozick, *Philosophical Explanations,* 29–70 (1981).
62. We might be able to work out a moral theory about the relations between earlier and later selves that would make something like hypothetical consent effective in some circumstances but not others. At best, however, we might need to rework the entire argument, and perhaps to abandon it, in multiple-selves situations. The obvious lesson is that we cannot count on the ex ante argument when substantial preference shifts are involved, and that the ex ante argument for the efficiency principle is consequently unreliable in those circumstances.
63. Another possibility is that the efficiency principle is not gravely defective but is weaker than some alternative approach. The most obvious alternative is utilitarianism, but it's

not clear that the distinction between the efficiency principle and utilitarianism is very significant once we take risk aversion and wealth distribution out of the picture. The efficiency principle also has the advantage of being more easily operationalized than utilitarianism.

It is also possible that, in addition to Rawls' two principles, there are other as yet unidentified principles of justice that rank higher than the efficiency principle. If so, these principles of justice would further constrict the scope of the efficiency principle. But it seems reasonable to put the burden of proof on anyone claiming that the rules of distributive justice are so detailed and universal as to dictate the correct decisions regarding creditor priority in bankruptcy, recording of liens, clearing of electronic funds transfers, and the other daily fare of commercial law.

64. For instance, suppose that the parties to a contract would in fact have agreed to a particular term, but only because one of the parties was intimidated by the other. This clearly has no moral force. Even if we assume that intimidation (within some bounds) is a legitimate bargaining tactic, it entitles its practitioners only to whatever favorable terms were actually gained through intimidation, not to those additional terms that they might have gained through further bullying given unlimited bargaining time.
65. If the parties can perfectly anticipate the court's decision at time 4, and if they know in advance that the court will apply the ex ante perspective, then the legal rule will be known in advance. This would obviously eliminate the ex ante issue, although it might still leave the question of whether economic efficiency is the right standard for issuing legal rules. What I am interested in, however, is the difficulty posed, as a matter of fairness, by the retroactive nature of the consequentialist judicial decision at time 4: The rule is designed to produce the best results in the future, at time 5, but is being applied to a transaction that took place earlier. For that reason, I will assume that the parties at time 3 either are unsure about whether the court will in fact utilize the ex ante perspective, or lack sufficient information to anticipate what legal rule the court will adopt in applying that perspective, perhaps because they do not have as much information about the rule's effects as the court will later have.
66. In the most extreme case, even the possibility that the ex ante perspective will be used is a surprise to the parties, who suffer from "amnesia" about the decisions made at the hypothetical constitutional convention. (More concretely, they did not anticipate Judge Easterbrook's appointment to the bench.)
67. Coleman, supra n. 33, at 131.
68. Dworkin, *Law's Empire,* supra n. 45, at 160.
69. Coleman, supra n. 33, at 131. See *United States v. Carroll Towing,* 159 F.2d 169 (2nd Cir. 1947).
70. Modern antitrust law is the great triumph of the Chicago school of economics, and of its legal advocates such as Posner and Robert Bork.
71. Much of this work can be found in updated and synthesized form in Richard A. Posner, *Economic Analysis of Law* (4th ed 1992).
72. Dworkin, *Law's Empire,* supra n. 45, at 254.
73. Shareholders should be indifferent to diversifiable risks (but not to risks that correlate with overall market shifts). The particular risk with which we are concerned here is diversifiable. In order to eliminate the risk of being on the losing side of intercorporate

litigation, it is only necessary to hold a broad portfolio including both potential plaintiffs and defendants. For example, if a legal rule increases the risk that debtor corporations will have to pay large sums of money to financial institutions, a shareholder in a debtor corporation will be protected if the shareholder also holds stock in financial institutions. Intercorporate litigation merely moves money between corporations, rather than affecting the overall risk of holding the market portfolio.

3

Constrained Optimization

Corporate Law and the Maximization of Social Welfare

LEWIS A. KORNHAUSER†

I. Introduction

How ought judges to decide cases? One answer, often associated with the economic analysis of law, asserts that judges ought to choose legal rules that are efficient or that maximize "wealth." This claim, which stirred great controversy in the late 1970s and early 1980s, has largely subsided into the background in areas outside of corporate and commercial law.[1] Within corporate and commercial law, however, academic legal discussion has increasingly adopted an economic perspective. The academic debate in the area of corporate and commercial law has thus largely focused not on whether the courts should pursue efficiency but on how the courts should promote this aim. Should any legal rules impose mandatory obligations on parties? What default rules are best? What is the optimal structure of priority rules in bankruptcy?

The discrepancy in the intellectual histories of efficiency as a judicial goal in corporate and commercial law and in the law more generally has some justification. The arguments against the general claim have less force against the claim restricted to corporate and commercial law. The argument for instance that law ought to pursue various conceptions of fairness has less force in the realm of corporate and commercial law, where transactions are at arm's lengths between well-informed parties, each of whom seeks to maximize its profit. More importantly, a reasonably straightforward institutional defense of the efficiency claim in corporate and commercial law can be mounted. Briefly, it has the following elements.

Law serves many objectives, but the promotion of the well-being of citizens is a central concern of law and legal institutions. This social concern has at least two aspects. First, society cares about the distribution of well-being among its citizens. Second, it cares about the general level of well-being. An institutional justification of wealth maximization (or efficiency) as a goal of corporate and commercial law then must establish that the pursuit of distributional (and other) goals ought to be institutionally divorced from the pursuit of increasing the general level of well-being.

Kaplow and Shavell have argued that the distributional goals of society are better (i.e., more efficiently) advanced through redistributive taxation and social welfare programs than through corporate and commercial law.[2] Basically, they show that any redistribution achieved through an inefficient rule of tort law (or, by implication, an inefficient contract or property rule) can be accomplished with less distortion through a redistributive tax scheme coupled with an efficient rule of tort law. The decrease in distortion implies that everyone could be made better off under the redistributive tax (and efficient tort rule) than under the redistributive (but inefficient) rule of torts. This argument thus supports a claim that the redistributive aims of law ought to be accomplished through legal institutions that are distinct from the institutions that maximize the general level of well-being.

To increase the level of well-being of citizens society must structure incentives for individual actors appropriately. It has two tools available: the imposition of primary obligations and the structuring of enabling regimes such as corporate and commercial law that harness the initiative and information of individuals. Certain obstacles to the enhancement of well-being, such as the costs of environmental degradation, are best handled through the imposition of primary obligations, i.e., by setting "prices" to economic actors appropriately. Put differently, the rules governing corporate governance, contract, and bankruptcy can be formulated without attention to externalities; these problems are adequately dealt with in separate bodies of law.[3] Finally, the self-interest of individuals pursuing their own aims within well-functioning markets will ensure that welfare is maximized. Corporate and commercial law, then, should simply provide a structure in which markets will function smoothly.

This argument seems both unproblematic and compelling. A conception of corporate and commercial law unconnected to increasing the general level of well-being is completely implausible. A conception that required legislatures and courts to balance every social value when society formulates or applies rules governing corporate and commercial conduct seems equally implausible. Furthermore, the division of labor among bodies of law that this argument assumes has strong intuitive appeal; it conforms to the interpretive inclinations of most lawyers.

The intuitive appeal of the argument, however, does not substitute for secure analytic foundations. This chapter reconsiders the normative foundations of corporate and commercial law. It raises three problems with the pursuit of efficiency or wealth maximization through corporate and commercial law. First, the chapter observes that the most efficient rule, or the wealth-maximizing rule, is always relative to some decision and to specified constraints. The best rule in a world of complete information, for example, may not be best in worlds with asymmetric information. Second, wealth maximization only provides an appropriate proxy for well-being under special conditions; these conditions need not always hold even in the context of corporate and commercial law. Third, the logic of maximization of well-being under uncertainty conceals as yet unsolved difficulties.

The discussion proceeds as follows. Part II investigates the concept of efficiency relative to a decision and to constraints. In particular, it emphasizes complexities introduced by various information structures. Part III turns to wealth maximization. It first connects this concept to the underlying goal of promoting well-being. It then investigates the extent to which wealth maximization implements the concept of maximization of well-being. Part III closes by linking the more specific aims of corporate and commercial law to wealth maximization. Part IV offers some concluding speculations on how these foundational problems alter the conception of corporate and commercial law.

II. Defining Efficiency

A definition of efficiency requires that one resolve at least three ambiguities. First, the contract paradigm in corporate and commercial law directs judges and other policymakers to announce efficient *rules*. The efficiency of a rule in turn depends on the *decisions* that agents make in response to these legal rules. A decision is efficient if there is no other decision that would make one individual better off without making any other individual worse off. This distinction between individual decision and legal rule requires attention in the definition of efficiency.

Second, a rule generally influences many decisions of each agent. A rule may be efficient with respect to one decision (e.g., breach) but not efficient with respect to another decision (e.g., precontractual reliance). The fact that a rule influences many decisions implies that one cannot determine whether a rule is efficient simply by determining whether the decisions it induces are efficient.

Third, the knowledge of individuals at the point of decision and of the courts at the time of the application of the rule will also influence one's evaluation of the legal rule. Again this influence works first through a reformulation of the efficiency of an individual decision that now must be understood as efficient relative to the information available to the agent at the time that the decision was made. The policymaker, in announcing the legal rule, will do so relative to its information at the time of announcement and in light of the information the parties will have when they make decisions in the shadow of this legal rule and in light of the information a court (or other law-applying agency) would have at the time it would apply the rule. This section elaborates briefly on each of these concerns.

A. *Efficiency Relative to the Class of Decisions*

The efficiency of a legal rule is then relative to the class of decisions under consideration. In general, a specific legal rule affects a large number of decisions that an agent might take. To determine the efficiency of a legal rule (or, more plausibly, of a set of legal rules), one must first identify the set of decisions that the legal rule might influence. The complexity of even simple economic transactions implies that a legal rule creates incentives that influence many decisions.

In commercial law, for example, the legal rules governing the consequences of nonperformance and of gap-filling in the contract influence a chain of decisions that begins prior to the formation of the contract and continues through its performance (or nonperformance). These legal rules influence the intensity of an individual's search for a contracting party (and hence the number of contracts formed), the extent to which a potential party to the contract invests in the potential relation during precontractual negotiations, the content of the contract actually drafted, the nature and extent of investments made by each party in reliance on the contract, whether and when to repudiate (or fail to perform) one's obligations under the contract, whether and how to modify the contract in light of changed circumstances, and the nature of a party's response to breach. The more closely one scrutinizes the contractual relation, the more decisions one can identify.

The decisions affected by the rules governing corporations are not less numerous or diverse. Corporate rules will influence the choice of investment opportunities to undertake, the allocation of resources across these projects, the skill and industry with which these projects will be pursued, whether and when to abandon these projects, and, more generally, which economic relationships will be governed by market transactions and which will be governed by hierarchy or other nonmarket mechanisms. The bankruptcy rules will influence all these decisions as well as decisions concerning whether to declare insolvency or not, which creditors to pay first when in financial straits, and how to continue the business in the face of insolvency.

B. *Efficiency of Rules, not Decisions*

A legal rule governs numerous transactions. In each transaction, individuals must make several decisions, each of which may be influenced by the legal rule. One may thus compare a legal rule R to a legal rule S in two ways. One might ask, for example, whether legal rule R induces better decisions of a given type, such as breach or search, over all transactions than rule S. In addition, one might compare rule R to rule S, all decisions considered, to determine which legal rule induces better outcomes over all decisions and transactions. Of course, a legal rule that is best all decisions considered need not be best for any specific decision. Nonetheless the academic literature tends to compare rules decision by decision rather than all decisions considered, and I begin in the same fashion.

Consider the efficiency of a legal rule relative to a decision regarding breach of contract. Consider some legal rule R. It will induce efficient breach decisions (conditional on the actual decisions previously made) for some set of contracts E_R and inefficient breach decisions for some other set of contracts I_R. A legal rule S is "breach" superior to legal rule R if and only if the set E_S of contracts for which S induces efficient breach decisions includes E_R (and correspondingly the set I_S of contracts for which S induces inefficient breach decisions is included in I_R). The legal rule S would be efficient relative to the decision to breach if there were no other legal rule that was "breach" superior to it.

Recall that an efficient decision was defined in terms of the welfare of individuals. The preceding definition of the breach efficiency of a legal rule does not quite reduce to considerations of individual welfare. If each individual were affected by only one contract,[4] then the efficiency of the legal rule would imply that no individual could be made better off without making some other individual worse off. If some individuals, however, are affected by more than one contract, then this reduction of the efficiency of a rule to individual welfare does not follow. Consider two contracts C_1 and C_2 between the same two parties, P_1 and P_2. Suppose that under an efficient rule R, the breach decision for C_1 is efficient but the breach decision for C_2 is not. If P_1 and P_2 value performance of C_2 more than the performance of C_1, both would prefer a legal rule S that induced an efficient breach decision in C_2 but not in C_1. If S induced identical decisions to R in every other contract, S would also be breach-efficient under the definition of the prior paragraph. But, in terms of individual welfare, S is Pareto-preferred to R by some individuals (i.e., P_1 and P_2) and dispreferred by no one.

Ideally, then, one should define the relation "breach superiority" in terms of individual well-being. A rule R is breach superior to a rule S if and only if no individual, all contractual behavior considered, prefers S to R and at least one person prefers R to S. This definition, however, is difficult for a policymaker to implement because it requires that the policymaker understand how the scope of contracting behavior of every potential contractor varies with the legal rule. The contract-by-contract (as opposed to individual-by-individual) definition seems less demanding and may be a reasonable proxy for the conceptually correct concept of efficiency.

The difficulties that confront the policymaker, however, extend beyond this shift in perspective from individuals to contracts. For each decision–search, precontractual reliance, formation, drafting, postcontractual reliance, breach, etc. – one might define an analogous relation of superiority among legal rules and consequently an analogous notion of efficiency. Two reasons, however, prevent a policymaker intent on inducing efficient (or even wealth-maximizing) decisions from proceeding decision by decision.

First, the desirability of certain decisions cannot be evaluated in isolation. Consider the decision to form a contract. As section C discusses at greater length, at the time of formation, a buyer may not know the value of performance and the seller may not know the cost. Whether it is desirable to form the contract will depend on the specific contents of any contract entered and on what happens after formation; the formation decision, too, is affected by the legal rule.

Second, a specific legal rule might be search-efficient but not breach-efficient or it might be reliance-efficient but not breach- or search-efficient. Presumably, the policymaker seeks the rule that is best, all decisions considered. How does it resolve conflicts that arise across legal rules?

If the policymaker adheres strictly to the criterion of efficiency and to a contract-by-contract perspective rather than an individual perspective, these different assessments of legal rules present no problems. The policymaker's criterion simply becomes less comprehensive; there are more and more rules which are not comparable all decisions considered. If R was breach-superior to S but S was reliance-superior to R, the policymaker might conclude that R is noncomparable to S, all decisions considered. Under this strategy, however, the policymaker will not be able to rank many rules. Thus, to make all decisions considered judgments, the policymaker may have to compare legal rules in terms of the effects on each individual.

C. Efficiency Subject to Constraints on Agents

Consider two individuals, Buyer and Seller, with an opportunity to make an exchange. Their ability to make efficient decisions depends on the environment in which they find themselves. Similarly, the ability of a policymaker to announce and of a law-applier such as a court to implement an efficient rule depends on the environment in which the policymaker or the court finds itself. An assessment of the efficiency of a legal rule should be responsive to the limitations placed on the agents, the policymaker, and the law-applier. When faced with constraints, one may be doing very well even though one is not doing as well as one could in an ideal world.

The analysis here grows complex because the legal rule announced by the policymaker and implemented by the law-applier constitutes part of the environment in which Buyer and Seller act. The legal rule thus constrains Buyer and Seller. Conversely, the policymaker only announces rules to which Buyer and Seller respond. The policymaker cannot command particular outcomes, it can only structure incentives for individuals. The interest and ingenuity of individuals pursuing their own goals thus constrain the policymaker in its pursuit of efficiency.

In this subsection, I consider constraints that may limit individuals in their efforts to find, negotiate, and perform desirable contracts. To begin, consider three nonexhaustive, and nonexclusive, categories of constraints: (1) resource constraints, (2) strategic constraints, and (3) information constraints. My primary interest lies in constraints imposed by information. A brief description of resource and strategic constraints, however, will facilitate understanding the role of information in the evaluation of legal rules.

Resource constraints arise from the direct expenditures that an agent must incur in order to conclude an exchange. Lawyers' fees for drafting the contract, the costs of searching for a contracting party, or time delays in reaching agreement are examples of resource costs.

It is easy to see how resource costs might prevent individuals from exhausting gains from trade. Suppose Buyer places a value v on a good G that Seller can produce for a cost c. In an ideal world, Seller should produce G if and only if $v \geq c$. Suppose in fact that $v > c$. If it costs Buyer and Seller more than $v - c$ to draft the contract, then it will not be drafted. Similarly, suppose there are many sellers each with a different cost c of production. On average, Buyer might have to find several sellers and engage in preliminary negotiations with each before identifying one who has costs $c < v$. If the expected cost of search exceeds $v - E[c]$, the expected gains from trade where $E[c]$ is the average cost of sellers, then Buyer will not enter the market.

"Strategic constraints" refer to those impediments to efficient bargains that arise merely from the strategic structure of the interaction. Since, as will be discussed below, the structure of information constitutes part of the strategic structure of a game, this discussion focuses on constraints that would arise even in a game of perfect information.

If one identifies "transaction costs" with resource and information constraints, then the Coase theorem – which states that parties will reach efficient bargains if parties can bargain freely and if such bargains were enforceable – implies that there would be no pure strategic constraints in the sense meant here. The category of strategic constraints would collapse into that of resource costs.

This argument, however, fails on several grounds. Most importantly, strategic constraints disappear only if the legal regime has a specific structure. The objection thus assumes the answer to the question of what legal regime will structure the parties' interaction efficiently. Consider Buyer and Seller from the earlier example. Suppose Buyer will receive value v with certainty; that Seller will incur cost c with certainty; that $v > c$ (so that the exchange is desirable); and that Buyer and Seller have common knowledge of these facts. Suppose further that production takes time so that any agreement must be executory. This "bargaining problem" poses, in the absence of the law, a standard prisoner's dilemma in which it is in each party's interest not to perform the contract. A law of contract that imposes sufficiently high damages for breach of contract permits Buyer and Seller to commit to performance and thus induces a desirable exchange.

Finally, consider information constraints. One should perhaps refer to information structures rather than information constraints. An information structure identifies what each relevant individual knows at each stage of the transaction. The structure of this information affects the ability of individuals to identify and to exhaust gains from trade.

Return to the earlier example of a buyer who would place a value v on a good G that Seller can produce at a cost c. One might identify three stages to the (potential) transaction: a formation stage (time 0) when the parties decided whether to contract and what clauses to include in any writing; a performance stage (time 1) when each party decides whether to perform, and a dispute stage (time 2) when a court or other law-applier resolves any disputes that arise. The information structure specifies what each actor – Buyer, Seller, and court-as-law-applier – knows at each stage of the process. In this subsection, I concentrate on the knowledge of Buyer and Seller at each stage.

Two distinctions are important. First, distinguish *symmetric* information structures from *asymmetric* information structures. As the name suggests, in a symmetric information structure, the parties at *each* stage have identical information about the values v and c. In an asymmetric information structure, Buyer at *some* stage has different information from Seller. Second, parties may have to act ex ante, before all relevant information is available, or ex post, after all information is available.

A large number of information structures are possible. Consider first symmetric structures. The simplest structure I_0 corresponds to complete information. Buyer and Seller each know both v and c at times 0, 1, and 2.[5] Consequently, both the formation decision and the performance decisions are made ex post, in light of all relevant information.

Two other symmetric structures merit attention.[6] In structure I_1, neither Buyer nor Seller knows either v or c at the time of formation. Rather, each knows that v is drawn from some known distribution F and that c is drawn from some other known distribution G. At times 1 and 2, the performance and dispute stages, however, both Buyer and Seller know both v and c. In I_1, the performance decisions are ex post but the formation decision is ex ante.

In structure I_2, as in structure I_1, Buyer and Seller know only the distributions F(v) and G(c) but not the actual realizations at time 0. At time 1, both know the realization of c but neither knows the realization of v. At time 2, both parties know v and c. In I_2, the formation decision is ex ante relative to both v and c while the performance decision is ex ante relative to the realization of v but ex post relative to the realization of c.

In each of these three situations, the ideal outcome requires that production occur if and only if $v \geq c$. Under I_0, in the absence of resource constraints and the presence of the correct damage rule (such as expectation damages), the agents face no difficulty in accomplishing the ideal. Under I_1, the parties can again achieve the ideal, if resource constraints are absent and an appropriate damage rule (such as expectation damages) is present.[7]

Under I_2, however, the parties face an information constraint. The parties do not know at the time of formation whether v exceeds c. Moreover, at time 1, though they will know c, they still do not know whether v exceeds c, because v remains unknown. One could hardly demand, given what Buyer and Seller know, that they form only those contracts in which $v \geq c$ or perform only when $v \geq c$.

Assume that parties may form contracts costlessly and that there are no costs to nonperformance (when $v < c$). Then the efficient formation decision requires that all contracts form. The "best" performance decision will be efficient ex ante: Seller should perform when and only when $c \leq E[v]$, the expected value to Buyer.[8] The information structure constrains the set of achievable outcomes, and one's concept of efficiency should reflect that constraint.

The information structure in I_2 constrained how well the parties could do but it did not have any strategic implications for the parties. An asymmetric information structure, by contrast, may constrain through its creation of additional strategic complications as well as through the straightforward limitations of knowledge present in symmetric information structures. Consider I_3 and I_4. In I_3, Buyer and Seller know only F(v) and G(c) at time 0, but at time 1, Buyer learns v and Seller learns c. At time 2, each learns the realization known by the other. Thus, in I_3, information at the formation stage is symmetric, though the formation decision must be made ex ante. At time 1, however, information is asymmetric, as each party knows something that the other party does not. Consequently, it is hard to classify the performance decision. Society (or the "market"), however, has all relevant information; the decision might seem ex post. If the parties do not communicate their private information to each other, then, from the perspective of each decisionmaker, the decision is ex ante with respect to one variable and ex post with respect to the other.

In I_4, information is asymmetric at time 0; Buyer knows v (and G(c)) while Seller knows c (and F(c)). At time 1, Buyer and Seller each have the information the party had at time 0. At time 2, each learns the realization known by the other. In I_4, then, if the parties do not fully reveal their private information, neither the formation nor the performance decisions are made from a wholly ex ante perspective. Nor is either made fully ex post because, again, the market has all the relevant information, but neither party does. Call decisions made in circumstances like I_3 and I_4 *interim*.

The information structures I_3 and I_4 are very similar, but legal rules do not induce behaviorally identical outcomes. One can argue that I_3 does not prevent Buyer and Seller from achieving the ex post efficient decisions if the court, knowing v and c at time 2, enforces a rule of expectation damages. Because the parties have symmetric information at time 0, they can agree on an appropriate price for the entire contract. Or they can draft a complete contingent claims contract that will specify a price for each realization (v,c). This price will depend on the distribution of (v – c), commonly calculated by the parties from F(v) and G(c), and their beliefs about whether performance will occur for each pair (v,c). Once the contract forms, the parties should anticipate that each will truthfully reveal the party's own realization to the other so that performance will in fact occur when and only when $v \geq c$. Truthful revelation is guaranteed by the court's ability to enforce (at no cost to it or to the parties) expectation damages.

I_4, however, does constrain the parties. Buyer and Seller can no longer agree on a price for a contract because, given private information, each has different beliefs about the distribution of v – c for the actual contract. Each wants to mislead the other in order to get more favorable terms. Not every desirable contract will form (although performance will occur in each contract that does form).

This discussion shows that some information structures constrain what the parties may achieve. Consequently the concept of efficiency must be relative to the information structure. How does the existence of information constraints affect the policymaker?

Three questions arise for policymakers. First, can the legal rule influence the information structure? Second, do different, exogenously given information structures demand different legal rules? Third, if legal rules do influence the information structure or if the legal rule should be contingent on the information structure, the policymaker must ask whether the law-applier will be able to observe the information structure applicable to a particular case accurately.

The debate over penalty defaults suggests that the answer to the first question is clearly yes. In a more elaborate model, the threat of legal liability might induce parties to reveal information private to them so a previously asymmetric information structure may become symmetric. (The argument concerning I_3, for example, implicitly assumed that, at time 1, each party disclosed his or her type to the other. In some instances, legal rules might induce such disclosure.) Conversely, the threat of legal liability might in some instances prevent the exchange of private information. The nature and extent of the influence, however, depend on a variety of ill-understood and complex factors. The same debate over penalty defaults has provided a more ambiguous answer to the second question.[9] The literature has remained largely silent concerning judicial competence to determine the relevant information structure in each case.

D. What Do Courts and Policymakers Know?

The law's capacity to induce efficient choices depends not only on the information structure faced by the parties to the transactions but also on the knowledge of the policymaker at the time it announces the legal rule and on the knowledge of the court (or other law-applier) at the time disputes are resolved. I discuss these concerns in reverse order.

1. WHAT DO COURTS KNOW? The discussion in Section C made two critical assumptions. First, it assumed that the court knew all relevant information at the time it resolved disputes. Second, it assumed that the parties faced no resource constraints – i.e., parties could litigate costlessly. Neither of these assumptions is plausible.

The literature in economics analysis of law often distinguishes *observable* actions (or other "payoff-relevant" factors) from *verifiable* actions (or other payoff-relevant factors). In general, observability implies that all parties have symmetric, ex post knowledge of the action (or other factor) at the dispute stage. Verifiability implies that the court also knows the ex post realization of the factor at the dispute stage. In the context of the examples in Section C, v (or c) is observable at time t if both parties know v (or c) at time t. v (or c) is verifiable if the courts can observe v (or c) at the time of dispute resolution. Similarly, each party's decision to perform or to breach is considered verifiable. Moreover, in each example, the parties can observe the factor before the courts can verify it. This sequence makes the assumption of verifiability somewhat more plausible though there are many actions observable by the parties that are not verifiable by the courts. Determinations of liability and assessments of damages must depend only on verifiable actions or factors.

Clearly, if v or c is unverifiable, legal rules are less likely to be able to induce efficient actions from the parties. One should not, however, underestimate the courts' ability to formulate efficient rules even when information is not verifiable (or even observable to both parties).

Suppose that only Buyer knows v. Implementation of expectation damages now becomes more difficult for a court; it cannot calculate directly the appropriate award v – p. In some circumstances, however, it will have a reasonable, even perfect, proxy. For example, cover, which allows the buyer to purchase an alternative on the market when the seller breaches, delivers v to Buyer without requiring the verifiability of Buyer's expectation v – p.[10]

If v (or c) is not fully verifiable either directly or indirectly, however, then the law's ability to induce efficient actions will be greatly limited. Suppose the court observes v only with error; the court gets an estimate of v. Assume, for example, that the court observes some signal $\sigma = v + \varepsilon$ where ε is symmetrically distributed with mean 0 and that the parties have entered a fixed-price contract. Then expectation damages will no longer be breach-efficient– i.e., for some values of v and c, Seller may breach even though $c < v$.[11]

Thus, a policymaker must consider not only what the parties know at each relevant time but also what the law-applier will know at the time of dispute resolution. In some circumstances, unverifiability of (legal) decision-relevant factors may force the policymaker to compare rules that are only second-best.

2. **WHAT DO POLICYMAKERS KNOW?** To formulate a legal rule, the policymaker must know what the law-applier will know at the time the dispute is resolved and what the parties will know at each stage. After all, courts will be unable to apply a legal rule conditioned on actions or other factors that are not verifiable. It seems equally evident that the policymaker must know the information structure of the contractual situations it seeks to regulate. In addition, however, it may appear that the policymaker must also know the distribution of values of Buyer and the distributions of costs of Seller.

If sufficient information is verifiable, however, the policymaker need not know anything about the distributions of Buyer value and Seller cost. Suppose that v and c are verifiable. Then, regardless of the distribution of Buyer and Seller types, the rule of expectation damages creates appropriate incentives on buyers and sellers to perform in the cases discussed in Section C.[12] Even in information structures such as I_2 and I_3, where Seller must decide prior to knowing the realization of v, expectation damages based on the ex post realization induce appropriate actions. After all, expectation damages based on ex post realizations present the deciding contracting party with the correct expected costs ex ante.

III. Wealth Maximization or Efficiency

The discussion thus far has enumerated a number of different conceptions of efficiency. Each of these conceptions is an elaboration of the general concept of Pareto efficiency. Economists, in making normative evaluations, generally invoke one of two welfarist criteria: Pareto efficiency or the maximization of social welfare. Welfarist evaluations are a class of consequentialist evaluations that evaluate actions in terms of their consequences for human well-being. The two criteria differ in one important respect: Pareto efficiency does not make any interpersonal comparisons of well-being, while social welfare maximization treats the well-being of each individual equally.[13] As efficiency imposes weaker constraints, economists have generally considered it a more basic and compelling criterion.[14]

The literature on economic analysis of law, however, has often argued that judges ought to pursue wealth maximization rather than either Pareto efficiency or the maximization of social welfare. Richard Posner, who first advanced wealth maximization as a judicial goal, defended it on a variety of nonwelfarist grounds such as consent.[15]

This section has two aims. First, it elaborates the wealth maximization criterion within a welfarist framework. Second, it addresses the discrepancy between "wealth maximization," as defined by Posner and as elaborated here, and various more specific "market value" criteria articulated in the domains of corporate and commercial law. In commercial law, for example, the courts might define wealth in terms of the market value of the goods exchanged in the transaction. In corporate law, the courts generally refer to maximization of firm value or of shareholder wealth (as measured by the value of the firm's equity). In bankruptcy law, the courts may seek to maximize the value of the debtor's estate. Specifically I identify conditions under which market measures of firm value correspond to the Posnerian definition of wealth.

A. Wealth Maximization as a Welfarist Criterion

The wealth maximization criterion is an attempt to implement the Kaldor-Hicks (K-H) potential compensation criterion. The K-H criterion itself attempts to extend the Pareto criterion from a partial ordering that permits comparison of only some social states to a complete ordering that permits comparison of all states. If successful, the K-H potential compensation test would then extend the theoretical independence from interpersonal comparisons of welfare from positive to normative economics.

Two concerns presumably motivated this attempted extension. First, many economists, particularly those with a radically subjectivist view of well-being, believed that such interpersonal comparisons were not conceptually possible. Second, even if interpersonal comparisons were conceptually possible, they were not practically achievable for purposes of public policy. Individuals would always have an incentive to misrepresent the relative intensity of their preferences.

This section begins with a recapitulation of the partial nature of the Pareto criterion. It then defines the K-H potential compensation test and argues that it fails to extend the Pareto criterion to a complete order. Third, wealth maximization, in the form of cost/benefit analysis, is considered as an attempt to implement the K-H potential compensation test. Finally, the information concerns of Section IIC are incorporated into the analysis of wealth maximization.

1. A PROBLEM WITH PARETO. To begin, consider an example that illustrates the failure of the Pareto criterion to provide a complete ordering of social states. Consider a society with two individuals, Ira and Jane. Society, i.e. Ira and Jane together, must rank three alternatives–A, B, and C. Suppose that Ira prefers A to B to C and that Jane prefers C to A to B. The Pareto criterion implies that A is Pareto-preferred to B but that C is Pareto noncomparable to A and that B is Pareto noncomparable to C. Notice that one cannot complete the Pareto criterion by defining all Pareto noncomparable pairs as socially indifferent. In this example, that definition implies first that C is socially indifferent to A and second that C is socially indifferent to B. Using the prior social comparison that A is Pareto-preferred to B, we have $C = A > B = C$, which is an intransitivity.

Incompleteness, of course, is an undesirable attribute in a normative criterion because it potentially leaves important issues unresolved. In the example of the prior paragraph, for example, a policymaker can only conclude that B is undesirable. Even that conclusion, however, could not be drawn if, for some reason, the choice A were unavailable and the policymaker were required to choose either B or C. The pressure to extend an incomplete ordering to a complete one is thus great.

2. DOES THE KALDOR-HICKS TEST EXTEND THE PARETO CRITERION?

The previous subsection showed that a more subtle method of completing the Pareto criterion is necessary to yield a complete order of social alternatives. Here I define the K-H potential compensation test and then consider whether the K-H potential compensation test completes the Pareto criterion.

Consider a distribution W of goods among a population. This distribution provides a complete description of the state. A second distribution, V, is K-H-superior to W if there exists a redistribution V′ of the goods available in V such that V′ is Pareto superior to W; that is, at least one person prefers V′ to W and no one prefers W to V′. A distribution V will be K-H-efficient if there is no distribution W that is K-H-superior to V.

To complete the Pareto criterion, the K-H test must (1) rank states A and B identically to the Pareto criterion if A and B are Pareto-comparable; (2) for every pair of states A and B, determine that A is K-H-preferred to B, B is K-H-preferred to A, or A and B are K-H-indifferent; and (3) these determinations must be transitive.

One can easily see that the K-H potential compensation test agrees with the Pareto criterion when two states V and W are Pareto-comparable. Suppose, without loss of generality, that V is Pareto-preferred to W. Because the potential compensation required in the definition of K-H superiority is measured in terms of well-being, this relation means that at least one person is better off in utility terms in V than in W, and no one is worse off. This satisfies the definition of K-H superiority.

To complete the Pareto criterion, however, the K-H test must provide unambiguous comparisons in two other types of cases: (a) Both V and W are Pareto-efficient states or (b) V and W are Pareto-noncomparable though at least one is not Pareto-efficient. Each of these cases presents a problem.

Consider case (a) first. If both V and W are Pareto-efficient distributions, neither is K-H-superior to the other. This conclusion follows immediately from the definitions of K-H superiority (which defines potential compensation in terms of well-being) and the definition of Pareto efficiency. Consider two Pareto-efficient allocations, V and W. By definition, there is no reallocation V′ of the goods available in V that is Pareto-preferred to W; similarly, there is no reallocation W′ of the goods available in W that is Pareto-preferred to V. This conclusion reflects the ordinalist underpinnings of the K-H compensation test. Classical utilitarianism would choose between V and W in terms of greater average (or total) "utility."

The situation is more complex if either V or W is not Pareto-efficient. Then, the K-H criterion might appear to rank V and W. This comparison, however, may not be meaningful. As Scitovsky noted,[16] the K-H potential compensation test does not necessarily yield an ordering of social states. A state V may be K-H-superior to a state W, and W may be K-H-superior to V. These two relations yield intransitivities. To eliminate this problem, Scitovsky proposed a potential compensation criterion in which V was Scitovsky-superior to W if V was K-H-superior to W and W was not K-H-superior to V. This modified criterion again agrees with the Pareto criterion but it clearly is not complete. It renders noncomparable not only all Pareto-efficient states but also those pairs of states that give rise to the Scitovsky paradox.

Examples of this Scitovsky paradox are easy to generate. Consider a simple, two-person, two-good exchange economy (i.e., there is no production). Assume more specifically that social resources consist solely of one hundred apples and one hundred oranges. An allocation in this economy consists of an allocation (a_1, o_1) to person 1 and an allocation (a_2, o_2) to person 2 such that $a_1 + a_2 \leq 100$ and $o_1 + o_2 \leq 100$. Assume further that the two individuals have identical preference relations with the property that each prefers the bundle (n,n) to (r,s) for $r + s \leq 2n$ and each prefers (r,s) to (r′,s′) if $r \geq r'$ and $s \geq s'$. (i.e., for a fixed number of pieces of fruit, each person prefers an equal number of each type of fruit to an unequal number, and each prefers more fruit to less). Consider the allocations V = [(100,0), (0,100)], which allocates all the apples to person 1 and all the oranges to person 2, and W = [(0,100), (100,0)], which allocates all the oranges to person 1 and all the apples to person 2. Note that neither V nor W is Pareto-efficient. Moreover, V is K-H-superior to W because the reallocation V′ = [(50,50), (50,50)] of V is Pareto-preferred to W. But equally, W is K-H preferred to V because V′ is also a reallocation of W and it is Pareto-preferred to V.

We have seen that the K-H criterion does not complete the Pareto criterion. In addition, it is unclear that K-H superiority is an ethically significant relation. Under the K-H criterion, compensation is potential rather than actual; an individual J may be worse off with distribution V than with distribution W. J would be at least as well off in V′ as in W but, though V′ is Pareto-superior to V, V′ is not the prevailing distribution. It is thus unclear why V is better than W.

3. IMPLEMENTING THE K-H POTENTIAL COMPENSATION TEST.[17] In this subsection, I shall ignore the problems raised in the prior section and consider a further problem. The K-H test considers potential compensation in terms of well-being, but well-being is not directly observable. Consequently, even if the K-H criterion did extend the Pareto criterion, one would still face problems of implementation. Wealth maximization is meant to solve these problems.

Cost/benefit analysis (CBA) attempts to implement the K-H potential compensation test. CBA uses market measures of "value" to estimate the welfare of each individual. It then aggregates these individual estimates into an aggregate measure of social value that also is a "potential compensation" test. Under CBA, however, potential compensation is in monetary, rather than welfare, terms. This measure is hence observable, but it does not perfectly implement the K-H potential compensation test. A perfect implementation would say that an option A was "CBA-preferred" to an option B if and only if A were K-H-preferred to B. More seriously and unfortunate, because the K-H potential compensation test is not itself an order, CBA need not provide an implementation of any social welfare function.[18]

Posner's wealth maximization criterion is essentially CBA. To understand it more clearly, begin with a comparison in market value terms of the welfare of an individual under two different economic states. Each economic state is identified with an allocation $(\mathbf{x}) = (\mathbf{x}^1, \mathbf{x}^2, \ldots, \mathbf{x}^n)$ of all commodities among each of the n individuals in the society and a price vector $(\mathbf{p})$. Consider an economic state $S_0 = (\mathbf{p}_0, (\mathbf{x}_0))$ and a state $S_1 = (\mathbf{p}_1, (\mathbf{x}_1))$.

CBA provides two measures of an individual's relative well-being in the two states. The *equivalent variation* (EV) calculates the change in income that would leave the individual as well off in S_0 as in S_1; EV uses the S_0 prices (and income calculated as $\mathbf{p}_0\mathbf{x}_0$) as the baseline. The *compensating variation* (CV) calculates the change in income (with the base income calculated as $\mathbf{p}_1\mathbf{x}_1$) that would restore the individual to the S_0 level of well-being; CV uses the S_1 prices as the baseline.[19]

If the individual prefers S_0 to S_1, then EV will be negative and CV will be positive; but, in general, the absolute value of CV will not equal the absolute value of EV. Each measure will rank the two states in the same way so that they are ordinally equivalent measures. They may differ in absolute value so that they are not cardinally equivalent.

The difference in absolute value may arise for at least two reasons. First, if the wealth of the individual varies greatly between S_0 and S_1, the difference may be attributable to wealth effects. Preferences for environmental quality, for example, are income-elastic; the wealthier the individual, the more the person is willing to spend on environmental quality. Second, goods with few substitutes, or relatively unique goods, may cause a discrepancy between CV and EV.[20] A policy may, for example, alter the risk of disability or death to an individual; both CV and EV measure this change in money terms even though the market does not provide ready substitutes for the good.

The inequivalence of individual EV and CV may lead to difficulties when one makes social (or aggregate) comparisons. The social comparison of S_0 and S_1 simply compares the sum of the individual EVs (ΣEV) or the sum of the individual CVs (ΣCV) to 0. In general, some individuals will prefer S_0 to S_1

and others will prefer S_1 to S_0. Because each individual's CV differs in size from the individual's EV, one sum, such as ΣCV, may indicate that, socially, S_0 is preferred to S_1 while the other sum, such aS ΣEV, indicates that, socially, S_1 is preferred to S_0.

One cannot resolve this conflict between the two market measures of well-being EV and CV by identifying one measure as the more appropriate one. This tactic fails because EV and CV are defined relative to the status quo. Suppose we choose EV as the "correct" basis for social comparison.[21] When we ask whether we should move from S_0 to S_1, ΣEV tells us to do so. Suppose the change is implemented. When S_1 is the status quo, the "new EV" is simply the measure CV when S_0 was the status quo. A situation analogous to the Scitovsky paradox thus arises. CBA may not yield a transitive order of all options that the agent considers.

Whether this problem arises in the context of corporate and commercial law is unclear. In close corporations, at least, and possibly in some bankruptcy situations and in some large publicly held corporations, control of the corporation may be a unique good to the owners or managers. So an individual might have different offer and asking prices – which can, with some care, be mapped into EV and CV – for control of the enterprise. A choice between legal rules will have two effects: one transitional on the individuals whose control is immediately determined by the rule, and one ex ante on individuals who will be similarly situated in the future. A CBA of the transitional effects may present the problem of inequivalence of ΣEV and ΣCV. Whether it arises in a CBA of the ex ante effect is less certain. If individuals know ex ante that they are more likely to be on one side of the transaction than another, then the discrepancy is possible.

These and other problems are avoided if the difference between the two economic states is small. In these circumstances, ΣEV and ΣCV will have the same sign and hence order the choice between S_0 and S_1 identically. CBA will thus provide a social order for choices close to one another.

4. ORDINALITY AND INTERPERSONAL COMPARABILITY OF CBA. At the outset, I described CBA as an attempt to implement the K-H potential compensation test, which itself was an attempt to maintain a purely ordinalist and interpersonally noncomparable welfare economics. One might ask, at this point, the extent to which CBA is ordinalist and eschews interpersonal comparisons of well-being. After all, one might argue that the dollar measures of CV and EV provide both a cardinal measure of intensity and a standard of interpersonal comparisons of well-being.

To begin, return to the procedure for eliciting an individual's EV. CBA assumes that the individual has preferences over states of the world that can be represented by a utility function u(S) such that the individual prefers state S_0 to state S_1 if and only if $u(S_0) > u(S_1)$. CBA then derives an equivalent utility function that uses a "money" index to represent the individual's preferences.

To derive this equivalent represent, CBA describes each state of the world S in terms of the individual's wealth w in that state and a vector **y** of other features of that state.[22] It then selects some baseline state $S_0 = (w_0, \mathbf{y}_0)$. For any state $S' = (w', \mathbf{y}')$, one may find the number m′ such that $U(w{-}m', \mathbf{y}_0) = U(w', \mathbf{y}')$. Notice that when $S' = S_0$, $m' = 0$, and that the agent prefers S′ to S if and only if $m' > 0$. Similarly, the agent prefers $S_1 = (w_1, \mathbf{y}_1)$ to $S_2 = (w_2, \mathbf{y}_2)$ if and only if $m_1 > m_2$. Thus, the individual's EVs are another representation of the individual's preferences, that, like the underlying preferences, carries only ordinal information. So , if we consider four states – S_1, S_2, S_3, and S_4, with $m_1 > m_2 > m_3 > m_4$, we cannot conclude from the fact that $m_1{-}m_2 > m_3{-}m_4$ that the individual's preference for m_1 over m_2 is more intense than (or greater than) her preferences for m_3 over m_4. EV thus provides only an *ordinal* representation of the agent's preferences.

One may understand the ordinal nature of the CBA representation in a different way. Each choice of a baseline state S induces a different representation of the individual's underlying preferences. Each representation will order states identically, but the monetary values assigned to each state will obviously differ: For example, each state will assign 0 to itself. More importantly, the monetary difference for two states will depend on the choice of baseline.[23] As before, one cannot infer intensity from difference in the EVs assigned to states; each individual's CBA ranking is ordinal only.

The discussion of the ordinal nature of the CBA ranking of an individual also clarifies the question of interpersonal comparability in cost/benefit analysis. I have already argued that each agent's EV provides only an ordinal ranking of her alternatives; it is thus not clear that the summation of these rankings is meaningful. The problems of interpersonal comparability, however, do not end here. Assume that the individual CBA rankings are induced by the choice of the same baseline state S for each individual. This summation assumes that the CBA ranking for individual j provides a scale identical to that of the CBA ranking for individual k. This assumption, however, seems implausible. After all, the prior argument concerning ordinality indicated that individual k's scale depended on her wealth or, equivalently, on the choice of the baseline state. More concretely, suppose that individual k is poor in the baseline state whereas individual j is rich in that state. For example, suppose that k has wealth of \$1,000 whereas j has wealth of 10,000,000. Then k's valuations are bounded above by \$1,000 whereas j's valuations are bounded above by \$10,000,000. It is difficult to see how a \$1 difference in valuation of two states can have the same significance for k as for j. There is no reason to think that a particular choice of baseline selects representations of each individual's preferences that are scaled appropriately.[24]

5. PROBLEMS INTRODUCED BY THE INFORMATION STRUCTURE. The discussion thus far has proceeded without regard to the complications in the concept of efficiency outlined in Section III C. The K-H compensation test was presented as an attempt at extending the partial order of the Pareto criterion. Implicitly, the discussion assumed that the relevant criterion was the ex post Pareto criterion. In this instance, all parties to the transaction, the court, and any other relevant decisionmaker are assumed to know the realization of all random variables at the time of decision. As Part II argued, this assumption of complete knowledge covers only a small number of transactional types.

Does it matter whether one seeks to extend the ex ante Pareto criterion or the interim Pareto criterion rather than the ex post Pareto criterion? Similarly, wealth maximization and CBA were presented as implementations of the K-H potential compensation test. Does implementability or the meaningfulness of the implementability depend on how one elaborates the concept of efficiency?

Two related problems arise. First, one must consider the accuracy of the information available to each of the parties (and to the policymaker). Second, in some instances, one must consider the ethical significance of expected measures of well-being. I investigate these questions in turn.

In analyzing the effects of the information structure on the welfare assessment of different rules, one must distinguish two questions: (a) On what information should the liability of a party be conditioned?; (b) on what information should the desirability of the legal rule be assessed? As will become evident, these two questions might receive radically different answers. The potential for divergent answers, however, should not surprise. The first question concerns how the *law-applier* should determine liability in a specific case. The second question confronts the *policymaker* who must rank different rules in order to announce the best one. Confusion not surprisingly arises when a single institution, a court, acts as both law-applier and policymaker in the context of a single case.

Consider the simpler, ex ante information structure first. To make the discussion concrete, recall one of the examples discussed in Section II C. There, an ex ante information structure meant that each party knew only the distribution from which the Buyer's value and the Seller's cost will be drawn. A court resolved disputes, however, with knowledge of the actual value and cost. Recall further that the prior discussion showed that a rule of expectation damages based on ex post information would induce the parties to take actions that were ex ante efficient. Thus, a rule that conditions liability on ex post information, information not available to the agents at the time they act, still induces ex ante efficient action.[25]

The situation for assessment of the legal rule, by contrast, is quite different. In this information structure, it seems clear that, for two reasons, the policymaker's assessment cannot rely only on an assessment of well-being in a specific, realized state. First, the policymaker's assessment of legal rules must in some way reflect the constraints under which individuals subject to the rule will act. The parties' lack of information constrains the parties at the time they form the contract and at the time they must decide whether to perform. Second, though the court (or other policymaker) may know that, at the time of rule application, the relevant information will be known, efficiency is a forward-looking criterion. Presumably, the policymaker, like the parties, does not know at the time it announces the rule which state will be realized. Unless it can identify a legal rule that will induce the correct decision ex post in each state of the world, the policymaker must somehow weight the well-being realized in each state.

Two different sets of weights naturally present themselves. The policymaker might use the weights employed by the parties themselves, i.e., each party's own beliefs about the likelihood of each state. This weighting is sometimes identified as an ex ante approach. Alternatively, the policymaker might use its *own* beliefs about the likelihood of each state. This weighting is sometimes (misleadingly) identified as an ex post approach.[26] The ex post identification is misleading because, in each scheme, the policymaker weights its judgments by a set of beliefs about the likelihood that each state might be realized. The ex ante approach might more accurately be considered the "actor-assessed" approach, while the ex post approach might be more accurately considered the "policymaker-assessed" approach.

When a policymaker conducts a cost/benefit analysis, it adopts the actor-assessed approach to social welfare. The cost/benefit analysis will ask individuals to compare states that differ in the legal rule that prevails and hence affect the payoffs that each receives in different states. The policymaker will thus elicit the equivalent variation of buyers and sellers for a move from the prevailing legal rule to the proposed alternative. Each EV depends on the ex ante beliefs of the individual. At least three concerns arise.

The first concern with EV-assessed ex ante arises when the parties' beliefs differ systematically. Are the equivalent variations of different individuals comparable (i.e., can they be summed in the usual way)? Consider Buyer's beliefs about the likelihood that Seller will be low-cost. It is clear that Buyer's comparison of two legal worlds will depend on her beliefs and that Buyer's EV based on a belief that low-cost Sellers are unlikely is not comparable to her EV based on a belief that low-cost sellers are highly likely.

This lack of comparability (between Buyer's EV based on beliefs B and her EV based on beliefs B') does not obviously transfer to the situation when Buyer's beliefs differ from Seller's, but it does raise concerns. The summation of EVs based on different beliefs conflates two judgments that ideally should be kept apart: a judgment concerning the effects of the policy on ex post well-being and a judgment concerning the likelihood that particular states will be realized. Summation might be the appropriate method for comparing Buyer's loss ex post to Seller's gain ex post. Normally, however, one would use a more complex procedure for resolving the conflict in beliefs. If one could induce each party to reveal his or her beliefs (and the information on which the beliefs are based), then each would reassess his or her own beliefs. This process of reassessment is not a simple sum.

Second, because EV depends on the beliefs of the party, one can change EV by changing the beliefs of the parties. This criterion therefore suggests that policies that produce optimistic (and incorrect) beliefs in the parties are desirable because they will increase actor-assessed social welfare as measured by the sum of the EVs. These policies, however, leave ex post social welfare at best unchanged.

The third concern asks whether well-being measured in terms of the beliefs of the parties is meaningful. To investigate this question, I examine the conceptually simplest setting in which the policymaker can measure and observe each individual's well-being directly. This setting ignores all problems of implementation and practicality.

In this purely (almost) "utilitarian" setting, the distinction between actor-assessed social welfare and policymaker-assessed social welfare remains. As before, actor-assessed social welfare evaluates social states in terms of the ex ante well-being of each individual in society; the proposed sum of the individual, ex ante EVs is thus a measure of actor-assessed social welfare. Similarly, policymaker-assessed social welfare evaluates social states in terms of the ex post well-being of each individual in society.[27]

One may illustrate the distinction through the contract examples of Section II C. There, one would assess the welfare of Buyer and Seller for each possible pair of realizations of Seller cost and Buyer value. In each state, one could determine the social welfare as a function of the well-being of Buyer and Seller in that state. Of course, one must now weight these ex post evaluations of social welfare by some assessment of the likelihood of that state arising. Actor-assessed social welfare weights each state by each actor's beliefs, calculates each actor's ex ante well-being, and sums the results. Policymaker-assessed social welfare sums the well-being of each individual in each state and then weights each sum by the policymaker's beliefs concerning the likelihood of that state. This weighted sum (of sums) is the policymaker-assessed social welfare.

Which perspective should the policymaker adopt? Unfortunately, there seem to be compelling arguments against both actor-assessed social welfare and policymaker-assessed social welfare.

When the policymaker and each individual in society share common assessments of the likelihood of each state,[28] actor-assessed social welfare will be identical to policymaker-assessed social welfare. Nevertheless, pursuit of actor-assessed social welfare may recommend different social policies than the pursuit of policymaker-assessed social welfare. As noted above, a policymaker seeking to maximize actor-assessed social welfare should attempt to alter the beliefs of the individuals in society. In the example in the text, the policymaker should seek to encourage the parties to believe that the gains from trade are more likely to be high than they actually are.

This incentive to deceive arises because concern for actor-assessed social welfare does not evaluate how individuals actually do but how they might do. This distinction between concern for final outcomes and concern for expectations manifests itself starkly even in a simple utilitarian setting.

To illustrate this point clearly, consider two individuals, Buyer and Seller, with identical preferences over certain outcomes. At time 0, there is some uncertainty about the allocation of goods between them at time 1. The assumption of diminishing marginal utility for money implies that, whatever state is realized, total (ex post) social utility will be maximized by an equal division of wealth available in that state. As is well known,[29] this ex post desirable equality may easily be Pareto-dominated at time 0 by some ex ante trade from equal positions. Individuals would be ex ante equal but would trade risks to ensure that they were ex post unequal. This shifting of risks may arise either because the parties have different beliefs about the likelihood of some event so that each profits ex ante from a bet or because they have different attitudes toward risk so that one of the parties may be willing to insure the other against some loss.[30]

Suppose, for example, that a risk-neutral Seller and a risk-neutral Buyer have equal shares in a single portfolio that consists of a risk-free bond with value 100 and a risky investment X. The risky investment will either have a value 0 or a value 100. Consequently, after the resolution of the uncertainty, total social wealth will be either 100 or 200. Assume not only that the parties have identical preferences but also that these preferences exhibit diminishing marginal utility for money.[31] These assumptions imply that to maximize ex post social welfare, wealth should be divided equally in each state: (50,50) if the investment pays 0, and (100,100) if it pays 100.

Suppose Seller believes that the value of X will be $100 with probability 1/2, and 0 with probability 1/2. Buyer believes X will have value $100 with probability .6, and 0 with probability .4. Clearly, Buyer should purchase Seller's half interest in X for somewhere between $25 and $30, such as $27.50. This trade improves the ex ante well-being of each party. It also ensures that they will have unequal wealth ex post. Seller will have a wealth of $77.50 regardless of what happens to the investment X, while Buyer will have a wealth of $122.50 if the investment pays out and a value of $22.50 if it does not pay out. Ex post wealth (and welfare) will be distributed unequally (and suboptimally).

Now suppose that Buyer and Seller have the same beliefs that X will have value $100 (suppose that Seller's belief that this will occur with probability .5 is correct) but that Seller is risk-averse but Buyer is risk-neutral. Again, Seller would like to sell his interest in X, and Buyer will be willing to purchase. Suppose, for example, that Seller would rather have $20 for certain than own a half interest in X (which has expected value $25). If a sale occurs at $22.50, then once the value of X is realized, Seller will have a wealth of $72.50 for certain, while Buyer will have a wealth of either $127.50 or of $27.50. Again, ex post wealth and welfare will be distributed unequally (and suboptimally).

In the first example where the parties' beliefs differ, maximization of policymaker-assessed social welfare would lead to a very different result. Recall that Buyer and Seller have identical preferences that exhibit diminishing marginal utility for money. Consequently, ex post, the best distribution is an equal division of total wealth. Regardless of the beliefs the policymaker assigns to the likelihood that the investment X will be profitable, the policymaker prefers that the Buyer and Seller not trade. This result follows because policymaker-assessed social welfare is a function of the ex post well-being of each individual; the earlier riskiness in outcome does not play a role.

The second example presents further complications. As before, the assumptions that Buyer and Seller rank certain outcomes identically and that this ranking exhibits diminishing marginal utility for money imply that the ex post best outcome remains equal wealth regardless of the profitability of investment X. From this perspective, the policymaker should continue to prefer that Buyer and Seller not trade. Yet Seller dislikes risk. Seller's well-being is adversely affected by a no-trade rule.

It is not clear how to evaluate Seller's loss in utility from the risk without reverting to actor-assessed social welfare. One might possibly reformulate the policymaker's objective function to maximizing the expected (discounted?) sum of each individual's well-being. In the simplest story, in which Buyer and Seller face a risk at time 0 that is realized at time 1, this story breaks down for two reasons. First, it double-counts the ex post realizations. Second, Seller's well-being at time 0 depends on the risk he perceives; thus Seller's time 0 well-being is measured ex ante.[32]

Thus, maximization of policymaker-assessed social welfare also presents dilemmas. In addition to the policymaker's difficulty in valuing losses in well-being due to risk, two other difficulties arise. The failure of policymaker-assessed social welfare to capture the effect of risk on well-being simply illustrates a more general problem. Society never reaches a truly ex post state. The "final consequences" considered by the policymaker will be subject to risk in the future. Thus, the assessments of each individual's well-being in the "final state" are in fact the individual's ex ante assessments of his or her well-being.

A further problem arises. Pursuit of policymaker-assessed social welfare will face the constraint that agents will make individual decisions to maximize their ex ante welfare. So the policymaker may be at odds with the citizenry.

The formulation of the policymaker's objective does not become easier when one moves from consideration of symmetric distributions of information to asymmetric information structures. Recall that in an asymmetric information structure, the parties have different information about the state of the world. This distribution of information highlights the difficulties that arise in the simpler ex ante, symmetric cases.

Consider, for example, case I_4, in which at the time of contract formation Buyer knows she has value v* and Seller knows he has cost c*. Actor-assessed social welfare criteria (such as cost benefit analysis) compare rules on the basis of the sum of each party's own assessment of his or her well-being. In this asymmetric case, the parties have different (and erroneous[33]) beliefs about the type of the other party. Clearly the appropriate way to aggregate their *beliefs* is not through a summation of the individual, ex ante measures of well-being.

On the other hand, the policymaker has *less* information than either party. It knows only the distributions. Maximization of policymaker-assessed well-being also relies on erroneous information. Indeed, the policymaker errs in both beliefs while each actor errs in only one. The choice between actor-assessed and policymaker-assessed well-being as the policymaker's maximand is thus deeply perplexing and problematic.

B. *Wealth Maximization in Corporate and Commercial Law*

Corporate law scholars often phrase the legal objective as the maximization of the value of equity or of the value of the firm understood as the sum of the value of equity and of debt. This characterization of the judicial goal superficially is at odds with the conception of wealth maximization elaborated in Section III A. In a world with sufficiently numerous and rich markets, however, the two characterizations, maximize firm value and maximize wealth, coincide.[34] In many instances, however, the two characterizations of value will diverge.

Consider first a world in which one can identify corporations with particular "projects" or investments. Each project generates a flow of costs and benefits. Assume that "project" returns are certain but differ with respect to the flow of costs and benefits. Consider corporation F. Which project should F undertake? If the corporation had a single owner-manager, the choice of project would be uncontroversial. Consider two cases. In one, no capital markets exist. The owner-manager then consults her own preferences for consumption across time and chooses the project that maximizes her own time preferences. In the second case, perfect capital markets exist[35]; the owner-manager can borrow or lend at the market rate of interest. In this instance, the owner-manager should choose the project that maximizes firm profits; she can then satisfy her own preferences for consumption across time through borrowing or lending on the capital markets. Notice that perfect capital markets imply that the owner-manager should maximize the value of the firm (because the value of the firm should reflect the flow of profits that the firm receives).

Suppose F has multiple owners. In general, these owners will have different time preferences. In the complete absence of capital markets, each would choose the project that maximized her time preferences; project choice would depend on which owner had the power to select the project. With perfect capital markets, however, owners would be unanimous. Each would choose to maximize the value of the firm and then borrow or lend on the capital markets in order to satisfy her own time preferences.

This argument extends to circumstances in which project returns are uncertain. Under these conditions, owners might differ not only in their time preferences but in their risk preferences and their beliefs about the world. In the absence of capital markets, a single owner would choose the project that was best given his or her time and risk preferences. So, two individuals with identical time preferences would choose different projects if they had different degrees of risk aversion. If a firm had multiple owners who had different attitudes toward risk, they would disagree over which project to adopt. Indeed their disagreement would persist as long as capital markets were imperfect.[36]

This disagreement would again dissolve if capital markets were "perfect." A perfect capital market now requires, in addition to sufficient markets to arbitrage time preferences, that the set of securities available on the market be sufficiently rich and diverse to generate competitive markets for "all risks."[37] In these circumstances, each owner will again agree that the firm should maximize the value of its securities and then adjust his or her portfolio to reflect his or her risk and time preferences.

Perfect capital markets, then, are a necessary condition for the equivalence of firm value maximization and wealth maximization more generally understood. When capital markets are imperfect, maximizing firm value need not maximize wealth or well-being. In this second-best world, however, no other clearly implementable objective for the policymaker is readily available.

Several conditions other than perfect capital markets are necessary as well. Recall, first, that the Posnerian definition of "wealth" differed from the market value of the goods consumed; rather, changes in "wealth" are measured by the equivalent (or compensating) variation. Firm value maximization, however, calculates firm value as the product of the prices of firm securities times the quantity of the securities issued. In most instances, a security holder will indeed value the security at its market price; after all, the security is simply a claim on assets, like money, and, except in specific circumstances, has no other inherent (or instrumental) value. So, for example, if each investor in the firm has a small interest, then market value will equal "Posnerian" wealth.

Note that the investor's interest must be small in two respects: It must be small in terms of the size of the firm and it must be small relative to the investor's own assets. If the investor holds a large interest in the firm, she may have control over it and control might have a value in addition to the market value of the securities. If the investor's share of the firm constitutes a large proportion of her own assets, then the market value of the securities may not accurately reflect her valuation of the securities. In particular, she may be inadequately diversified and the market value of the firm overstates her valuation of the assets.

A third necessary condition for the equivalence of wealth and firm value maximization requires that agency costs be zero. Shareholder unanimity theorems or the second separation theorem[38] assumes that management conscientiously implements the agreed upon aim of maximizing firm value. Managers, however, have their own aims, which may diverge from or conflict with the maximization of firm value. The maximization of firm value consequently comes at the cost of well-being to managers. Managers, that is, might be willing to pay more for a legal regime that permits some divergence from the maximization of firm value than shareholders would be willing to pay for the firm value maximizing regime.

IV. Concluding Remarks

In the recent academic literature, the normative foundations of corporate and commercial law are largely uncontroversial. Policymakers in announcing rules and courts in applying them ought to promote efficiency or wealth maximization. This essay has argued that this goal is easier to endorse than to articulate precisely and to justify.

The structure of the argument is straightforward. Efficiency and wealth maximization are both instrumentally but not intrinsically valuable. Law ought to pursue them only to the extent that they provide reasonable and practical proxies for individual well-being. Unfortunately, these goals require further clarification in at least three ways before they can provide reasonable guidance to a policymaker.

First, legal rules influence a large number of decisions made by commercial and corporate actors. A rule that is best with respect to one decision need not be best with respect to a second decision. This conflict poses a dilemma for policymakers. The determination of the most efficient (or of the wealth maximizing) rule all decisions considered may be a task beyond the competence of either courts or legislatures. On the other hand, courts and legislatures may not be able to develop and apply doctrinal tools that permit proceeding separately with respect to each individual decision.

Second, the information possessed by corporate and commercial actors as well as by the policymaker and the courts is likely to be both imperfect and distributed asymmetrically. This asymmetry and imperfection constrain the policymaker to seeking second- or third-best alternatives. In addition, if the "best" legal rule varies with the structure of information, then courts must be able to classify cases according to their underlying information structure correctly.

Third, and conceptually most serious, the specification of the appropriate maximand under uncertainty presents unresolved difficulties. In many information structures, the agents must act without knowledge of the realization of all decision-relevant factors. In these circumstances, the evaluation of a legal rule depends on the appropriate weighting of each potential outcome. Usually, evaluations weigh each possible outcome either by the beliefs of each agent that that outcome will occur or by the policymaker's belief that it will occur. Neither an actor-assessed conception of social welfare nor a policymaker-assessed conception of social welfare, however, is fully satisfactory.

These foundational difficulties raise two distinct questions concerning claims about the judicial goal of wealth maximization. First, they suggest that an interpretation of current judicial rulings as in fact maximizing wealth requires that one identify the mechanism that produces this result. It is implausible to believe that judges consciously aiming at efficiency or wealth maximization, as appropriately understood in the complex commercial world that judges confront, could actually achieve it. It is equally implausible to interpret the opinions as aiming directly at this goal.

Second, and related, the foundational concerns raise doubts about the wisdom of the courts as policymakers directly pursuing efficiency or wealth maximization. Generally, courts have inadequate information about the distribution of agent types and too little sophistication concerning these economic goals to succeed in formulating rules that seek directly to promote them. This claim, of course, does not deny that courts might have appropriate information to apply rules that are efficient or wealth maximizing. Part of the elegance of expectation damages based on actual damages lies in the informational economy of the rule.

Arguments against the direct pursuit of efficiency do not indicate how courts might indirectly pursue the same goal. The most compelling defense of wealth maximization as a judicial goal relies on the desirability of using one instrument – tax – to pursue distributional goals, a second instrument – e.g., tort or regulation – to ensure that agents internalize costs to third parties, and a third instrument – corporate and commercial law – to promote the general level of well-being through exchange and cooperation. This strategy suggests that the law might pursue efficiency relative to a specific decision in distinct doctrinal domains.

This strategy requires not only that the law develop distinctive doctrines concerning each relevant decision, but also that remedies vary across doctrinal areas. Corporate and commercial law has clearly developed doctrines specific to at least some of the decisions outlined in Section II A. The range of remedies, however, is quite narrow. Contract law, for example, generally denies enforcement or provides expectation damages. Occasionally, it offers reliance damages. This menu of remedies may be too sparse to create a legal regime that maximizes wealth, all decisions considered.

Notes

† The Filomen d'Agostino and Max E. Greenberg Research Fund of the NYU School of Law provided financial support. I thank Barry Adler, Liam Murphy, Alan Schwartz and participants at the Stanford Law and Economics Workshop for comments on an earlier draft.

1. This sentence somewhat overstates the current status of debate. Economic analysts of law continue to address a broad range of legal questions from tort law to issues in constitutional law. These studies often adopt an "efficiency" perspective but do not generally argue strongly against alternative normative perspectives.

   See Louis Kaplow and Steven Shavell, *Why Is the Legal System Less Efficient Than the Income Tax in Redistributing Income,* 23 J. Legal Stud. 667 (1994). *Should Normative Analysis of Law Be Solely Economic or Include Consideration of Fairness?* (manuscript 1996), however, has recently revived the claim, on grounds of institutional competence, that tort law in particular should seek to promote efficiency. For a brief summary of their position, see Lewis A. Kornhauser, *Wealth Maximization,* 3 *New Palgrave Dictionary of Economics and the Law* (P. Newman, ed., 1998).
2. See Kaplow and Shavell. For an earlier argument to the same effect, see Steven Shavell, *A Note on Efficiency vs. Distributional Equity in Legal Rulemaking: Should Distributional Equity Matter Given Optimal Income Taxation,* 71 Am. Econ. Rev. 414 (Papers and Proceedings, 1981).
3. These separate bodies of law include antitrust law to ensure that product and input markets are competitive and, in some circumstances, consumer protection laws that correct or ameliorate certain informational problems present in those markets.
4. "Affected by" includes relations other than "party to" a contract. The intensity of search for a contracting party, for instance, will affect individuals not party to any final contract actually made. A buyer who searches intensively for a low-cost seller may negotiate with and then abandon many moderately low-cost sellers before concluding a contract. Conversely, a buyer who conducts a superficial search may conclude a contract with a much higher-cost seller, and this superficiality of search may harm a lower-cost seller who would have gotten the contract. See Peter Diamond and Eric Maskin, *An Economic Analysis of Search and Breach of Contract, I: Steady States,* 10 Bell J. Econ. 282–316 (1979); Peter Diamond and Eric Maskin, *An Economic Analysis of Search and Breach of Contract, II: A Non-Steady State Example,* 25 J. Econ. Theory 165–95 (1981).
5. It might seem that if a party knows a fact at time 0, it knows that fact at each later time. In some circumstances, however, a party may "forget" its prior information. In the game of bridge, for example, if one considers North-South one player and East-West a second player, the knowledge of each player changes from move to move. A related situation may arise in litigation that typically occurs long after various events that were common knowledge to the parties at the time. The verifiability of these actions to a court often rests on the documentation that survives.
6. The three symmetric information structures considered here do not exhaust the possibilities, but the structures not discussed do not present any issues that do not arise in the present discussion.
7. For example, the parties might simply draft a complete contingent claims contract that, for each possible pair (v,c) of realizations, specifies whether performance should occur and a transfer price from Buyer to Seller. As long as the court observes v and c at time 2 and enforces a rule of expectation damages, Buyer and Seller will make efficient decisions.

Notice that even when it is costly to draft contracts, the rule of expectation damages may still elicit efficient decisions from Buyer and Seller.

8. The efficient "contract" can be viewed as a complete contingent claims contract that specifies for each possible realization c whether Seller should produce, given the distribution of values. Clearly, Seller must be compensated for his costs of production. A contract that specified production when $c > E[v]$ would not be ex ante efficient. Seller must receive some price $p \geq c$ to compensate for his costs, but this price exceeds the expected value of performance.
9. The debate in the law and economics literature has focused on the rule of *Hadley v. Baxendale* 9 Ex. 341, 145 E no. Rep. 145 (1854). The importance of information structure was first addressed by Ian Ayres and Robert Gertner, *Filling Gaps in Incomplete Contracts: An Economic Theory of Default Rules,* 99 Yale L.J. 87 (1989). In a subsequent article, responding to Jason Johnston, *Strategic Bargaining and the Economic Theory of Contract Default Rules,* 100 Yale L.J. 615 (1990) (arguing for a different default rule), Ian Ayres and Robert Gertner, *Strategic Contractual Inefficiency and the Optimal Choice of Legal Rules* 101 Yale L.J. 729 (1992) conjectured that the legal rule would matter only if resource constraints differed across potential rules.
10. The buyer pays price p' for the alternaive performance and receives damages of $p'-p$ from the seller. The buyer thus receives the expectation $v-p$.
11. Suppose (a) $F(\varepsilon)$ is the distribution function for ε; (b) Seller has a cost c and (c) $v > c > p$. Thus, efficiency requires production but, under a rule of expectation damages, Seller would prefer to breach. If Seller performs he loses $c - p$ with certainty. If Seller breaches he pays $\sigma - p$ as long as $c < \sigma - = v + \varepsilon$. Otherwise Seller pays nothing (as there was no damage). Seller's expected damages from breach are therefore less than $v - p$. For v sufficiently close to c, the probability that Seller will escape without liability approaches 1/2. His expected damages correspondingly fall. At some point he will prefer to breach.

    Of course, to the extent that parties anticipate the court's inability to verify v, they will take the expected court error into account in the decision to form a contract and in the price that should be set. See Aaron Edlin, *Cadillac Contracts and Upfront Payments: Efficient Investment under Expectation Damages,* 12 J. L., Econ. + Org. 98–118 (1996) constructs, on the assumption that parties are risk-neutral and the court measure of damages is an unbiased estimate of actual damages, an efficient contract in a more complex setting.
12. Correct incentives to perform are even created in C_4; the difficulty there lies in the decision to form a contract, not to perform it.
13. In a world of certainty, the two criteria differ in another respect. Efficiency requires only an ordinal measure of well-being but social welfare maximization generally assumes that well-being is cardinally measurable. In the presence of uncertainty, as in the definitions of ex ante and interim efficiency, the criterion of efficiency requires that well-being be cardinally measurable though it insists that risk provide the appropriate index.
14. For others, by contrast, the lack of interpersonal comparability undermines rather than advances the ethical attractiveness of efficiency. See, for example, Lawrence Sager, *Pareto Superiority, Consent and Justice,* 8 Hofstra L. Rev. 913 (1980).
15. For references, see Kornhauser, *Wealth Maximization,* supra n. 1.
16. Tibor Scitovsky, *A Note on Welfare Propositions in Economics,* 9 Rev. of Econ. Stud. 77–88 (1941).
17. This section draws on Kornhauser, *Wealth Maximization,* supra n. 1.

18. See Charles Blackorby and David Donaldson, *Consumers' Surpluses and Consistent Cost-Benefit Tests,* 1 Soc. Choice and Wel. 252–62 (1985). "Social welfare function" here means a Bergson-Samuelson social welfare function, not an Arrovian one.
19. For technical details, see Hal R. Varian, *Microeconomic Analysis* (2d ed., 1984).
20. W. Michael Hanemann, *Willingness to Pay and Willingness to Accept: How Much Can They Differ?* 81 Am. Econ. Rev. 635 (1991).
21. EV, in fact, is the more appropriate choice of measure. Suppose one must compare three options S_0, S_1, and S_2 with S_0 the status quo. If one adopts EV as the measure, the comparison of S_0 and S_1 will be made in terms of S_0 prices; similarly the comparison between S_0 and S_2 will be made in terms of S_0 prices. If each comparison suggests that a shift from S_0 is desirable, then one could compare the ΣEV_0s of S_1 and the ΣEV_0s of S_2 to decide which change from S_0 is best.

    If one adopts CV as the measure, however, the comparison between S_o and S_1 will be made in terms of S_1 prices while the comparison between S_0 and S_2 will be made in terms of S_2 prices. In the event that each comparison implies that S_0 should be abandoned, the analyst has no common baseline with which to compare S_1 and S_2.
22. In the prior discussion, each state was represented by a price vector **p** and an allocation (**x**) of all commodities among each of the n individuals in the society. Individual k haaas wealth w_k defined by the value of the marketable assets in k's allocation $\mathbf{x}^k$.
23. If the agent's preferences are independent of wealth, then the CBA representation of the underlying preferences for one baseline will be a linear transformation of the representation induced by another baseline state. When preference depends on wealth, however, the situation is different. Consider two states S and S′. Suppose that, using state R as a baseline, CBA assigns the values r and r′ to the two states, and that when using the state T, CBA assigns the values t and t′. Then r – r′ will have the same sign as t – t′ but differ in absolute value.
24. In general, an individual's preferences are equivalently representable by a large number of utility functions. Interpersonal comparability essentially requires that one specify the representation of individual j's preferences using the same "scale" as a specified representation of agent k's preferences.
25. Two collateral points merit mention. Legal rules based on ex ante information might also induce the appropriate actions. To induce efficient action, each agent must see the expected cost that failure to perform imposes on the other party. If damages equal this amount regardless of the actual damage incurred by the promisee, efficient incentives are created. This rule, however, requires that the court know the ex ante distributions as well as the ex post realizations. It may be more reasonable to suppose that the court knows only the ex post realizations. (It will be unable to learn the ex ante distributions from its experience of litigated cases because it will see the realizations only for transactions in which a breach occurred.)
26. See Peter Hammond, *Utilitarianism, Uncertainty and Information,* in *Utilitarianism and Beyond* 85–102 (1982).
27. Hammond, supra n. 26, has a clear and insightful analysis of the issues raised by the two different perspectives from which one might evaluate well-being. He calls "actor-assessed" social welfare "ex ante" social welfare, and "policymaker-assessed" social welfare "ex post" social welfare.

28. Identity between the two measures requires some additional restrictions on the form of the social welfare function. See Peter Diamond, *Cardinal Welfare, Individualistic Ethics, and Interpersonal Comparisons of Utilities: A Comment,* 75 J. of Pol. Econ. 765–6 (1967).
29. See Diamond, supra n. 28 and Amartya Sen, *Collective Choice and Social Welfare* (1970).
30. Both possibilities are raised by Hammond, supra n. 29.
31. In expected utility theory, diminishing marginal utility for money is a consequence of risk-aversion. Thus the assumption of risk-neutrality implies that each individual has preferences that are linear in money. The additional assumption that each individual has preferences that exhibit diminishing marginal utility for money must thus mean that the preferences over risk are not over money directly but over a strictly concave transformation of money into "certain utils." On this assumption, ex post well-being is maximized when wealth is divided equally between the parties. (If preferences were linear in money, any division of ex post wealth would yield the same total well-being.)
32. One might object that the discussion of risk in the text confuses the appropriate locus of well-being. In the formalism, the only relevant stage at which to assess well-being is at time 1, after the realization. This objection fails for several reasons. First, as the text suggests, individuals experience well-being over time; an overall assessment of well-being should consider this flow. Even if one evaluated lives as a whole at their end, the nature and extent of risks experience would enter into one's assessment of an individual's lifetime well-being.
33. Buyer believes that Seller has cost c* with some probability less than 1 even though Seller has cost c*.
34. Of course, financial, product, and input markets must be perfectly competitive, and externalities must be priced appropriately through other bodies of law.
35. A perfect capital market satisfies three conditions: (a) Individuals and firms have equal access to the market; (b) each market participant is "small" relative to the market so that prices (i.e., interest rates) are competitive; and (c) there are no transaction costs to borrowing or lending.
36. Peter DeMarzo, *Majority Voting and Corporate Control: The Rule of the Dominant Shareholder,* 60 Rev. of Econ. Stud. 713–34 (1993).

    Note that the disagreement might result from a divergence in beliefs about the likelihood that specific states will be realized as well as from differences in preferences over risk.
37. That is, the set of securities must span the states of the world that might be realized, and the market for each security must be competitive.
38. The first separation theorem states that, under appropriate conditions, the total market value of any firm in equilibrium is independent of its capital structure (e.g., the division between debt and equity). This theorem requires that certain rules of priority as between early and later creditors apply. Obviously, the structure of legal rules will matter here.

    The second separation theorem – or shareholder unanimity theorems – states that all security holders will agree that the firm should maximize firm value.

4

Do Trade Customs Exist?

RICHARD CRASWELL†

I. Introduction

The question, of course, is semifacetious. Trade customs – and related concepts such as trade usage, course of dealing, and course of performance – play a central role in Article 2 of the Uniform Commercial Code. They played an equally important role in the work of Karl Llewellyn, one of Article 2's principal drafters.[1] Customs are also invoked, at least occasionally, in analyses of corporate law.[2] And there is surely *some* sense in which trade customs actually do exist.

Nevertheless, I argue here that the exact sense in which customs exist deserves closer examination. Customs can be thought of as a kind of pattern or regularity in prior behavior, much as common law doctrines can be thought of as a pattern or regularity in court decisions. In jurisprudence, however, it would be controversial to claim that patterns in court decisions have an existence of their own, or that those patterns can be identified independently of the goals and beliefs of the person doing the identifying. In this paper, I argue that the existence (and identification) of customs should be subject to exactly the same controversy. In particular, I suggest that the goals, beliefs, and other normative premises of the person doing the identifying must inevitably play a role in the interpretation and application of customs.

Part II of this chapter defines the issue more precisely by distinguishing it from much of the recent literature on norms and customs in commercial law. That literature not only takes the identification of a custom to be relatively unproblematic, it also suggests that reliance on custom can actually free a court from the need to engage in any normative or policy analysis of its own. Parts III and IV consider two possible but (in my view) unpersuasive ways of conceiving of customs: as a pattern or regularity in merchants' behavior, which can be discerned from the objective record of past behavior; or as beliefs held subjectively by industry members, in the form of bright-line rules about how merchants ought to behave. Part V then argues for a different view of custom that assigns a greater role to industry members' own case-by-case judgments about proper behavior, where those judgments take a form that often cannot be reduced to bright-line rules. This view of custom casts doubt on, or at least raises new questions regarding, the conventional argument that the judgment of industry members is likely to be more reliable than the courts' own judgments about proper behavior, or than the judgments of economists or philosophers. Part V also surveys some appellate decisions, showing that (as might be expected) the courts' own judgments do in fact play an influential role.

II. Some Current Issues Distinguished

The academic interest in norms and customs (and in their relation to commercial law) has experienced a resurgence in recent years. With few exceptions, however, this resurgence has centered around questions very different from those I address here.

For example, a recent exchange between Lisa Bernstein, on the one hand, and Jody Kraus and Steven Walt, on the other, has questioned the extent to which many commercial practices are uniform across significant geographic regions.[3] While this is an interesting and important empirical question, it is not the question that I am addressing here. Instead, my concern is not with the degree of uniformity of business behavior, but rather with the interpretation of any given uniformity. That is, even in a region where (for example) there is a uniform pattern or regularity in business behavior, we still must decide which aspects of that pattern to select as defining features of the custom, and which to dismiss as irrelevant.

Unfortunately, most prior work on customs has completely overlooked this question. Indeed, most of the prior literature assumes that the custom in question has already been interpreted or articulated, and proceeds to the question of whether the law should follow that custom. In this respect, most of the prior literature is implicitly prefaced with the statement, "Assume the following custom. . . ."

For example, consider a case where a custom is known to one party to a transaction but not to the other, and where the courts must decide whether to use the custom to bind both parties (by interpreting their contract to accord with it). The law's treatment of such cases can have many possible consequences, including an effect on everyone's incentive to become informed about customs in the future.[4] But this issue does not even arise unless and until it is determined that a custom does in fact exist (and, of course, that it was known to only one party). And analyses of these incentives generally do not concern themselves with the question of how the existence of the custom might have been determined in the first place. Instead, these analyses implicitly assume that the custom has *already* been identified, and focus only on the question of what the law should do with it.

The same is true of a more general debate about whether courts should give legal effect to customs that seem unfair or inefficient. One early and frequent criticism of Llewellyn was that his apparent endorsement of trade custom would give legal effect to entrenched practices that benefited merchants at the expense of other social goals.[5] Similar criticisms are often made in tort law, arguing that compliance with prevailing custom should not establish the reasonableness of a party's behavior.[6] Whatever the merit of these criticisms, the point of interest here is that they address an issue that arises only after the existence of a custom has already been established. In other words, the question raised by this debate is what the law ought to do with a *given* custom, not how to identify the custom in the first place.

The same is true of a more recent body of literature that attempts to identify the conditions under which customs are likely to be efficient. For example, several authors have argued that customs are most likely to be efficient in communities whose members interact frequently and are well-informed about the matters governed by the custom, and when the costs and benefits of the custom are felt primarily by the members of the community themselves rather than being externalized to outsiders.[7] The suggested legal (as opposed to merely anthropological) relevance of this analysis is that it could enable judges or legislators to adopt efficient rules of law even if they lack the economic expertise to design efficient rules on their own. As long as judges or legislators can identify those communities whose customs are likely to be efficient (the argument goes), they can simply adopt legal rules that mimic those communities' customs, without having to analyze the efficiency of the resulting rules.[8]

In short, this literature too is concerned entirely with what to do with a custom once it has been identified, not with how to identify the custom in the first place. In addition, this literature implicitly assumes that a community's custom can be identified by judges or legislators in a relatively unproblematic way. At the very least, it assumes that a custom can be identified in a way that is *different* from and places fewer demands on decisionmakers than would be the case if decisionmakers were required to analyze the efficiency of legal rules directly. Otherwise, if efficiency analysis were required even to identify the custom, there would be no point in looking to custom as a way of bypassing the decisionmaker's own efficiency analysis.

Indeed, a similar point could be made about some writers who urge reliance on trade customs for reasons other than efficiency. For example, Randy Barnett has argued that when a contract fails to address some issue explicitly, the law should supply a default rule that matches the parties' tacit assumptions, at least in cases where the same tacit assumptions are shared by both parties. He also suggests that, in the absence of any other evidence about what the parties tacitly assumed, their assumptions should be taken to match the customs (or "commonsense expectations") within "the relevant community of discourse."[8]

Barnett bases his recommendation not on any claim that these customs are likely to be efficient, but merely on the claim that these customs are most likely to correspond to the subjective intentions of the parties, since the subjective intentions of the parties are what his autonomy-based theory of contract law would (ideally) respect.[10]

This recommendation, too, presupposes that there is some relatively unproblematic way for courts or legislatures to identify the customs or commonsense expectations of the relevant community. In particular, it presupposes that courts can identify the relevant custom without substituting their own preferences for those of the parties, for that would be to do what an autonomy-based theory does not permit. In Barnett's theory, for example, the principal argument for respecting the parties' subjective intentions is the Hayekian claim that only in this way can the parties' own "local knowledge" (knowledge of their own needs, desires, etc.) be brought to bear, thereby producing fairer and more accurate allocations than a central planner could ever achieve.[11] Barnett thus shares with many efficiency theorists the premise that customs can serve as a guide to something that courts would face great difficulty identifying on their own. But this argument has force only to the extent that the identification of customs places demands on courts that are less stringent than, or at least are different from, the demands courts would face if they tried to allocate risks based on their own judgments of fairness or efficiency.[12] Ultimately, then, the force of this argument depends on just how the customs are to be identified.

It is this question – how are customs to be identified? – that has largely been ignored in the recent literature. To address that question, however, we must first be clear about what we mean by a "custom," or what must be true for a custom to "exist." These logically prior issues are what I address here.

III. Customs as Patterns of Behavior

One possible view of customs is that they represent a pattern or regularity in prior commercial behavior. For example, it might be said that there is a custom of free delivery just in case it is true that sellers have always (or nearly always, or usually) delivered their products without any charge. To be sure, a more complete statement of this position would require spelling out the exact degree of regularity that is required – always, nearly always, or usually? – in order to count as a custom.[13] But however that issue is resolved, the key for my purposes is that under this approach, the existence of a custom is to be determined by looking for patterns in actual commercial behavior.

Framed in this way, the task of identifying customs has much in common with the task of identifying common law rules. Common law rules are often described as reflecting the pattern of prior instances of *judicial* behavior – to wit, the rulings of earlier judges. For example, it might be said that the common law standard of care is one of negligence just in case it is true that prior judges have always (or nearly always, or usually) found liability when and only when the defendant was negligent. On this view, the search for common law rules – like the search for customs – is also seen as a search for patterns or regularities in prior events.[14]

In jurisprudence, however, it has long been recognized that this sort of pattern must be "constructed" by judges, and cannot simply be "found" empirically. In a nutshell, the problem is that any history of prior decisions will always underdetermine the possible patterns that might be ascribed to that history. For example, even if courts have applied a negligence standard in every single prior decision, that history will still be consistent with an entire family of possible rules:

1. Always apply a negligence standard.
2. Apply a negligence standard if the case arises before January 1, 2010 (a date that is not yet here), but apply strict liability if the case arises after that date.
3. Apply a negligence standard if the case arises before March 14, 2117, but apply strict liability if the case occurs after that date.[15]

And in most real situations, where the historical record is rather more mixed, there will be no need to resort to such extreme examples to show that the same set of prior cases is consistent with more than one possible rule. Of course, the range of possible rules is particularly broad if the classifier is free to set aside certain prior decisions as "erroneous" – or, in the case of customs, if certain actions can be dismissed as aberrations by "dissidents ready to cut corners."[16] But even if we set aside this source of flexibility, it is still true that no finite hisory of cases can uniquely determine an appropriate generalization.

As a consequence, most jurisprudential accounts of common law rules have recognized that a later court's selection from among the possible generalizations will depend at least in part on the later court's normative or political views. For example, in Ronald Dworkin's famous account, his idealized judge, Hercules, must construct a rule that is consistent, or achieves a maximal degree of "fit," with both (1) the existing caselaw and (2) some broader political or philosophical theory that could justify the cases the new rule fits.[17] In most settings, though, there will be several possible rules that satisfy these two dimensions of fit with varying success. For example, one rule might be consistent with almost all of the prior caselaw, but might be a very poor fit with the most plausible political theory. Some other rule might fit better with an attractive political theory, but might fit a smaller percentage of the prior caselaw. In selecting one of these possible rules, therefore, Hercules will have to trade off some kinds of "fit" against others. And while the exact nature of this trade-off remains mysterious,[18] it is clear that Hercules' own views of the merits and importance of the political theories involved (and, hence, about the acceptability of various degrees of less-than-complete fit) must play an important role.

While other jurisprudential accounts do not demand that the judge engage in such a systematic analysis, they still recognize that the judge's normative views will influence the rule that he or she ultimately selects. For example, if judges decide cases by picking the prior precedent most closely *analogous* to the current case, they then face the problem that every prior case will be analogous in some respects but not in others. In other words, the task of picking the most apt analogy is essentially equivalent to the task of picking those dimensions of similarity that are most (or least) important. But picking the dimensions that are "most important" requires, at least implicitly, a normative judgment, not merely an empirical enquiry into prior behavior.[19] Thus, in this account as well, the pattern or analogy that is selected will depend at least in part on the judge's normative views.

Obviously, the same problems are present when the task is to identify patterns in a prior record of commercial behavior. Indeed, many cases involving trade customs raise issues of distinction and analogy that are virtually identical to those discussed in the jurisprudential literature. For example, if a seller has routinely granted price adjustments in response to changed market conditions, but if these past adjustments all took place when the market was in a slump and the seller was in need of customers, should this "custom" require a similar adjustment in another instance when the market is more favorable to the seller?[20] If parties to fertilizer contracts have often treated stated quantities as nonbinding estimates, should it matter if all of the past instances involved standard form contracts, while the current case involves a contract that was the result of extensive negotiations?[21] If the parties to construction contracts with an open delivery date have always requested delivery within three or four months, should a similar limit be understood as applying to a new contract involving a much larger quantity?[22] And if sellers of corporate jets, when they agree to provide free training for the buyers' flight crews, have provided training to only a single crew for each plane, should they also have to train only a single crew when an identical plane is sold for use not as a corporate jet but as a cargo plane by a delivery service? Should it matter if most corporate jets are used infrequently and by only a single flight crew, thus making it sensible to train just a single crew, even though cargo services use their jets more heavily and routinely employ several crews?[23]

In each of these cases, the court (in effect) had to decide how broadly or narrowly the custom ought to be framed. Moreover, in each case the prior pattern of behavior could not itself speak to the question of how broadly or narrowly the custom ought to be framed, for the pattern itself would have been consistent with either a broad or a narrow articulation. Indeed, if these cases had involved common law precedents rather than business dealings, it would be obvious that the key questions concerned the breadth of the "holding" of the prior precedents, and whether the new circumstances were sufficiently different to permit the prior cases to be "distinguished." The fact that these cases actually involved prior business dealings, rather than prior court decisions, should not blind us to the essential similarity of the problem.

Indeed, the impossibility of inferring patterns from behavior alone affects another issue that has been much discussed in the recent commercial law literature: how to decide whether an admitted regularity in commercial behavior was meant to be legally binding.[24] For example, suppose that it is clear that sellers have always provided free delivery in the past (and suppose, too, that we have already decided that it is appropriate to generalize their behavior in this way, rather than as "free delivery under the following circumstances"). Even so, this stipulated pattern of free delivery will still be ambiguous between the following rules:

1. Sellers should provide free delivery, but buyers have no right to any legal recourse if they do not.
2. Sellers should provide free delivery, and buyers are entitled to take them to court and collect damages if they do not – but buyers are also free not to bring suit, if they so choose.

Obviously, we have no basis for choosing between these rules if sellers have *always* provided free delivery in the past, for in that event the issue of the buyer's remedies will never have arisen.[25] The pattern would also be ambiguous even if sellers occasionally had not provided free delivery, if in those cases no buyer had ever brought suit. That is, a history of no lawsuits would obviously be consistent with buyers having no right to sue (rule 1), but it would also be consistent with buyers having a right to sue but choosing not to exercise that right (rule 2). In this case, too, the pattern itself cannot determine which rule or generalization is most appropriate.[26]

Indeed, even if there were instances in which disappointed buyers *did* file suit when sellers failed to provide free delivery, that would not eliminate all of the ambiguities surrounding the question of legal enforceability. True, a sufficient number of buyer suits would let us reject rule (1) in the preceding list – but consider the following possibilities that would still remain:

2a. Sellers should provide free delivery, and if they fail to do so, then buyers have absolute discretion in deciding whether to seek legal remedies.

2b. Sellers should provide free delivery, and if they fail to do so, then buyers have absolute discretion to decide whether to seek legal remedies if their relationship with the seller has ended, but not if they still have an ongoing relationship with the seller.

2c. Sellers should provide free delivery, and if they fail to do so, then buyers have absolute discretion to decide whether to seek legal remedies if the lack of delivery created an undue hardship, but not if the lack of delivery did not cause undue harm.

Moreover, this is only part of an infinitely long list that could be generated by varying the exact conditions in rules like (2b) or (2c). True, if buyers have sued in a sufficiently large number of cases, this would probably let us reject some of the more ridiculous possibilities (e.g., "buyers should not seek legal remedies if the refusal to deliver occurred on a Thursday"). But no finite set of cases will ever be sufficient to eliminate all of the possible conditions. Once again, something other than the bare empirical record will have to be consulted in order for a court (or any other outside observer) to select one of these possible generalizations as the best statement of the custom. And one obvious candidate is the court's own normative view: its view about when it would make *sense* for buyers to be allowed to sue. As I discuss in Part V, courts often seem to be influenced by exactly that.

IV. Customs as Subjective Beliefs

A different approach would locate customs in the subjective beliefs of industry participants, rather than in the objective record of their prior behavior. That is, even if (as the preceding section argued) a bare record of prior behavior cannot itself determine a single generalization, there could still be cases where everyone in the industry *believed* that he or she was governed by a particular rule or generalization. If so, it might make sense to speak of that rule as a custom that existed in the industry members' beliefs.

To be sure, from a jurisprudential perspective this approach to identifying customs might seem strange. If the same approach were used to identify common law rules, that would imply that the "real" rule is whichever rule most lawyers and judges currently *believe* the precedents to stand for. Most scholars in jurisprudence would resist such a conclusion, in part because it precludes any possibility of arguing that current lawyers and judges are simply wrong. In sociology, however, and in other empirical social sciences, this approach to identifying customs is widely employed. For example, sociologists and anthropologists rely heavily on surveys and other forms of self-reporting to identify the customs (or norms) that are perceived by members of the relevant community. This view of customs is also consistent with the way that customs are usually established in litigation, where members of the industry testify as to *their own beliefs* about the industry's customs.

It might seem, then, that courts could often identify customs by a purely empirical enquiry into the beliefs of industry members. However, there are two separate reasons that this form of inquiry will not necessarily produce results that allow cases to be decided by rote application of custom, without any direct normative analysis. First, in many cases the industry members' beliefs may take the form of very general standards, which still require normative analysis to be applied to any particular case. Second, even when industry members' beliefs are expressed in the form of a more specific rule, that expression may itself be the product of prior normative analysis by the industry members, in the course of their decision to select that particular rule as the expression of their custom. Each of these possibilities is discussed below.

A. Beliefs in the Form of Vague Standards

In some cases, the beliefs of industry members may not take the form of bright-line rules, which (once identified) can be applied unproblematically to any particular case. Instead, the industry members' beliefs may take the form of more general standards – for example, "sellers should provide free delivery unless they have a *good-faith* reason for not doing so," or "sellers should provide free delivery whenever it would be *efficient* for them to do so." If the industry members' beliefs take this form, then even a court that is committed to following those beliefs will still have to make its own assessment of a seller's efficiency or good faith, in order to decide whether the seller violated the custom.

To be sure, in some of these cases it might be possible to elicit more specific guidelines from industry members, if their beliefs include detailed rules about what counts as "efficiency" or "good faith." Detailed guidelines such as these would effectively make the case one where the industry members' beliefs took the form of bright-line rules rather than vague standards, and I will address this case in the following subsection. My point here is simply that, in those cases where the beliefs of industry members do *not* include any such detailed rules, the court may be left with nothing but a vague standard that it will have to apply on its own.

One interesting question, then, is how often merchants' beliefs do take the form of unqualified, bright-line rules. This is an empirical question that can be answered only by investigating merchants' beliefs in a large number of industries, to see how often their beliefs do in fact take the form of bright-line rules.[27] In the absence of conclusive evidence, however, the complexity of most commercial issues provides some reason to be sceptical of any claim that merchants' beliefs will always take this form. Obviously, when the behavior that is most efficient (or is otherwise most appropriate) depends on an entire set of situational variables, bright-line rules will be seriously over- and under-inclusive. To be sure, bright-line rules also have their advantages (ease of application, predictability, etc.), so there will undoubtedly be at least some cases where bright-line rules would be superior on balance to vague standards. My only point here is that there is no a priori reason to suppose that this will *always* (or even often) be the case, and thus no a priori reason to predict that merchants' beliefs will often take the form of bright-line rules. Indeed, recent work by Lisa Bernstein suggests that merchants' customs often do *not* take the form of bright-line rules – or, at least, that merchants' beliefs about the appropriate rules are rarely uniform even within a given industry.[28]

B. Beliefs in the Form of Bright-Line Rules

In this section, I will focus exclusively on those cases where merchants' beliefs *do* take the form of bright-line rules (and where those beliefs are uniform across all industry members), since this is the only situation where a court could even conceivably apply those beliefs without any further normative analysis. Even in these cases, there are still interesting questions to be asked about how those rules came to be recognized by the industry members, or about how their beliefs were formed. My claim is that, while bright-line rules may eliminate the need for *courts* to engage in normative analysis, they often do so by substituting the analysis of the individual merchants who testify regarding the existence of the bright-line rules. In other words, what courts are relying on in these cases may be better described as the judgments of individual merchant witnesses, rather than any time-tested rules developed over the generations. If so, this will have important implications for theories about the evolution of custom, as well as for the role of merchant witnesses compared to other, nonindustry experts.

To understand the role played by merchants' individual judgments, consider how a given merchant might choose to articulate the custom in his or her industry. I will discuss below some factors that might produce a uniformity of articulation, in which every industry member articulated the custom in the same way. Absent such factors, however, even merchants who agreed about the application of the custom to every possible case might still articulate the custom in different ways. For example, some merchants might frame the custom as a bright-line rule: "Sellers should always provide free delivery, no matter what the circumstances." Some might frame it as a bright-line rule qualified by an open-ended exception: "Sellers should *normally* provide free delivery, but in extreme circumstances this obligation might not apply." And some might frame it as a completely general standard – for example, "Sellers should provide free delivery whenever failure to do so would amount to bad faith" (or, even more generally, "Sellers should never take *any* action that amounts to bad faith"). These merchants might still agree about any particular application of the custom: For example, even the merchant who originally stated the custom it as a bright-line rule might be willing to recognize exceptions if she were presented with cases she had not considered before. My point is that, even among merchants *who agree about every concrete case,* there could still be differences in how those merchants articulated their practice.

If various formulations of their practice are possible, how could we arrive at a state in which most or all merchants formulate it using the same bright-line rule? One possibility is that every member of the industry may have learned the rule in a single, canonical form. For example, if everyone in the industry has had a particular formulation of the rule drummed into them since birth – "Never, under any circumstances, should a seller fail to provide free delivery" – they would probably all describe the custom in the same way. In such an industry, then, the canonical formulation of the custom would have been settled by the industry's socialization process.

But how likely is it that most industry members will have had a single formulation drummed into them? It seems at least as plausible that, in most industries, the customs will have been learned by more indirect means: by observing the behavior of others, or by listening to instructive parables and case studies. In that event, industry members who are asked to state the custom will have to *decide* which formulation is most appropriate. For instance, if sixteen sellers who failed to provide free delivery have been held up as bad examples, should the resulting lesson be stated as a bright-line rule that sellers should always provide free delivery? Or should it be stated as a more general standard (e.g., "Provide free delivery unless there is a good-faith reason for not doing so")? Or is the real lesson a standard of even broader applicability ("Never do *anything* unless there is a good faith reason for doing it")? As these examples show, when a custom has been taught and learned by indirect means, the task of selecting an articulation of a custom is very similar to the task of selecting a common law rule, as discussed in Part III. In such an industry, the individual merchants will be the ones who must decide what generalization to ascribe to the relevant historical precedents. If they choose a bright-line version of the rule (rather than a vague standard), that choice will itself reflect an implicit normative judgment.

Indeed, even in industries where everyone initially learned the custom as a particular bright-line rule, a similar normative judgment will have been required at an earlier stage, by whichever industry member first chose to express the custom in that form. Moreover, each succeeding industry member may still have to exercise judgment to decide how to apply the rule to new circumstances. Suppose, for example, that every industry member initially learned an unqualified rule: "Sellers should always provide free delivery." But suppose they are then asked about a case that had not arisen before – for example, a case where the buyer prefers to have his or her own employees transport the goods – and suppose they all respond, "In that case, of course the seller would not have to provide the delivery services." Obviously, such a response requires the industry members to decide whether the new circumstances are *sufficiently* different as to require a reformulation of the rule. Moreover, the same sort of analysis will have been required (if only implicitly) even when the industry members all decide that the bright-line rule should still apply, and that no exception should be created for the new circumstances. That is, even when the bright-line rule survives unmodified, the industry members will still have had to choose whether to stick with the bright-line rule, or whether instead to recognize an exception for the particular case. In this situation, too, the task of choosing which articulation to stick with bears a striking similarity to the task faced by common law courts.

The lesson I draw from this is that, in many industries, any merchant testifying as a witness will have had to exercise some judgment (if only implicitly) in the very process of articulating a sensible formulation of the custom. Once the industry witnesses have chosen their formulation, it may then be possible for a court simply to accept that formulation without the need for any further judgment on the part of the court (as long as the industry members' formulation takes the form of a bright-line rule). But this just means that the locus of the judgment has shifted, and that the judgment is now being exercised by the industry members rather than by the court. To be sure, there may well be advantages to this shift: I will consider that issue in Part V. My point now is simply that judgment must still be exercised somewhere in the process. When a court searches for customs in industry members' beliefs, it will rarely be the case that both the court *and* the industry members can be blindly following a rule.

C. An Analogy to Languages

To better understand the importance of individual judgment, it may help to consider an analogy drawn from the use of language. Obviously, much of what is communicated by language depends on shared customs or conventions.[29] For example, the period of the earth's orbit around the sun is written as *year* in English, as *año* in Spanish, and as 年 in Chinese; and we can use those words to communicate only if these definitions are shared by our fellow speakers. Moreover, many of these definitions take the form of bright-line rules that can be learned and applied in a relatively unproblematic way. When an English-speaker who is studying Spanish learns that *año* means the same as *year,* she does not need to consider whether the purposes of the language would be better served if *año* were given a broader or narrower definition. Nor does she need to construct a Herculean theory designed to achieve the best fit between all prior uses of *año* and some broader political or moral theory. While there are, of course, many words whose definitions are more open-ended, most people assume that there are a large number of semantic and syntactic rules that can be applied without anything resembling normative analysis.

This understanding of bright-line semantic customs may lead some readers to think that trade customs, when they exist, must always take a similar form. However, even within the domain of language, linguists and philosophers of language have long recognized that much of what is communicated depends on more than bright-line rules. This is the branch of linguistics usually referred to as *pragmatics*. For example, if someone asks how I feel and I pull out a bottle of cold medicine and show it to them, I will have effectively communicated that I have a cold, even if there is no prior rule that "showing a bottle of cold medicine means that the person has a cold."[30] Similarly, if someone tells me that his or her car is out of gasoline, and I reply that there's a gas station three blocks away, I will usually be taken as implying that the gas station is still in business (or, at least, that I do not *know* that it is out of business).[31] This effect, too, is produced without there being any predefined, bright-line rule that mentioning the location of a gas station implies that the gas station is still in business.

Indeed, whenever the message conveyed depends heavily on context, it will often be through this sort of pragmatic effect. For example, the same statement ("There's a gas station three blocks away") would *not* imply that the gas station was still in business if it were made in response to any of several different questions (e.g., "Where do I make a right turn to get back on the freeway?" or, "Are there any abandoned businesses in this town?"). Similarly, displaying a bottle of cold medicine could also communicate any of several messages, depending on the question to which it responds (compare, "How are you feeling today?" with, "Have you forgotten your cold medicine again?" or, "I have a cold, too: what brand of medicine do you think is best?"). It is highly unlikely that there could be pre-established rules defining every possible message that might be conveyed by showing a medicine bottle, or by uttering the expression, "There's a gas station three blocks away." Indeed, one of the contributions of modern pragmatics has been to demonstrate how often information is conveyed by means that cannot usefully be analyzed as the application of predefined rules.[32] Researchers in artificial intelligence have discovered much the same thing, as a result of their efforts to write rule-based programs allowing a computer to understand natural language utterances in more than a crudely literal fashion.[33]

Of course, if many messages are communicated *without* their meanings being defined by any preexisting rules, this raises the question of how such messages *are* communicated. One theory, first advanced by Paul Grice, posits that listeners use an interpretive strategy based on assumptions about the speaker's interests and motives. In particular, Grice suggested that many pragmatic implications (or "implicatures") could be derived by listeners on a case-by-case basis, by assuming that speakers were following what he called the Cooperative Principle: "Make your conversational contribution such as is required, at the stage at which it occurs, by the accepted purpose or direction of the talk exchange in which you are engaged."[34] Grice then formulated more specific maxims that he saw as implications of the Cooperative Principle – for example, "Make your contribution as informative as required (for the current purposes of the exchange)," "Be brief," and, "Do not say that for which you lack adequate evidence."[35] Grice's thesis was that the information conveyed pragmatically by any utterance is the information that must be assumed in order to rule out what would otherwise be a violation of these maxims.

For example, consider the utterance about the gas station three blocks away, made to a person who both parties know to be in need of gas. A speaker who made such an utterance while knowing that the gas station was out of business would be violating the maxim requiring him to be as informative as necessary, as well as the maxim requiring him to be relevant. But there would be no such violations if the speaker knew that the gas station was still in business, for in that case the utterance would be both informative and relevant. This, Grice said, explains why virtually everyone who hears such an utterance would assume that the speaker did know the gas station was still in business (or, at least, that the speaker had no knowledge that it had gone out of business).[36] In short, even if there is no specific *rule* that requires gas stations to be mentioned only when they are still in business, there is a general *principle* of helpfulness or cooperation in conversation. That general principle, according to Grice, is what allows listeners to retrieve various pragmatic implications in particular contexts.

Of course, as many pragmaticists have pointed out, Grice's maxims leave a good deal to be determined in any particular instance.[37] Indeed, many of the maxims are not only vague, but are also contradictory (or could be in particular contexts). For example, suppose that a speaker says that there is a gas station three blocks away (to someone who is known to be in need of gasoline), but fails to mention the brand of gasoline, its price, and the name of the gas station's owner. Does the speaker's silence on these points pragmatically imply that the speaker lacks any information about these topics? If the maxim of informativeness required speakers to disclose *every* fact known to them, such an inference would indeed be expected (under Grice's theory), for a speaker who knew such information but failed to disclose it would be violating this interpretation of the maxim of informativeness. But Grice clearly did not believe that the maxim of informativeness was this broad, for his other maxims enjoin the speaker to be relevant, to be brief, and not to make the contribution any more informative than is required. In order to apply Grice's maxims in any particular context, then, trade-offs will often be required between the goals that each of the maxims serve. In this respect, Grice's maxims are more like general standards than like bright-line rules.

Interestingly, at least some of the trade-offs required to apply Grice's maxims could be described as a form of cost/benefit or efficiency analysis. For example, one way to determine what information must be disclosed in order to be "as informative *as required*" is by reference to the value that any given piece of information would have to the listener. That value could then be compared to the cost of explicitly disclosing that information, both in terms of prolonging the conversation and (in some cases) in terms of possibly distracting the listener from other, more important matters. Indeed, Grice subsequently analyzed the tension between informativeness, brevity, and relevance in just these terms. He noted that listeners do not always draw inferences about the speaker's lack of knowledge just because certain information has been omitted, and suggested that this makes sense if "the gain [from mentioning the information] would have been insufficient to justify the additional conversational effort."[38]

A similar tension can arise between the duty to be as informative as required and another of Grice's suggested maxims: "Do not say that for which you lack adequate evidence."[39] The latter maxim can explain why an unqualified assertion implies pragmatically that the speaker has adequate evidence in support of the assertion; otherwise, the speaker would be violating the maxim about adequate evidence. However, the question of how much evidence is "adequate" is hard to answer without making some kind of trade-off in the nature of a cost/benefit analysis. If the information about the gas station three blocks away would be extremely valuable if true – for example, if there is no other source of gasoline within fifty miles – the speaker might then be justified in mentioning that gas station even if there were only a slight chance that it was still open for business. But if there is another gas station only slightly farther away in the opposite direction, and this second gas station is *known* to be open for business, that could suggest that the speaker should not have mentioned the first gas station unless he was absolutely sure that it, too, was open.[40] In other words, the amount of certainty needed to justify an assertion – and, hence, the evidence that an assertion pragmatically presupposes – would seem to depend on a balance between the value the asserted information would have if true, and the potential harm that would be caused if the assertion turns out to be false.[41]

This similarity between cost/benefit trade-offs and pragmatic implications is not coincidental. Grice himself suggested that his Cooperative Principle could be thought of as "a quasi-contractual matter" with parallels to any other cooperative enterprise, even those not involving interpretation or speech.[42] Indeed, the Cooperative Principle itself – "make your conversational contribution such as is required by the accepted purpose or direction of the talk" – could be thought of as a commitment to maximizing the expected value of the parties' conversation, just as economists speak of maximizing the expected value of a transaction or of a business enterprise. To be sure, the exact nature of the costs and benefits being traded off (to say nothing of their respective magnitudes) is often difficult to assess in speech situations. But the important point is not whether these trade-offs are best described in terms of costs and benefits or in terms of other competing values, but simply that *some* such trade-offs are required, in both the commercial and the conversational spheres. Indeed, scholars who have modeled pragmatic implications more formally than Grice did have had to incorporate such trade-offs into their models quite explicitly. As Atlas and Levinson put it, informativeness (in the Gricean sense) is "part of an account of efficient communicative behavior."[43]

If this is true, then many linguistic customs should not be conceived as an extended set of bright-line rules, which any competent language speaker will already have learned.[44] Instead, at least where pragmatic implications are concerned, the only "rules" that exist are extremely general ones, which leave much of the balancing to be done by individual speakers and listeners on a case-by-case basis. To be sure, in some cases the pragmatic implication may be so frequently used or so well established that it hardens into a more specific rule – an idiom – that need not be recalculated on every subsequent use.[45] For example, the question, "can you open the door?" is now routinely interpreted as a request that the door be opened, not as a mere inquiry about the other party's capabilities. (Analogously, Oliver Wendell Holmes expected that common law doctrines would harden into greater specificity over time, thus sparing courts from having to resolve difficult issues in subsequent cases.[46]) Clearly, though, this hardening process has taken place for only a tiny fraction of the infinitely many bits of information that might be conveyed pragmatically (just as it has taken place for only a fraction of common law doctrines). And the fact that pragmatic implications are often misunderstood suggests both that much is still left to case-by-case balancing, and that this balancing is not always easy.[47]

Indeed, even when pragmatic implications have hardened into an accepted idiom, case-by-case adjustments may still be required in individual cases. While it is true that "Can you open the door?" is now routinely interpreted as a request that the door be opened, even this interpretation would change if the context indicated that some other interpretation was more relevant to the parties' purposes – for example, if the same question were put to an adventurer standing in front of the spellbound portal of a magic castle.[48] In other words, even those implications that have become entirely customary or conventional will normally be defeasible in particular circumstances. It will therefore be up to the listener to decide anew, in each individual case, whether the circumstances are such as to require a departure from the usual interpretation.

This view of language is similar, though not identical, to that of Stanley Fish, whose claims that "context matters" have become familiar in the legal literature.[49] Fish is more controversial in his assertion that there is *no* purely literal or semantic meaning that can be attached to utterances independently from their context (a claim that most pragmaticists would reject). Pragmatics treats the literal or semantic meaning of an utterance as a kind of trigger that can lead listeners to draw any number of pragmatic implications, so pragmaticists have to assume that the trigger itself has some semantic content. For present purposes, however, this difference is not very significant, for pragmaticists would agree with Fish (or he with them) that the bulk of what is conveyed by most utterances lies in the context-dependent pragmatic implications, not in the bare semantic meaning.

Instead, the more fundamental difference between Fish and the pragmaticists is that Fish seems largely uninterested in the exact process by which any given utterance triggers any particular set of pragmatic implications – while the exact details of this process are precisely what pragmatics as a field attempts to identify. That is, Fish seems content simply to posit a set of "practices" or "traditions" that competent listeners have internalized, which somehow enables them to retrieve all context-dependent implications. In this respect, much of Fish's analysis could aptly be prefaced (or concluded): "Assume a practice."

Nevertheless, when Fish invokes particular practices to use as examples, his discussion is generally consistent with the pragmatic analysis discussed above. The following analogy is apt:

> Suppose you were a basketball coach and had taught someone how to shoot baskets and how to dribble the ball, but had imparted these skills without reference to the playing of an actual basketball game. Now you decide to insert your student into a game, and you equip him with some rules. You say to him, for instance, "Take only good shots." "What," he asks reasonably enough, "is a good shot?" "Well," you reply, "a good shot is an 'open shot,' a shot taken when you are close to the basket (so that the chances of success are good) and when your view is not obstructed by the harassing efforts of opposing players." Everything goes well until the last few seconds of the game; your team is behind by a single point; the novice player gets the ball in heavy traffic and holds it as the final buzzer rings. You run up to him and say, "Why didn't you shoot?" and he answers, "It wasn't a good shot." Clearly, the rule must be amended, and accordingly you tell him that if time is running out, and your team is behind, and you have the ball, you should take the shot even if it isn't a good one, because it will then be a good one in the sense of being the best shot in the circumstances. . . . Now suppose there is another game, and the same situation develops. This time the player takes the shot, which under the circumstances is a very difficult one; he misses, and once again the final buzzer rings. You run up to him and say "Didn't you see that John (a teammate) had gone 'back door' and was perfectly positioned under the basket for an easy shot?" and he answers "But you said. . ." Of course, there will eventually come a time when the novice player (like the novice judge) will no longer have to ask questions; but it will not be because the rules have finally been made sufficiently explicit to cover all cases, but because explicitness will have been rendered unnecessary by a kind of knowledge that informs rules rather than follows from them.[50]

In other words, following the "practices" or "customs" of basketball involves both an understanding of the goals of the game and an ability to weigh each action's costs and benefits (defined relative to those goals) in any possible circumstance that might arise. To paraphrase Atlas and Levinson, good shot selection is part of an account of efficient basketball strategy. Moreover, competence in carrying out that strategy does *not* depend on having access to a set of rules that, once learned, will free the actor from the need for case-by-case balancing.

I suggest that what is true of pragmatic implications (and of basketball) may also be true of trade customs. That is, many customs may be internalized by merchants only in their most general forms, like the Gricean maxims, "Be as informative as required," or, "Do not make assertions without adequate evidence" (or, "Do not take bad shots"). The merchants may still be able to use those maxims to reach decisions in particular cases, and there may even be a large degree of uniformity in the decisions that various merchants reach – but this will be because each is exercising his or her judgment in a similar way, not because each is following a bright-line rule that eliminates any need for judgment. In fact, even in the case of customs that appear to have hardened into more specific rules, merchants may still have to exercise their judgment to decide whether the circumstances of the case justify any departure from the bright-line rule. In short, many industry customs will require a considerable amount of case-by-case judgment on the part of the industry members. If courts rely on the members' testimony about what a particular custom requires, they will be relying on the industry members' own judgments, and not on a set of rules that makes such judgments unnecessary.

V. Customs as Intuitive Judgments

As noted earlier, there is nothing necessarily objectionable about having courts rely on industry members' judgments. To be sure, if the industry members' judgments serve unacceptable goals – private profits versus general welfare, for instance – that could provide a reason not to rely on industry members' judgments. But this argument would apply equally against relying on any form of industry guidance, be it in the form of individual members' judgments or in the form of judgment-free rules (as the usual models of custom would have it).

In this section, however, I argue that the case for relying on industry guidance takes on a different light if that guidance is now seen as the judgment of individual witnesses about particular contexts, rather than as crystallized rules that have been handed down through generations. In particular, if individual witnesses must draw on their own analysis of particular contexts, then they are providing an assessment that is not entirely different from what would be provided by any other expert whom a court might consult, such as an economist or a philosopher.[51] The judgment of the industry expert might of course be either wiser or less wise than that of the outside economist or philosopher – but the comparison is still between two forms of individualized, case-by-case judgments, rather than between case-by-case judgments on the one hand and bright-line rules on the other.[52]

Instead, on this view the two forms of judgment may be more usefully distinguished along a dimension running from explicit analysis, at one end, to more intuitive judgments at the other. Outside experts such as economists or philosophers will usually have a relatively explicit normative framework that enables them to recommend one outcome over another. By contrast, while industry experts may be *implicitly* making trade-offs (as described in the preceding section), they often do so on a more intuitive basis, without an explicit normative framework.

That is, nothing in the preceding section's analysis presupposed that participants in a practice or industry necessarily engaged in any *conscious* balancing of costs and benefits. An expert basketball player, for example, must make immediate judgments about shot selection without anything approaching the time needed to weigh consciously each of the alternatives. The same is true of ordinary conversation: A stranded motorist who is told, "There's a gas station three blocks away," will normally assume at once that the speaker thinks the gas station is still in business, without stopping to work out the implicature in Gricean terms. (Actually, the motorist may not initially make any conscious assumption at all – but if she travels the three blocks and finds a gas station that clearly has been abandoned for years, she will instantly blame the speaker for having misled her.) Similarly, when judges and lawyers are asked what doctrine best states "the rule" of a given line of cases, they often give intuitive but quite confident answers, without engaging in anything like the kind of reasoning that Dworkin demanded of Judge Hercules.

The fact that expert practitioners do not consciously make this sort of calculation is not a criticism of any of the theories advanced in the preceding section, for those theories were not meant to be a description of anyone's actual mental processes. Still, the fact that expert practitioners seem to be able to reach such judgments without any conscious weighing of pros and cons does suggest a rather different way of asking which form of judgment is likely to be superior. The traditional view, which assumes that customs take the form of judgment-free rules, often frames the choice between customs and outside analysis as a choice between individual judgments, on the one hand, and the accumulated wisdom of an evolutionary process, on the other. But the view I have advanced here suggests that the choice is often between individual judgments that are made analytically, by outside experts, and individual judgments that are made intuitively, by industry practitioners. If so, this has several implications for commercial law scholarship.

A. Intuitive Versus Explicit Normative Judgments

First, this way of framing the question should make it possible to look more closely at the possible grounds for preferring one of these methods over the other. It is easy to see that there are some cases (such as basketball shot selection) where an intuitive assessment may be superior to an analytic one, especially if the decision must be made in a limited time. But it is easy to romanticize about the accuracy of intuitive assessments, and to forget that there may be other situations (especially when time is not so limited) where analytic methods are likely to give better results.

Even in sports, careful statistical analysis has cast doubt on propositions that had seemed unquestionably true to practitioners.[53] More important, there are also many commercial propositions that were accepted uncritically for years, but which economic analysis has shown to be dubious at best. Consider, for example, the number of people who still believe that buyers are unequivocably better off if sellers provide more generous warranties (while failing to consider the price increase that a better warranty may trigger), or who still believe that anything that increases sales must therefore be good for the economy. John Maynard Keynes's aphorism – that "so-called practical men . . . are usually the slaves of some *defunct* economist"[54] – should serve as a warning here. When beliefs and values are allowed to remain intuitive, rather than being made explicit (and therefore subject to scrutiny), there is always a danger that the lack of explicit scrutiny will permit the survival of assessments that ought to become defunct.

B. *The Significance of Uniformity*

The choice between explicit and intuitive judgments might also be affected by the extent to which practitioners of either method agree in their assessment of any particular case. From this standpoint, it may be significant that testimony as to industry custom is accorded weight only when industry members are unanimous (or nearly unanimous) in their testimony about what their custom requires. For example, if all industry members testify that their their custom is a bright-line rule ("always provide free delivery"), rather than a bright-line rule with an open-ended exception ("unless it would be unusually expensive to do so"), this suggests that they all regard the advantages of the bright-line rule as sufficiently strong to outweigh the benefits of an occasional exception. And while a court might well be sceptical about the instinctive judgment of *one* industry member on such an issue, it might be much more comfortable if everyone in the industry agreed. After all, if an entire panel of basketball experts agrees that a particular shot was a good one, this should give a lay observer much more confidence in reaching the same conclusion.

By contrast, we are all used to the fact that economists do not always agree (especially in hard cases), and that in many cases expert economists testify on both sides of a disputed issue. This may lead to an inappropriate comparison between (a) relying on industry members' intuitive judgments, in cases where the entire industry is in agreement, and (b) relying on the more explicit analyses of outside experts, in cases where the outside experts disagree among themselves. When the comparison is skewed in this way, it is only natural to think that the intuitive judgments of industry members might quite often be a better guide than the more explicit analyses of outside experts.

The reason this comparison is skewed, of course, is that it is also possible for industry members to disagree among themselves, or even for economists to agree. That is, if the view I have advanced here is correct, there are likely to be just as many hard cases where industry members themselves are divided in their judgment – or, what amounts to the same thing, cases where industry members (if they testified at all) would have to testify that no uniform custom exists.[55] And we could skew the comparison in the other direction by comparing (a) these hard cases, in which industry members disagreed as to the appropriate custom, to (b) the easy cases in which virtually all economists agreed about what practice would be most efficient. Such a comparison would then suggest an opposite but equally flawed conclusion, that expert economic testimony was inherently more reliable than that of industry members.

In short, the question of which method of analysis is most useful – intuitive judgments by industry members, or more explicit analyses by outside experts – is logically distinct from the question of how much unanimity should be required among experts in either camp. In easy cases, there is likely to be a high degree of unanimity; in harder cases, there is likely to be more diversity of opinion. A high degree of uniformity can thus enhance the credibility of either group of experts – but it does not provide any systematic reason for thinking one group is more useful than the other.

C. The Evolution of Intuitive Judgment

My emphasis on the importance of intuitive judgments also suggests an important limitation of most current models of the evolution of customs. These models inevitably portray customs as bright-line rules, and then posit that the rules will survive (or fail to survive) depending on the frequency with which they are followed in various situations.[56] In these models, though, the only decision the actors have to make is the simple decision about whether to follow the rule. If the rule "survives," by being followed in a particular case, its actual application to that case is always assumed to be unproblematic.

On the view taken here, this is an oversimplification, at least as applied to those customs that do not take the form of bright-line rules. If customs are not bright-line rules, and cannot be followed without making individualized judgments in the process of doing so, then the evolutionary path of any custom will depend critically on the skill or judgment with which it is applied. But little is known about how skills or judgments (as opposed to bright-line rules) are transmitted from generation to generation – and much less about whether those skills tend to improve with time. For example, today's basketball players clearly are bigger and stronger than those of thirty years ago – but are they actually any better at shot selection? Similarly, today's businesses have access to better technologies and better means of communication – but are their judgments about how to resolve disputes better, too? None of the existing models of evolution sheds any light on this question.

D. Customs in the Caselaw

A final implication of my analysis is best presented by returning to some actual cases. If industry witnesses are seen as simply presenting their own intuitive judgment about how best to resolve a particular case, and if there are doubts about whether such judgments are systematically more reliable than more explicit forms of analysis, then one should expect courts to rely on explicit normative analysis as well as on the judgments of industry experts. Indeed, if the analysis presented here is correct, one would expect explicit normative analysis to enter in even when the court is deciding what the industry custom *is,* and not merely when the court is deciding whether to follow a custom that has already been independently identified. While it is difficult to be certain, there is some evidence that courts are doing exactly that.

The reason it is difficult to be certain is that courts rarely address these issues directly. Even if trial judges are in fact influenced by their own views about which reading of a custom would be most sensible, such influences are more likely to be unexpressed (or even subconscious) than to be explicitly stated in an opinion. And appellate judges are rarely asked to decide the basic issue of whether a custom exists, since the UCC assigns such issues to the trier of fact.[57] Thus, appellate opinions reach these issues only indirectly, either in deciding whether there is sufficient evidence to uphold the fact finder's decision, or in deciding "legal" issues such as whether interpreting the contract in light of an alleged custom would violate the UCC's parol evidence rule.[58]

Still, in spite of these difficulties, it is easy to find cases where the court's own view of the merits of a practice has clearly influenced its ruling on the legal issues involving customs. One recurring example concerns clauses allowing a creditor to accelerate the entire debt if a single payment is late. If the creditor has accepted late payments in the past without demanding that the entire debt be paid at once, the debtor will often point to this as a "course of performance" that should bind the creditor in the future. The creditor, on the other hand, typically argues that its past behavior is best interpreted as a series of voluntary waivers of its acceleration rights, no one of which extended past the particular instance in which a late payment was accepted. In choosing between these interpretations, courts often rely explicitly on their hostility to acceleration clauses. As one court put it, "acceleration is a harsh remedy which should be allowed only if there is some reasonable justification for doing so, such as a good faith belief that the prospect of payment is impaired" (which the court did not find in the case before it).[59] As a result, the court was quite willing to interpret the creditor's past behavior as a custom that the debtor was entitled to rely on, not as a mere series of voluntary waivers.

A similar pattern can be observed in the interpretation of contracts that state a fixed quantity, in industries where deviations from the stated quantities have been allowed in the past. Courts have split on the question of whether such a custom would "contradict" the written contract, in which case the custom would be inadmissible under the parol evidence rule, or whether such a custom would instead "supplement" the written contract. Significantly, many courts' position on this issue seems to match their view of the wisdom of the alleged custom (i.e., on the wisdom of allowing stated quantities to fluctuate). For example, in one case refusing to admit evidence of such a custom, the court thought that allowing stated quantities to fluctuate "might jeopardize the certainty of the contractual duties which parties have a right to rely on."[60] By contrast, many decisions that allowed such evidence also endorsed what they saw as the reason for the custom, as in the following example:

> Because potatoes are a perishable commodity and their demand is dependent upon a fluctuating market, and because the marketing contracts are signed eight or nine months in advance of the harvest season, common sense dictates that the quantity would be estimated. . . .[61]

Even when one party has claimed that the custom allowed reductions in quantity all the way to zero (thereby canceling the contract entirely), decisions can be found on either side of the question, based at least in part on the court's view of the wisdom of permitting such cancellations, and the effect on the resulting allocation of risks.[62] The courts may or may not have been right in their assessments of the wisdom of these practices, of course – but their assessments do seem to have influenced the outcomes.

More generally, many other decisions have found the existence of a custom (or have permitted the introduction of a custom over objections based on the parol evidence rule) when the custom quite clearly matched the court's own view of the proper result. In one case, the court recognized a custom in the horse trade that sellers did not warrant the soundness of a horse, and observed that this custom made sense "because horses are fragile creatures, susceptible to myriad maladies, detectable and undetectable. . . ."[63] In another case, the court agreed with a purported custom in the retail clothing industry – to wit, that the phrase "June-August delivery" required the bulk of the deliveries to come in June and July – because the court understood that clothes had to arrive then to be in time for the back-to-school shopping season.[64] In still another case, involving sellers who had delayed price increases to paving contractors on certain jobs, the court had to decide whether the past delays were a binding custom or merely a series of voluntary waivers. The court treated them as a binding custom, based at least in part on its own belief that these delays were "a realistic necessity to operate in that market and thus vital to [the buyer's] ability to get large government contracts and to [the seller's] continued business growth."[65]

Indeed, recent decisions have often employed an explicitly economic analysis to evaluate the alleged custom. In one case, a bank had occasionally supplied indorsements that had been omitted by depositors of its checks, but the court declined to interpret this practice as a binding custom. In doing so, the court was influenced by its view that such an obligation would be inefficient:

> It is a well known principle of tort law that the risk of loss should be borne by the one who can most economically avoid the loss. . . . [I]mposing such a duty on depository

banks to find all missing indorsements would be extremely costly for the banks and would ultimately diminish the efficiency of the check collecting system as a whole.[66]

In another case, a court refused to turn a bank's prior practices of extending time for repayment (or, at least, of not rejecting requests for extensions without a good-faith reason for doing so) into a binding custom, pointing to similar economic objections.[67] In still another case, a court used its own assessment of the proper risk allocation as one ground for refusing to interpret a party's practice of conducting its own title searches as a binding custom that would free the other party from liability if the title turned out to be defective.[68]

An even more explicit economic analysis can be found in a recent opinion of Judge Posner. The case involved the sale of custom-made welding equipment, pursuant to a written contract that was ambiguous as to whether the seller had excluded liability for any loss to the buyer's business if the machines failed to work as expected. The seller offered to testify that such exclusions were customary in the industry, and that liability for consequential damages was "unheard of," but the trial court refused to admit that testimony.[69] The appellate court reversed, relying partly on general doctrines about the admissibility of industry custom, but also on its own economic analysis of the custom in question. As Judge Posner saw it:

> That contractual liability for such damages . . . is of relatively recent vintage, that many breaches of contract are (as here) involuntary, that only the sky would be the limit to the amount of consequential damages that manufacturers of machinery indispensable to their customers' businesses might run up, that those customers not only have a better idea of what the potential injury to them might be but also might be able to avert it more easily than their supplier – all these things make it not at all incredible that a custom might have evolved in this industry against a buyer's getting consequential damages in the event of a breach.[70]

In this case, then, the court explicitly relied on economic analysis as a form of corroborative support for the testimony of the industry experts regarding their own interpretation of the custom.[71]

What lessons should be drawn from these examples? The most obvious lesson is a practical one: Any litigant who wants to introduce a trade custom into evidence should be prepared to explain why that particular custom makes sense. That is, it will rarely be enough to simply claim that "*x* is the custom in our industry," and to expect that the court will therefore enforce *x* regardless of how unattractive *x* might seem. Unless the court is also persuaded that *x* is a sensible practice, the court will probably be reluctant to believe that *x* is in fact the custom. From this standpoint, then, persuading the court that the alleged custom is sensible will be a crucial part of any litigant's case.

Whether this kind of evidence ought to be *required* (required practically, even if not doctrinally) will be more controversial. Obviously, courts can err when they attempt their own assessments of the merits of a practice, and judicial unwillingness to recognize any custom that the courts do not themselves believe to be desirable could retard the growth of useful customs.[72] On the other hand, *some* assessment of the merits of a practice will often be inevitable, for all of the jurisprudential reasons discussed in the preceding sections of this chapter. If so, then we are left with the question raised at the end of Part V: Are these assessments better left to the intuitive judgments of experienced practitioners, or to the analytic skills of other specialists? Without further evidence bearing directly on this question, it is hard to avoid concluding that both kinds of expertise can have their uses – and that our confidence in an outcome should be strongest when the judgments of both groups happen to converge. Arguably, this use of both methods is exactly what the judges were doing in each of the cases described above.

VI. Conclusion

The nature of contractual customs has been alluded to in the philosophical literature on promising. In an early article, John Rawls recognized that the obligation to keep a promise was limited by implicit qualifications and exceptions.[73] Rawls assumed that those exceptions were defined by the social *practice* of promising, which he seems to have conceived as a kind of custom.[74] But Thomas Scanlon responded with a more sceptical view:

> [W]hen, for example, I try to determine whether a promise to do *x* obligates a person to do *x* even at the cost of *y* – it seems clear to me that I am engaging in moral reflection, not an inquiry into what the accepted rules of our social practice of agreement-making are. . . . [W]hile a social practice of agreement-making *could* shape the content of particular obligations arising under it in this way, I am unable to identify any such limitations built into our particular practice of promising.[75]

My argument here is that Scanlon is correct, and that appeals to custom in commercial law often turn out to be appeals to a kind of "moral reflection." Sometimes the reflection is performed by the reviewing court; sometimes the court (in effect) delegates the job of reflection to the industry witnesses who testify concerning the custom; but in either case the reflection will have to come somewhere. My hope is that if we recognize and understand the nature of the reflection that is required, the choice between these and other forms of reflection (such as explicit economic or philosophical analysis) can more sensibly be made.

Notes

† I have benefited from comments by Lisa Bernstein, Robert D. Cooter, Jody S. Kraus, Jack L. Goldsmith, Gregory C. Keating, Clayton P. Gillette, Mark A. Lemley, Richard H.

McAdams, Elizabeth Mertz, Eric A. Posner, Richard A. Posner, Richard J. Ross, and participants in workshops at the Stanford, University of California, University of Chicago, University of Virginia, and Chicago-Kent law schools.

1. On the role of custom in Llewellyn's thought, and its effect on Article 2 of the UCC, see Richard Danzig, *A Comment on the Jurisprudence of the Uniform Commercial Code,* 27 Stan. L. Rev. 621 (1975); James Whitman, *Commercial Law and the American* Volk: *A Note on Llewellyn's German Sources for the Uniform Commercial Code,* 97 Yale L.J. 156 (1987); Zipporah B. Wiseman, *The Limits of Vision: Karl Llewellyn and the Merchant Rules,* 100 Harv. L. Rev. 465 (1987). See also Alan Schwartz, *Karl Llewellyn and the Origins of Contract Theory* (Chapter 1 in this volume).
2. E.g., Robert C. Clark, *Contracts, Elites, and Traditions in the Making of Corporate Law,* 89 Colum. L. Rev. 1703 (1989).
3. Lisa Bernstein, *The Questionable Empirical Basis of Article 2's Incorporation Stategy: A Preliminary Study,* 66 U. Chi. L. Rev. 710 (1999); Jody S. Kraus and Steven D. Walt, *In Defense of the Incorporation Stategy,* Chapter 6 of this volume.
4. For an analysis of these issues, see Elizabeth Warren, *Trade Usage and Parties in the Trade: An Economic Rationale for an Inflexible Rule,* 42 U. Pitt. L. Rev. 515 (1981).
5. See Danzig, supra n. 1, at 627–31, and the sources cited there.
6. For a discussion of this issue, see Richard A. Epstein, *The Path to the* T. J. Hooper*: The Theory and History of Custom in Torts,* 21 J. Legal Stud. 1 (1992).
7. See generally Robert C. Ellickson, *Order without Law: How Neighbors Settle Disputes* (1991); Robert D. Cooter, *Decentralized Law for a Complex Economy: The Structural Approach to Adjudicating the New Law Merchant,* 144 U. Pa. L. Rev. 1643 (1996); Robert D. Cooter, *Structural Adjudication and the New Law Merchant: A Model of Decentralized Law,* 14 Int'l Rev. L. & Econ. 215 (1994). For less optimistic views of the evolution of custom, see Eric A. Posner, *Law, Economics, and Inefficient Norms,* 144 U. Pa. L. Rev. 1697 (1996); Jody S. Kraus, *Legal Design and the Evolution of Commercial Norms,* 26 J. Legal Stud. 377 (1997).
8. For explicit endorsements of this strategy, see Cooter, supra n. 6; Epstein, supra n. 5, at 9–10; and Charles Goetz and Robert E. Scott, *The Limits of Expanded Choice: An Analysis of the Interactions between Express and Implied Contract Terms,* 73 Calif. L. Rev. 261, 278 (1985).
9. Randy E. Barnett, *The Sound of Silence: Default Rules and Contractual Consent,* 78 Va. L. Rev. 821, 876–82 (1992).
10. Ibid. For a similar autonomy-based view of the authority of customs, at least in cases where the same custom supplies both parties' tacit expectations, see Steven J. Burton, *Default Principles, Legitimacy, and the Authority of a Contract,* 3 S. Cal. Interdisc. L.J. 115, 164 (1994).
11. Barnett, supra n. 8, 78 Va. L. Rev. at 831–55.
12. Interestingly, Barnett suggests that if there is no other evidence bearing on the nature of a custom, a court could consult its own practical wisdom, or even an economist's efficiency analysis, as evidence of what the custom probably is (and, hence, as evidence of what the parties probably intended subjectively). Ibid. at 907–9. He acknowledges, however, that this is "a funny kind of 'evidence'" (ibid. at 909). I will return to this point infra in note 51.
13. See, for example, UCC §1–205, comment 5 ("[I]t is not required that a usage of trade be

'ancient or immemorial', 'universal' or the like. [F]ull recognition is thus available for new usages and for usages currently observed by the great majority of decent dealers, even though dissidents ready to cut corners do not agree."). I will return to this issue infra in Section VB.

14. I exclude from my analysis cases where the relevant custom has been "codified" by a trade association or other formal body, thus producing something more analogous to a statute passed by a legislature. As the codified version of such a custom will clearly *exist,* such codifications raise few of the difficulties that I address here. To be sure, interesting questions can still be asked about whether courts should follow such a codified custom – but these are the sort of questions already explored by the literature surveyed earlier in Part II.
15. This problem is well known in the philosophy of induction. See, e.g., Ludwig Wittgenstein, *Philosophical Investigations* ¶¶185–9, 198–201 (1945) (G. E. M. Anscombe trans., 3d ed. 1972); Nelson Goodman, *Fact, Fiction, and Forecast* 74 (4th ed. 1983).
16. See n. 12 supra. For a criticism of this aspect of the UCC's use of custom, see Danzig, supra n. 1, at 629.
17. Ronald Dworkin, *Law's Empire* (1987). See also Ronald Dworkin, *Is There Really No Right Answer in Hard Cases?* in *A Matter of Principle* (1985); Ronald Dworkin, *Taking Rights Seriously* (1977).
18. For criticisms of Dworkin's theory in this regard, see, e.g., Andrew Altman, *Legal Realism, Critical Legal Studies, and Dworkin,* 15 Phil. & Pub. Aff. 205 (1986); Gregory C. Keating, *Fidelity to Pre-Existing Law and the Legitimacy of Legal Decision,* .69 Not. Dame L. Rev. 1 (1993).
19. See, e.g., Cass R. Sunstein, *On Analogical Reasoning,* 106 Harv. L. Rev. 741, 756 (1993) ("Different factual situations are inarticulate; they do not impose order on themselves. Patterns are made, not simply found."). For an earlier discussion, see Edward H. Levi, *An Introduction to Legal Reasoning,* 1–6 (1949).
20. *H&W Industries, Inc. v. Occidental Chemical Corp.,* 911 F.2d 1118, 1112 (5th Cir. 1990) (refusing to require similar adjustments under the new market conditions).
21. Compare R. W. Kirst, *Usage of Trade and Course of Dealing: Subversion of the UCC Theory,* 1977 Law Forum 811, 847 (arguing that the extent of negotiations should make a difference), with *Columbia Nitrogen Corp. v. Royster Co.,* 451 F.2d 3 (1971) (failing even to discuss any possible difference in the extent of negotiations).
22. *Capital Steel Co. v. Foster & Creighton Co.,* 264 Ark. 683, 687; 574 S.W.2d 256, 258 (1978) (refusing to apply a similar time limit to the larger contract).
23. *Federal Express Corp. v. Pan American World Airways, Inc.,* 623 F.2d 1297 (8th Cir. 1980) (ruling that the seller should only have to train a single crew, even when it knew the plane was being bought for use as a cargo jet).
24. Recent discussions include Lisa Bernstein, *Merchant Law in a Merchant Court: Rethinking the Code's Search for Immanent Business Norms,* 144 U. Pa. L. Rev. 1765, 1787–95 (1996); Jason Scott Johnston, *The Statute of Frauds and Business Norms: A Testable Game-Theoretic Model,* 144 U. Pa. L. Rev. 1859 (1996); Eric A. Posner, *The Regulation of Groups: The Influence of Legal and Nonlegal Sanctions on Collective Action,* 63 U. Chi. L. Rev. 133 (1996). For an early sociological study, suggesting that businesses often do not seek legal enforcement, see Stewart Macaulay, *Noncontractual Relations in Business: A Preliminary Study,* 25 Am. Soc. Rev. 55 (1963).

25. Cf. *Kunststoffwerk Alfred Huber v. R.J. Dick, Inc.*, 621 F.2d 560, 564–5 (3d Cir. 1980) (past practice of giving buyer a price credit for defective merchandise failed to establish a practice of *not* providing compensation for consequential damages, as there was no evidence that the buyer had requested compensation for consequential damages in any of the prior instances).
26. A number of cases have raised just this question: whether a history of prior instances in which one party failed to take some action is best interpreted as a customary understanding that the party had no right to take that action, or merely as a series of one-time waivers of the right to act (without giving up the right to act in the future). Compare *Columbia Nitrogen Corp. v. Royster Co.*, 451 F.2d 3, 10 (4th Cir. 1971), and *Nanakuli Paving & Rock Co. v. Shell Oil Co.*, 664 F.2d 772, 794 (9th Cir. 1981) (permitting juries to find a custom limiting the party's rights), with UCC § 2–208, comment 3 (preferring interpretation as a waiver); *Terrebonne Fuel & Lube, Inc. v. Placid Refining Co.*, 681 So.2d 1292, 1297–8 (La. App. 1996) (same). For a useful discussion of this issue, see Bernstein, supra n. 23, at 1807–15.
27. Richard McAdams has suggested – plausibly, though without any empirical evidence – that the beliefs (or "norms") most likely to be internalized by real actors are those articulated in very general terms, as vague standards. Richard H. McAdams, *The Origin, Development, and Regulation of Norms*, 96 Mich. L. Rev. 338, 383 (1997).
28. Lisa Bernstein, *The Questionable Empirical Basis of Article Two's Incorporation Strategy: A Preliminary Study*, 66 U. Chi. L. Rev. 710 (1999).
29. For a more extended discussion of this claim, see David K. Lewis, *Convention: A Philosophical Study* (1969), especially Chapters 4 and 5.
30. This example is taken from Dan Sperber and Deirdre Wilson, *Relevance: Communication and Cognition* 25 (1988).
31. This example is taken from Paul Grice, *Logic and Conversation* [1967], reprinted in Paul Grice, *Studies in the Way of Words* 32 (1989).
32. For general discussions of this issue, see Sperber and Wilson, supra n. 29, ch. 1; François Récanati, *The Pragmatics of What Is Said*, 4 Mind & Language 295 (1989); Geoffrey Nunberg, *Validating Pragmatic Explanations*, in *Radical Pragmatics* 192 (Peter Cole, ed., 1981); J. L. Morgan, *Two Types of Convention in Indirect Speech Acts*, in *Syntax and Semantics* 9: *Pragmatics* 261 (Peter Cole, ed., 1978). For a less technical discussion, see Stephen Pinker, *The Language Instinct* 222–30 (1994).
33. See, e.g., Roger C. Schank, *Dynamic Memory: A Theory of Reminding and Learning in Computers and People* (1982).
34. Grice, supra n. 30, at 26.
35. Ibid. at 26–7.
36. Ibid. at 32.
37. E.g., Sperber and Wilson, supra n. 29, at 36–7; Jerold M. Sadock, *On Testing for Conversational Implicature*, in *Syntax and Semantics* 9: *Pragmatics* 281, 285–6 (Peter Cole, ed., 1978).
38. Paul Grice, *Further Notes on Logic and Conversation* [1978], reprinted in Paul Grice, *Studies in the Way of Words* 42 (1989).
39. Grice, supra n. 30, at 27.
40. In either situation, a possible alternative is for the speaker to try to describe the evidentiary basis for his beliefs, thereby letting the other party decide for herself which gas

station to try first. The attractiveness of this alternative depends on how easily and accurately the information about the speaker's evidentiary basis can be communicated – in other words, it depends on the optimal balance between being informative and being brief, as analyzed in the preceding paragraph.

41. Interestingly, the Federal Trade Commission Act has been applied to advertisements in a very similar way: An advertiser who makes an assertion thereby implies the existence of "adequate" evidence to support that assertion, so the absence of adequate evidence has been held to make the advertising misleading. The Federal Trade Commission has been quite explicit that the amount of evidence deemed "adequate" must be determined by a cost/benefit analysis. *Thompson Medical Co.,* 104 F.T.C. 648, 823 (1984). For a general discussion of this point, see Richard Craswell, *Regulating Deceptive Advertising: The Role of Cost-Benefit Analysis,* 64 S. Cal. L. Rev. 549, 555–6 (1991).
42. Grice, supra n. 30, at 29.
43. Jay David Atlas and Stephen C. Levinson, *It-Clefts, Informativeness, and Logical Form: Radical Pragmatics (Revised Standard Version),* in *Radical Pragmatics* (Peter Cole, ed., 1981). See also Sperber and Wilson, supra n. 29, at 123–32; Asa Kasher, *Gricean Inference Revisited,* 29 Philosophica 25, 31–40 (1982).
44. Compare the discussion in Lewis, supra n. 28, which focuses almost entirely on the *semantic* aspects of language, or those conventions that *can* be captured by relatively bright-line rules.
45. For a discussion of this process, see Morgan, supra n. 31, at 269–75.
46. Oliver Wendell Holmes, *The Common Law* [1881] 89–91 (M. Howe, ed., 1963).
47. Sperber and Wilson make the interesting claim that pragmatic implications are often used – especially in the case of metaphors and other forms of literary or figurative speech – precisely in order to convey an entire range of *possible* implications, many of which will not be certain, and will be reconstructed differently by different listeners. This, they suggest, explains why something is inevitably lost when those forms of speech are translated into explicit prose assertions. Sperber and Wilson, supra n. 29, at 217–43; Dan Sperber and Deirdre Wilson, *Loose Talk,* 86 Aristotelian Soc'y 153 (1986). Significantly, this effect would be impossible to achieve if pragmatic implications could always be identified by very specific rules that left no room for case-by-case interpretation.
48. This example is due to Peter Meijes Tiersma, *The Language of Offer and Acceptance: Speech Acts and the Question of Intent,* 74 Calif. L. Rev. 194, 206 (1986). For pragmatic analyses of questions such as "Can you open the door?" in their more usual context, see, e.g., Morgan, supra n. 31; Sadock, supra n. 36, at 289–90.
49. E.g., Stanley Fish, *Doing What Comes Naturally: Change, Rhetoric, and the Practice of Theory in Literary and Legal Studies* (1989); Stanley Fish, *Fish vs. Fiss,* 36 Stan. L. Rev. 1325 (1984); Stanley Fish, *How Come You Do Like You Do? A Reply to Dennis Patterson,* 72 Tex. L. Rev. 57 (1993).
50. Fish, supra n. 48, 36 Stan. L. Rev. at 1329–30. For a similar analogy drawn from a different sport, see Stanley Fish, *Dennis Martinez and the Uses of Theory,* 96 Yale L.J. 1773 (1987).
51. As most of the arguments in this section would apply whether one takes the goal of commercial law to be efficiency or something else, I will not distinguish between economists and philosophers in what follows.

52. Cf. Randy Barnett's analysis (supra at n. 11) of explicit economic or philosophical analysis as evidence of what the trade custom might be, but nevertheless a "funny kind" of evidence. On the view taken here, the testimony of industry experts and the testimony of economists or philosophers are both evidence of something, and neither is more "funny" (except perhaps unintentionally) than the others.
53. See, e.g., Thomas Gilovich, Robert Vallone, and Amos Tversky, *The Hot Hand in Basketball: On the Misperception of Random Sequences,* 17 Cognitive Psych. 295 (1985).
54. John M. Keynes, *The General Theory of Employment, Interest and Money* [1936] 383 (1964) (emphasis added).
55. See, e.g., *Frigaliment Importing Co. v. B.N.S. Internat'l Sales Corp.,* 190 F. Supp. 116 (S.D.N.Y. 1960). See also Bernstein, supra n. 27.
56. See the sources cited supra n. 6.
57. UCC § 1–205(2).
58. UCC § 2–202.
59. *Williamson v. Wanlass,* 545 P.2d 1145, 1149 (Utah 1976). For a similar analysis, and a similar result, see *McGowan v. Pasol,* 605 S.W.2d 728, 732 (Tex. Civ. App. 1980).
60. *Southern Concrete Services, Inc. v. Mableton Contractors, Inc.,* 407 F. Supp. 581, 584 (N.D. Ga. 1975); aff'd, 569 F.2d 1154 (4th Cir. 1978).
61. *Heggblade-Marguelas-Tenneco, Inc. v. Sunshine Biscuit, Inc.,* 59 Cal. App.3d 948, 957, 131 Cal. Rptr. 183, 189 (1976). See also *Columbia Nitrogen Corp. v. Royster Co.,* 451 F.2d 3, 7 n.3 (4th Cir. 1971) (quoting with apparent approval the expert witness's explanation of *why* the custom was to treat stated quantities as estimates).
62. Compare *Atlantic Track & Turnout Co. v. Perini Corp.,* 989 F.2d 541, 544–5 (1st Cir. 1993) (permitting a reduction to zero by interpreting the contract as an outputs contract, and analyzing the resulting allocation of risks), to *Snyder v. Herbert Greenbaum & Assocs., Inc.,* 38 Md. App. 144, 151–2, 380 A.2d 618, 623 (1977) (refusing to permit such a reduction, on the ground that this would leave the other party's substantial reliance completely unprotected).
63. *Sessa v. Riegle,* 427 F. Supp. 760, 766 (E.D. Pa. 1977) (footnote omitted).
64. *Warren's Kiddie Shoppe, Inc. v. Casual Slacks, Inc.,* 120 Ga. App. 578–9, 171 S.E.2d 643–4 (1969).
65. *Nanakuli Paving & Rock Co. v. Shell Oil Co.,* 664 F.2d 772, 780 (9th Cir. 1981).
66. *Charter Title Corp. v. Crown Mortg. Corp.,* 67 Wash. App. 428, 434, 836 P.2d 846, 850 (1992).
67. *Badget v. Security State Bank,* 16 Wash.2d 563, 571 n.3, 807 P.2d 356, 361 n.3 (1991) ("[A] duty to consider proposals might easily lead to a duty to negotiate such proposals. This, in turn, will increase transaction costs for the parties and decrease economic efficiency."). See also *Terrebonne Fuel & Lube, Inc. v. Placid Refining Co.,* 681 So.2d 1292, 1297 (La. App. 1996) (refusing to interpret as a binding course of dealing a lender's prior practice of not foreclosing on its security whenever payment was only slightly late, and explicitly recognizing the commercial importance to the lender of maintaining the right to foreclose immediately).
68. *Kirby Forest Indus., Inc. v. Dobbs,* 743 S.W.2d 348, 356 (Tex. App. 1987) ("To hold in cases such as the one before us that title checks are not only required, but are required to

be 100% successful, would shift the risk that title is defective from the warrantor back to the warrantee. This is not a desirable result.").

69. *Western Indus., Inc. v. Newcor Canada Ltd.*, 739 F.2d 1198, 1202 (7th Cir. 1984).
70. Id. at 1204.
71. Id. at 1203.
72. For an analogous criticism of courts' use of their own analysis when interpreting the parties' written contract, see Charles J. Goetz and Robert E. Scott, *The Limits of Expanded Choice: An Analysis of the Interactions between Express and Implied Contract Terms,* 73 Cal. L. Rev. 261, 290–1 (1985).
73. John Rawls, *Two Concepts of Rules,* 64 Phil. Rev. 3 (1955).
74. Id. at 17 ("Is this to say that in particular cases one cannot deliberate whether or not to keep one's promise? Of course not. But to do so is to deliberate whether the various excuses, exceptions and defenses, which are understood by, and *which constitute an important part of the practice,* apply to one's own case.") (emphasis added).
75. Thomas Scanlon, *Promises and Practices,* 19 Phil. & Pub. Aff. 199, 215–6 (1990).

5

The Uniformity Norm in Commercial Law

A Comparative Analysis of Common Law and Code Methodologies

ROBERT E. SCOTT†

I. Introduction

One of the central norms of the Uniform Commercial Code is "to make uniform the law among the various jurisdictions."[1] Nowhere in the Code, however, is the substance of the uniformity norm of commercial law explained or justified. Moreover, in the thirty years following the remarkable success of the codification enterprise in achieving formal uniformity – the widespread adoption of the Code in all American jurisdictions[2] – there has been virtually no academic or judicial analysis of whether this grand experiment in the uniform codification of American commercial law has, in fact, produced the social benefits that are presumed to follow from uniformity. Instead, there is a broad consensus, uninformed by evidence or analysis, that formal uniformity has led as well to substantive uniformity, to the certainty, predictability and stability that are the bedrock desiderata of commercial law.[3]

This uncritical acceptance of the notion that uniform codification best promotes the substantive goals of uniformity is puzzling. Large areas of commercial contract law and corporate law remain outside the Code and have evolved in a formally nonuniform fashion through the process of common law adjudication and statutory enactments in various states. In the case of corporate charters, a robust literature has focused on the substantive benefits inherent in jurisdictional diversity – stimulating a "race to the top" as states compete among themselves to capture the economic rents from incorporation.[4] Many of these substantive benefits, such as predictable interpretation of corporate charters and the promulgation of standardized contract terms, are precisely the values that inhere in any sensible conception of what the uniformity norm entails.[5]

Clearly, then, uniform codification of large segments of commercial law is not the only means of promoting the substantive goals of uniformity. Nor is the codification enterprise a priori preferable to or superior to the evolving common law of contract. Nevertheless, the uncritical assumption that formal uniformity necessarily leads to substantive uniformity has been the stimulus behind the efforts to expand the jurisdiction of the Code to commercial activities that heretofore have been regulated by the common law of contracts.[6] Before contract law is entirely absorbed into the Code, it is at least prudent to ask whether the codification enterprise has accomplished its intended purposes. The experience of the last thirty years does provide an opportunity to conduct a natural experiment: to compare outcomes under the uniform code and the common law against plausible optimality criteria that undergird the norm of uniformity. This chapter begins that project.

I begin with the claim that the state's primary substantive role in uniformly enforcing commercial contracts is to regulate incomplete contracts efficiently. This role requires the state to perform two interdependent but conceptually distinct functions. The first is an interpretive function – the task of correctly (or uniformly) interpreting the meaning of the contract terms chosen by the parties to allocate contract risk. The second is a standardizing function – the task of creating broadly suitable default rules and/or "labeling" widely used contract terms and clauses with standard meanings.[7] Uniform interpretation argues for *formalism,* for a "textualist" or plain-meaning interpretation of the (facially unambiguous) express terms used in incomplete contracts.[8] On the other hand, the task of generating useful defaults argues for *functionalism,* for contextualizing incomplete contracts.[9] The defaults will naturally come from commercial practice, and context evidence is the way courts find out about commercial practice. Thus, the first goal seems to require keeping context out as often as possible, and the second goal seems to require incorporating context whenever as possible. As a consequence, the law is apparently forced to trade off one goal against the other.

The UCC has quite clearly chosen the functionalist strategy of incorporation. In addition to specifying a broad definition of what constitutes a legally binding agreement,[10] the Code adopts a pervasive standard of commercial reasonableness that requires context to supply meaning to many of its generic default rules. The incorporation strategy is most evident in sales law under Article 2. This is perhaps not surprising, as Karl Llewellyn was the principal drafter and Article 2 was the apotheosis of his jurisprudence. But curiously, an analysis of Article 2 cases reveals that the Code fails even at the one task it was explicitly designed to do. Under Article 2, there has been very little production of standardized default rules and other standard form prototypes. Moreover, Article 2, intent on incorporation, also fails at the first enterprise – reliable and predictable interpretation of contractual text. On the other hand, the development of standardized terms has been much more successful under the common law, in those areas of contract law such as commercial services to which the Code does not extend. And these courts, constrained by more traditional plain-meaning and parol evidence rules, have maintained a textualist interpretive strategy. The result is that both kinds of efficiency gains – the creation of a fairly uniform menu of standardized terms, with regular additions of new terms to the menu, and stable (i.e., uniform) interpretation of express terms – are seen much more in the common law than under the Code.

In sum, the great exercise in promoting codified uniformity and predictability has instead produced variety and greater contracting risk. In part, this is a problem caused by the way in which the Code is drafted and especially with the pervasive emphasis on commercial reasonableness. But in a larger sense, the inefficiencies of the Code are a product of the codification enterprise itself – of trying to introduce a civil law approach into a largely successful common law system. A code remains at all times *its own* best evidence of what it means. Thus, decisions interpreting specific contract terms and default rules of the Code do not as easily become part of the understood, standardized meaning. Because gaps are filled with reference to the internal policy of the Code rather than the external contractual context, interpretation is both contextual and self-referential – the worst of both worlds.

This chapter proceeds as follows. Part II specifies the efficiency objectives of a uniform commercial law. Part III compares the experience of contracting parties under the Code (with particular emphasis on sales law) with the roughly parallel experience of commercial parties who negotiate and litigate contracts for services under the common law. I evaluate the results of this natural experiment in terms of the uniformity criteria developed in Part II. Surprisingly, uniform codification appears to be inferior to the modern common law alternative as a means of uniformly (i.e., efficiently) regulating incomplete contracts. In Part IV, I argue that a principal reason that the UCC is less "uniform" than the common law stems from the uniquely different interpretive methodology and institutional design that is dictated by a code. Thus, while the Code has achieved a formal, jurisdictional uniformity, it has failed to enhance substantive uniformity: The Code forces a contextualist interpretation of express terms in incomplete contracts, but it does so without securing the offsetting benefits of standardization. I conclude, in Part V, that the proponents of the Code would do better to attend to the efficiency values of uniformity and to the larger issues of institutional design rather than to the relentless pursuit of formal uniformity for its own sake.

II. The Role of the State in Uniformly Regulating Incomplete Contracts

The central task of a uniform commercial law is to specify the appropriate role of the state in regulating incomplete contracts. A contract is incomplete when it fails to specify the outcomes for all contingent states of the world and/or fails to specify an appropriate sanction for nonperformance in each contingent state. From the perspective of legal design, all contracts can be regarded as incomplete. Complete contracts (to the extent that they exist in the real world) are rarely, if ever, breached since the payoffs for every relevant action and the corresponding sanctions for nonperformance are prescribed. In the case of incomplete contracts, however, parties have incentives to breach to exploit the contractual gaps. Making the verifiable terms of the contract legally enforceable and regulating incompleteness consistently or uniformly reduces these incentives to breach. Legal enforcement of incomplete contracts, in turn, requires the state to interpret the signals the contracting parties have used to allocate contractual risk. Interpreting disputed contracts also presents the state with the opportunity to protect (and even improve) the efficacy of those signals for future contractors. If the state performs this function inconsistently, the costs of contracting will rise.

A. The Efficiency Values of Uniformity

To regulate incomplete contracts efficiently, the state must perform two interdependent functions consistently. The first is an interpretive function – the task of uniformly interpreting the contract terms chosen by contracting parties to allocate contract risk. An interpretation is "uniform" when it is transparent to the litigating parties and predictable to other parties.[11] An important point, often lost on those who promote formal uniformity, is that uniform interpretation is both a temporal as well as a jurisdictional matter. Thus, one efficiency value is for parties to know at the time they write contracts that their verifiable obligations will be interpreted in the same manner by courts of different jurisdictions (jurisdictional uniformity). In addition, efficiency is enhanced if parties are certain that courts in any given jurisdiction will interpret their verifiable obligations uniformly over time (temporal uniformity).

The interpretive task is made difficult in incomplete contracts because the causes of incompleteness are not known to the interpreter. Did the parties fail to complete the contract deliberately or inadvertently? Is the incompleteness a product of high transaction costs, asymmetric information, or other factors? If the incompleteness is a result of private information, those asymmetries may be the inability of the contracting parties to observe relevant variables or their inability to verify those variables to courts, or they may be the unwillingness of the parties to disclose to others the relevant information necessary to verification. For these reasons, an interpreter seeking to understand the causes of incompleteness in any particular case can only sensibly rely on the signals chosen by the parties. Predictability of meaning is the bedrock of any signaling system. This latter requirement argues for the use of objective interpretive methodologies so that parties can predict over time the effect to be given to the words used to create obligations. Thus, objective modes of interpretation and temporal uniformity go hand in hand.

The second function of uniform state regulation is standardization. At least to the extent that this task is also performed by courts, it is interdependent with and derivative of the interpretive function. The state facilitates the contracting process to the extent that courts in the process of interpretation create standardized (or "uniform") terms that parties can use in signaling their intentions so as to remove the uncertainties attendant on interpretation. Those signals can be developed in two ways. The first is through a process of "gap-filling," where courts interpreting incomplete contracts elect to condition or qualify the express terms of the contract by specifying default rules that complete the contract. These default rules can be broadly suitable "majoritarian" defaults that apply to the largest set of heterogenous contractors, or they can be "tailored" defaults that apply to smaller subsets of homogeneous parties (such as merchants in a particular trade or business). The second method of standardization occurs when courts interpret authoritatively the meaning of *invocations* – standard form terms or clauses that parties frequently use in incomplete contracts. In either case, the key to this process is the standardization of the meaning and jurisdiction of the state-supplied defaults and the privately provided invocations from which parties can customize their contracts.

As a matter of institutional design, these two functions can be performed separately – e.g., where courts interpret incomplete contracts and legislators generate useful defaults and menus of invocations – or they can be performed in combination – e.g., where courts fill gaps and interpret litigated contracts and thereby attach standard meanings to defaults and invocations. But in either case, the performance of the one role necessarily affects the performance of the other. Evaluating these efficiency objectives of state regulation is further complicated in American law because, as I suggested above, there are two quite different dimensions of uniformity. The first dimension is principally temporal. It assumes a single state decisionmaker and looks to consistency and standardization over time. A quite different dimension of the problem is embodied in jurisdictional uniformity, which focuses on consistent decision making by different courts in different jurisdictions. For expository clarity, I will designate both dimensions as comprising "substantive" uniformity. Substantive uniformity should be distinguished from purely formal uniformity, e.g., the coincidence of similar rules across time and across jurisdictions.

While the complexity of the task of uniformly regulating incomplete contracts is better understood today, policymakers have long seen the critical importance of predictability of outcomes and certainty of meaning given to both the express and implied terms in commercial contracts. Indeed, perhaps the oldest aphorism in commercial law is that in commercial contexts it is more important for the law to be certain than to be right. This aphorism has its roots in the law merchant and found new voice in the United States where commercial law was first established in the diversity of different states accepting the English common law at different times and with different interpretations of the content and meaning of that law.[12]

B. The Uniformity Movement in Commercial Law

Despite the diversity of jurisdictions and of legal heritage, a recognizable trend toward uniformity in commercial law quickly took hold in the United States. Grant Gilmore noted the effects of *Swift v. Tyson* on commercial law in the nineteenth century:

> During the second half of the nineteenth century, the Supreme Court of the United States became a great commercial court. The rules which it announced were, in nine cases out of ten, gladly followed by the state courts as well as, of course, by the lower federal courts. A remarkable degree of national uniformity in the law applicable to commercial transactions was in fact achieved over a remarkably long period of time.[13]

Nevertheless, in the view of influential academics and practitioners, this "common law" process failed to achieve an adequate degree of uniformity. Significant diversity in the commercial law of various states led to proposals for the enactment of a federal commercial code to govern interstate commercial transactions.[14] In turn, the proposals calling for a federal code stimulated the formation of the National Conference of Commissioners on Uniform State Laws (NCCUSL) in 1892.[15] Rather than accepting federal intrusions into a traditional preserve of state authority, the National Conference proposed to formulate and seek adoption of various uniform laws governing different aspects of commercial law. Each state was then encouraged to adopt these uniform statutes. Unhappily for the Conference, the uniform acts that purported to regularize commercial law received a mixed reception in the states. All states adopted the Uniform Negotiable Instruments Law and the Uniform Warehouse Receipts Act. But only thirty states adopted the Uniform Sales Act and only ten enacted the Uniform Conditional Sales Act.[16]

Many, if not most, observers, regarded the first efforts to produce uniform state commercial law as unsatisfactory. There were numerous local amendments to uniform acts and some state courts interpreted uniform provisions differently than other courts. The perceived failure of the states' processes to perform adequately the purposes underlying the drive for uniformity stimulated reform initiatives. In 1940, the Federal Sales Act was introduced in Congress. The federal act received strong support from influential academics and practitioners.[17] The National Conference reacted to the threat of federalization with predictable speed. The commissioners lobbied against federal enactment, began drafting a revised Uniform Sales Act, and, perhaps most significantly, recruited to their task Karl Llewellyn, one of the strongest advocates for the federalization of sales law.

By 1945, the NCCUSL had formed a collaboration with the American Law Institute (ALI)[18] and, working in tandem, they expanded the revised sales act project to include the drafting of a comprehensive Uniform Commercial Code.[19] Llewellyn and the other proponents of the project sought to avoid the difficulties with the previous experiment in state law uniformity by creating a "code" – a systematic, preemptive, and comprehensive enactment of a whole field of law.[20] The decision to produce a code was primarily instrumental. The ALI and NCCUSL believed that this consolidation would enable them to sell the entire project to the states on a "take it or leave it" basis and thus avoid the selective enactment that had occurred with the earlier uniform acts.[21] The strategy worked. By 1967, every American state except Louisiana had adopted the Code.[22]

In a formal sense, uniformity in commercial law has been achieved. Indeed, the formal uniformity of the UCC has been maintained even as its proponents have supported wide ranging and comprehensive efforts over the past twenty years both to revise existing provisions and to add new ones covering commercial activity previously governed by the common law of contract. What is not so clear is whether achieving – and then working to maintain – this degree of formal uniformity has required sacrificing the efficiency values of substantive uniformity. To appreciate the reasons why that might be so, one must first understand the peculiar process by which Code revisions are proposed and enacted and the political economy of the private legislative groups that control that process.

The UCC projects proceed under the general direction of a Permanent Editorial Board, composed of representatives from NCCUSL and the ALI. In addition to issuing periodic commentary on particular problems of interpretation, the Board sends recommendations for Code revisions to NCCUSL and the ALI. If both groups agree that a revision is or may be desirable, the ALI president appoints a "study group" that prepares a report that is sent to both the ALI and NCCUSL for approval.[23] Following the approval of the study group report by both bodies, the NCCUSL, in consultation with the ALI, then appoints a "drafting committee" that is responsible for putting the recommendations of the study group into statutory form. Once the drafting committee's product is finally approved by the Conference, it then lobbies for adoption by the states.[24]

Alan Schwartz and I have studied the political economy of the NCCUSL and the ALI using the techniques of positive political theory.[25] Our analysis suggests that the institutional dynamics of the ALI and NCCUSL law making process strongly influence the design of their legislative products. In cases where a single interest group dominates (such as in the revisions to Article 9), this private legislative process generates a large number of bright-line rules.[26] These rules preserve the victory of the dominant interest group in the legislative process and confine the discretion of courts that are subsequently asked to interpret the rules. On the other hand, when there is competition among interest groups (as in the case of the revisions to Article 2 and the proposed Article 2B), the process results in vague and imprecise rules that delegate broad discretion to courts. These rules result, not because of their intrinsic merits, but because academic "reformers" propose them when they are unable to get bright-line rules adopted.[27] Thus, the pressure to formulate rules that will be uniformly adopted distorts the rules themselves in ways that may, quite perversely, undermine the very objectives of a uniform law.

In short, the success of the Code in gaining widespread and "uniform" adoption has disguised a deeper jurisprudential question: To what extent have the efficiency values of substantive uniformity – predictability of interpretation and standardization of widely useful terms – been served by the experiment in codification of commercial law? In particular, since my focus here is on the legal regulation of incomplete contracts, how has the uniform codification of sales law, and the ongoing efforts at its revision, affected the costs of contracting? Before we can address that question systematically, we must first examine more carefully the interdependencies that affect the two central functions of state regulation.

C. *The Dilemma of Substantive Uniformity*

The traditional assumption that formally uniform law straightforwardly promotes the efficient regulation of incomplete contracting is, at best, simplistic and, at worst, seriously misleading. To the extent that the uniformity norm purports to embrace both predictable interpretations of incomplete contracts as well as the standardization of contract terms, it is subject to an apparent dilemma: Achieving predictability in interpretation appears to undercut the process of standardization, and vice versa. This dilemma is rooted in the fundamental tensions that exist between unconventional or atypical forms of agreement on the one hand and conventional norms and understandings on the other.

To the extent that these tensions have been understood at all, the major attempt to harmonize them relies on what I have elsewhere termed the expanded choice postulate.[28] The postulate maintains that legal promulgation and recognition of default rules (as well as menus of standardized contract terms) are normatively desirable because these terms expand the choices available to contracting parties. Providing standardized and widely suitable contract terms reduces both the resource and error costs involved in negotiating a contract. This expanded choice thesis implicitly presumes a neutral stance toward individualized agreements: Atypical parties lose nothing, since they remain free to opt out of the standard defaults and/or design customized provisions to replace the state-sanctioned terms.[29]

But the seductive appeal of the expanded choice postulate serves to disguise an underlying question: To what extent do express terms and default rules, and standardized and individualized forms of agreement, function in antagonistic rather than complementary ways? For example, courts frequently are called upon to interpret the apparently fixed price and quantity terms of a supply contract together with contextual evidence of a customary understanding that such terms are only "fair estimates"[30] or that "reasonable variations"[31] should be permitted. In such cases, creating useful defaults by filling gaps in the incomplete contracts with the prevailing custom or usage may lead to misinterpretation of the express terms of the contract. On the other hand, strict adherence to a textualist or plain-meaning interpretation of the express terms in such a contract may diminish the supply of useful defaults that will have received official "recognition."[32] To better understand these tensions, let's focus for a moment on the benefits (and the costs) of standardization.

1. THE BENEFITS OF STANDARDIZATION. Standardized terms exist both as default rules and as standard form terms and clauses (or *invocations*). The state, by announcing standardized defaults and assigning a standard meaning to invocations, reduces many errors that inhere in incomplete contracting. Providing a menu of signals from which parties can choose greatly simplifies and reduces the resource costs of contracting. More importantly, however, the process by which standardized terms mature and are recognized by the state provides a collective wisdom and experience that parties are unable to generate individually.

A principal effect of this evolutionary process is the testing of combinations of express terms and default rules for latent defects. Combinations of terms in incomplete contracts are unlikely to be carefully pretested by individual contractors. Testing involves substantial risks, and private parties who develop successful packages of contractual terms cannot capture much of the benefit that will accrue to subsequent users. Thus, the state's recognition of the evolutionary trial-and-error process functions as a regulatory scheme – analogous to the Food and Drug Administration regime for testing new drugs – designed to promote these public goods. Just as the FDA tests drugs beyond any level of precautions that are sensible for any particular individual, the consequences of standard contractual formulations are observable over a wide range of transactions. This permits the elimination of latent design defects that cannot be avoided by simply encouraging individuals to exercise greater care in the contracting process. In that sense, these standardized terms are "safer" than the customized express terms chosen by the parties.[33]

Standardization thus supports a reliable and uniform (and therefore intelligible) system of signaling the nature of the contractual risk assumed by each party. It also contributes to the evolutionary enrichment of the supply of novel terms through the selection and announcement of specific experiences that can be generalized to particular classes of transactions. By expanding the stock of such tailored defaults, the state provides parties with better-fitting default choices. Taken in combination, these several benefits argue for more rather than less standardization.

The gains from standardization are purchased at considerable cost, however. First, standardization increases the risk that courts will misinterpret the meaning of the express terms that parties use to opt out of the standard defaults. Second, standardized defaults increase the difficulty in coordinating a move to novel default terms. The first problem undermines the objective of predictable interpretation, while the second threatens the future supply of useful default terms.

2. THE COSTS OF STANDARDIZATION: BARRIERS TO OPTING OUT. Privately developed prototypes are incorporated into the stock of useful default rules through a process of "gap-filling," where courts elect to condition or qualify express contract terms by declaring the prototype to be a default term of an otherwise incomplete contract. It follows that the production of these widely useful defaults is facilitated by theories of interpretation that use context evidence liberally to supplement both the express terms and the existing stock of state-supplied default rules. This incorporation objective clashes, however, with the demands of the interpretive function: correctly (i.e., predictably) interpreting the verifiable express terms in the contract.

A single-minded focus on increasing the supply of standardized defaults through incorporation necessarily threatens the integrity of the express terms in the contract. The interpreter will be reluctant to give express terms' meanings that conflict with the apparent factual and legal context. In interpreting the meaning of the contract's express terms, courts typically look to the very same commercial context that they use to incorporate emerging default understandings. To be sure, the contractual context may often be helpful in clarifying meaning. But context evidence can also be misused, for example, where a court decides that, no matter what the express terms seem to say, the apparent meaning is simply implausible when viewed in its context.[34] One response to this conundrum is for courts to insist – through the rules of interpretation – on certain standards of artful wording.[35] The bias against giving verifiable express terms the nonstandard meaning that the text appears to prescribe will diminish if key words are given well-defined meanings. But this method of protecting the building blocks of express agreement also requires the interpreter to restrict the weight accorded to any extrinsic evidence that vitiates the predefined or "plain" meaning of certain terms.

3. THE COSTS OF STANDARDIZATION: BARRIERS TO INNOVATION. Even assuming that parties can rely on textualist modes of interpretation to opt out of the standard defaults and the commercial context, standardization impedes the development of novel or innovative terms. A transition to new contractual formulations requires individuals to first develop and then groups of contractors to coordinate their joint adoption of a standard formulation of the novel terms. The limits of copyright law create an initial barrier to innovation by denying parties substantial property rights in their formulations.[36] Individual contractors must incur whatever costs are necessary to identify novel contract terms with potential advantages over the status quo. So long as individual contractors must bear the costs of novelty but are incapable of capturing the full benefits of their innovative expressions, novel formulations will be underproduced.[37] An inherent collective action problem thus retards the production of novel terms for emerging relationships. Moreover, learning effects (the costs involved in learning how best to use and deploy the novel terms) will discourage parties from adopting the novel terms once they are developed.[38] Thus, even if private parties could costlessly develop novel uniform terms, they cannot readily coordinate any general move to the new forms by other contractors.

The twin problems of misinterpretation and uncoordinated behavior that are by-products of the state's effort to provide uniform and standardized terms are a classic illustration of the optimal solution for one segment of a multidimensional problem being inconsistent with the optimal solution for the whole. Standardization, which aims to reduce the costs of contracting, indirectly produces negative effects in a related dimension of the regulatory process. This fact does not, of course, imply that the state's role in facilitating standardized terms is on balance undesirable. It does suggest, however, that the drive toward uniformity in American commercial law has ignored significant tradeoffs in the state's regulatory process.[39] Determining how best to optimize these tradeoffs requires a better understanding of contacting behavior. What are the causes of incompleteness in contracts, and how can the state best assist parties as it performs the dual roles of interpretation and standardization?

D. *Theoretical Solutions to the Uniformity Dilemma*

Assuming that substantive uniformity is a desirable objective for the state, a plausible strategy is to maximize the net social benefits to contracting parties that derive from the dual regulatory functions of interpretation and standardization. But operationalizing this formulation poses significant difficulties. Even assuming that the gains to contractors from "better" interpretation of incomplete contracts can be compared ordinally to the gains to parties from increased standardization, the question remains: how best to strike the balance? And can some types of institutional design achieve that optimum better than others?

The recent theoretical literature on the economics of incomplete contracting offers some valuable insights into the reasons for incompleteness and, in turn, suggests a modest and circumscribed role for courts in generating default rules and an expansive role in "recognizing" privately developed standard form terms. The analysis begins with a simple puzzle. Incomplete contracts carry imbedded risks of misinterpretation as courts are asked to fill gaps and to assess the meaning of the contract's explicit terms. Why then don't parties reduce those risks by writing (more) complete contracts? Broadly speaking, transactions costs and asymmetric information are the two classes of reasons that explain why parties might not write complete contracts (contracts that prescribe the relevant actions, including sanctions, for every possible state of the world). Each of those explanations has been the subject of sustained analysis in the literature. While the debate continues, a review of the principal contributions does permit some (tentative) assessments.[40]

Transactions costs explanations of incompleteness have formed the basis for much of the law-and-economics analysis of contract law. On this account, parties write incomplete contracts because: a) the resource costs of writing complete contingent contracts would either exceed the expected gains or exceed the costs to the state of creating useful defaults[41]; or b) the parties are unable to identify and foresee uncertain future conditions or are incapable of characterizing complex adaptations adequately.[42]

If transactions costs are preventing the parties from completing contracts with efficient terms, then the state properly should supply defaults to solve those problems when the state's costs are lower than the parties'. Indeed, this condition is most plausibly satisfied in the set of "majoritarian" defaults familiar to any student of contract law. The existing stock of default rules in contract law is typically framed in terms of generalized, categorical, winner-take-all risk allocations. Consider, for example, the doctrines of perfect tender, mistake, excuse, and breach. These rules are simple and binary and apply to large populations of parties. But what about the production of more tailored defaults, contract terms that would apply to particular classes of parties or transactions? Much of the recent contract theory literature supports the claim that, in a large and complex economy with heterogeneous parties, the state is only rarely capable of supplying tailored defaults that optimally solve contracting problems.[43] Under these conditions, many factors suggest a modest state role – the more heterogeneous are the contracting parties, the less the scale economies for any default and the less likely that the state is more capable than the parties themselves in solving their contracting problems.[44]

In short, the state can sensibly specify default rules when a large number of parties face the same problem and the state-supplied solution costs less than the total benefit to the affected class of parties. This condition explains both the set of majoritarian default rules that have evolved under the common law as well as the virtual absence in the common law of tailored defaults. But what does this say about the incorporation project embraced by the Code? At a minimum, it argues for caution. Unless the contracting solution is immanent in the commercial practice and relationship of the parties (as Llewellyn believed it was), and a court can identify and standardize the practice or experience as a default, a court is likely to create ill-fitting defaults in complex commercial environments.

The contract theory literature also suggests that parties may write incomplete contracts as a means of coping with the problems caused by asymmetric information. Under these accounts, parties would not write complete contracts even if transactions costs were zero and they were able to describe costlessly all contingencies and their corresponding consequences.[45] There are several reasons that parties might choose voluntarily to discard information that could be used to complete the contract. Such a contract may be incomplete because one of the parties cannot observe key economic conditions either at the time of contracting or upon renegotiation. Alternatively, even if key conditions can be observed by both parties, the parties may not be able to verify those conditions to courts. Finally, even if such conditions are observable and verifiable, parties might choose for strategic reasons not to disclose private information about themselves. When any of these conditions obtain, the literature predicts that parties will choose to write incomplete contracts even if they were able to describe costlessly all possible contingencies in advance.[46]

The possibility that contracts may also be incomplete because of hidden information urges even greater modesty about the state's role in creating useful default rules. The state would be incapable of completing contracts with useful defaults whenever the problems caused by private information led the parties to write contracts that were incomplete.[47] Under these circumstances, a default would have to be conditioned on information that is either unobservable to the parties and/or unverifiable to the courts. Since the parties themselves will not condition their contracts on information that is unobservable or unverifiable, they would, a fortiori, choose to opt out of any such state-supplied default. Under conditions of "hidden" information, therefore, the state simply cannot provide parties with useful defaults that solve their contracting problems.[48]

This analysis suggests that the role courts may have traditionally assumed in specifying default rules for contracting parties may be far less useful in a large, complex economy with heterogeneous parties, *unless the courts have the capacity to craft tailored defaults by efficiently incorporating commercial practice and experience for commercial subgroups*. Moreover, the invitation to courts to seek to advance the standardization goal by creating broadly useful defaults threatens the parallel goal of predictable interpretation, especially when incompleteness is a product of asymmetric information. For example, parties may write incomplete contracts that look to renegotiation as the mechanism for achieving ex post efficiency. Under these conditions, the verifiable price and quantity terms in an otherwise incomplete contract may well be designed to form the basis for a subsequent renegotiation. A court that conditions the enforceability of the price and quantity terms by completing the contract with a default rule is changing the agreed upon parameters of the anticipated renegotiation.

Does this mean that there is no role for state-facilitated standardization in a complex environment of incomplete contracting? The answer is certainly no. A clue to a solution to the vexing problem of regulating incomplete contracts lies in the fact that heterogeneity of both contracting behavior and of contracting parties argues for preserving the objective instruments for interpreting contracts. Given the difficulty of identifying whether incompleteness is a consequence of high transactions costs or of asymmetric information, and assuming that the state cannot efficiently incorporate the commercial norms necessary to supply useful tailored defaults, the best option may be for courts to interpret the facially clear and unambiguous terms of the contract *without recourse to extrinsic evidence.*[49] Thus, a given form of words will come to have a given meaning that will hold across cases. A rigorous application of the plain-meaning rule will reduce interpretation error by encouraging more careful choices of clear, standardized signals. Moreover, over time, a menu of standard form invocations will be developed by private parties, authoritatively interpreted by the courts, and made available for widespread adoption by other parties with similar contracting problems.

The cost of this strategy is that courts will have fewer opportunities to incorporate the customary prototypes that typify a particular commercial context and that might emerge as tailored defaults. As a result, contracting parties will be required to incur the costs of developing standard form specifications for the many customary understandings that might otherwise have been incorporated by default.[50] The merits of the strategy thus turn on a straightforward empirical question: To what extent does (or can) efficient incorporation occur? In the absence of efficient incorporation, a strategy of plain-meaning interpretation would maximize the interpretation and standardization values inherent in the uniformity norm. On the other hand, evidence that courts under the Code do not (or cannot) use the incorporation mechanism to create tailored defaults would lend credence to the more modest role suggested by the contract theory literature.

III. Evaluating Substantive Uniformity Under the Code and Common Law

A. The Common Law Versus the Code: Formalism or Functionalism?

The question of whether the Code or the common law best achieves the efficiency goals that inhere in uniformity is amenable to observation since we now have thirty years experience with sales law under the Code against which we can compare a roughly parallel experience with the common law regulation of commercial services contracts. The state plays a relatively restrained role in supplying standardized defaults under the traditional common law approach to interpretation and incorporation. The common law interpretive approach, as reflected in its parol evidence and plain-meaning rules, focuses intensively on the written agreement.[51] If the writing appears to be a complete expression of the parties' agreement, the common law parol evidence rule bars introduction of contextual evidence to contradict or even supplement the written terms.[52] Only the established set of judicially or legislatively recognized default rules (the law of contract) is automatically incorporated into the agreement. In addition, the traditional plain-meaning rule bars parties from using contextual evidence to aid in the interpretation of contract terms that appear clear and unambiguous on their face, giving instead a lay or "dictionary" meaning to the words used.

Quite clearly, the traditional common law approach to interpretation and incorporation resolves the uniformity dilemma by sacrificing the possible benefits from increasing the supply of standardized defaults in order to preserve the benefits from predictable, "objective" interpretation. But what if the incorporation process could be deployed efficiently to discover, and then promulgate as tailored defaults, experiences and practices derived from the general commercial environment? Such useful defaults might include trade usages regarding the existence of warranties, commonly accepted quality tolerances, and circumstances under which price and quantity terms that appear to be fixed are in fact subject to some variation. These customary norms can serve as prototypes – as temporal precursors to formal legal recognition. If these norms could be efficiently incorporated as disputed contracts are interpreted, it would argue for a more balanced approach to maximizing the benefits of substantive uniformity – trading off some of the gains from plain-meaning interpretation so as to facilitate incorporation of useful defaults for commercial subgroups.

It is precisely that intuition that appears to undergird Karl Llewellyn's notion of "immanent" law. Llewellyn saw the law as the crystallization of slowly evolving social mores. A just law was inherent in the patterns of relationships that one could observe and record in the commercial environment.[53] From this perspective, the role of courts was not deductive, but inductive: to observe and record what was already there. Thus the Code, buttressed by Llewellyn's jurisprudential intuitions, purports to offer a dramatically different, activist approach to the uniformity dilemma. The Code reverses the common law presumption that the parties' writings and the official majoritarian default rules (the law of contract) are the definitive elements of the agreement. Rather, the Code explicitly invites incorporation by defining the content of an agreement to include trade usage, prior dealings, and the parties' experiences in performing the contract. Indeed, the Code rejects the plain-meaning rule,[54] and its parol evidence rule admits inferences from usage, prior dealings, and contractual performance even if the express terms of the contract seem perfectly clear and are apparently integrated.[55]

Following the adoption of the Code, a number of common law courts (encouraged perhaps by the Second Restatement of Contracts[56]) have adopted the more activist interpretive methodology. But the tide of expansive incorporation has not swept away the restrained approach of the common law tradition. Thus, the two systems continue in an uneasy coexistence and provide a unique opportunity to observe how different methods of institutional design influence the social benefits that inhere in uniformity.

B. Substantive Uniformity Under Article 2 of the Code

In this section, I evaluate the extent to which courts, adjudicating disputed sales contracts under the Code, have been successful in implementing the approach that Llewellyn seems to have envisaged: balancing the predictability (and standardization) benefits of uniform interpretation against the standardization benefits from activist incorporation.[57]

1. THE INCREASE IN BIASED INTERPRETATION. The activist approach to incorporation adopted by the Code necessarily increases the stress on courts seeking to minimize errors in interpretation. Parties must communicate the express terms of their agreement through the inherently imperfect mediation of words, actions and other manifestations that admit of varying interpretations. As the arbiter of disputed interpretations, the state determines the meaning of whatever signals the parties exchange. While the state presumably knows what it means by the default rules that it implies in every contract, it does not know the intended meaning of the express terms chosen by the parties. Thus, privately formulated express terms are always subject to an additional risk of unpredictable (or nonuniform) interpretation. Contracting parties face an inherent risk that an express term that was designed to trump the default terms of the contract will be interpreted instead as merely supplementing the default understanding.[58]

Casual observation strongly suggests that the risk of unpredictable interpretation has greatly increased for commercial parties under the Code. Courts under the Code have, consistent with its institutional design, interpreted the meaning of express terms in a contract by looking to precisely the same commercial and legal context they use to determine whether to incorporate custom and usage as default rules.[59] While this may seem perfectly logical (the parties negotiated the contract in a particular context, so courts should look to the context to determine what the parties meant by the words they used), it injects a bias into the interpretive process. Giving the commercial context interpretive priority subverts the efforts of those parties who seek to opt out of the context. Thus, for example, the Code directs courts to construe express terms and the commercial context as consistent with each other.[60] While this presumption is limited by the corollary that inconsistent usages and experiences should give way, courts have frequently abandoned this principle on the grounds that there is almost always some contextual argument upon which seemingly inconsistent terms can be rationalized. In practice, therefore, the presumption of consistency in the Code has placed a considerable additional burden on parties seeking to opt out of either the legally supplied defaults or the commercial context.[61]

The effects of interpretation bias under the Code are not limited to the error costs of unpredictable interpretation. A contextualized strategy of interpretation also undermines the ability of courts to increase the supply of officially recognized (and standardized) invocations and other privately supplied standard terms. The abandonment by the Code of the plain-meaning rule has resulted in decisions that strip terms of their meanings and thus erode the reliability of standardized express terms.

In one illustrative case, the seller attempted to introduce evidence of a course of performance between the parties to suggest that the buyer had implicitly agreed to pay for unloading and storage charges.[62] The court admitted the evidence despite the presence in the contract of an express F.A.S. shipment term that, in standard meaning, requires the seller to pay for unloading and storage charges. The court apparently believed that it was incorporating the course of performance as a tailored default to redesign the somewhat ill-fitting conventional meaning attached to F.A.S. by the Code. However, this legal recognition of a prevailing contextual pattern threatens the parallel process by which courts recognize (and standardize) similarly useful express signals. In order to protect invocations such as F.A.S. from interpretive bias, the course of performance must be seen as trumped by the talismanic meaning attributed to the standard form term. After all, if parties are to use express language to opt out of custom, the language they use for this purpose must be insulated from the context they are seeking to escape. On this view, an invocation selected by the parties can be modified only by additional, express language. Otherwise, incorporation of the factual context will create a presumptive answer to the very question being asked.

2. THE RESULTS OF THE INCORPORATION STRATEGY. The increase in interpretation bias reflected in decisions by courts following the activist methodology prescribed by the Code is predicted by the analysis developed in Part II. The central question remains, are the costs of unpredictable interpretation justified by offsetting gains that result from the incorporation of useful tailored defaults from the commercial context?

While the Code was explicitly designed to incorporate evolving norms into an ever-growing set of legally defined default rules, incorporation as such has simply not occurred. To be sure, courts have interpreted contracts in which context evidence has been evaluated together with the written terms of the contract. The invitation to contextualize the contract in this manner is explicitly embodied in the Code's definition of "agreement,"[63] and it is amplified by § 1–205(3), which specifies that courses of dealing and usages of trade give particular meaning to, and qualify terms of, an agreement.[64] But while such judicial decisions affirm the institutional bias toward contextualizing the contract, the fact-specific nature of the contract dispute leaves, in virtually every case, little opportunity for subsequent incorporation as tailored defaults.

The limited role played by usage and course of dealings per se is not surprising. These questions typically arise as interpretive disputes over the meaning of express terms and particular usages and not as the means of specifying a more precise or tailored meaning of the substantive obligations embodied in the Code's numerous default rules. The vehicle for this latter aspect of the incorporation project, in Llewellyn's mind, was the pervasive direction to courts (found in a majority of the specific provisions of Article 2) to apply the default provision in question according to the norm of commercial reasonableness.[65]

The supereminent norm of commercial reasonableness was seen by Llewellyn as a key incorporating mechanism – one that would function as an empirical direction. To decide whether the parties have acted in a commercially reasonable manner as to any particular contractual obligation, the court is asked to look to the commercial environment and observe the relevant commercial behavior. Once revealed (and mediated through the normative "purposes" of the Code), this standard would then provide the legal norm to be published as an appropriately tailored default for the relevant class of contracting parties.[66]

Thus, for example, § 2-609 provides that "when reasonable grounds for insecurity arise with respect to the performance of either party the other may in writing demand adequate assurances of due performance and until he receives such assurances may if commercially reasonable suspend his own performance. . . . "[67] Generations of law students have begun their study of the Code by confronting the facially vacuous nature of that default provision. As a majoritarian default, it offers little in the way of a standardized contractual risk assignment since it carries no predictable meaning. But Llewellyn understood this point as well. UCC § 2-609 was never intended to operate as a useful default on its face. Rather, the key instructions – "adequate assurances," "reasonable grounds for insecurity," and "commercially reasonable" suspension – were intended to direct courts to examine the relevant contracting environment and then (presumably over time) publish meaningfully tailored defaults that would apply to particular populations of commercial parties.

This was a revolutionary idea, and one that seemed to anticipate the theoretical objection to state-supplied default rules raised by the recent literature on incomplete contracting. But the project has failed in implementation. A systematic examination of the litigated cases interpreting the "reasonableness" standards of Article 2 reveals that courts have consistently interpreted these statutory instructions not as inductive directions to incorporate commercial norms and prototypes but rather as invitations to make deductive speculations according to "Code policy" or other noncontextual criteria.[68] I evaluate the reasons for the failure of the Code's incorporation strategy in Part IV. But the empirical point is that, for whatever reason, courts charged with the responsibility of implementing the Code's activist policy toward incorporation have declined to do so.[69]

Thus, the costs of a strategy of incorporation – a highly contextualized interpretive methodology that seeks to embed the explicit terms of a contract within a larger commercial context – seem not to be justified by corresponding enhancements in the supply of useful defaults for appropriate subsets of commercial contractors. At least according to the uniformity criteria developed above, the results of thirty years of codified uniformity suggest that formal uniformity has masked a general deterioration in the efficiency values that stimulated the search for a uniform law in the first instance. The final question, of course, is whether the parallel experience of courts interpreting commercial services contracts under the common law has been more or less "uniform" than the results under the Code.

C. Substantive Uniformity Under the Modern Common Law

It is striking to contrast the experiment in codified uniformity with the experience of common law enforcement of commercial services contracts over the same thirty-year period. The interpretive methodology of the common law has stubbornly resisted the contextual interpretation adopted by the Code and the Second Restatement of Contracts. A strong majority of jurisdictions continues to adhere to textualist interpretation of contract terms, primarily through a rigorous adherence to the plain-meaning rule. Indeed, the continuing vitality of the traditional parol evidence and plain-meaning rules cannot be overestimated.[70] In numerous cases, common law courts interpreting commercial contracts have been unwilling to accept the implications of contextualization; in one guise or another, they continue to invoke the primacy of express, verifiable contract terms and of the written agreement between the parties.

Two uniformity values are served by the common law courts' insistence on preserving the traditional approach to contractual interpretation. First, a rigorous application of the plain-meaning rule reduces the errors caused by unpredictable interpretations of incomplete contracts, encouraging parties to use clearer, predefined signals of the reasons for contractual incompleteness. Second, plain-meaning interpretation facilitates that portion of the standardization function that promotes the recognition of privately supplied customary terms. These invocations then carry a standard meaning whenever they are used, even if their use is not so customary as to warrant automatic incorporation as default rules.[71] As suggested previously, the legal recognition of these talismanic words and phrases greatly facilitates the contracting process. Definitional recognition does not change the optional character of these terms, but it does confer upon them a *status* so that, once expressly incorporated into a contract, they will have a legally circumscribed meaning that will be heavily and perhaps even irrebuttably presumed.

As one might predict, a study of the evolving common law of commercial services contracts does not reveal the incorporation by courts of novel default rules. Incorporation is stymied by an interpretive methodology that systematically excludes reference to the commercial context. But the past thirty years have nonetheless seen a remarkable harmonization in contract terms through the development of a detailed menu of invocations.[72] Standardization of express terms has been stimulated in construction contracting, for example, through the offices of key intermediaries such as the American Institute of Architects and the Associated General Contractors.[73] One particularly instructive example is the response of these two trade organizations to the contracting challenges produced by the development of fast-track construction and the construction management model of design and construction contracting.[74] Each of these two rival organizations produced during the 1970s a competing set of model forms that defined the contractual obligations and risks associated with the use of a construction manager.[75] Versions of these forms have been widely adopted by contracting parties and subsequently have been tested both in litigation and consensual arbitration proceedings.[76] Out of that process, a set of standardized "official" terms continues to emerge that collectively reduce the risks of writing contracts to govern these novel contractual relationships.[77]

In short, trade organizations and other private intermediaries have developed and promulgated model contract terms and forms that are widely and successfully used by parties to construction contracts and that have been subject to remarkably uniform interpretation by state courts. These model or standard forms provide a mechanism for internalizing at least some of the benefits from contractual innovation and standardization that private parties are otherwise unable to capture. In instances where the intermediary organization represents a significant subset of the potential users of the standard terms, such a form can supply the coordination necessary to overcome the collective action problems discussed earlier.

Perhaps surprisingly, the maintenance of rigorous rules of objective interpretation seems to have stimulated the development of novel standard terms by trade groups and other intermediaries. These kinds of standardized options have been far slower to develop under the Code. Indeed, Lisa Bernstein notes the phenomenon of a key commercial subgroup under the Code – The National Grain and Feed Association – choosing to opt out of the Code entirely in order to secure the kind of plain-meaning interpretation necessary to the promulgation of standardized norms.[78]

Thus, the common law regulation of commercial contracts seems to have created a hospitable legal environment, one that facilitates the development of intermediaries to overcome the collective action problems that otherwise retard the development of novel uniform terms. Moreover, additional harmonization of noncode commercial law has resulted from the jurisdictional diversity that the Code drafters sought so vigorously to overcome. New York, for example, has solidified its position as the jurisdiction of choice for commercial contractors by enacting a choice of law selection statute that permits parties ex ante to choose New York contract law as the uniform source of interpretation.[79]

But does jurisdictional diversity impose (offsetting) costs? There are, after all, measurable efficiency gains that inhere in jurisdictional uniformity. Prime among these are "learning effects" that result from a common legal language and method of categorization of legal rules.[80] Here the formal uniformity of the Code might seem to offer a significant advantage over the common law. Indeed, the notion of a uniform "filing system" that permits the storage and retrieval of key legal information remains one of the strongest justifications offered by Karl Llewellyn for a uniform sales law.[81] Under the Code's cataloging system, specific court decisions are filed under the broad rubric of Code-defined categories such as rejection, cure, etc. Systematizing the retrieval of legal rules reduces the learning effects imposed by jurisdictional diversity. Presumably, information costs would be greater if the decisions were not organized systematically.

Despite the jurisdictional diversity that remains under the common law, there is reason to believe that learning effects and legal information costs are not significantly greater than under the Code. Economic and cultural forces may well have contributed to the evolution of interjurisdictional substantive uniformity during this same period. Indeed, the past fifty years have witnessed a remarkable degree of harmonization of American commercial common law. The variations in contract law from state to state today are relatively small and insignificant. There are few instances where a state persists over time in applying a widely variant "rule" of contract law. The result is "substantive harmony without uniformity."[82]

This result should not be surprising. Powerful market forces push toward harmonization across jurisdictions. Judges, especially in commercial cases, want to please the practicing bar; they benefit from favorable evaluations of their work from insiders. The practicing bar, meanwhile, prefers law that is (1) predictable, so that lawyers are better able to advise their clients, and (2) substantively right, insofar as there is a substantively right answer. Quite obviously, these two factors coalesce. Where the law is uncertain, but there is a strong substantive case for one legal rule rather than another, the practicing bar would like to be able to predict the outcome by discerning the substantively better rule. Thus, both factors push toward harmonization, probably with a tendency to follow those state courts with special expertise and prestige.[83] In short, while the risks of casual empiricism argue for tentativeness in advancing empirical claims, nevertheless all the available evidence points to the fact that the Uniform Commercial Code has been far less successful than the common law alternative in promoting the efficiency values of uniformity.

IV. The Causes and Effects of the Failure of Codified Uniformity

Why has the experiment with uniform codification of contract law performed so poorly in terms of the substantive objectives of a uniform law? And what are the effects of that failure? In this part, I explore both of these questions.

A. Why the Code Has Failed to Produce Substantive Uniformity

There are doubtless many reasons for the failure of the Code to achieve the objectives of its drafters. Quite clearly, one central reason was the failure of the other Code drafters to adopt Llewellyn's proposal that commercial disputes under the Code be resolved by merchant juries. Llewellyn believed that a major purpose of the Code was to resolve disputes according the "best" commercial norms. In his view, the task of the courts was to identify and select the best commercial prototypes that were revealed in a particular commercial environment. One obvious objection to this strategy, of course, is that courts lack the expertise to observe and evaluate merchant practice. To respond to this concern, Llewellyn designed the supereminent norm of commercial reasonableness as an empirical direction: to delegate discretion to expert bodies, not judges and lay jurors.[84] Eliminating the merchant jury while retaining the pervasive notion of commercial reasonableness was, in consequence, a drafting disaster.

But the failure to provide for the merchant jury is but a symptom of a larger jurisprudential mistake for which Llewellyn must be held at least partly responsible. Llewellyn believed (or at least acquiesced in the belief ascribed to him) that moral norms can be derived from actual practices.[85] But how is this to be accomplished? After all, the evaluator must have some moral criteria, derived independently from the practice, in order to extract the "ought" from the "is." [86] For example, assume a court is faced with the question of good faith in the case of a merchant under § 2-103(1)(b).[87] The subject of the dispute is the merchant's business practice which is followed by some, but not all, of the participants in the trade. Whether this practice reflects "the observance of reasonable commercial standards of fair dealing in the trade" cannot be answered by the mere existence of the practice. The court must, therefore, have some criteria, derived independently from the practice, by which to decide whether the practice is "reasonable" and "fair" under the legal standard.

It seems quite clear that this point was not lost on Llewellyn either. He had an answer: The moral norms used to sort good practices from bad ones were to come from the purposes of the Code itself. Llewellyn, like most realists, wanted courts to choose purpose over rule language: To do this is to judge in the "grand style."[88] Thus, Llewellyn wanted particular Code sections interpreted in light of the purposes underlying the Code itself. This preference explains, in part, the decision to retain the supereminent norm of reasonableness even after the proposal for merchant juries was abandoned. Llewellyn wanted courts to understand that it was desirable to decide specific cases in light of the Code's general purposes. To do that, he joined, enthusiastically, those of his colleagues who were promoting (for instrumental reasons)[89] the idea of a "true commercial code" to replace the checkered pastiche of prior uniform statutes. Thus, instrumental and jurisprudential considerations were united. [90]

The decision to create a code was a fateful one.[91] A central difference between the uniform commercial statutes that preceded the UCC and the new Code lay in the different interpretive methodologies that are dictated by a code. A code is a preemptive, systematic, and comprehensive enactment of a whole field of law.[92] It purports to give the answers to all relevant questions. Thus, when a court confronts a gap in an incomplete contract, its duty in interpreting a code is to use the processes of analogy and extrapolation to find a solution consistent with the purposes and policy of the codifying law. In this way, the code itself provides the best evidence of what it means. Thus, the decisions interpreting provisions of a code do not as easily become part of the understood meaning of its terms as they do in the case of an ordinary statutory enactment.[93]

In order to promote its purposes, a code must have a systematic method of filling gaps by a self-referential process that divines the purposes of the enactment. In the UCC, this methodology is specified in § 1-102, which directs courts to liberally construe and apply the specific provisions of the act "to promote its underlying purposes and policies."[94] The effect of this language is that the Code not only has the force of law, but is itself a source of law.[95] In important respects, therefore, Llewellyn's Code displaced the legal method of the common law and substituted the legal method of the civil law. [96]

To construct the Code in the tradition of continental codifications required the development of supereminent "safety valve" provisions designed to fill gaps and to mitigate the harshness of bright-line rules that would otherwise be asked to govern "hard" cases.[97] Gaps are to be filled through recourse to the purposes enumerated in the Code and, in specific provisions, by recourse to the overarching injunction to follow the norms of "reasonableness." The net effect of this institutional design is a highly contextualized interpretive methodology, one that seeks to embed the explicit terms of a contract within the larger jurisprudential context of the Code as well as within the specific commercial context being regulated.

The result, in terms of maximizing the benefits of substantive uniformity, could hardly have been much worse. First, the rejection of the common law plain-meaning and parol evidence rules was an open invitation to courts to abandon any meaningful constraints on the interpretation of language. Over time, the uniformity value of predictable interpretation has been eroded. While courts under the Code are uniformly using the same interpretive rules, the results they reach are anything but uniform. Thus, the Code quite self-consciously has squandered whatever efficiency gains are achievable through uniform, objective methods of contract interpretation. Second, the standardization process has failed to evolve. Recall that standardization comes in two forms: the promulgation of useful default rules by incorporating commercial practice into commercial law, and the official recognition and interpretation of privately supplied customary terms. Neither of these processes has occurred with the same vigor in the Code as in the parallel common law process.

One reason for the unwillingness of the courts to embrace incorporation may be the lack of information regarding the effects of novel, tailored defaults in different settings and among heterogeneous parties. But another reason seems to be the peculiar distortions created by code methodology: Courts are required to create default rules with reference to the hermetic regulatory framework of the Code itself.[98] The process of Code interpretation inevitably resists the dynamic process inherent in standardization.[99] A comprehensive Code means that, for any given issue, courts will be driven to adopt a rule that will then be treated as, in effect, a part of the Code. Parties under the Code are thereby pushed toward arguments that are based on one or another "Code rule." Contracting out of the rule, in turn, is made difficult by the abandonment of the common law parol evidence and plain-meaning rules. Thus, code methodology tends to produce a stasis that impedes the evolution and promulgation of novel default rules and contract terms.[100] Under the common law, on the other hand, the parol evidence and plain-meaning rules make it fairly easy for parties to generate new terms that can then acquire standard interpretations. Those sorts of legal rules are not so *enveloping;* they are significantly easier to opt into or out of.

B. The Effects of a "Nonuniform" Uniform Code

The promulgation of a uniform code that reduces rather than enhances the economic benefits from uniformity has had several significant effects. The first is the observed practice of groups of commercial parties opting out of the Code entirely in important classes of cases. Lisa Bernstein notes an important illustration: the decision by the members of the National Grain and Feed Association to opt out of the Code and create a private legal system to resolve contract disputes among themselves.[101] One of the principal reasons for the Association's decision to abandon the Code was its desire to have written express terms subject to a formalist and objective interpretive methodology and not to be trumped by relevant evidence of course of dealing or usage of trade. Bernstein suggests that the explanation for this practice lies in the parties' desire to separate the legal norms that govern their written agreements from the informal social norms that govern their actions.[102] An alternative (and complementary) explanation, however, is that opting out of the Code permits the grain and feed merchants to secure the economic benefits of uniformity by substituting a private common law process for the state-subsidized mechanism under the Code.[103]

Whether the practice by homogeneous groups of commercial parties of opting out of the Code reflects an underlying inefficiency in the law is, of course, an empirical question. We would have to know how widespread is the practice that Bernstein and others have observed before passing judgment on the Code's inefficiency.[104] Nevertheless, the evidence is sufficiently striking to undermine the uncritical assumption of the academic and professional proponents of the Code that it serves its purported purposes efficiently.

The second effect of the stasis in the supply of Code defaults is even more dramatic. The principal source of novelty in the stock of Code default rules has been the process of comprehensive revision of the Code under the auspices of the ALI and NCCUSL.[105] Technological change and the need for new legal instruments to accommodate that change have been among the driving forces behind the current revisions of the UCC. Electronic funds transfers, for example, stimulated revisions in Articles 3 and 4. Changing business practices led to Article 2A and revisions in Articles 5, 6, 8, and 9.[106] Article 2, the provision most clearly designed by Llewellyn to evolve through dynamic renewal, has been in the process of revision for the past decade with no end in sight.[107]

Relying on the Code revision process to generate novel default rules is worrisome on several grounds. First, the process is slow, cumbersome and costly. To the extent that there is a lag in the evolution of new contractual forms, parties with emerging needs face a difficult choice. Either they can rely upon ill-fitting rules and/or standard terms that secure less than maximum trading gains or they can incur the costs of crafting new forms of agreement that are better adapted to the evolving conditions. To the extent that Code methodology impedes the development of privately supplied invocations, commercial parties are often left with the option of lobbying in the revision process as the only viable response to the problem of lags.

Interest group influence on the private legislative process that produces Code revisions raises a further set of concerns. The work on the political economy of these private legislative bodies suggests that the rules they produce are driven more by institutional factors than by their social desirability.[108] There are good reasons to believe that private lawmaking bodies such as the ALI and NCCUSL will have a strong status quo bias and will sometimes be captured by powerful interests. More important, when interest groups compete, the legal rules that are produced will frequently be characterized by vague and imprecise standards, not because open-ended standards are optimal, but because of the particular institutional dynamic.

In the case of Article 2, this analysis predicts that, *despite the possible economic advantages of a return to a formalistic, common law approach to interpretation,* the forthcoming revision to Article 2 will contain the same methodological characteristics as its predecessor: many vague rules that invoke the animating purposes of the Code coupled with open-ended, contextual modes of interpretation. These rules will dominate, not because of their intrinsic virtues, but because they are proposed by reformers (i.e., legal academics) who are unable to get clear, bright-line rules enacted. This is because the effects of sales law do not fall systematically on any single interest group, and thus interest group competition leads to successful efforts to block bright-line rules that a given interest group opposes, and thwarts efforts of a given group to lobby for bright-line rules in its favor.[109]

These predictions seem to be confirmed in the work to date of the Article 2 drafting committee. According to the reporter of the drafting committee, the committee "preserved the original approach to contract formation and interpretation attributable to Karl Llewellyn. This approach minimizes formality. . . . [T]he emphasis is upon flexible standards, mutual conduct and the intention of the parties."[110] Ironically, even this strategy was insufficient to overcome interest group opposition to particular proposed revisions. The opposition of various industry groups led to an indefinite postponement of the final approval of Revised Article 2.[111] Following the resignation, in protest, of the reporter and associate reporter, the drafting committee was "reconstituted" with the direction to accommodate the strong interest group opposition.[112] In all likelihood, therefore, the Revised Article 2 will not address the underlying causes of the failure to achieve substantive uniformity. Even if most contracting parties would benefit from an institutional design that promoted the objective interpretation of express contract language and the recognition and promulgation of privately developed standard terms, there are good reasons to believe that the institutional dynamic of the lawmaking process will result in a recodification of the status quo. Whether it is socially optimal or not, opting out of the Code and into the common law may be the only recourse for cohesive, homogeneous commercial groups.

V. Conclusion

The Uniform Commercial Code is a project of many parts and it resists generalizations. The time is much too premature, therefore, to declare the entire experiment with codified uniformity a failure.[113] Nevertheless, there is growing evidence that the effort to unify sales and related contract law through codification is seriously flawed. Article 2 and its progeny are driven by the motivation to achieve formal uniformity *über alles*. The push for formal, jurisdictional uniformity leads Code proponents to accommodate sharp differences over value choices and interest group conflicts with vague statutory provisions that delegate broad discretion to courts. In turn, courts operating within the Code scheme are instructed to supply content to otherwise vacuous default rules by incorporating custom, trade usage, and other immanent patterns of commercial exchange. The methodological conception that undergirds the norm of commercial reasonableness is that an open-textured, functionalist interpretive methodology generates properly tailored default rules that clarify the meaning of incomplete contracts. So long as its central premises are unquestioned, this methodological conception is normatively plausible, indeed perhaps even compelling. But evidence continues to accumulate that the Article 2 methodology is premised on courts being able to discover patterns of behavior that do not, in fact, exist.[114] And, in any event, courts are instructed to deploy a methodology that would not succeed in discovering these patterns even if they existed.

The claim that the foundations of Llewellyn's Code are built on clay does not come easily to one who has spent a lifetime with the UCC. It is clear that more analysis, both theoretical and empirical, is required before anyone can safely call for radical reform. There are, however, low-cost, intermediate responses to the interpretation conundrum that are likely to reduce contracting costs and to shed further light on party preferences. At a minimum, commercial parties should be free to choose, by appropriate contractual language, either a functionalist or formalist legal interpretation of the terms of their contract. If the interpretive methodology is made a default rule rather than a mandatory rule, the costs of continued allegiance to the incorporation strategy could be reduced at the same time that parties could avoid the risks of encrustation and rote usage resulting from exclusive reliance on formalism.[115]

In any event, it is time to recognize that the efficiency goal of maximizing the value of contractual relationships is served by the substantive norms of uniformity – predictability and standardization – and not by the mere formality of different jurisdictions enacting rules that are facially the same. Rather than relentlessly pursuing formal uniformity for its own sake, the proponents of the Code and the law reform groups responsible for its revision would do better to attend to the efficiency values of uniformity and to the larger issues of institutional design.

Notes

† I am thankful to Lisa Bernstein, Clay Gillette, John Jeffries, Kevin Kordana, Jody Kraus, Paul Mahoney, Alan Schwartz, Paul Stephan, Bill Stuntz, Steve Walt, and the participants in law and economics workshops at the University of Chicago, Columbia University, New York University, and the University of Michigan for their helpful comments on prior drafts.

1. UCC § 1-102 (2)(c).
2. By 1967, the Code had been adopted in forty-nine states and the District of Columbia. The only exception to formal uniformity was Louisiana, where adoption of most parts of the Code has occurred more recently. Moreover, the uniformity objective has been maintained even as the Code has undergone significant revisions to Articles 3 (Commercial Paper), 4 (Bank Deposits), 5 (Letters of Credit), 6 (Bulk Transfers), 8 (Investment

Securities) and 9 (Secured Transactions) and the adoption of new Article 2A (Leases) and 4A (Funds Transfers). The major challenge to formal uniformity remains the proposed revisions to Article 2 (Sales) and 2A (Leases) and the proposal for a new Article 2B (Licenses). See n. 27 infra.

3. A similar consensus has supported the parallel goal of unity and harmonization in international commercial law. Efforts toward this goal over the past fifty years have produced conventions governing international sales of goods, bank credits and payments, and contracts of carriage, as well as a large body of procedural rules regulating disputes between international traders. See, e.g., *Convention on Contracts for the International Sale of Goods,* Apr. 10, 1980, UN Doc. A/Conf./97/18; *Convention for the Unification of Certain Rules Relating to Bills of Lading,* Aug. 25, 1924, 51 Stat. 233, 120 L.N.T.S. 155; *Convention for the Unification of Certain Rules Relating to International Transportation by Air,* Oct. 12, 1929, 49 Stat. 3000, 137 L.N.T.S. 11; *Convention on the Recognition and Enforcement of Foreign Arbitral Awards,* June 10, 1958, 21 U.S.T. 2517, 330 U.N.T.S. 3. For a sceptical view of the presumed benefits of formal unification of international business law, see Paul B. Stephan, *The Futility of Unification and Harmonization in International Commercial Law,* 39 Va. J. Int'l. L. 743 (1999).
4. See, e.g., Roberta Romano, *Law as a Product: Some Pieces of the Incorporation Puzzle,* 1 J. Law, Econ. & Org. 224 (1985); William J. Carney, *The Production of Corporate Law,* 71 S. Cal. L. Rev. 715 (1998); Roberta Romano, *The Genius of American Corporate Law* (1993); Ronald J. Daniels, *Should Provinces Compete?: The Case for a Competitive Corporate Law Market,* 36 McGill L.J. 130 (1993). There is a debate among corporate law scholars as to whether the value generated by jurisdictional diversity takes the form of enhanced value to firms or stimulates a rent-seeking "race to the bottom" by corporate managers searching for corporate law rules that permit managerial entrenchment. See e.g., Lucian Bebchuk, *Federalism and the Corporation: The Desirable Limits on State Competition in Corporate Law,* 105 Harv. L. Rev. 1435 (1992); Lucian Bebchuk and Allen Farrell, *Federalism and Takeover Law: The Race to Protect Managers from Takeovers* NBER Working Paper 7232 (July 1999). A recent empirical study by Robert Daines adds valuable evidence supporting the "race to the top" hypothesis. See Robert Daines, *Does Delaware Law Enhance Firm Value?* (unpublished manuscript on file).
5. Marcel Kahan and Michael Klausner, *Standardization and Innovation in Corporate Contracting (or "the Economics of Boilerplate"),* 83 Va. L. Rev. 713 (1997).
6. The first step in the expansion of the jurisdiction of the UCC occurred with the promulgation of Article 2A governing contracts to lease personal property. Thereafter, Article 4A, covering electronic transfers, was promulgated, and Article 2B, purporting to regulate software licensing contracts, was brought forward by the drafting committee for final approval by the American Law Institute (ALI) and the National Conference of Commissioners on Uniform State Laws (NCCUSL) in 1999. The decision by the ALI not to endorse proposed Article 2B (Licenses) (which is being reissued by NCCUSL as the Uniform Computer Information Transactions Act) and the approval of an alternative provision that repeals Article 6 (returning the law of bulk transfers to common law and statutory regulation) offers some evidence that the expansion of the Code's jurisdiction is not unambiguously regarded as a social benefit.
7. The two central functions of the legal regulation of contract – predictable interpretation of contract terms and the provision of broadly useful default rules – are the functional applications of the two core processes of contractual formulation: generalization and

particularization. Thus, the search for widely suitable default rules in the contractual context is the key element in the process by which evolving customary norms of *general* application are recognized and officially adopted. On the other hand, the effort to impose predictable interpretation on express contract terms is the mechanism whereby *particularized* contractual understandings are protected from contrary inferences that emerge from context. Charles J. Goetz and Robert E. Scott, *The Limits of Expanded Choice: An Analysis of the Interactions Between Express and Implied Contract Terms,* 73 Calif. L. Rev. 261, 308–9 (1985).

8. For an interpretation to be uniform, it must be both transparent to the contracting parties and predictable to other parties. The uniformity values of transparency and predictability are the normative underpinnings of the "objective" theory of contract interpretation. This preference for objective modes of interpretation is most clearly manifest in the common law plain-meaning rule. The rule requires a court to make a preliminary finding that the contractual text is ambiguous or unclear before admitting extrinsic evidence that varies the text's apparent meaning. See, e.g., *Watkins v. Petro-Search, Inc.* 689 F.2d 537 (5th Cir. 1982) (unambiguous writing will be accorded the meaning apparent on its face; objective and not subjective intent controls). See the discussion in n. 11 infra.

   For many of the same reasons, textualists in other areas of law, such as statutory interpretation, argue against using context evidence such as legislative history to illuminate the text. The preference for predictability that underlies the goal of uniformity thus implies as well a preference for formalist modes of interpretation and analysis generally. See Thomas Grey, *The New Formalism* (unpublished manuscript on file). Grey identifies three specific doctrinal tendencies as the forming the underpinnings of the "new formalism" 1) *textualism* – the preference for text-based over purposive modes of interpretation; 2) *objectivism* – the preference for determinate, rule bound law over open-ended standards; 3) and *conceptualism* – the preference for treating abstract categories – such as contract – as coherent structures of concepts and principles. See Grey, *The New Formalism,* supra at 2–4.

9. Functionalism is the mirror opposite of formalism. It expresses a preference for purposive interpretation over textualism, open-ended standards over bright-line rules, and contextualism over conceptualism. Ibid. at 19–27.

10. See UCC § 1-102(3). An "agreement" means "the bargain of the parties in fact as found in their language or by implication from other circumstances including course of dealing or usage of trade or course of performance. . . ." Comment 3 explains that the Code's concept of agreement is intended to include full recognition of all context evidence and the surrounding circumstances.

11. Transparency and predictability are the functional underpinnings that justify the "objective" theory of contract. Under the objective theory, the outward manifestations of agreement between contracting parties determine legal consequences, despite evidence that either or both contractors may have had different, subjective understanding of the meaning and legal consequences of the terms used or the context in which they were employed. See Robert E. Scott and Douglas L. Leslie, *Contract Law and Theory* 21–23, 207–09 (1993). This principle is vividly captured in Judge Learned Hand's famous dictum: "A contract has, strictly speaking, nothing to do with the personal, or individual, intent of the parties. . . . If it were proved by twenty bishops that either party, when he used the words, intended something else than the usual meaning which the law imposes upon them, he would still be held. . . ." *Hotchkiss v. National City Bank,* 200 F. 287, 293

(S.D.N.Y. 1911), aff'd, 201 F.2d 664 (2d Cir. 1912), aff'd, 231 U.S. 50 (1913). See also, the court's statement in *Chernohorsky v. Northern Liquid Gas Co:*

> The language of a contract must be understood to mean what it clearly expresses. A court may not depart from the plain meaning of a contract where it is free from ambiguity. In construing the terms of a contract, where the terms are plain and unambiguous, it is the duty of the court to construe it as it stands, even though the parties may have placed a different construction on it.

Chernohorsky v. Northern Liquid Gas Co., 268 Wis. 586, 68 N.W. 2d 429 (1955); Restatement of Contracts § 230 comment b (1932); S. Williston, *A Treatise on the Law of Contracts,* § 609, at 403–4 n.2 (citing supporting cases).

12. Ford W. Hall, *The Common Law: An Account of Its Reception in the United States,* 4 Vand. L. Rev. 791 (1951).
13. Grant Gilmore, "Commercial Law in the United States: Its Codification and Other Misadventures," in Jacob S. Zeigel and William F. Foster, eds. in *Aspects of Comparative Commercial Law: Sales, Consumer Credit, and Secured Transactions* 449, (1969).
14. See, e.g., Committee on Commercial Law, Report, 10 ABA Rep. 332–44 (1887); See, generally, E. Hunter Taylor, Jr., *Federalism or Uniformity of Commercial Law,* 11 Rutgers-Camden Law Journal, 527 (1980).
15. Handbook of the National Conference of Commissioners on Uniform State Laws (1892).
16. Taylor, *Federalism or Uniformity,* supra n. 14. In general, the track record of NCCUSL in getting its uniform laws enacted over the past 100 years has been decidedly mixed. Of more than two hundred proposed uniform acts, 107 have been adopted in fewer than ten states and seventy-seven in fewer than five. See James J. White, *Ex Proprio Vigore,* 89 Mich. L. Rev. 2096, 2103 (1991). On the other hand, the Conference's most sustained success has been in the commercial area. Of the twenty-two uniform laws enacted by more than forty states, nine have been commercial. See White, at 2103–5 n. 35–40.
17. See, generally, Karl N. Llewellyn, *The Needed Federal Sales Act,* 26 Va. L. Rev. 558 (1940); Hiram Thomas, *The Federal Sales Bill as Viewed by the Merchant and the Practitioner,* 26 Va. L. Rev. 537 (1940).
18. The ALI is a private law-reform group that chooses its own members, typically lawyers, legal academics, and judges. The ALI proposes restatements of the law, sponsors special projects, and, in collaboration with the NCCUSL, promulgates the UCC and its revisions.
19. The marriage between the ALI and NCCUSL was proposed and arranged in the 1940s by William Schnader, a prominent attorney who belonged to both organizations. See Kathleen Patchel, *Interest Group Politics, Federalism, and the Uniform Commercial Code,* 78 Minn. L. Rev. 83, 98 (1993) (providing history of the UCC).
20. See n. 91 infra for a discussion of the status of the UCC as a "code."
21. William D. Hawkland, *The Uniform Commercial Code and the Civil Code,* 56 La. L. Rev. 23–5 (1995).
22. By 1975, Louisiana had enacted Articles 1, 3, 4, and 5. Subsequently, Article 9 and parts of Article 2 were enacted as well.
23. The study group is appointed on the recommendation of the ALI director, who consults with NCCUSL and the ALI Council. The latter body must approve its membership. A study group typically meets two to three times a year over a several-year period. Although it has an academic reporter, the study group as a whole, rather than the reporter, has the final say as to the contents of a draft report. Robert E. Scott, *The Politics of Article*

9, 80 Va. L. Rev. 1783, 1805–10 (1994). Study group reports are very influential in determining the content of proposed UCC legislation. Ibid.

24. Over time, the internal procedures and processes of the Conference have become regularized, thus creating, in effect, a private legislative body. The Conference is composed of roughly three hundred "commissioners" who are members of the bar appointed for three-year terms by the governors of their states. Since the appointment is viewed as "nonpolitical," the commissioners are frequently reappointed. Each state can have as many commissioners as it wants, but voting on proposed laws is done by states. Uniform laws are drafted by designated committees. The Conference then meets annually for a week to consider and vote on the proposed uniform law, with approval by a majority of the states represented at the meeting. See *Handbook of the National Conference of Commissioners on Uniform State Laws and Proceedings of the Annual Conference Meeting in Its Ninety-Eighth Year* 400 (citing NCCUSL constitution § 2.4) (1994).
25. Alan Schwartz and Robert E. Scott, *The Political Economy of Private Legislatures,* 143 U. Pa. L. Rev. 595 (1995).The analyst using these tools identifies the utility functions that participants in the legislative process maximize, specifies the institutional structures that transform participant preferences into legislative outcomes, and then shows what outcomes these preferences and structures will produce.
26. Ibid. at 637–50; Scott, *The Politics of Article 9,* supra n. 23 at 1818–21.
27. The decision by NCCUSL to postpone indefinitely final approval of revised Article 2 and revised Article 2A offers some especially vivid evidence to support this theory. Opposition to the proposed revisions to Articles 2 and 2A by various affected industries at the NCCUSL meeting in Denver in July 1999, where final adoption of the new Article 2 had been expected, led instead to the postponement of formal approval for at least another year. The postponement was apparently agreed to in order to protect the objective of securing uniform adoption of the revisions in state legislatures. Note, for example, the remarks of Arizona Commissioner James M. Bush, that any revised Article 2 must have a reasonable chance of being enacted in substantial numbers of jurisdictions. Mr. Bush stated that the current draft didn't meet that test and that "uniformity would be lost." *Record of Proceedings, NCCUSL Plenary Session, July 1999.* This action, in turn, prompted the Reporter and Associate Reporter for the revised Article 2 to resign and the drafting committee to be reconstituted (the Article 2 and Article 2A drafting committees have been consolidated into a single committee).

    Although the postponement action and the reaction it caused was a dramatic occurrence in the normally sedate processes of NCCUSL, it should not have been unexpected by any student of the codification process. The work that Schwartz and I have done on the political economy of the ALI and NCCUSL predicts that efforts by Code proponents to pursue the goal of formal uniformity will inevitably lead, in the forthcoming revisions to Article 2, to even greater reliance on vague statutory language in lieu of the bright-line rules that stimulate interest group opposition. In turn, crafting statutory provisions in vague language delegates considerable law making discretion to courts. Reliance on such vague and open-ended statutory language is not a product of a conscious choice of standards over rules, but rather is a product of the interactions between interest group opposition and the interests of Code proponents (mostly the academic reporters and other "reformers") in getting codifications enacted. See Schwartz and Scott, *The Political Economy of Private Legislatures,* supra n. 25 at 615–38. The central question that this chapter seeks to address is whether the drive for formal uniformity and the concomitant promulgation of vague statutory provisions actually undermines, rather than advances, the underlying objectives which the uniformity norm seeks to advance.

28. Goetz and Scott, *The Limits of Expanded Choice,* supra n. 7 at 262.
29. The expanded choice postulate thus rests primarily on a straightforward autonomy claim. People make binding commitments via contract in order to engage in voluntary, cooperative activity that advances their individual purposes. The law enhances the value of these individual pursuits by facilitating the contracting process for those who choose typical forms of agreement without interfering with the ability of individuals to pursue atypical contractual relationships.
30. See, e.g., *Columbia Nitrogen Corp. v. Royster Co.,* 451 F.2d 3 (4th Cir. 1971) (course of dealing and usage of trade admitted into evidence to show that express price and quantity terms in a written contract were only fair estimates).
31. See, e.g., *Modine Mfg. Co. v. North E. Indep. School Dist.,* 503 S.W. 2d 833, 837–8 (Tex. Civ. App. 1973) (trade usage admissible to show that express terms should be interpreted as permitting reasonable variations).
32. See, e.g., *Southern Concrete Servs. v. Mableton Contractors,* 407 F. Supp. 581 (N.D. Ga. 1975), aff'd 569 F.2d 1154 (5th Cir. 1978) (express term requires exclusion of evidence of prevailing usage).
33. See Goetz and Scott, *The Limits of Expanded Choice,* supra n. 7 at 286–7. The claim here is only that standardized defaults that emerge from the commercial context and are incorporated by courts are, on average, less prone to error in their formulation than individually crafted express terms. This does not imply that the standardized prototypes are "optimal." There is, in theory, room for "intelligent design" by legal actors that may well improve on the evolutionary process. See Jody S. Kraus, *Legal Design and the Evolution of Commercial Norms,* 26 J. Legal Stud. 377 (1997). Moreover, the customary prototypes may themselves be differently understood by individual contractors, and by courts, especially prior to any official "recognition." See e.g., Richard Craswell, *Do Trade Customs Exist?* in Chapter 4 in this volume. Nevertheless, careful analyses of the evolutionary story in specific contexts provide continuing evidence of its vitality. For an excellent example in the context of incorporating international custom into the international sales law, see Clayton P. Gillette, *Harmony and Stasis in Trade Usages for International Sales,* 39 Va. J. Int'l L. 707 (1999).
34. See, e.g., *Brunswick Box Co. v. Coutinho, Caro & Co.,* 617 F.2d 355 (4th Cir. 1980) (course of performance and surrounding context suggest that the understood meaning of the F.A.S. term in the contract should not govern).
35. See Edwin W. Patterson, *The Interpretation and Construction of Contracts,* 64 Colum. L. Rev. 833 (1964).
36. See, generally, Robert E. Scott, *The Case for Formalism in Relational Contract,* 94 Nw. U. L. Rev., n., 24 (forthcoming, 2000). The federal copyright statute offers a seemingly broad and expansive protection for all "original works of authorship." 17 U.S.C. 102 (1982). Nonetheless, it is unclear whether a contract form or term is copyrightable at all. Where, for example, an uncopyrightable idea is so straightforward or narrow that there are necessarily only a limited number of ways to express it, any particular form of expressing that idea will also be uncopyrightable. The rationale for this limitation is to prevent the underlying idea from being monopolized. See *Morrissey v. Proctor & Gamble Co.,* 379 F.2d 675 (1967). Moreover, even if copyright protection is available for a particular innovative contractual clause, the substantive ideas that it expresses remain

public goods. Thus, other parties are free to embody similar contractual provisions in their agreements and may use suitable words to express such provisions. See, e.g., *Dorsey v. Old Surety Life Ins. Co.*, 98 F.2d 872 (10th Cir. 1938). Trade secret rules offer no alternative protection for innovative contract terms since it is the breach of confidence by unauthorized disclosure, rather than infringement of a property right that is the gravamen of trade secret liability. See, e.g., *Wilkes v. Pioneer Am. Ins. Co.*, 383 F. Supp. 1135 (D.S.C. 1974). Cf Mark A. Lemley and David McGowan, *Legal Implications of Network Economic Effects,* 86 Cal. L. Rev. 479, 571 n. 399 (1998) (patent or copyright protection is "theoretically possible" for contract terms individually drafted, but in practice lawyers copy contractual innovations).

37. The costs of innovation include the uncertainty costs of interpretation. New terms, no matter how apt for the parties' contracting purposes, carry an enhanced risk that they will be interpreted by courts in a manner different from that intended by the parties. Novel terms also carry a heightened risk of latent ambiguity and other errors of expression. These costs are borne by the initial drafters and remain until the terms have survived litigation and been "authoritatively" interpreted. See Goetz and Scott, *Expanded Choice,* supra n. 7 at 283–6.
38. See Steven Walt, *Novelty and the Risks of Uniform Sales Law,* 39 Va. J. Int'l L. 671 (1999); Kahan & Klausner, supra n. 5 at 719–20; Michael Klausner, *Corporation, Corporate Law, and Networks of Contracts,* 81 Va. L. Rev. 757, 786–9 (1995).
39. See also Eric Posner, *The Parol Evidence Rule, the Plain Meaning Rule, and the Principles of Contractual Interpretation,* 146 U. Pa. L. Rev. 533 (1998) (framing this dilemma as a choice between a "hard parol evidence rule" and a "soft parol evidence rule").
40. Much of the incomplete contracts literature can be seen as a natural extension of the transactions costs literature most associated with the work of Oliver Williamson. See Oliver Williamson, *Markets and Hierarchies: Analysis of Antitrust Implications* (1975); Oliver Williamson, *The Economic Institutions of Capitalism* (1985). These models focus on the costs of describing or specifying ex ante all of the contingencies for every possible state of nature. Owing to these costs, parties write incomplete contracts and then renegotiate when a particular state of nature is realized. See, e.g., Oliver Hart and John Moore, *Foundations of Incomplete Contracts*, 66 Rev. Econ. Stud. 115 (1999); Oliver Hart and John Moore, *Incomplete Contracts and Renegotiation,* 56 Econometrica 755 (1988); Oliver Hart, *Incomplete Contracts and the Theory of the Firm,* 4 J. L. Econ., and Org. 119 (1988). The inability of exogenous transactions costs explanations of incompleteness to predict the contracts that we see in the world has led to efforts to explain incompleteness in a world where transactions costs are zero. These models explain incompleteness as endogenous owing to asymmetric information. Under these circumstances, parties choose not to complete contracts so as to avoid moral hazard or adverse selection problems. See, e.g., J. Thomas and T. Worrall, *Income Fluctuations and Asymmetric Information,* 51 J. Econ. Theory 367 (1991); Benjamin Hermalin aqnd Michael Katz, *Moral Hazard and Verifiability: The Effects of Renegotiation in Agency,* 59 Econometrica 1735 (1991), M. Dewatripont and E. Maskin, *Contractual Contingencies and Renegotiation,* 26 Rand J. Econ 704 (1995); B. Bernheim and M. Whinston, *Incomplete Contracts and Strategic Ambiguity,* 88 Am. Econ. Rev. 432 (1998). Most recently, models have made transactions costs endogenous by focusing on factors such as the limited attention of decision makers, Sharon Gifford, *Limited Attention and the*

Optimal Incompleteness of Contracts, 15 J. L. Econ. & Org. 468 (1999), or on the complexity of the contracting environment, Ilya Segal, *Complexity and Renegotiation: A Foundation for Incomplete Contracts,* 66 Rev. Econ. Studies 57 (1999).

41. See Charles J. Goetz and Robert E. Scott, *Liquidated Damages, Penalties and the Just Compensation Principle: Some Notes on a Theory of Efficient Breach,* 77 Colum. L. Rev. 554 (1977). For formal analyses that appeal to exogenous transactions costs to explain incomplete information, see G. Huberman and C. Kahn, *Limited Contract Enforcement and Strategic Renegotiation,* 78 Am. Econ. Rev. 471 (1988); K. E. Spier, *Incomplete Contracts and Signaling,* 23 Rand J. Econ. 432 (1992).
42. See Robert E. Scott and Charles J. Goetz, *Principles of Relational Contracts,* 67 Va. L. Rev. 1089 (1981). For formal analyses of the effects of uncertainty and complexity, see W. B. MacLeod, *Decision, Contract, and Emotion: Some Economics for a Complex and Confusing World,* 29 Canadian J. Econ. 788 (1996); and Ilya Segal, *Complexity and Renegotiation: A Foundation for Incomplete Contracts,* 66 Rev. Econ. Studies 57 (1999).
43. Alan Schwartz, *The Default Rule Paradigm and the Limits of Contract Law,* 3 S. Cal. Interdisciplinary L. J. 389 (1994).
44. Consider first the case of a default where the cost of specification for any individual contractor is less than the corresponding gains and less than the cost to the state of creating a public default. Here the efficiency advantage in a state-created default is that all subsequent parties of the relevant type can costlessly use the public default. In this case, the parties would specify a contract term if the state does not provide a default. Thus, as the number of parties covered by the default grows smaller, so does the probability that the state can provide a solution superior to one the parties themselves would supply. On the other hand, assume the cost to individual contractors of creating a contractual solution exceeds the gain. Here parties would write incomplete contracts. But to supply an optimal default, the state would have to estimate the total private gain to all affected parties and create a default when the state's creation costs were less than the total gain. This condition also becomes more difficult to satisfy as the number of parties in the relevant preference set declines. See Schwartz, *The Default Rule Paradigm and the Limits of Contract Law,* supra n. 43 at 402–10.
45. For formal analyses of the effects of asymmetric information on incomplete contracting, see Benjamin Hermalin and Michael Katz, *Judicial Modification of Contracts Between Sophisticated Parties: A More Complete View of Incomplete Contracts and their Breach,* 9 J. L. Econ. & Org. 98 (1993); J. Thomas and T. Worrall, *Income Fluctuations and Asymmetric Information,* 51 J. Econ. Theory 367 (1991); B. Bernheim and M. Whinston, *Incomplete Contracts and Strategic Ambiguity,* 88 Am. Econ. Rev. 902 (1998).
46. Alan Schwartz, "Incomplete Contracts," *The New Palgrave Dictionary of Economics and Law* (1997); Ian Ayres and Robert Gertner, *Strategic Contractual Inefficiency and the Optimal Choice of Legal Rules,* 101 Yale L. J. 729 (1992); Hermalin and Katz, *Judicial Modification of Contracts,* supra n. 45.
47. A qualification to that general statement is the possibility that the state could construct "information forcing" defaults designed to encourage one party to share key information with the other. The rule of *Hadley v. Baxendale* is often used as the paradigmatic illustration of such a default rule. See, e.g., Robert E. Scott, *A Relational Theory of Default Rules for Commercial Contracts,* 19 J. Legal Stud. 597, 609–11(1990); Ian Ayres and Robert Gertner, *Filling Gaps in Incomplete Contracts: An Economic Theory of Default Rules,* 99 Yale L. J. 87, 101–4 (1989); Jason Johnston, *Strategic Bargaining and*

the Economic Theory of Contract Default Rules, 100 Yale L. J. 615 (1990); Lucian A. Bebchuk and Steven Shavell, *Information and the Scope of Liability for Breach of Contract: The Rule of Hadley v. Baxendale,* 7 J. L. Econ. & Org. 284 (1991). The discussions in the literature demonstrate, however, that such defaults are optimal only if courts possess very specific information about the strategic and market positions of the parties. It is unlikely that courts would be in a position to craft many such defaults with any confidence that they would successfully stimulate parties to share private information voluntarily. Indeed, were they able to do so, presumably the parties would craft such information-forcing terms themselves. But information-forcing terms are almost never observed in expressly negotiated contracts.

48. Schwartz, *Incomplete Contracts,* supra n. 46. Note again that it is a separate question as to whether the state, in lieu of supplying "problem-solving defaults," can craft defaults that encourage parties to share private information voluntarily. See note 47 supra.
49. This formalist approach to interpretation in contract law was first suggested in the legal literature by Alan Schwartz. See Schwartz, *Incomplete Contracts,* supra n. 46; Schwartz, *The Default Rule Paradigm,* supra n. 43. For a more complete discussion of the relative merits of formalism and alternative activist interpretation strategies, see Scott, *The Case for Formalism,* supra n. 36.
50. See, generally, Jody S. Kraus and Steven D. Walt, *In Defense of the Incorporation Strategy,* Chapter 6 of this volume (arguing that critics of incorporation ignore these "specification" costs). Beyond the increase in specification costs, a return to formalism will have other costly effects. In particular, there will be (at least) a short-term increase in the number of disputed contracts where enforcement is denied because the contract is found to be fatally incomplete and/or ambiguous. See Scott, *The Case for Formalism,* supra n. 36 at 17.

In theory, the costs of pursuing a single-minded formalist interpretation of incomplete contracts can be avoided by a more complex strategy, one in which courts interpret contracts either formalistically or functionally depending on the simplicity of the contract and the causes of simplicity. See Karen Eggleston, Eric A. Posner, and Richard Zeckhauser, *Simplicity and Complexity in Contracts* (unpublished manuscript on file). As Eggleston et al. recognize, this "mixed" strategy requires that two key conditions be satisfied: (1) Parties are able to opt in or out of strict or liberal modes of interpretation at relatively low cost; and (2) courts are sufficiently competent to undertake an analysis of the causes of incompleteness and then select the appropriate strategy depending on the clues that are revealed by those causes. The analysis that follows in Part IV supra suggests that neither condition is satisfied in many commercial environments today. The alternative strategy, suggested by this chapter, depends on the evolutionary development of a detailed menu of predefined contract terms that parties, both sophisticated and unsophisticated, could employ in optimally specifying their contract terms. Determining which strategy has the less restrictive conditions is, of course, an empirical question. In either case, both the Eggleston approach and the one suggested in this chapter would coalesce around a single normative conclusion: Parties should be allowed to choose, at the time of contracting, to have their legal obligations determined according to either a formalist or functionalist method of interpretation. Treating the interpretive methodology as a default rule rather than a mandatory or immutable rule is simply a logical corollary to the instrumental justification for uniformity: to maximize the ex ante value of contractual relationships. See Part V supra.

51. See, e.g., *Henrietta Mills Inc. v. Commissioner,* 52 F.2d 931, 934 (4th Cir. 1931) ("the courts will not write contracts for the parties to them nor construe them other than in accordance with the plain and literal meaning of the language used"); See also, E. Allen Farnsworth, *Disputes over Omission in Contracts,* 68 Colum. L. Rev. 860, 862–4 (1968).
52. See, e.g., *Smith v. Abel,* 316 P. 146, 148 (Ore. 1957) ("While custom, if sufficiently shown, might be used to interpret an ambiguous term in the contract, it could not be used to make a contract or to add to or contradict the terms of the contract"); *Swiss Credit Bank v. Board of Trade,* 597 F.2d. 146, 148 (9th Cir. 1979) (ambiguity is necessary to admission of usage evidence).
53. Robert E. Scott, *Chaos Theory and the Justice Paradox,* 35 W & M L. Rev. 329, 341 (1993); Richard Danzig, *A Comment on the Jurisprudence of the Uniform Commercial Code,* 27 Stan. L. Rev. 621 (1975). But see Alan Schwartz, *Karl Llewellyn and the Origins of Contract Theory,* Chapter 1 in this volume (arguing that Llewellyn believed that custom had only epistemological rather than normative relevance).
54. UCC § 2-202, comment 1: "This section definitely rejects . . . any premise that the language used has the meaning attributable to such language by rules of construction existing in the law rather than the meaning which arises out of the commercial context in which it was used." See also UCC § 1-205, comment 1: "This Act rejects both the 'lay dictionary' and the 'conveyancers' reading of a commercial agreement."
55. UCC § 2-202 and comments 1, 2 (1994). "[W]ritings are to be read on the assumption that the course of prior dealings between the parties and the usages of trade were taken for granted when the document was phrased."
56. See Restatement (Second) of Contracts, § 204, 221–3 (1979).
57. I have chosen to examine the results of cases decided under Article 2 both because it is the foundation of Llewellyn's activist strategy and it offers the best point of comparison with common law contract interpretation. The selection does have a bias, however. Many of the provisions in Articles 3 and 9, for example, are more rulelike and rely less on vague directives that delegate discretion to courts. Incorporation of the relevant context in those settings may not be stymied by the self-referential interpretive methodology that is characteristic of Article 2. See Part IVA supra.
58. See, e.g., *Publicker Indus., Inc. v. Union Carbide Corp.,* 17 UCC Rep. Serv. 989 (Pa. 1975); *Missouri Pub. Serv. Co. v. Peabody Coal Co.,* 583 S.W.2d 721 (Mo. 1979).
59. See, e.g., *Brunswick Box Co. v. Coutinho, Caro & Co.,* 617 F.2d 355 (4th Cir. 1980); *Steuber C. v. Hercules, Inc.* 646 F2d. 1093 (5th Cir. 1981); *Nanakuli Paving & Rock Co. v. Shell Oil Co.,* 664 F2d. 772 (9th Cir. 1981); *Columbia Nitrogen Corp. v. Royster,* 451 F2d. 3 (4th Cir. 1971); *Modine Mfg. Co. v. North E. Independent School Dist.,* 503 S.W. d. 833 (Tex. Civ. App. 1975).
60. UCC § 1-205 (4) (1978).
61. This interpretive error is both "unpredicted" and also "unpredictable." Courts sometimes commit the reverse error of interpreting express terms that seem intended by the parties as merely supplementary to the standard default rules as trumping those defaults. Thus, the bias is both skewed in favor of the standard norms and uncertain in its application to particular cases.
62. *Brunswick Box Co. v. Coutinho, Caro & Co.,* 617 F.2d 355 (4th Cir. 1980).
63. UCC § 1-102(3) defines "agreement" as "the bargain of the parties in fact as found in their language or by implication from other circumstances including course of dealing or usage of trade or course of performance as provided in this Act."

64. UCC § 1-205(3) (1994) comment 1 to § 1-205 provides that:

    This act rejects both the "lay-dictionary" and the "conveyancer's" reading of a commercial agreement. Instead the meaning of the agreement is to be determined by the language used by them and by their action, read and interpreted in the light of commercial practices and other surrounding circumstances. The measure and background for interpretation are set by the commercial context, which may explain and supplement even the language of a formal or final writing.

65. The norm of commercial reasonableness is variously expressed in Article 2, sometimes just with the injunction "reasonable," but always directed to or qualified (usually explicitly) by a broader reference to commercial practice. See, e.g., §§ 2-103(1)(b), 2-204, 2-205, 2-206, 2-208, 2-305, 2-308, 2-309, 2-311, 2-402, 2-503, 2-510, 2-513, 2-603, 2-604, 2-605, 2-607, 2-608, 2-609, 2-610, 2-614, 2-706, 2-709, 2-710, 2-712, and 2-714.
66. Alan Schwartz and Robert E. Scott, *Commercial Transactions: Principles and Policies* 5 (2d ed. 1991).
67. UCC § 2-609 (1994).
68. A LEXIS search for cases of the past ten years that invoke commercial reasonableness in close conjunction with mention of at least one Article 2 section returned 164 hits. A detailed examination of fifty-five cases randomly selected from this base pool revealed two cases where the court viewed the commercial reasonableness question as requiring inductive evaluation. See *Havird Oil Co. v. Marathon Oil Co.*, 149 F.3d 283 (4th Cir. 1998); *Cattle Fin. Co. v. Boedery, Inc.*, 795 F. Supp. 362 (D. Kan. 1992). In eighteen other cases, a deductive approach was used in the evaluation of commercial reasonableness. See *Meyer v. Norwest Bank Iowa*, 112 F.3d 946 (8th Cir. 1997); *U&W Indus. Supply v. Martin Marietta Alumina, Inc.*, 34 F.3d 180 (3d Cir. 1994); *Bausch & Lomb, Inc. v. Bressler* (2d Cir. 1992); *Bill's Coal Co. v. Board of Pub. Utils. of Springfield*, 887 F.2d 242 (10th Cir. 1989); *Canusa Corp. v. A&R Lobosco, Inc.*, 986 F. Supp. 723 (E.D.N.Y. 1997); *Spanierman Gallery Profit Sharing Plan v. Arnold*, 1997 U.S. Dist. LEXIS 3547 (S.D.N.Y. Mar. 27, 1997); *Waldorf Steel Fabricators v. Consolidated Sys.*, 1996 U.S. Dist. LEXIS 12340 (S.D.N.Y. Aug. 23, 1996); *Wayman v. Amoco Oil Co.*, 923 F. Supp. 1322 (D. Kan. 1996); *RW Power Ptnrs., L.P. v. Virginia Elec. & Power Co.*, 899 F. Supp. 1490 (E.D. Va. 1995); *Twin Creeks Entertainment, Inc. v. U.S. JVC Corp.*, 1995 U.S. Dist. LEXIS 2413 (N.D. Ca. Feb. 22, 1995); *BAII Banking Corp. v. ARCO*, 1993 U.S. Dist. LEXIS 14107 (S.D.N.Y. Oct. 7, 1993); *J. Moreria, LDA. v. Rio Rio, Inc.*, 1992 U.S. Dist. LEXIS 19088 (S.D.N.Y. Dec. 15, 1992); *Larsen Leasing v. Thiele, Inc.*, 749 F. Supp. 821 (W.D. Mich. 1990); *Danish Fur Breeders Assn. v. Olga Furs, Inc.*, 1990 U.S. Dist. LEXIS 4779 (S.D.N.Y. Apr. 24, 1990); *in re Narragansett Clothing Co.*, 138 B.R. 354 (Bankr. D.R.I. 1992); *Bockman Printing & Servs. v. Baldwin-Gregg, Inc.*, 572 N.E.2d 1094 (Ill. App. Ct. 1991); *Touch of Class Leasing v. Mercedes-Benz Credit of Canada, Inc.*, 591 A.2d 661 (N.J. Super. Ct. App. Div. 1991); *Hornell Brewing Co. v. Spry*, 664 N.Y.S.2d 698 (N.Y. Sup. Ct. 1997). Of the remaining thirty-five cases, nineteen touched only tangentially upon the issue of commercial reasonableness, while sixteen dealt principally with commercial reasonableness under other sections of the Code or other areas of the law, e.g., Articles 2A, 3, 9, and common law real property. See also Imad D. Abyad, Note, *Commercial Reasonableness in Karl Llewellyn's Uniform Commercial Code Jurisprudence*, 83 Va. L. Rev. 429 (1997), for a systematic review of the interpretation and use by courts of the supereminent notion of commercial reasonable-

ness under the Code. Abyad finds that courts predominantly apply a deductive approach to the determination of commercial reasonableness. But he also notes and examines some striking exceptions to this general rule in courts' treatment of certain provisions within Articles 3 and 9 of the Code.

69. It is a separate and independent question whether, had the results of the Code's experiment with incorporation been different, the tailored defaults that were announced and standardized would have been either optimal or efficiently promulgated by courts. See generally Kraus, *Legal Design and the Evolution of Commercial Norms,* supra n. 33 (arguing that evolutionary norms are not likely to be optimal and suggesting the continuing utility of intelligent institutional design). See also Scott, *A Relational Theory of Default Rules,* supra n. 47 at 613–15 (suggesting that a positive explanation for the absence of tailored defaults lies in the parties' preferences to be governed under separate regimes of bright-line majoritarian default rules and flexible extralegal norms that are not legally enforceable. "It may be that the great lesson for the courts is that any effort to judicialize these social rules will destroy the very informality that make them so effective in the first instance." Ibid. at 615); Lisa Bernstein, *Merchant Law in a Merchant Court: Rethinking the Code's Search for Immanent Business Norms,* 144 U. Penn. L. Rev. 1765 (1996) (same); Omri Ben-Sharar, *The Tentative Case against Flexibility in Commercial Law,* 66 U. Chi. L. Rev. 781 (1999) (arguing that incorporating flexible adjustments as legal rules increases enforcement costs to promisees).

70. See, e.g., *Watkins v. Pedro Search, Inc.,* 689 F.2d. 537 (1982) (unambiguous writing will be accorded the meaning apparent on its face; objective and not subjective intent controls); *Mellon Bank v. Aetna Business Credit, Inc.,* 619 F. d. 1001 (3d Cir. 1980) (same); *Lee v. Flintkote Co.,* 593 F. 2d 1275 (D.C. Cir. 1979) (plain-meaning rule bars evidence of meaning of unequivocal contract terms); *Reed, Wible & Brown, Inc. v. Mahogany Run Dev. Co.,* 550 F. Supp. 1095 (M.D. La. 1982) (same); *Acree v. Shell Oil Co.,* 721 F.2d. 524 (5th. Cir. 1983); *William B. Tanner Co. v. Sparta-tomah Broadcasting Co.,* 543 F. Supp. 593 (W.D. Wis. 1982) (unambiguous contract language should be given its plain meaning, with no need to consider extrinsic evidence or rules of construction); *Berry v. Klinger,* 225 Va. 201 (1983) (plain-meaning rule controls interpretation of unambiguous written contract) (same result in New York, North Carolina, Illinois, Oklahoma, and Pennsylvania; see cases cited in Goetz and Scott, *The Limits of Expanded Choice,* supra n. 7 at 124).

71. See Goetz and Scott, *The Limits of Expanded Choice,* supra n. 7 at 281–3. See also Posner, *The Parol Evidence Rule,* supra n. 33 at 533.

72. Apt examples of standardized invocations are "Incoterms," the international rules for the interpretation of trade terms. See International Commerce Commission Incoterms (1980). Each of the fourteen Incoterms attempts to set forth a number of substantive rules. These rules were well known and widely used terms of international trade before their formal codification by the International Chamber of Commerce. Additional examples include corporate indentures, bond covenants, and most of the standard features of corporate financial agreements. See, generally, Kahan and Klausner, *Standardization and Innovation in Corporate Contracting,* supra n. 5.

73. See American Institute of Architects, General Conditions of the Contract for Construction (14th ed 1987); Associate General Contractors, Standard Form of Agreement between Owner and Construction Manager (1979). The standard form terms produced by these trade groups (especially the AIA) are widely used in the construction industry. The

AIA standard form terms, now in their fourteenth edition, have been tested and refined through litigation and arbitration in many jurisdictions over an extended period of time. Stuart Macauley et al., *Contracts: Law in Action* 1021–5 (1995); Justin Sweet, *Sweet on Construction Industry Contracts* (1987).

74. Under the fast-track method of phased construction, many construction tasks are initiated before overall design is complete. The economic motive for this accelerated procedure is to minimize both financing costs and inflation of labor and material costs during the construction period. The consolidation of the design and building process is typically combined with the use of a construction manager (CM). The CM combines functions traditionally performed separately by the design architect and the contractor. Using the CM, with its hybrid characteristics, poses difficult contracting problems for the parties. Most importantly, it departs from the traditional owner/architect/contractor structure in which the mutual relationships and obligations have been thoroughly worked out and defined over time. Furthermore, the fast-track procedure is often unusually contentious, placing stress on the legally defined terms of the agreement. The procedure is thus inherently susceptible to contractual disputes over change orders and whether they represent true alterations in the scope of the original work or are merely the finalization of the original plans. See *City Stores Co. v. Gervais F. Favrot Co.*, 359 So. 2d 1031 (La. Ct. App. 1978); *Daugherty Co. v. Kimberely-Clark Corp.*, 14 Cal. App. 3d 151, 92 Cal. Rptr. 120 (1971).
75. American Institute of Architects, General Conditions of the Contract for Construction, Docs. Nos. A101/CM, A201/CM, B141/CM, B801(1980); Associated General Contractors, Standard Form of Agreement Between Owner and Construction Manager, Doc. No. 8a (1977), 8d (1979–80).
76. For an example of this testing process in litigation, See, e.g., *Bolton Corp. v. T.A. Loving Co.*, 94 N.C. App. 392, 380 S.E. 2d 796 (N.C. Ct. Appeals 1989). For a thorough review of the testing of contract terms through arbitration, see Thomas J. Stipanowich, *Beyond Arbitration, Innovation and Evolution in the United States Construction Industry,* 31 Wake Forest L. Rev. 65 (1996).
77. See, generally, Victor G. Trepasso, *The Lawyer's Use of AIA Construction Contracts,* 19 Prac. Law 37 (1973); John Michael McCormick, *Representing the Owner in Contracting with the Architect and Contractor,* 8 Forum 435 (1973).
78. Bernstein, *Merchant Law,* supra n. 69.
79. McKinney's General Obligations Law, § 5-1401; McKinney's Consolidated Laws of New York Annotated (1989):

> The parties to any contract . . . in consideration of a transaction covering in the aggregate not less than two hundred fifty thousand dollars, including a transaction otherwise covered by subsection one of section 1–105 of the uniform commercial code, may agree that the law of this state shall govern their rights and duties in whole or in part, whether or not such contract . . . bears a reasonable relation to this state. . . .

There is some evidence that New York courts, intent on capturing a market position as the arbiters of commercial disputes, are more likely to adopt formalist modes of interpretation even when applying Article 2 provisions. A particularly salient example is *Intershoe, Inc. v. Bankers Trust Co.*, 77 N.Y. 2d 517, 571 N.E. 2d 641, 569 N.Y.S. 2d 333 (Ct App. 1991), in which the court held that Article 2 applied to foreign exchange contracts and insisted on a high level of formality in contract terms.

80. See, generally, Klausner, *Corporations and Networks of Contracts,* supra n. 38.
81. Karl N. Llewellyn, *Why We Need the Uniform Commercial Code,* 10 U. Fla. L. Rev. 367, 369 (1957).
82. Arthur Rosett, *Unification, Harmonization, Restatement, Codification, and Reform in International Commercial Law,* 40 Am. J. Comp. L. 683 (1992).
83. Jonathon Macey and Geoffrey Miller have shown how states compete for the economic rents from increased litigation and transactional business for members of the practicing bar. See Jonathan Macey and Geoffrey P. Miller, *Toward an Interest-Group Theory of Delaware Corporate Law,* 65 Tex. L. Rev. 469 (1987).
84. See Note, *Commercial Law and the American Volk: A Note on Llewellyn's German Sources for the Uniform Commercial Code,* 97 Yale L. J. 156 (1987).
85. There is a debate in the literature over the nature of Llewellyn's views on contract theory. Modern scholars have tended to infer Llewellyn's views on contract theory from his later jurisprudential writings and from his (perhaps instrumental) statements during the process of drafting and seeking enactment of the Code. See, e.g., Zipporah B. Wiseman, *The Limits of Vision: Karl Llewellyn and the Merchant Rules,* 100 Harv. L. Rev. 465 (1987). In Chapter 1 of this volume, Alan Schwartz argues that Llewellyn's earlier writings on contract reveal a much more nuanced view of the appropriate role of custom and practice. Schwartz asserts that Llewellyn believed that custom had only epistemological and not normative relevance, and that courts should (and could) infer the efficient rule from the standard practice. Alan Schwartz, *Karl Llewellyn and the Origins of Contract Theory,* this volume. Granting Schwartz's claim, nevertheless Llewellyn in his later work on the Code was quite prepared to acquiesce in the normative views commonly ascribed to him.
86. To do otherwise requires overcoming a naturalistic gap. It risks committing what arguably is the naturalistic fallacy. See G. E. Moore, *Principia Ethica* 10–4 (1971 ed). For a recent assessment that doubts the existence of the fallacy, see Stephen Darwall, Allan Gibbard, and Peter Railton, *Toward Fin de Siecle Ethics: Some Trends,* 101 Phil. Rev. 115, 115–20 (1992).
87. UCC § 2-103(1)(b) provides that "'good faith' in the case of a merchant means honesty in fact and the observance of reasonable commercial standards of fair dealing in the trade."
88. See Karl N. Llewellyn, *The Common Law Tradition* (1960).
89. See text accompanying notes 107–12 infra.
90. The decision to create a code was combined with the political instincts not to publicize the project as a codification. William Hawkland, who served as Llewellyn's research assistant, suggests that if Llewellyn had publicized his intention to codify the commercial law, the UCC would "probably have died aborning." Hawkland, *The UCC and the Civil Codes,* supra n. 21 at 233. But, nevertheless, a code by any other name. . . .
91. One can debate the point of whether or not the Code is a "true code." There is respectable academic argument either way. On the side of the "true code" advocates can be placed the strong set of normative principles to guide in Code interpretation that § 1-102 provides, the uniform jurisprudential underpinnings generated by systematic recourse to commercial context, and the pervasive reliance on "reasonableness and other supereminent norms." See, e.g., Richard Buxbaum, *Is the Uniform Commercial Code a Code?,* Rechtsrealismus, multikulturelle Gesellschaft und Handelsrecht, 197, 220 (Duncker & Humbolt, Berlin 1994) (arguing that the UCC is a code "within the American frame of

reference"); William D. Hawkland, *Uniform Commercial "Code" Methodology,* 1962 U. Ill. L.F. 291 (same). On the other side, one can invoke § 1-103, which purports to make the UCC dependent on extra-UCC law. See Homer Kripke, *The Principles Underlying the Drafting of the Uniform Commercial Code,* 1962 U. Ill. L.F. 321. For further views, see John Gedid, *UCC Methodology: Taking a Realistic Look at the Code,* 29 W & M L. Rev. 341 (1988); Robert A. Hillman, *Construction of the Uniform commercial Code: UCC § 1-103 and "Code" Methodology,* 18 B.C. Indust. & Com. L. Rev. 655 (1977).

But § 1-103 is a slim reed on which to hang the argument that the Code is not a "code." The provision does not operate as a dynamic incorporation mechanism. Recourse to the law merchant and to the "law relative to capacity to contract, principal and agent, estoppel, fraud, misrepresentation, duress, coercion, mistake, bankruptcy, or other validating or invalidating cause" is only appropriate "unless displaced by the particular provisions of this Act." UCC § 1-102, which specifies liberal construction to promote the underlying policies of clarification, expansion of commercial practices, and uniformity, is precisely the sort of "particular provision" that displaces the common law. Thus, the primary effect of § 1-103 is to incorporate noncontroversial default rules and subject them to the very same interpretive methodology that influences the interpretation of the Code-supplied defaults. In the sense that it matters here, therefore, the Code is a "true code" in that it has a self-contained mechanism for interpretation and expansion of internally generated rules and principles of interpretation.

92. Grant Gilmore, *Legal Realism: Its Cause and Cure,* 70 Yale L.J. 1037, 1043 (1961); Hawkland, *The UCC and the Civil Codes,* supra n. 21at 235 et seq.; Hawkland, *Uniform Commercial "Code" Methodology,* supra n. 91 at 291.
93. Grant Gilmore, *Legal Realism,* supra n. 92 at 1043.
94. UCC § 1-102 (1994). One of the profound ironies of the Code is that among the enumerated purposes of § 1-102 is to "make uniform the law among the various jurisdictions." The very provision that led to this purpose being fulfilled in a formal sense sows the seeds for failure in a substantive sense.
95. Mitchell Franklin, *On the Legal Method of the Uniform Commercial Code,* 16 Law & Contemp. Prob. 330, 333 (1951). This claim seems confirmed by comment 1 to § 1-102: "This Act is drawn to provide flexibility . . . to make it possible for the law embodied in this Act to be developed by the courts in the light of unforeseen and new circumstances and practices."
96. One obvious question, given the decision by the Code's proponents to adopt a civil law approach, is to ask how the civil law countries treat the creation and interpretation of commercial law. Here it is significant to note that in countries with a civil code, commercial relations are not typically governed by the civil code. Transactions among commercial actors typically are governed by separate laws, and even when they are denominated "codes" are less codelike in the sense of being hermetic and self-contained. Moreover, cases frequently come before specialized courts or industry-based arbitration. Ugo Mattei, *Efficiency and Equal Protection in the New European Contract Law: Mandatory, Default and Enforcement Rules,* 39 Va. J. Int'l L. 537, 540–3 (1999); Rudolf B. Schlesinger et al., *Comparative Law: Cases-Text-Materials* 276–9 (6th ed. 1998). In a sense, therefore, the marriage of code form with the making of commercial law was without precedent elsewhere. My tentative claim, moreover, is that the marriage is suboptimal in several respects: (1) common law courts are being asked to perform tasks

under the UCC that they don't do very well, and (2) given that Llewellyn envisioned a completely different dispute resolution system, it is folly to separate substantive methodology from the dispute resolution mechanism.

97. Hawkland, supra n. 21 at 235 et seq.
98. The tension that underlies this approach is revealed in § 1-102, which purports to set out the general purposes and interpretive framework of the Code. Thus, § 1-102 declares that "[t]his act shall be liberally construed and applied to promote its underlying purposes and policies," which include "(b) to permit the continued expansion of commercial practices through custom, usage and the agreement of the parties," *and* "(c) to make uniform the law among the various jurisdictions." UCC § 1-102(2)(b), 1–102(2)(c). Unhappily, these two statements of purpose are not harmonious. The incorporation goal of § 1-102(2)(b) asks courts to engage in an exercise in particularization: to interpret specific Code provisions according to the particular practices of specific commercial subgroups. The uniformity goal of § 1-102(2)(c), on the other hand, asks courts to engage in an exercise in generalization: to interpret particular Code provisions according to the general purposes and policies of the Code itself. The result has been a confusing signal to courts, which have generally chosen the worst of both worlds.
99. Recall that efficient standardization requires not only that the present stock of standard terms and defaults be preserved but that, as they become incrusted with rote usage over time and as new practices develop that demand new legal arrangements, the standardization process evolves new forms and coordinates the move to the novel terms. See Goetz and Scott, *The Limits of Expanded Choice,* supra n. 7 at 288–9.
100. Another virtue of the common law, given these factors, is that litigation and legal argument are much less costly under the common law scheme. For example, as between context-free arguments about what "F.A.S." ought to mean, and arguments about what the relevant commercial customs are, the former are significantly cheaper than the latter. Moreover, litigating commercial reasonableness is costly in another way – there is a substantial error cost, a risk that courts will not get the custom right. Commercial arrangements, after all, are anchored in industries with which courts may have little familiarity. See, generally, Craswell, *Do Trade Customs Exist?,* supra n. 33.

    The combination of these costs quite probably impel some commercial actors to invest, not in producing evidence and argument about new commercial customs for incorporation into the Code, but rather in avoiding the Code altogether, by arbitration or choice-of-law agreements or by other, more informal, means. In sum, perhaps the Code doesn't incorporate new defaults because the mechanism by which the defaults are produced is too costly and that cost drives parties more to litigation avoidance than to law production. See text accompanying notes 107 to 113 infra.
101. See Bernstein, *Merchant Law,* supra n. 69.
102. Bernstein, *Merchant Law,* supra n. 69. I advanced this explanation for the dichotomy between bright-line default rules and flexible commercial practice in an earlier paper. See Scott, *A Relational Theory of Default Rules,* supra n. 47 at 613–5.
103. Cf. David Charney, *The New Formalism in Contract,* 66 U. Chi. L. Rev. 842, 854–7 (1999) (suggesting that the formalist trade rules may instead reflect the capture of these trade organizations by large firms that use formal rules to appropriate rents from smaller firms within the industry).
104. There are other illustrations of commercial parties opting out of ill-fitting default rules

by developing standard terms that create customized risk allocations. Perhaps the best example is the common practice in the purchase and sale of hard goods of using standard form contract terms that trump the Code's warranty scheme for allocating quality risks as well as the Code's scheme for salvaging broken contracts through the mechanisms of rejection, acceptance, revocation of acceptance, cure, etc. In the place of Code warranties and the rules for rejection et al., parties who trade in hard goods typically substitute standardized "repair and replacement" clauses. Such clauses purport to divide quality risks between buyer and seller and to displace the binary default rules governing revocation of acceptance and cure (and perhaps rejection as well). See Alan Schwartz and Robert E. Scott, *Sales Law and the Contracting Process* 204–9, 308–9 (2d ed. 1991). Unfortunately, the standard repair and replacement clauses have been subject to disparate interpretations under the Code, producing exactly the kinds of jurisdictional uncertainty costs that the Code was designed to reduce. Compare, e.g., *Myrtle Beach Pipeline Corp. v. Emerson Electric Co.*, 843 F. Supp 1027 (D. S.C. 1993) to *Earl M. Jorgensen Co. v. Mark Construction, Inc.*, 540 P.2d 978 (Haw. 1975) and *International Financial Services, Inc. v. Franz,* 23 UCC Rep 2d 1078 (Minn. 1994) to *Chattlos v. NCR,* 635 F.2d 1081 (3d Cir. 1986).

105. Revisions have either been promulgated or are planned for every article of the UCC, save Article 7 (Documents of Title). At least one scholar predicts that, "in all probability," Article 7 will be revised as well. Richard E. Speidel et al., *Studies in Contract Law* 9 (1997).
106. Fred H. Miller, *Realism Not Idealism in Uniform Laws – Observations from the Revision of the UCC,* 39 So. Tex. L. Rev. 707 (1998).
107. See discussion in n. 27 supra.
108. See Schwartz and Scott, *The Political Economy of Private Legislatures,* supra n. 25 at 637–50; Scott, *The Politics of Article 9,* supra n. 23 at 1818–21. For applications of this analysis to international lawmaking, see Paul Stephan, *Accountability and International Lawmaking: Rules, Rents and Legitimacy,* 17 Nw. J. Int'l L. & Bus. 681 (1997).
109. In other words, interest group competition in this setting leads to defensive rather than offensive lobbying strategies. See, generally, Schwartz and Scott, *The Political Economy of Private Legislatures,* supra n. 25.
110. Richard E. Speidel, *Contract Formation and Modification Under Revised Article 2,* 35 W & M L. Rev. 1305, 1311 (1994).
111. See discussion in n. 27 supra.
112. As reported by the director of the ALI to the members, the drafting committee has been asked "to preserve the substantive gains in the (earlier) version . . . while restoring some of the language of the original Article 2 with which lawyers and business people are comfortable." Letter from Lance Liebman, ALI Director, to the Members of the ALI, September 17, 1999.
113. In particular, Articles 3,4,5,8, and 9 that purport to regulate credit, payment, and financing transactions are different in kind and conception from Article 2 and its progeny. These provisions are characterized, for example, by many more bright-line rules rather than vague standards. The appearance of many precise, bright-line rules may well result from the desire of a dominant interest group to preserve its victory in the legislative process by confining the discretion of the courts. See Schwartz and Scott, *The Political Economy of Private Legislatures,* supra n. 25 at 624–33. While interest

group dominance raises difficult policy issues, these are different questions from the kind that are stimulated by the vague rules that interest group competition produces in the Article 2 context.

114. See Lisa Bernstein, *The Questionable Empirical Basis for Article 2's Incorporation Strategy: A Preliminary Inquiry,* 66 U. Chi. L. Rev. 710 (1999). But see Jody S. Kraus and Steven D. Walt, *In Defense of the Incorporation Strategy,* this volume (arguing that Bernstein's empirical data show at most the dearth of uniform, trade-wide customs in the early part of the twentieth century but do not exclude the possibility that relevant trade practices do, in fact, exist in particular subgroups today).

115. The repetitious use of express terms generates two special problems: *rote use* and *encrustation.* Each of these is a feature of what is commonly designated as "boilerplate." Rote usage may develop as a kind of "contractual overkill" in which terms are used by rote so consistently that they are robbed of their meaning. For example, the recitation of the phrase "signed and sealed" continues to be prevalent in contracts that are already enforceable and where the "seal" has no legal effect. Nonetheless, rote terms such as these are repeated because the parties have no incentive to eliminate a term that is seen as costless to include, especially if they thereby incur a risk, albeit a small one, of jeopardizing the formally understood meaning of their agreement. Needless repetition pf such phrases imposes a cost on those parties who actually seek to use the formal term operationally only to discover that its meaning has been emptied by prior, needless repetition. A related problem with the maintenance of the stock of express, formal terms is encrustation, or the overlaying of legal jargon to the point where the intelligibility of language deteriorates. This sort of jargon-laded boilerplate robs words and phrases of their communicative properties, making them less reliable as true signals of what the parties really intended. See Goetz and Scott, *The Limits of Expanded Choice,* supra n. 7 at 288–9.

6

In Defense of the Incorporation Strategy

JODY S. KRAUS AND STEVEN D. WALT†

I. Introduction

Contract law must provide rules for interpreting the meaning of express terms and default rules for filling contractual gaps. Article 2 of the Uniform Commercial Code provides the same response to both demands: It incorporates the norms of commercial practice.[1] This "incorporation strategy" has recently come under attack. Although some question the incorporation strategy for gap-filling, recent scholarship criticizes the incorporation strategy for interpretation as well.[2] Critics charge that the expected rate of interpretive error under an incorporationist interpretive regime is so excessive that almost any plain-meaning regime would be preferable.

The attack on the incorporation strategy for interpretation is fundamentally flawed. The best interpretive regime is one that, all else equal, minimizes the sum of interpretive error costs and the costs of specifying contract terms.[3] Critics of the incorporation strategy have focused exclusively on the former and completely ignored the latter. Yet the chief virtue of the incorporation strategy for interpretation is its promise to yield specification costs well below that of plain-meaning regimes. Even if plain-meaning regimes have lower interpretive error costs, the incorporation strategy is superior if its lower specification costs outweigh its higher interpretive error costs. Moreover, most critics treat their objections to Article 2 as objections to the incorporation strategy generally. But Article 2 is just one possible institutional variant of the incorporation strategy. All of the sources of interpretive error critics identify can be substantially reduced, if not avoided, by making feasible alterations to Article 2 that nonetheless preserve its incorporationist character.

This chapter defends the incorporation strategy as a method of contractual interpretation. Part II analyzes the debate between incorporation and plain-meaning regimes. After explaining the comparative and empirical nature of this debate, we present the intuitive empirical case for believing that incorporationist interpretive regimes will yield significantly lower specification costs than plain-meaning regimes. Part III considers recent objections to the incorporation strategy for interpretation. These objections identify several potential sources of interpretive error and offer both a priori and empirical arguments to suggest these errors are likely to be extensive in any incorporation regime. We argue that these criticisms overstate the probable extent of interpretive error under Article 2, and that all of the kinds of interpretive errors identified can be significantly reduced by feasible changes to Article 2. Part IV describes the salient features in Article 2 that implement the incorporation strategy and presents possible amendments to reduce the extent of the interpretive errors identified in Part III. Given the distinction between the incorporation strategy and its implementation, Article 2 can accommodate these amendments without abandoning the incorporation strategy. Part V concludes by summarizing the argument for favoring the incorporation strategy for interpreting contracts among a heterogeneous group of contractors: Because the lower contract specification costs of a carefully designed incorporation regime will outweigh its higher interpretive error costs, it is likely to have a lower sum of specification and interpretive error costs than a plain-meaning regime.

II. The Structure of the Incorporation Debate

The contemporary debate about the role of commercial norms in contract interpretation typically pits the incorporation strategy against a plain-meaning regime. Although the notion of plain-meaning at work is seldom clarified, for our purposes we need only roughly describe it. We understand "plain meaning" to be rule- or convention-based sentence meaning independent of the particular context of sentence use. Plain meaning is literal sentence meaning.[4] We also count as plain-meaning approaches ones that exclude commercial custom, even if they rely on other contextual evidence to determine meaning. This extension of "plain meaning" preserves the contrast between the incorporation strategy and plain-meaning regimes. It is of course another matter whether literal sentence meaning exists or is useful in resolving the range of interpretive disputes litigated. In the course of defending the incorporation strategy against plain-meaning regimes, we take into account the possibility that the plain meaning of terms sometimes will not be clear, and in some cases may not exist. We do not, however, take a position on debates over the inherent limitations of plain-meaning regimes.

We should note at the outset, however, that the contest between incorporationist and plain-meaning regimes arises most directly when contractual disputes pit an interpretation based on an ideally precise and unique commercial norm against an interpretation based on an equally precise and unique plain meaning. In such cases, the different results under each interpretive strategy are clear. But in many cases, the commercial norm and "plain-meaning" candidates will be somewhat vague and ambiguous. In these cases, even the proper application of either strategy will serve at best to limit the range of interpretive disagreement. Neither strategy will be useful in choosing among the possible interpretations within the remaining range of interpretations they identify. Some other interpretative strategy would be necessary to resolve disputes within that range. Similarly, in some extreme cases, there will be no relevant commercial norms or plain meaning to apply. Obviously, in these cases the proper application of either strategy will not yield an interpretation. In one sense, then, the debate between incorporationist and plain-meaning regimes is limited to the domain of interpretive questions susceptible, at least in part, to proper resolution by both approaches.

However, the merits of both approaches turn not only on the likelihood and seriousness of the interpretive errors that result when each is applied to resolve a dispute that at least in principle it can be used properly to resolve. The merits also turn on the likelihood and seriousness of the interpretive errors that result when each approach is applied to resolve a dispute that even in principle it cannot be used properly to resolve. Where commercial norms or plain meaning are indeterminate or do not bear on the interpretive issue in question, neither approach can select among possible meanings. Each approach will yield an expected aggregate cost of interpretive error both in cases where commercial norms or plain meaning are determinate and relevant and in cases where they are not. The approach that has the lower cost, all else equal, is superior. Of course, even if analysis reveals one regime to be superior to the other on these grounds, a third approach is necssary for resolving interpretive questions to which that strategy cannot be properly applied, such as when commercial norms or plain meaning are not available. We set this question aside, however, to focus exclusively on the relative merits of the incorporation and plain-meaning interpretive strategies.

Although the contemporary incorporation/plain-meaning debate arises in response to Llewellyn's explicit adoption of the incorporation strategy in Article 2, it has precisely the same structure as the classic and familiar debate between the subjective and objective theories of intent in the common law of contract. The same considerations that easily vindicate the objective theory of intent in contract law structure the debate between plain-meaning and incorporation interpretive regimes in both contract and sales law. However, because plain-meaning and incorporation regimes are both versions of objective theories of intent, these considerations do not so easily settle this debate.

The first lesson taught in first-year contracts is that contractual intent is objective rather than subjective. Even though one of the parties can prove that he or she understood the contractual term "dog" to mean cat, courts will interpret the term "dog" to mean dog. The lesson seems counterintuitive. The law of contract is designed to vindicate parties' intent, yet one party's subjective understanding of the meaning of the terms of the contract is, by itself, irrelevant to a court's interpretation of those terms.[5] The counterintuition rests on the erroneous presumption that subjective intent is static rather than dynamic. The party who assigns an idiosyncratic meaning to a contractual term might be surprised the first time he learns his subjective view is irrelevant to its judicial interpretation. But he will not be surprised again. The next time he enters into an agreement, the party will be careful to use terms according to the interpretation a court is likely to give them. Thus, if courts refuse to interpret terms according to the parties' subjective intent, parties will align their subject intent with the "objective" intent courts enforce. Contractors' choice of terms and the subjective meaning contractors assign to them are therefore a function of the contractors' expectation of how courts will interpret contractual terms. Contractual behavior can be explained and predicted only by a dynamic rather than static model.

The purpose of a theory of contractual interpretation therefore is not merely to select an interpretive rule that is most likely to reflect the parties' subjective intent. This goal can be secured by any interpretive rule that allows parties to predict the likely interpretation of their contractual terms with reasonable certainty. When there are equally predictable interpretive rules, the best rule allows the parties to secure their desired interpretation at the lowest cost. Consider an interpretive regime, for example, that enforced key contractual terms only if they appeared on an extensive menu of judicially constructed terms of art. A court would find an agreement that did not use these terms to specify its key provisions too indefinite and therefore unenforceable. Such a regime would provide an extremely high degree of predictability of judicial interpretation of contract terms. But this predictability would come at a price. Parties would be forced to choose between creating a legally unenforceable agreement or incurring the costs of learning and using the terms on the judicial menu, which might nonetheless vary from the terms they most prefer in their contract. The price of predictability, therefore, is the inefficiency of the resulting contract: Whenever the terms of a contract are at variance with the parties' most preferred terms, the expected joint value of the contract at the time of formation will be suboptimal.[6]

Thus, a perfect interpretive rule not only enables parties to predict a court's interpretation of contractual terms with complete certainty, but also allows parties to specify their desired contract at no cost. Real-world interpretive regimes therefore face an unavoidable trade-off between maximizing the predictability of contractual interpretation and maximizing the ability of the parties to specify the most efficient terms for their contracts. To maximize the ability of the parties to specify their most preferred terms, the parties' costs of specifying their most preferred terms must be minimized. Thus, all else equal, the optimal regime minimizes the sum of interpretive error and specification costs.[7] The costs of interpretive error consist of the losses due to both the prospect and actual incidence of interpretive error. The prospect of interpretive error leads to suboptimal reliance losses. These losses consist of the foregone benefits of the increased reliance that would be efficient in a regime of interpretive certainty, and the direct and opportunity costs of taking affirmative precautions to hedge against the prospect of interpretive error. The actual, rather than prospective, incidence of interpretive error leads to detrimental reliance losses. Specification costs are the costs parties incur in specifying their most preferred terms, such as learning and selecting from a judicially chosen menu of express terms.[8]

The justification for the objective theory of contractual intent is based not merely on the claim that it yields a high degree of predictability of contractual interpretation and thus a low prospect of interpretive error. It also turns on the low specification costs produced by the objective theory. The proposition that the objective theory will yield a high degree of interpretive predictability is based on two claims. The first is that most terms have a relatively clear, objective "plain" meaning, which consists of their most common interpretation. Because most people know the common interpretation of most terms, both contractors and judges ordinarily will be able to determine accurately objective meaning, and contractors will be able to predict accurately the likely interpretation of their contractual terms. The second claim is that the costs of learning a term's plain meaning will be lower on average than the costs of learning any alternative meaning these terms might be given. This second claim also supports the proposition that the objective theory of intent will yield low specification costs. The lower the costs of learning the judicially recognized meaning of terms, the lower contractors' specification costs. Further, under the objective theory, parties in principle will always be able to include any term they prefer in their contract. Unlike the hypothetical interpretive regime that limits parties to a finite list of judicially recognized key contractual terms, the objective theory offers contractors all the English language, which presumably provides an array of terms, each with plain meanings, sufficient to specify virtually any term parties might prefer.

At bottom, the case for the objective theory of intent is comparative. The objective theory of intent will yield an equilibrium producing a sum of interpretive error and specification costs. The choice between the objective theory and any competing theory is decided by determining which theory is expected to yield the equilibrium producing the lower sum of interpretive error and specification costs. If most English language terms have a clear, common, "plain" meaning known to most contractors and judges, or learned at low cost, these costs will not be great. Whether an alternative regime can produce an even lower sum of these costs remains an open empirical question.

The case for the objective theory of intent is traditionally made by comparing it to a purely subjective theory of intent. The objective theory of intent is defended on the ground that it yields an equilibrium with lower total interpretive error and specification costs than a purely subjective theory of intent. The case is easily convincing. Contractors and courts cannot determine or verify purely subjective intent. Because the interpretive error rate by courts and contractors under a subjective intent regime would be high, the total interpretive error costs would be high. Contract specification costs would also be high because parties would have great difficulty specifying terms with meanings that courts would reliably enforce. In contrast, if terms have an objective and verifiable plain meaning, the objective intent regime will clearly lead to an equilibrium with much lower aggregate interpretive error and specification costs. The move from subjective to objective intent in first-year contracts takes a class or two at most.

But the choice between objective and purely subjective theories of intent presents a false dichotomy. Most terms have multiple meanings that can be described along continua of objectivity and verifiability. If many terms have multiple objective meanings, the issue is not whether objective theories of interpretation should be preferred over subjective theories. Rather, it is how we should choose among various possible objective theories. The main objective competitors to plain-meaning regimes are incorporation regimes. Incorporation regimes, like plain-meaning regimes, are objective because they interpret contractual terms in light of objective and verifiable commercial practices. Thus, unlike the debate between objective and purely subjective theories of intent, the intramural debate between plain-meaning and incorporation regimes is far more difficult to assess. Both regimes constitute objective theories of interpretation and both require trade-offs between reductions in interpretive error costs and reductions in specification costs. The debate is a contest between competing empirical intuitions.

Intuitively, plain-meaning regimes are likely to lead to lower interpretive error costs than the incorporation regimes. Plain-meaning regimes posit a fairly clear set of non-domain-specific, common meanings associated with most terms, whereas incorporation regimes posit a set of fairly clear but domain-specific meanings. Even assuming both the generic "plain" meaning and the more specialized domain-specific meanings are equally clear, we would expect a higher rate of interpretive error under incorporation regimes because they require judges (and contractors) to choose among the various possible meanings of terms. Under a plain-meaning regime, the judicially recognized meaning of every term is unique. The only possible source of interpretive error is a misinterpretation of the plain meaning by contractors or judges. Under an incorporation regime, however, contractors and judges can mistakenly identify the domain for which a term's meaning is determined, in addition to misinterpreting the meaning of the term within that domain. Thus, there is only one opportunity for interpretive error under plain-meaning regimes. Incorporation regimes, however, present a second opportunity for interpretive error in addition to the same opportunity presented under plain-meaning regimes. Because the two types of mistakes are not correlated, incorporation regimes would be expected to have a higher rate of interpretive error than plain-meaning regimes, all else being equal.

But the comparative strength of the incorporation strategy is its potential for producing lower specification costs than the plain-meaning rule. The key presumption of the incorporation strategy is that contractors naturally and costlessly use terms that have domain-specific meanings. These terms presumably have evolved to address the particularized needs and expectations of contractors within a given domain. Their efficiency is analogous to the efficiency of terms of art within academic and technical disciplines. Terms of art allow participants familiar with a particular discipline effectively to communicate a complex thought with the ease of one specially defined word or phrase that is widely understood within the discipline.[9] Similarly, it would sometimes be cost-ineffective for some contractors to restate their understanding of all the dimensions of their contractual agreement using the plain meaning of terms. Indeed, some specialized or context-specific terms carry with them an array of implications that might be difficult even to bring to mind, let alone commit to paper. Nonetheless, just as the full connotations of even the plain meaning of terms can be specified by English speakers only when presented with a particular contextualized application, the implications of specialized contractual terms will be clear to the contractors, and every other participant in their trade or industry, only when particular contingencies arise in their relationship. They will nonetheless "know it when they see it."[10]

If courts interpret contractual terms by attempting to determine whether the parties intended to invoke their plain or domain-specific meaning, the specification costs for parties might be lower than under a plain-meaning regime. Under an incorporation regime, contractors can use the terms that express their intent most effectively at the lowest cost. Contractors will choose a less efficient term over a more efficient term whenever the additional cost of specifying the most efficient term exceeds the gains from using the more efficient term instead of the less efficient term. The incorporation strategy can save contractors specification costs by allowing them to use domain-specific meanings customized to suit the needs and expectations of their contracting context. A plain-meaning regime imposes on parties the additional costs of either translating the understandings already carried by the domain-specific meanings of available specialized terms into an equivalent statement using the plain meaning of terms, or settling on a less efficient contractual term that can be specified at a lower cost.

Moreover, the plain-meaning rule requires contractors to make sure they are not mistakenly relying on a domain-specific meaning rather than a plain meaning. In a complex contractual setting, it may prove extremely costly, and perhaps impossible, to identify all the unwritten interpretations of contractual terms that the contractors naturally and unconsciously presume to be mutually understood. Even when contractors knowingly operate under a plain-meaning regime, they will sometimes fail to realize that their understanding of the meaning of a term, particularly commonly used industry terms, will nonetheless not be judicially recognized. To be sure, such mistakes might be less frequent over time. But as long as domain-specific meanings exist, such mistakes are unlikely to disappear entirely.

Thus, the contest between plain-meaning and incorporation regimes turns on competing empirical hunches. Which is larger, the interpretive error costs saved under a plain-meaning regime or the specification costs saved under an incorporation regime? Any comparative analysis of plain-meaning and incorporation regimes that focuses exclusively on relative interpretive error costs is seriously incomplete. It must also take into account relative specification costs. The case for the incorporation strategy rests on its claim to significantly lower specification costs than plain-meaning regimes.

In Part III, however, we set aside this comparative question to consider the likelihood of interpretive error under incorporation regimes. The criticisms that allege extensive interpretive error under the incorporation strategy, we argue, are overdrawn and one-sided. They either exaggerate the likely extent of interpretive error under incorporation regimes or fail to acknowledge that the sources of interpretive error they identify apply equally to plain-meaning regimes.

III. The Critique of the Incorporation Strategy

Three different sorts of charges have been made against the incorporation interpretive strategy and in favor of a plain-meaning regime. Although often not distinguished from each other, each charge asserts the likelihood of a particular form of interpretive error. For ease of reference, we refer to the charges respectively as the "*existence,*" "*informal norms,*" and "*encrustation*" critiques. The existence and informal norms critiques are supported by both a priori reasoning and empirical studies. For each critique, we describe the kind of interpretive error it identifies. Our objective is to isolate the sources of these errors in order to clarify how they might be reduced by the amendments to Article 2 that we suggest in Part IV or by an alternative incorporation regime. Where appropriate, we also argue that these critiques either exaggerate the likely extent of interpretive error under an incorporation regime or fail to acknowledge that similar errors are likely to be equally extensive under a plain-meaning regime.

A. The Existence Critique

The existence critique argues, on both an empirical and a priori basis, that commercial practices might be less extensive and less clear than proponents of the incorporation strategy have supposed.[11] The extreme form of this critique suggests that commercial practices suitable for incorporation might not even exist. Were this the case, the incorporation strategy at best would be a useless interpretive strategy. Attempts to employ the strategy would end in a vain attempt to identify relevant commercial practices. At worst, fact finders might wrongly believe that a commercial practice exists and thus mistakenly interpret a contract term in light of the nonexistent commercial norm. But the extreme critique must overcome an extremely strong pretheoretical empirical presumption that widespread, identifiable, and effective commercial practices do exist. The near-universal insistence by merchants of all kinds that their conduct is governed, in large measure and important respects, by relatively clear commercial norms justifies a demand that evidence be presented for their nonexistence. To date, only one empirical study has been presented in support of the existence critique.

Lisa Bernstein has recently offered a case study to support the claim that "the pervasive existence of usages of trade and commercial standards, whose geographic reach is coextensive with the reach of the relevant trade, is a legal fiction rather than a merchant reality."[12] Her study examines the debates surrounding merchant industry efforts to codify commercial customs in the hay, grain and feed, textile, and silk industries near the turn of the century. She argues that these debates, as well as interview evidence and testimony of merchant associations when Article 2 was proposed, reveal widespread disagreement among merchants regarding the commercial customs in their trade. Specifically, Bernstein claims her evidence "casts doubt on the systematic existence of industry-wide unwritten customs that are generally known, geographically coextensive with the scope of trade, and implicitly assented to be market transactors."[13] Bernstein uses her evidence to argue primarily against the existence of what she calls "strong form Hayekian customs whose existence is assumed by the Code."[14] Although Bernstein allows that "some industry-wide usages of trade do exist, and highly local customs might have existed,"[15] she claims that her evidence nonetheless "strongly suggests that the types of customs that exist, even in these rather well-defined merchant communities, do not amount to anything close to the all-pervasive sets of implicit gap-filling provisions and dictionary-type interpretive guides assumed by the Code."[16] Instead, Bernstein claims that commercial customs that do exist at best constitute "weak-form customs" that "play an important role in the development of commercial relationships,"[17] but fall far short of the kind of customs required by the incorporation strategy.

Bernstein's study constitutes a worthwhile preliminary effort to uncover the nature and extent of commercial custom. But it does not make a convincing case against the existence of the kind of commercial practice posited by the incorporation strategy. The most important limitation of Bernstein's study is that, even by its own lights, it demonstrates at most that there were few, if any, uniform national customs in many commercial industries around the turn of the century. If the incorporation strategy required such customs to exist, Bernstein's study might provide reason to doubt the strategy's viability at least at the time Article 2 was created. But neither the incorporation strategy in general nor

Article 2 in particular requires that uniform industrywide commercial practices exist. Indeed, the commentary to Article 2 itself states that usage of trade should be used to interpret the language in contracts so that it means "what it may fairly be expected to mean to parties involved in the particular commercial transaction *in a given locality* or in a given vocation or trade."[18] If Bernstein's study is correct, the incorporation strategy at the turn of the century would have had limited value in interpreting contracts between merchants in localities with different customs. If local customs existed, however, the incorporation strategy would have been a viable strategy for interpreting local contracts.

But the evidence Bernstein presents to demonstrate the nonexistence of nationally uniform customs provides equally compelling support for the existence of precisely the extensive and robust local customs the incorporation strategy anticipates. Indeed, most of Bernstein's evidence of lack of nationally uniform customs is based on industry members' assertion that different customs existed in different locales.[19] The very codification efforts giving rise to the debates Bernstein examines presuppose the existence of extensive and important local customs. The objective of the codification efforts typically was not to create trade rules out of whole cloth but to *unify* industry customs and thereby eliminate preexisting, widespread differences between local customs.

As a critique of the incorporation strategy, Bernstein's study has at least two other weaknesses. First, the dearth of uniform, tradewide customs in the early part of the century provides poor evidence that such customs do not exist now.[20] Changes in the size and structure of the national economy make extrapolation to the present unsafe. By the end of the nineteenth century, extensive changes in transportation produced a national market in agriculture and manufacturing.[21] The national market expanded significantly throughout the first half of the twentieth century, as shown by indexes such as freight-tonnage and freight-mileage shipped by commercial carriers.[22] Merchants' desire at the turn of the century to replace local with uniform custom is completely consistent with uniform customs now existing. As Bernstein repeatedly acknowledges, the express purpose of the codification efforts she studied was to replace local custom with uniform industry custom.[23] In order to better compete in a geographically larger market, merchants likely felt they could not wait for a nationally uniform customary practice to evolve at the rate at which local customs had evolved. An expanding national market is likely to increase the desire for a single industry custom. Codification efforts at the turn of the century suggest only that commercial custom lagged behind changes in patterns of distribution. They do not show that nationally uniform custom does not exist today. Thus, earlier trade practices are bad indicators of contemporary industry practices bearing on custom.

Second, although Bernstein claims the evidence she considers demonstrates that industrywide customs did not exist, much of the evidence at most establishes that some customs were not ideally precise. For example, Bernstein reports that members of the National Hay Association disagreed over whether the term "carload" meant ten tons or twelve tons.[24] Such evidence at most establishes that customary understanding was not always sufficiently precise to resolve any possible interpretive dispute. Assuming the debates accurately reflect the lack of consensus in the industry over the definition of a "carload," custom could not be invoked to adjudicate a dispute between merchants over whether a contract calling for a carload of hay to be delivered would be satisfied by a ten ton rather than twelve ton shipment of hay. But on this evidence, it is plausible to suppose that custom does establish that an eight ton shipment would not constitute a "carload" and that a twelve ton shipment would constitute a "carload." Thus, evidence of imprecise customs is not evidence of no custom at all. The incorporation strategy is useful even if it incorporates imprecise customs, so long as those customs serve at least to define a range of reasonable and unreasonable disagreement over the meaning of contract terms.[25] Bernstein's empirical case against the existence of commercial practice is unconvincing.

However, the existence critique, in either its empirical or a priori form, can be stated more modestly. Richard Craswell offers an a priori version of the modest critique.[26] Craswell's target is the view that the incorporation strategy is justified because it "enable[s] judges or legislators to adopt efficient [or fair] rules of law even if they lack the economic [or ethical] expertise to design efficient [or fair] rules on their own. As long as judges or legislators can identify those communities whose customs are likely to be efficient [or fair] (the argument goes), they can simply adopt legal rules that mimic those communities' customs, without having to analyze directly the efficiency [or fairness] of the resulting rules."[27] Craswell believes that this justification implicitly presumes that customs take the form of bright-line rules, which require little if any exercise of individual judgment to identify and apply. But Craswell argues that customs by their nature can be identified and applied only by the case-specific exercise of individual judgment. If courts must engage in individual judgments of their own, or defer to individual judgments of others, in order to identify and apply a custom, then, he concludes, the incorporation strategy cannot be justified on the ground that it enables courts to avoid making or relying on such judgments.[28] Further, once it is conceded that custom identification and application requires at least the individual judgment of merchants, Craswell argues that custom no longer provides an alternative to interpretation based on substantive, normative analysis. If the justification for reliance on customs is efficiency, courts might consult efficiency experts directly, rather than attempting to identify and apply customs, which in turn ultimately requires the same individual efficiency judgments to be made. Similarly, if the justification for reliance on customs is fairness, ethics experts might be consulted directly.[29]

Craswell's argument can be put succinctly as follows: Because the process of incorporating commercial custom inevitably relies on the exercise of individual judgment, rather than the judgment-free application of bright-line rules, the incorporation strategy does not avoid the need for courts, directly or indirectly, to rely on individual judgment to decide cases. But if courts are going to rely on individual judgment to decide cases, it is no longer clear they should rely on the judgments of merchants, as incorporation strategies typically require, rather than the judgments of nonmerchant experts such as economists or philosophers.

The central premise of Craswell's argument is, we believe, uncontroversial. Identifying and applying custom requires individual judgment. The question is how the need for individual judgment bears on the viability of the incorporation strategy. Its most obvious implication is that in order to identify and apply the custom relevant to interpreting a disputed contract, the incorporation strategy requires courts to rely on the exercise of their own or others' individual judgment. But the need for individual judgment is not only congenial to existing and proposed incorporationist regimes, it is in fact presupposed by them. Article 2 contemplates the use of testimony by experienced merchants to identify and apply relevant custom, and as Craswell notes, judges exercise their own judgment in deciding Article 2 cases. Further, Llewellyn's original proposal for implementing the incorporation strategy contemplated that Article 2 cases would be decided by merchant juries. Presumably, the members of such juries would use their individual judgment to identify and apply custom relevant to resolving the dispute before them. Craswell's argument also suggests incorporationist regimes might do best by relying on the judgment of nonmerchant experts rather than merchants or judges. But even this argument recommends that incorporationist regimes take a particular form, not that incorporation ought to be abandoned.

There is, however, a fundamental criticism of the incorporation strategy embedded in Craswell's argument. Despite his claim that his title, "Do Trade Customs Exist?," is "semifacetious," Craswell's argument can be read as denying the idea of custom itself. Craswell suggests that abandoning the notion that custom consists in bright-line rules, and acknowledging the inevitability of using individual judgment to interpret custom, makes custom-based interpretive methodologies equivalent to interpretive methodologies based solely on individual judgment. Thus, when the incorporation strategy adverts to custom to interpret or fill a gap in a contract, it is equivalent to an interpretive strategy that simply requires the exercise of individual judgment without invoking the notion of custom at all. Thus, according to Craswell, there is then no appreciable difference between the incorporation strategy and nonincorporationist interpretive regimes that rely on the individual judgments of experts, such as economists or philosophers: "if individual witnesses must draw on their own analysis of particular contexts, then they are providing an assessment that is not entirely different from what would be provided by any other expert whom a court might consult, such as an economist or a philosopher."[30]

The critical flaw in Craswell's argument is in his description of the interpreter's individual judgment. Craswell claims that the judgments of merchants and nonmerchant experts are "not entirely different." In fact, they are entirely different. Two important differences distinguish the judgments made by each group: their likely reliability and what is being judged. As to reliability, first note that interpreting custom requires a preliminary determination of the instances of past commercial behavior that in part constitute the relevant custom. These instances constrain interpretations of relevant custom. The worth of competing interpretations in part will be a function of their fit with these instances. This means that an analysis counts as an interpretation of custom only if it adequately fits relevant commercial behavior and attitudes. Otherwise, the analysis is not an interpretation of anything. It instead serves as a recommended decision rule, not a description of a going convention. Thus, even if the interpretation of custom relies on efficiency judgments, it cannot rely exclusively on them. Further, the preliminary determination of past commercial behavior must be based on pretheoretical intuitions informed by experience. The use of a particular theory to select behaviors and attitudes that constrain the interpretive process would be question-begging.[31] The question therefore is whether merchants' judgments identifying the relevant commercial behavior underlying custom are likely to be more reliable than the judgments of nonmerchant experts.

Merchants' judgments in the matter are likely to be more reliable. Their familiarity with the typical behavior and attitudes of other merchants in a particular trade make it so. To be sure, individual judgment plays other roles besides determining the instances of commercial behavior and attitudes that interpretations of custom must fit. For example, the choice between interpretations satisfying the criterion of fit might turn in part on the application of some normative principle such as efficiency. Craswell therefore might be correct that an economist would do at least as well as a merchant noneconomist in determining the implications of the efficiency principle. But even then the economist has a disadvantage in judging how prior commercial practice trades off efficiency for fit, making its judgments of fit less reliable than the judgments of the merchant. Any advantage its expertise gives in applying an efficiency principle does not improve the reliability of its judgments about commercial practice.

Craswell muddies this assessment of comparative reliability by the example he uses. He focuses on the rare case in which the best interpretation of custom requires exclusive application of a single principle, such as efficiency or fairness. Given the nature of the principle, the judgments necessary to interpret the custom's application in a particular case are reliably made by the expert, –

an economist or philosopher, respectively. Merchants plausibly have no particular advantage given by their greater exposure to commercial practice. But most customs are more complex in their underlying principles than the ones Craswell discusses. They often involve multiple, competing principles in which the difficulty of application need not derive from a vagueness of their terms. For example, a commercial custom of price adjustment in response to cost increases might require efficiency to be balanced against a norm of equality or risk sharing. Although an economist might make superior efficiency judgments, and a philosopher superior distributional judgments, only merchants in the trade have exposure to instances in which both values constituting the custom are in play. Greater exposure to the more complex principle makes their individual judgments about custom more likely to be accurate.

Finally, even if the best justification of a custom is based on efficiency, it does not follow that the best interpretation of custom is itself based on efficiency. A custom justified by efficiency concerns might require individuals to make only non-efficiency-based judgments when interpreting custom. Rawls famously illustrated this point by imagining an institution of punishment based exclusively on deontic rules but justified entirely on consequentialist grounds.[32] To identify and apply the rules of the institution of punishment correctly, participants in that institution, such as judges and jury members, can engage only in deontic reasoning. Despite the consequentialist justification of their institution, the individual judgments of participants in the institution of punishment necessary for the correct interpretation of the rules of punishment do not, because they cannot, consist of judgments about the consequences of their decisions. Similarly, even if the best justification for commercial customs is based on their efficiency, the individual judgments necessary for the correct interpretation of custom need not therefore consist of judgments about the efficiency of possible decision rules. Indeed, such judgments might consistently yield incorrect interpretations of commercial customs. Because an economist could judge only efficiency, his or her judgment would likely be less reliable than the non-efficiency-based judgment of an experienced merchant.

As to what is being judged, it should now be evident that nonmerchant experts are ordinarily most competent to make judgments only within their area of expertise, but not about a custom per se. Merchants ordinarily are most competent to make judgments concerning commercial practice, but not about efficiency per se. If the latter requires exclusively the former, as it does in Craswell's example of an atypical custom, both merchants interpreting a practice and economists analyzing the efficiency of possible contract terms are in some sense making judgments about the same thing: A judgment interpreting the custom is reducible to a judgment of the efficiency of contract terms. Except in this rare instance, however, the interpretive judgments of merchants and the efficiency judgments of economists are about different things. Thus, ordinarily there will be no difficulty in discerning the difference between an interpretive methodology that incorporates custom and one that need only take into account the individual judgments of nonmerchant experts.

However, suppose Craswell's extreme, reductivist account of custom were correct. The individual judgments required for interpreting custom might then be equivalent to the individual judgments of nonmerchant experts. This fact might undermine the economic justification of the incorporation strategy for gap-filling. Suppose that justification holds that incorporating custom allows courts to avoid reliance on individual efficiency judgments, which are likely to be less efficient than evolved customary practices. Obviously, if the process of interpreting these practices itself requires reliance on individual efficiency judgments, the incorporation strategy cannot constitute an alternative to deciding cases by reliance on individual efficiency judgments. But even if this critique were accepted, it would not similarly undermine the justification we have presented for the incorporation strategy for interpretation. That justification holds that interpreting contractual terms according to their customary meaning will save parties the costs of specifying the same contract provisions using terms that will be interpreted according to their plain meaning. The potential savings in specification costs created by the incorporation strategy does not depend on the extent to which the interpretation of custom relies on individual judgment, nor on whose individual judgment it relies. As long as the parties prefer their terms to be given a customary interpretation, rather than a plain-meaning interpretation, and the incorporation strategy accurately interprets terms according to their customary meaning, the incorporation strategy will economize on specification costs.

Craswell's a priori existence critique properly dispels the naive conception of custom as bright-line rules and raises the interesting question of how individuals exercise the judgment necessary to interpret custom. It also rightly points out that the judgment of experts, in addition to merchants, might be relevant to the interpretation of some customs, and in extreme cases, might be dispositive. But the critique is wrong to the extent that it suggests that the need for individual judgment eliminates any relevant differences between interpretation by custom and interpretation by nonmerchant experts. Moreover, even if this conclusion could be sustained, it would not threaten the viability of the incorporation strategy for interpretation.

B. *The Informal Norms Critique*

The informal norms critique points out that not all commercial practices provide good evidence of the intended meaning of contractual terms. Some commercial practices are indicative of "formal" norms, which parties intend to be given legal effect, while others indicate "informal" norms, which parties intend not to be given legal effect. The paradigm evidence of a formal norm is provided by tradewide contractual practices. For example, suppose that 90% of a representative sample of contracts for the sale of horses disclaimed the warranties of merchantability and fitness for a particular purpose. There is little question that this evidence establishes the existence of a commercial norm of warranty disclaimer in sales of horses and that this norm is intended by contractors to be given legal effect.

In contrast, informal norms are common commercial practices that are intended by their practitioners not to be given legal effect. The paradigm evidence of an informal norm is provided by tradewide testimony that a practice is not intended to be given legal effect. For example, suppose that horse sellers routinely exchange or return the price for lame horses that were accepted by their buyers. But every horse seller will testify that this practice constitutes a legally optional accommodation rather than a legally binding obligation. In fact, sellers might well claim that the desirability of the accommodation practice turns crucially on the availability of the legally enforceable right to enforce the original trade. Such an informal practice might arise in order to preserve an ongoing relationship with a set of repeat buyers.[33] But the same transactors who follow these norms might do so only because they take themselves to have preserved the option of enforcing their more stringent contractual rights – in this case, refusing to exchange or refund the price of the horse. Contractors might invoke their stricter, contractual rights whenever they consider their contracting partner to be behaving opportunistically. Such behavior is more likely at the end of a contractual relationship, when further contractual interaction between the parties is unlikely, rather than in the middle of an ongoing relationship.[34] In specifying the terms of their contract, parties attempt to create an optimal mix of formal and informal norms to mediate their relationship. The informal norms critique argues that the incorporation strategy, as implemented in Article 2, undermines this optimal mix by formalizing informal norms.

Thus, the informal norms critique presupposes that contractors intentionally select from a rich set of formal and informal norms an optimal combination of norms to regulate their conduct. If the premise of the critique is that incorporation of informal norms undermines this optimal mix, there must be many formal and informal norms for courts to confuse with one another. After all, if there are few commercial norms of any sort, as the existence critique maintains, incorporating informal norms would hardly present a serious problem.

Like the existence critique, the informal norms critique has both an a priori and an empirical form. The a priori informal norms critique simply relies on the presence of some informal norms to conclude that an incorporation regime such as Article 2 might incorporate an informal rather than a formal norm. Clearly, the possibility exists that informal norms sometimes will be incorporated under an incorporation regime, and clearly such incorporation is undesirable in any interpretive regime. But in order to constitute a critique of the incorporation strategy, much more is required than establishing the mere possibility that an incorporation regime might incorporate some informal norms. The informal norm critique must instead show that even well-designed incorporation regimes inevitably would so frequently incorporate informal norms that they would be inferior to most plain-meaning regimes on that account alone. There is, however, no reason to believe that all incorporation regimes would incorporate informal norms frequently, let alone so frequently that the entire incorporation approach must be rejected. In fact, there is no reason to believe that Article 2 itself frequently incorporates informal norms, or that feasible revisions to Article 2 could not ensure that such instances would be rare.

Article 2 does not explicitly direct courts to distinguish between formal and informal norms. However, Article 2 clearly does not contemplate or condone the incorporation of informal norms. No court applying Article 2 would intentionally incorporate informal norms. This is because an informal norm cannot be evidence that the term is intended to be enforced. In other words, the evidence goes to something that is not a term of the contract. Indeed, the informality of a norm entails that no term in the contract at issue can be interpreted as having a meaning governed by the norm. It is simply no part of the parties' enforceable set of obligations. Thus, any court that identified a norm as informal must already have concluded that the norm cannot be used as a basis for interpreting the meaning of the contract. The court's prior determination of the norm's informality would constitute its finding that the norm does not inform the meaning of any of the contract's terms.

Accordingly, the incorporation strategy is not embarrassed by commercial practices reflecting both formal and informal norms. Instead, these practices simply raise another potential source of interpretive error. Under Article 2, for example, judges might mistakenly incorporate an informal norm in the process of interpretation. The possibility is unexceptional. Judges can make mistakes in passing on any aspect of the sales contract, from formation questions to remedies. So the question is whether this kind of interpretive error will be so extensive and costly that Article 2 and other incorporation regimes will be less efficient than available nonincorporation interpretive regimes. The answer depends on the precise design of the incorporation process and on the base rate of observable contractual activity that is inconsistent with the legal duties contractors intentionally undertake in their contracts. When both variables are taken into account, the probability of erroneous incorporation of informal norms is unlikely to be as extensive as the current literature suggests.

Consider how Article 2 directs courts to determine the existence of a commercial norm in the process of interpreting contractual terms. The predicate for a finding that a usage of trade exists is an empirically observable regularity in the conduct of a majority of contractors in the relevant trade.[35] The predicate for a finding that a course of dealing or course of performance exists is a pattern of observable behavior by the parties.[36] Before the finder of fact can incorporate a norm under Article 2, it must first have evidence of observable regularities in the conduct of merchants or the parties to the contract in dispute. Unless the finder of fact ignores this requirement, no norm, whether informal or formal, can be incorporated into an agreement in the absence of a prior finding of the existence of a pattern of observable conduct that serves as evidence of the norm. Therefore, in order for an informal norm to be incorporated under Article 2, there must be some pattern of behavior of merchants in the relevant trade or the parties to the contract in dispute that provides observable evidence of the norm.

Erroneous incorporation of informal norms is possible only to the extent that such norms are evidenced by observable patterns of behavior. The existence of informal norms not evidenced by observable patterns of behavior has no effect on the probability of erroneous incorporation of informal norms. Therefore, the probability of courts mistakenly incorporating informal norms is a function of the ratio of observable patterns of behavior in which contractors are entitled to engage under their contract to observable patterns of behavior in which contractors are not entitled to engage under their contract. All else equal, the higher this ratio, the lower the rate of mistaken incorporation of informal norms will be. If this ratio is very low, however, the likely rate of mistaken incorporation of informal norms, all else equal, will be much higher. At some point, the probability of such errors might be so high as to call into question the viability of the incorporation strategy itself, and thus Article 2 as well.

There is no empirical study that attempts directly to measure the proportion of formal to informal norms evidenced by observable patterns of behavior in commercial settings. Thus, in estimating the likelihood of mistaken incorporation of informal norms under the incorporation strategy, lawmakers must speculate about the proportion likely to obtain. Our speculation is that observable patterns of commercial behavior more often than not reflect formal rather than informal norms.[37] We base our speculation on two considerations. First, the literature suggests that informal norms most commonly will develop in the context of relational, rather than discrete, contracts. Many, perhaps a majority, of the transactions governed by Article 2 are discrete.[38] Because informal norms are less likely to play a significant role in discrete contracting, the risk of erroneous incorporation of informal norms in this context is relatively low.

Second, we suspect that the material terms in most commercial contracts are known in advance by the contractors to have a vague or ambiguous plain meaning, or no plain meaning at all, over a large range of possible contingencies.[39] If our suspicion is correct, then most contractual disputes concern matters that cannot be resolved by using plain meaning. In most cases, then, contractors would have anticipated that a third-party adjudicator would be required to interpret these terms either in light of observable regularities in commercial practice or in light of some alternative method of judicial construction. It is difficult in any event to predict with precision a court's likely interpretation of any contract term. But it is surely far easier to predict how a court using a plain meaning regime will interpret a term with clear and unambiguous plain-meaning, or how a court using an incorporation regime will interpret a vague and ambiguous term in light of relevant commercial practice, than it is to predict how a court will interpret a term when it can advert neither to plain meaning nor commercial practice. Absent a compelling reason to the contrary, we predict that parties will choose express terms for their contracts that have meanings informed by either relatively clear plain meaning or relatively robust commercial practice. As a rule, contracting parties would avoid using language that a court must interpret without adverting to plain meaning or commercial practice.

Given that we believe contractors often, even typically, use express terms with vague or ambiguous plain meaning, we infer that they intend these terms to be interpreted in light of commercial practice. If contractors were intentionally to use express terms with vague and ambiguous plain meaning, and yet not intend each other and courts to interpret them in light of commercial practice, they would be sacrificing their own likely mutual understanding of their contract requirements and their ability to predict a court's likely interpretation of their contract. In short, rational parties would not sacrifice the benefits of predictable meaning unless doing so made possible even greater benefits of a different sort. Invoking express terms with vague and ambiguous meaning, and yet excluding commercial practice as an interpretive device, severely diminishes the predictability of a contract's requirements and the utility of the contract itself.

There are two reasons that might explain why parties would invoke vague and ambiguous terms and yet exclude interpretations based on commercial practice. The first is that, contrary to our assumption, a court's likely interpretation of such terms is in fact equally as predictable as their plain-meaning interpretations of terms with clear plain meaning or their incorporationist interpretations of terms informed by clear commercial practice. However, our reading of contracts and sales caselaw suggests this is not the case. Alternatively, even though a court's interpretation of such terms is difficult to predict, the court's independent interpretation of the terms will provide such superior content to the contract that its benefits will outweigh the loss of predictability. The plausibility of this claim depends on what method courts would use to interpret such terms. Although we cannot explore all the possibilities here, we are dubious that any practical method could provide such benefits. Quite apart from how a court could achieve such a feat, it is unclear how *any* interpretation of a term could significantly benefit parties who have little prospect of predicting that interpretation in advance.

The second explanation of why parties might intentionally specify vague and ambiguous terms and yet exclude interpretations based on commercial practice is that, as we have seen, parties might rationally intend to create a dual regime of contractual regulation in which the expected (informal) contractual performance is at odds with the (formal) contractual requirements. Such an arrangement might prove optimal if an informal regime of commercial practices provides the most efficient regulation of transactions among contractors acting in good faith, while a formal contractual regime provides the optimal protection to a nonbreacher if his or her contracting partner acts in bad faith. Of course, if the parties intend to create a dual regime of contractual regulation, they must exclude the possibility that their contractual terms will be interpreted in light of commercial practice. The goal of such a regime is to create contract requirements that are inconsistent, rather than consonant, with informal commercial practice. But if this were their objective, we suspect that they would choose express contract terms with a clear plain meaning. By doing so, they would ensure that they, and a third-party adjudicator, would understand the difference between their informal (unenforceable) practices and their formal (legally enforceable) rights and duties.

The chief advantage of a dual regime is that it enables a nonbreacher with the ability to police against bad faith conduct by invoking a legal right to performance not otherwise required by informal practice. If that legal right itself is subject to good faith disagreement between the parties, as well as relatively unpredictable judicial interpretation, the utility of the dual regime will be defeated. The predictability of contractual interpretation is therefore especially important under a dual regime of contractual regulation. Contractors concerned to create such a regime for their contract would therefore be at pains to provide express terms with relatively clear and unambiguous plain meaning. And in the event they could not provide such terms, they would be unlikely to attempt to regulate their transaction with a dual regime. They would take advantage of the relative certainty of commercial practice in place of the relative uncertainty of judicial construction unguided by either plain meaning or commercial practice.[40]

We conclude that most observable regularities of commercial behavior are intended by contractors to inform the meaning of most of the material terms of their contracts. This conclusion is based on our speculation that the material terms of most commercial contracts are vague or ambiguous, and our argument that contractors typically will include such terms only if they intend them to be interpreted in light of commercial practice. If we are right, then most of the observable regularities of commercial behavior evidence formal rather than informal norms. On this view, relatively few patterns of behavior are understood by contractors as exceeding their contract entitlements and therefore requiring permissions or waivers of rights.[41] The existence of informal norms establishes that some observable patterns of behavior fall into the latter category. But not all informal norms are evidenced by observable patterns of behavior. And we suspect those that are correspond to a relatively small proportion of observable regularities in commercial behavior.[42]

Thus, even if the Code indiscriminately incorporated all norms evidenced by observable regularities of conduct, we suspect that most of the norms incorporated would be formal. Even if fact finders inferred formal norms from behavioral regularities in all instances, they would be right more often than wrong. But of course, the fact finder under the Code does not indiscriminately apply norms to the contract. Evidence of a norm's informality is relevant to persuading the fact finder not to incorporate it. Under Article 2, there are two principal methods of demonstrating the existence of an observable regularity of conduct: expert testimony and evidence about statistical regularities. Expert testimony sometimes can straightforwardly ascertain whether most transactors regard the norm as legally binding. The experts will presumably speak directly to that question. Disagreement among experts is no more of a problem here than elsewhere. But much of the evidence of commercial norms might consist simply in the presentation of evidence of statistical norms – mere frequencies of a given behavior in the trade, in past dealings between the parties, or in the course of performance under the contract in question. This evidence will not settle whether there is an informal, or formal norm. The rate of erroneous incorporation of informal norms will be directly affected by the manner in which the trier of fact seeks to determine whether such statistical norms are informal or formal. Our speculation is that, as a statistical matter, there is a high probability that the regularity indicates the existence of a formal, rather than informal norm. But when the reverse is true, the only method for reducing the probability of erroneous incorporation is either to seek expert testimony or require that the trier of fact have some level of relevant expertise itself.

Apart from establishing the proportion of informal to formal norms generally, empirical studies might be used to demonstrate the prevalence of interpretive error in Article 2 resulting from the incorporation of informal norms. They could therefore provide either direct or indirect evidence of the efficiency of one kind of regime over the other. Direct evidence of the regimes' comparative efficiency is a basis for inferring either the absolute or relative costs of interpretive error and specification costs under either kind of interpretive approach. Evidence of the absolute costs of interpretive error and specification under only one regime by itself allows no inference about the relative merits of the two approaches. To determine which regime is likely to be more efficient, one must estimate the absolute costs of interpretive error and specification under the alternative approach. Only partial and inconclusive evidence of the relative merits of each regime is given by an empirical study presenting data on the relative costs of interpretive error, for example, but not specification under each regime. To determine which regime is likely to be more efficient, we would need data concerning the relative costs of specification under each regime.

An empirical study, however, might reveal only indirect evidence of the comparative efficiency of these regimes. If both regimes are available to contractors, and the majority of contractors choose one consistently over the other, where the only plausible explanation for the choice is that contractors prefer it, then that regime is likely to be the most efficient. Similarly, if only one regime is made available without cost, and a second regime can be created by contractors willing to incur the costs of its creation, choice of the second regime by the majority of parties is strong indirect evidence of its superior efficiency.[43]

The only empirical evidence offered to refute the incorporation strategy has been Bernstein's data.[44] She presents them as a challenge to "the fundamental premise of the Uniform Commercial Code's adjudicative philosophy, the idea that courts should seek to discover 'immanent business norms' and use them to decide cases."[45] Bernstein studied the arbitration system adopted by the National Grain and Feed Association (NGFA). The NGFA opted out of the Code's interpretive regime and created its own formalistic arbitration system. Its system substitutes trade rules and a formalistic interpretive system for the Code's reliance on usage of trade, course of dealing, and course of performance. Indeed, according to Bernstein, arbitrators sometimes even note that they are prohibited from taking into account trade usage inconsistent with the express terms of the contract. Her interviews with grain and feed merchants suggest that members of the NGFA prefer their formalistic system to the Code's regime because it allows them to achieve their most desired mix of informal and formal norms to govern their contractual relationships. There is no question that the likelihood of interpretive error due to incorporation of informal norms is much lower for contracts adjudicated under the NGFA regime than for contracts adjudicated under the Code's regime.

Bernstein's case study might be taken to provide direct or indirect evidence of the relative size of interpretive error costs in incorporation and nonincorporation regimes. The NGFA study gives direct evidence that one kind of interpretive error is less under the NGFA regime than under the Code regime. If the incidence of other kinds of interpretive error is the same in both regimes, the study would provide incomplete but direct evidence bearing on the relative efficiency of both regimes. The study is incomplete because it does not purport to determine the relative specification costs under each regime. But even without an empirical study of relative specification costs, it seems clear that the specification costs under the NGFA regime will be no greater, and in fact will probably be much less, than the specification costs NGFA members would face if forced to adjudicate their contracts under the Code regime.

Ordinarily, an interpretive regime that excludes extrinsic evidence of the meaning of contract terms increases specification costs relative to a regime that does not. This is because parties under a nonincorporation regime will have to incur the costs of using terms with plain or predefined meanings to express ideas more easily expressed using terms with context-specific meaning, or settle for less efficient contractual terms. But the NGFA provides its members with an extensive set of predefined terms whose meanings are entirely derived from common commercial practice in the grain and feed industry. By providing such a tailored list of predefined express terms, the NGFA eliminates the chief advantage of incorporation regimes over nonincorporation regimes. The specification costs for NGFA contractors under the NGFA regime are certain to be lower than under any incorporation regime. This is because contractors achieve all the benefits of incorporation by incorporating all relevant commercial practice in their predefined trade rules and terms rather than in the course of adjudication. The adjudicatory process therefore can be dedicated solely to the task of enforcing predefined terms, without thereby imposing on contractors any additional costs of aligning their contractual practices with these predefined terms. Because the NGFA intentionally selects the predefined terms its members most prefer – terms with meanings reflecting the most common commercial practices in the grain and feed industry – a strict construction rule in favor of the predefined meanings for these terms can be adopted without increasing contractors' specification costs. In this way, the NGFA system thereby eliminates the ordinary tension in adjudication between interpretive strategies that minimize interpretive error costs and those that minimize specification costs. The NGFA's strict construction regime, then, appears to have both lower interpretive error costs and lower specification costs than the incorporation strategy. Thus, it might appear that the NGFA study provides good evidence that nonincorporation regimes are likely to be superior to incorporation regimes.

The NGFA study, however, establishes only that the NGFA provides a superior interpretive regime for the members of the NGFA. It says nothing about the majority of contractors whose agreements are governed by Article 2. The NGFA study illustrates the well-known efficiencies of custom-tailoring rules of contractual interpretation to the needs of specific kinds of contractors. If all contractors shared the same commercial understandings, needs, and practices, as do the members of the NGFA, the incorporation strategy would serve no purpose. An NGFA-like regime instead could be employed to govern all sales contracts. There would not be an unavoidable trade-off between customizing contractual terms in the process of adjudication, thereby reducing specification costs, and reducing interpretive error by adhering to the strict construction of predefined terms. Instead, the predefined terms themselves could be customized to suit all parties' contractual preferences, eliminating the need to attempt such customization during the course of adjudication. Thus, if contractual preferences are homogeneous, customization can be achieved ex ante, at the stage of predefining a menu of contractual terms, rather than ex post, during the adjudicative process. If customization is achieved ex ante, there is no need to attempt customization ex post, and therefore no need to introduce the additional risk of interpretive error associated with ex post customization attempts.

More generally, if contracting parties shared a narrow set of commercial understandings, needs, and practices, there would be no need for a generalized sales law such as Article 2. Of course, an NGFA-like regime that combined custom-tailored, predefined terms with strict construction adjudication would optimize contractual interpretation for such a homogenous group.[46] But the point of the incorporation strategy is to accommodate the impossibility of ex ante customization in a sales law designed to govern an extraordinarily heterogenous population of contractors. The incorporation strategy is explicitly designed to trade off the risk of increased interpretive error in order to capture some of the efficiencies of custom-tailored interpretive rules. Llewellyn's gambit is that the efficiency gains the incorporation strategy makes possible will outweigh the interpretive error costs it occasions. The NGFA example provides a perfect solution to the Code's interpretive challenge by assuming away the problem.

The NGFA example also might be indirect evidence of the superior efficiency of a nonincorporation regime over an incorporation regime. The willingness of NGFA members to incur the costs of creating the NGFA strict construction regime to opt out of the Code's incorporation regime might be taken to indicate the superiority of strict construction regimes over incorporation regimes. But no such inference is justified. First, opting out by the NGFA members at most is evidence of the NGFA's superior efficiency over Article 2's particular version of the incorporation strategy. It provides no evidence that a strict construction regime other than the NGFA is superior to Article 2's incorporation strategy or even that the NGFA is more efficient than any incorporation regime other than Article 2.

Second, and more important, the NGFA study does not even demonstrate that the NGFA regime is superior to Article 2. As explained above, the superiority of the NGFA for NGFA members has no bearing on the merits of Article 2's incorporation strategy. Indeed, Article 2 explicitly invites contractors to opt out of the Code's regime when doing so would be efficient. The ability of NGFA members to opt out of the Code's regime in part vindicates, rather than refutes, the design of Article 2 by demonstrating the efficacy of its opt-out provisions. This is because the Code anticipates that groups of homogenous contractors sometimes will be able to secure gains from forming a distinct adjudicative regime, exploiting the advantages of ex ante customization, that exceed the costs the contractors must incur to form and operate such a regime. The Code does not try to provide a more efficient regime for such contractors than they can provide for themselves. Instead, it is designed to be the most efficient regime for governing a set of heterogenous contractors whose contracting preferences cannot, except in very broad terms, be effectively anticipated in advance. The Code's comparative inefficiency would be indirectly shown only if some individuals with largely heterogenous preferences would opt out of the Code for a private interpretive regime. Instead, the NGFA example proves the unsurprising exception but leaves the rule of incorporation completely intact.

C. The Encrustation Critique

The final critique of the incorporation strategy focuses on the mechanics of the incorporation process of Article 2. Article 2 requires judges to interpret contractual terms in light of commercial practice. But once courts have made an initial determination of the meaning of a term, based at least in theory on an inquiry into relevant commercial practices, they appear reluctant to engage in that inquiry again. Instead, they appear to treat such determinations as canonical. Thus, although courts might initially employ the incorporation strategy, their initial interpretations become "encrusted" as virtual precedents. Courts subsequently disfavor any interpretations inconsistent with these encrusted interpretations.[47] One suggestion is that courts are predisposed to treat statutory interpretation in a static, precedent-bound fashion, rather than the dynamic fashion contemplated by the incorporation strategy. Thus, incorporation implemented by Article 2, rather than through a common law system, might account for this judicial interpretive intransigence.

The judicial practice of one-time incorporation is inconsistent with the goal of interpreting contractual terms in light of their evolving meanings. If parties understand their contractual terms in light of evolving commercial practices, encrustation will lead to interpretive error. If parties recognize and respond rationally to the judicial practice of one-time incorporation, costs of specifying their most preferred terms will increase. If courts will not interpret contractual terms in light of current commercial practices, parties will have to incur the costs of making explicit any of their understandings at variance with outdated practice, or settle for the suboptimal interpretation of their contractual terms according to the outdated practice. The costs of "opting out" of the encrusted interpretations of their terms are exacerbated by the tendency of courts to disfavor such opt-outs. If courts refuse to interpret terms in light of evolving commercial practice, the value of attempting to "opt out" of encrusted interpretations is reduced. Even if parties incur the costs to provide an otherwise clear opt-out, courts might nonetheless refuse to enforce the parties' interpretation. This practice thus reduces the expected joint value of all contracts by depriving parties of the ability to specify their most preferred terms.

Encrustation is a potentially serious problem for incorporationists. The tendency of courts to make one-time interpretations of terms instead of continually updating their interpretations in light of evolving practice is inconsistent with the implementation of the dynamic incorporation process contemplated by Article 2's incorporation strategy. The tendency to disfavor even clear efforts to opt out of encrusted interpretations constitutes simple interpretive error. How serious a problem encrustation presents depends on the relative frequency of interpretive error resulting from a failure to recognize changes in commercial practice or a bias against clear opt-outs. These in turn depend on how the incorporation strategy is implemented.

But plain-meaning regimes are likely to suffer from shortcomings similar to those caused by encrustation. First, encrustation undermines the incorporation strategy because it prevents parties from easily invoking the current customary meanings attached to their contract terms. It thus raises the parties' specification costs. But plain-meaning regimes do not even attempt to enable parties to invoke customary meanings at minimal cost. They instead require parties to communicate their customary understandings according to the plain meaning of the terms they use. Thus, although encrustation erodes some of the expected savings in specification costs under the incorporation strategy, the expected specification costs under plain-meaning regimes will be even higher. Second, encrustation undermines the incorporation strategy because judges refuse to honor parties' attempts to opt out of the customary meanings assigned to their contract terms. Again, this judicial practice raises expected specification costs under the incorporation strategy. But if judges favor the customary meaning of contract terms when they interpret under an incorporation regime, we would expect them to favor the plain meaning of terms under a plain-meaning regime. For example, if contractors state that their quantity terms are estimates, judges might nonetheless hold the parties to the plain meaning of their quantity term. It is difficult to understand why judges would be biased in favor of the customary meaning of terms under an interpretive regime that accords primacy to customary meaning while not exhibiting a similar bias in favor of the plain meaning of terms under a regime that accords primacy to plain meaning.

E. Summary

Each critique correctly identifies the possibility of one kind of interpretive error but fails to estimate its likely extent. Because every interpretive regime produces some interpretive error costs in order to reduce specification costs, the only relevant question is whether the incorporation strategy has greater aggregate interpretive error and specification costs than alternative interpretive regimes. The question therefore is a comparative one. We have speculated that the kinds of interpretive error identified are unlikely to be so great as to clearly disqualify the incorporation strategy outright. Indeed, if the error rate were so high, most merchants would at least attempt to opt out of most of the Code's provisions. By comparing the evolution of the Code to the common law over the last forty years, Robert Scott has argued, in effect, that the sum of specification and error costs is lower under a common law plain-meaning regime than under an incorporation strategy.[48] But even Scott acknowledges that the interpretive error rate under the Code in large measure can be attributed to obvious flaws in its particular design rather than to shortcomings endemic to the incorporation strategy itself.[49] There is no doubt, however, that the chief liability of the incorporation strategy is its vulnerability to interpretive error. Part IV canvasses measures that might be taken to improve the interpretive error rate under Article 2. We argue that such changes are entirely feasible and realistic. Once in place, these changes could dramatically reduce the current interpretive error rate under Article 2.

IV. Implementing a Defensible Incorporation Strategy

The incorporation strategy for interpreting contracts directs courts to interpret the meaning of contract terms in light of relevant extrinsic evidence, such as trade usage, course of dealing, and course of performance. But it does not specify how a court is to take such evidence into account. Interpretive regimes can implement the incorporation strategy in many different ways. They can vary along a number of crucial dimensions of institutional design. First, they might allocate the responsibility for deciding whether a usage of trade, course of dealing, or course of performance exists to different decisionmakers. The decision could be allocated to the court, a lay jury, or a merchant jury. Second, they might apply different standards for proving the existence of extrinsic evidence. Although precise formulations of such standards are notoriously difficult, familiar standards range from a "preponderance of evidence" to "clear and convincing evidence." And they might apply different standards for the kind of proof that can be offered to prove the existence of extrinsic evidence. For example, one regime might require evidence of statistical regularity, while another might require expert testimony. Third, some regimes might provide a menu of safe harbors that allow the parties to signal reliably their preference for having their contract interpreted by a particular sort of extrinsic evidence. Finally, some regimes might add presumptions to aid in justifiably inferring facts that are difficult or costly to determine. Thus, every incorporation regime will permit extrinsic evidence to be used to interpret contract terms only when a fact finder finds that the party with the burden of proof sustains its burden by offering admissible evidence satisfying the relevant standard of proof. But each regime can specify different fact finders, burdens of proof, standards of proof, safe harbors, and presumptions.

Article 2 explicitly or implicitly specifies the fact finder, burden of proof, standards of proof, safe harbors, and presumptions for the incorporation of extrinsic evidence. Article 2's core interpretive provisions are § 1-205(3) and its parol evidence rule, § 2-202. Section 1-205(3) states the order of priority given to different sorts of evidence in interpreting contract terms. It requires express terms to be construed as consistent with course of dealing and trade usage "wherever reasonable."[50] Express terms control only when a consistent construction is "unreasonable." Fairly understood, § 1-205(3) gives priority to the plain meaning of a term over trade usage, course of performance, and course of dealing in such cases. Section 2-202 states what sort of evidence is admissible to interpret contract terms. The section instructs courts to allow trade usage, course of performance, and course of dealing to "explain or supplement" the terms of even an integrated writing. Official comments explicitly reject the "lay dictionary" and the "conveyancer's" reading of terms in commercial agreements.[51] Article 2 allows parties a safe harbor by which they can limit the sort of evidence used to interpret their agreement. They can do so by "carefully negat[ing]" any usage of trade, course of performance, or anticipated course of performance they prefer not to have applicable to their deal.[52]

Article 2 relies on a mix of Code and extra-Code law to set the other elements needed for interpretation. Interpretation of contract terms is allocated to the fact finder, except when the court finds a writing to be integrated.[53] The existence and content of trade usage, course of performance, and course of dealing also are left to the fact finder.[54] Article 2's definition of trade usage places a modest constraint on fact finding, requiring that it have a "regularity of observance in a place." The associated official comment makes clear that only statistical regularity, not longevity, is required for a finding of trade usage.[55] Although Article 2 sometimes expressly allocates the burden and standards of proof,[56] it does not do so in the case of the interpretation of contract terms. Burdens and standards of proof therefore are implicitly left to extra-Code law, presumably applicable under § 1-103. The few presumptions that bear on the interpretation of contract terms, such as *contra proferentum* rules or the bindingness of trade usage on newcomers, are products of decisional law, not Article 2's provisions.

A fair assessment of the incorporation strategy requires a clear distinction between the incorporation strategy itself and the many possible incorporation regimes that might implement it. Because the incorporation strategy does not require a single specification of any particular institutional element, many different incorporation regimes are possible. A criticism of one particular incorporation regime therefore does not by itself constitute a criticism of the incorporation strategy generally. A defect in one incorporation regime does not demonstrate that all other possible and feasible incorporation regimes are likely to have a similar defect.[57] Moreover, even if a criticism is effective against a particular incorporation regime, that regime might be amended to address the particular defect the criticism identifies. Thus, because Article 2 describes just one way in which the incorporation strategy can be implemented, criticisms of it neither condemn Article 2 itself nor the incorporation strategy generally. After all, if Article 2 is subject to compelling criticism, it might be amended to avoid the criticism. The resulting interpretive regime might well be sufficiently similar to the original Article 2 regime that we would not say the criticism required abandoning the regime. More important, whether or not Article 2 survives its own amendment, the resulting regime might not only qualify as incorporationist but constitute a more thoroughgoing incorporationist regime than Article 2.

The incidence of the interpretive errors identified by the critiques we have considered can be significantly reduced by including a number of feasible provisions in incorporation regimes such as Article 2. The existence and informal norm critiques are each directed at interpretive error produced by faulty inferences from regularities in behavior, either under a contract or in similar contracts. The existence critique holds that trade usage sometimes or often does not exist where the incorporation strategy finds it. The informal norm critique maintains that courts sometimes or often fail to distinguish formal from informal norms, wrongly interpreting the contract to include norms not intended by the parties to be enforceable. Both critiques charge that incorporation induces courts to find commercial practice where there is none.

Under Article 2, the interpretive errors identified are the product of a trier of fact (or a court, if the agreement is integrated) drawing incorrect inferences based on particular sorts of evidence. These errors can be reduced by selecting a better decisionmaker or requiring that interpretation be based on more reliable evidence. Accordingly, a combination of a superior fact finder, superior evidentiary bases, or higher standards of evidence can be specified. As with any interpretive approach, a combination of devices is available to the incorporationist. Contract interpretation therefore could be allocated away from relatively inexpert, generalist trial courts or juries and toward specialist courts or merchant juries. The Delaware Court of Chancery illustrates the former possibility. This court hears most of the corporate cases brought in Delaware, acts as a fact finder, and has a developed expertise in corporate matters. It is well positioned (and motivated) to understand the background against which corporate matters appear. In the case of contract interpretation, such specialized courts are well positioned to understand when parties are likely to incorporate commercial practice and when not.[58] At the very least, they are better positioned than generalist trial courts or juries. Interpretive error thereby can be reduced by the choice of judicial interpreter.

Merchant juries are another possibility. They can be assigned the task of interpreting the terms of the contract, taking into account commercial practices of which they are familiar. In early drafts of Article 2, Llewellyn proposed a merchant jury.[59] The elimination of his proposal from the final version of Article 2 means that inexpert fact finders both find commercial practice and interpret the terms of a sales agreement in light of it. This sort of institutional design is not inevitable. Merchant juries, potentially familiar with the commercial practices in issue, arguably make fewer interpretive errors than lay juries. They are less likely to wrongly find trade usage, for instance, where none exists or a "thick" and detailed practice where there are only "thin" and sparse regularities of behavior. Merchant juries, potentially being industry experts, are less likely to mistake local trade usage for widely shared commercial practice. Certainly parties often select arbitrators familiar with the practices surrounding the transaction for which the parties have contracted. The reasons for doing so are complex and sometimes have nothing to do with knowledge of the decisionmaker selected. However, the contracting parties' choice of arbitration is consistent with a preference for the interpretive advantage provided by an expert familiar with the relevant commercial practices.[60] Merchant juries, which reduce the rate of interpretive error, make litigation a closer substitute for arbitration.

Restricting evidence, raising standards of proof, and adopting stronger legal criteria for commercial custom also can reduce interpretive error. If the existence critique is correct, regularities in industry practice are seldom pronounced or detailed enough to be trade usage. An appropriate response to such paucity of trade usage might be to restrict evidence of industry practice to written industry codes or corroborative testimony by industry experts.[61] This makes good sense given a general regulatory and contractual preference for conditioning obligations on verifiable variables. Alternatively, admissible evidence could be restricted to terms appearing in standard form contracts in the relevant trade.[62] Another response would be to require more regularity of commercial practice, both in scope and longevity. Pre-Code law apparently did this, by requiring that trade usage be "ancient or immemorial" and prevalent.[63]

The amendments to Article 2 that would be expected to reduce the interpretive errors identified by the existence critique would also be expected to reduce the interpretive errors identified by the informal norms critique. But the problems each critique identifies are importantly different. Whereas the existence critique calls for measures to ensure that fact finders do not find custom where it does not exist, the informal norms critique calls for measures to ensure that fact finders do not find formal norms where only informal norms exist. Thus, unlike the existence critique, the informal norms critique does not deny that there are regularities in commercial behavior generally, and in the contracting parties' behavior in particular, that reflect enforceable obligations. It notes that these regularities sometimes will reflect unenforceable obligations instead (informal norms). The problem therefore is not to design rules in the face of an assumed infrequent phenomenon such as formal trade usage. It is to design rules to induce the accurate detection of a frequent phenomenon: formal norms evidenced by usage of trade, course of dealing, and course of performance. If party-specific behavior is more likely to reflect informal norms than general commercial behavior, an incorporation regime might well assign different burdens and standards of proof to trade usage than for course of dealing and performance. For example, a bare statistical regularity might suffice to prove a formal usage of trade exists, while both a statistical regularity and expert testimony might be required to prove the existence of a formal course of dealing or course of performance.

Reduction of the interpretive errors identified by the encrustation critique requires altering another way in which the incorporation strategy is implemented. The critique speculates that the self-contained nature of Article 2 induces courts to rely on precedent, interpreting Code provisions dependent on commercial custom, and to ignore changes in that custom.[64] Because the tendency postulated is not irreversible, encrustation can be avoided by altering the way in which courts regard Article 2. Accordingly, the incorporationist response is similar to its other responses: altering the particular way in which Article 2 is implemented. A straightforward alteration is to make Article 2 even less self-contained by making it more reliant on extra-Code developments in commercial custom. It is common for treaties lacking a mechanism for centralized implementation to include provisions calling for national courts to interpret them with an eye to uniformity.[65] Article 2 could be amended in the same sort of way. It could contain an explicit injunction to courts to avoid relying on caselaw to determine trade usage, for instance. The injunction would help force them to gauge trade usage by looking to contemporary commercial practice. It more effectively vindicates the incorporationist strategy.

The variety of feasible ways of implementing the incorporation strategy means that it has resources to adjust to the presence of interpretive error costs. This is illustrated by specific strategies for pursuing incorporation that arguably *fail* to take interpretive error seriously. Robert Cooter, for example, proposes that courts proceed by identifying existing commercial norms and discerning the likely strategic structure of interactions in which the norms arise.[66] If the strategic structure of interactions tends to produce efficient outcomes, courts should use the commercial norms identified to interpret or supplement parties' contracts. By doing so, according to Cooter, courts need not inquire directly into the efficiency of contract terms or interpretation of them. Cooter's proposal arguably induces high interpretive error costs (as well as high administrative costs). Although courts need not inquire directly into the efficiency of terms, Cooter requires them to assess two variables: relevant commercial norms and the strategic structure of likely interactions. Because the variables are independent, the likelihood of judicial error is greater than if courts were directed only to identify commercial norms. Further, error in detecting the strategic structure of interactions probably is itself high. This is because the strategic structure of an interaction sometimes must include the way in which parties describe the array of payoffs and strategy choices. The mathematical structure of interactions, such as payoffs and strategy choices, is not enough always to explain equilibrium outcomes.[67] Because judicial access to parties' descriptions of their interactions is at best imperfect and can be gamed by parties in litigation, the interpretive error costs associated with Cooter's proposal are likely to be significant. Whether they are higher than the costs associated with directly inquiring into the efficiency of terms or their interpretation needs to be determined.

The proposal still might produce lower aggregate interpretive error costs than its competitors. If it does not, then, holding specification costs constant, Cooter's specific suggestion for incorporation of course should be rejected.

However, the failure of the suggestion still leaves a range of other feasible ways of implementing the incorporation strategy. And they might well fare better by producing greater reductions in interpretive error costs. For instance, a variant on Cooter's suggestion recommends that courts determine only relevant commercial custom, rather than the strategic structure of interactions. By not requiring that courts detect strategic structures, this strategy eliminates a likely and significant source of interpretive error. The recommendation also clearly provides recognizable means of implementing the incorporation strategy. Even if unsuccessful, Cooter's proposal therefore is only one of a number of ways in which incorporation can proceed, and its rejection does not condemn the incorporation strategy generally.

The array of possible ways of implementing particular incorporationist strategies does not undermine their incorporationist character. Each implementation still requires that commercial practice inform the meaning assigned to contract terms. They differ only in how commercial practice enters in the interpretive process. Of course, devices such as burdens of proof have effects on whether contract terms will bear the meaning given them by customary practice. An assignment of burden of proof to one who wants to introduce trade usage, for instance, might make it more unlikely that trade usage will be considered in interpreting a term. However, the reduced likelihood does not mean that trade usage will not be successfully introduced. It will depend on whether the evidence is available to the party having the burden. Alternatively, a statutory menu of language that if used by contracting parties will be taken to make trade usage inapplicable is possible.[68] This limits without eliminating the circumstances under which commercial practice will be used. Certainly both approaches remain significantly different from plain-meaning approaches to interpretation. According to them, commercial practice is never relevant to interpret the plain meaning of contracts. Even impeccable evidence of relevant industry practice is to have no effect on interpretation. Thus, implementing incorporation by adjusting interpretive devices does not destroy the distinctiveness of incorporationist strategies.

V. Conclusion

Incorporation of commercial practice in contract interpretation is best suited to generalist commercial statutes or rules. Generalist commercial laws cover a wide variety of transactions among contracting parties having heterogeneous, transaction-specific preferences. In these circumstances, interpretative approaches must take into account both interpretive error costs as well as specification costs. The case here for incorporation in interpretation argues that an incorporation strategy optimally minimizes the sum of interpretive error and specification costs associated with contract interpretation. The argument rests principally on four sensible empirical assumptions.

First, where party preference is heterogeneous, contracting parties face high costs in signaling to third parties their understanding of contract terms. Thus, specification costs are a variable that interpretive approaches cannot ignore. By interpreting contract terms according to commercial practice, the incorporation strategy saves parties most of the cost of having to signal the aspects of that practice they want applicable to their contract.

Second, despite the arguable lack of uniformity of trade custom at the turn of the century, contemporary local and national trade customs are likely to be quite extensive. Third, where norms exist governing heterogenous transactions covered by a generalist law, they are more likely to be formal norms, intended by the parties to be enforceable, than informal norms, not intended for enforcement. On the whole, formal norms are likely to outnumber informal norms because transactions cover both discrete and relational contracts, informal norms are unlikely to govern discrete contracts, relational contracts are unlikely to predominate discrete contracts, and even within relational contracts, formal norms are likely to predominate informal norms. Thus, the rate of interpretive error in mistaking informal for formal norms probably is low.

Fourth, error costs associated with interpreting terms in light of commercial practice can be reduced by adjusting the way in which incorporation is implemented. This means that mistakes due to bias against opt-outs of trade usage, misidentification of informal for formal norms, or identification of trade usage where there is none can be reduced by altering burdens of proof, evidentiary bases and standards of proof, and the like. Adjustment of these elements to affect legal error rates therefore can be made, taking into account their effect on specification costs. In this way, marginal interpretive error and specification costs can be gauged so as to obtain optimal levels of both. The case for the incorporation strategy claims that, given these four sensible assumptions, aggregate interpretive error and specification costs are lower than under plain-meaning interpretive approaches.

The a priori case against the existence of custom raises fair questions about the kinds of judgment necessary to implement the incorporation strategy, but does not undermine the prospect of incorporation itself. However, empirical studies concerning the existence of trade usage or the rates of informal and formal norms in particular industries are important for incorporationists. In fact, they are essential to the incorporation strategy because they affect the way in which it is implemented. For example, the adjustment of standards of proof and evidentiary bases depends on the likely rates of interpretive error. Thus, if trade usage is mostly local or "thin," or if most norms in a particular industry are informal, as Bernstein's data might suggest, then raising a standard of proof or restricting evidentiary bases might be appropriate. Far from being incompatible with the incorporation strategy, empirical data about the rate of informal norms or the limitations of trade usage are necessary for an intelligent implementation of the incorporation strategy. At the very least, the data require that incorporationists be sensitive to interpretive error and specification costs. Our objection to the critiques of incorporation is not that they fail to identify possible sources of interpretive error associated with consulting commercial custom. It is that the critiques either ignore specification costs, which favor incorporation, or ignore the resources available to incorporation strategies to reduce the interpretive errors they identify.

Notes

† We thank Ian Ayres, Lisa Bernstein, Douglas Cole, Richard Craswell, and participants at the 1999 Canadian Law and Economics Association Annual Convention in Toronto, Canada, for very helpful comments.

1. The incorporation strategy is also adopted in the sales law of other legal systems and in some treaty law. See, e.g., Belgian Civil Code art. 1134 (1982), United Nations Convention on Contracts for the International Sale of Goods art. 9(2), 19 Int. Legal Mat. 668 (1980); International Institute for the Unification of Private Law, UNIDROIT Principles of International Commercial Contracts art. 1.8(2) (1994).
2. In our view, contractual interpretation is logically prior to gap-filling. Whether a contract contains a gap depends on the interpretation given its express and implied terms. We define contractual gaps as issues not resolved by the terms of a contract properly interpreted. Under a plain-meaning regime, once a contract's terms have been given their plain-meaning interpretation, issues not addressed by these terms would constitute contractual gaps. Thus, under a plain-meaning regime, there may be a contractual gap with respect to an issue even if the contract contains a term purportedly governing the issue. If the plain meaning of that term is ambiguous or does not exist, the proper interpretation of that term fails to resolve the issue it purports to govern. Therefore, in our definition, there is a contractual gap with respect to that particular issue despite the existence of a contractual term purporting to govern it. Obviously, a plain-meaning rule cannot be used to fill contractual gaps so defined because gap-filling is required if and only if the plain-meaning rule cannot be used to resolve an issue. Unlike the plain-meaning rule, the incorporation strategy provides a methodology both for interpreting actual contract terms and filling in contractual gaps.

   Criticism of the incorporation strategy for gap-filling is based on the likely suboptimality of evolved custom, the difficulty of accurately identifying and incorporating custom, and the possibility that courts, legislatures, or private lawmaking bodies can create more efficient default rules for filling in contractual gaps. For the claim that the evolution of commercial practice is not likely to be optimal and therefore might be improved by legal designers, see Michael Klausner, *Corporations, Corporate Law, and Network Externalities,* 81 Va. L. Rev. 757 (1995); Marcel Kahan and Michael Klausner, *Standardization and Innovation in Corporate Contracting (or the Economics of Boilerplate),* 83 Va. L. Rev. 713 (1997); Jody S. Kraus, *Legal Design and the Evolution of Commercial Norms,* 26 J. Leg. Stud. 277 (1997). See also Eric Posner, *Law, Economics, and Inefficient Norms,* 144 U. Pa. L. Rev. 1697 (1996). For the claim that the process of identifying and applying custom potentially undermines the usefulness of the incorporation strategy for both interpretation and gap-filling, see Richard Craswell, "Do Trade Customs Exist?," Chapter 4 of this volume [hereinafter *Trade Customs*]. For the claim that the incorporation strategy undermines the ability of contractors to create an optimal mix of legally enforceable and legally unenforceable norms, see Lisa Bernstein, *Merchant Law In a Merchant Court: Rethinking the Code's Search for Immanent Business Norms,* 144 U. Pa. L. Rev. 1765 (1996) [hereinafter *Merchant Law*]. For the claim that the kind of custom required by the incorporation strategy does not exist, see Lisa Bernstein, *The Questionable Empirical Basis of Article 2's Incorporation Strategy: A Preliminary Study,* 66 U. Chi. L. Rev. 710 (1999) [hereinafter *Questionable Empirical Basis*]. For the claim that the common law plain-meaning rule better promotes uniform and predictable contract interpretation than the incorporation strategy, see Robert E. Scott, *Rethinking the Uniformity Norm in Commercial Law,* Chapter 5 of this volume [hereinafter *Rethinking Uniformity*].

3. If an interpretive regime that minimizes the sum of interpretive error and specification costs has higher administration costs than a regime with higher total interpretive error and specification costs, the latter may be the preferable regime. See Richard A. Epstein, *Simple Rules for a Complex World* 30–6 (1995). The "all else equal" proviso allows for this possibility. Our case for incorporation is not based on a complete analysis of all relevant variables. Interpretive regimes affect a number of decisions of actual and potential contracting parties, including whether to contract at all, the type of contract, contract performance, and the decision to breach. The decision to contract, for instance, is not an exogenously fixed variable. Where performance deviates from the express terms of a contract, use of commercial practice to interpret terms can increase the cost of performance over the life of the contract. In some circumstances, this prospect can make not contracting the preferred decision. A complete analysis of equilibria under different interpretive regimes must estimate the aggregate effect of an interpretive regime on all variables, not just on specification and interpretive error costs. This chapter holds the parties' preferences for contracting and contract terms constant and estimates the effect of choice of regime on two important variables. Its analysis is more manageable because the estimation is of the effect of interpretive regimes on the likely costs of making particular decisions. The full case for and against incorporation would estimate the range of decisions affected by such regimes.
4. Philosophers standardly assume that literal sentence meaning exists, as do some legal theorists. See, e.g., Donald Davidson, *Truth and Interpretation* 247 (1984); John R. Searle, *Speech Acts* 19 (1969): Larry Alexander, *All or Nothing at All? The Intention of Authorities and the Authority of Intentions,* in Andrei Marmor, ed., *Law and Interpretation: Essays in Legal Philosophy* 356, 363–5 (1995); Frederick Shauer, *Statutory Construction and the Coordinating Function of Plain-Meaning,* 1990 Supr. Ct. Rev. 213, 251–3. For scepticism about the existence of plain-meaning, see Stanley Fish, *Doing What Comes Naturally: Change, Rhetoric, and the Practice of Theory in Literary and Legal Studies* 508 (1989); Sanford Levinson, *Law as Literature,* 60 Tex. L. Rev. 373, 378 (1982). Contrary assessments of the trend in recent caselaw appear in Margaret N. Kniffin, *A New Trend in Contract Interpretation: The Search for Reality as Opposed to Virtual Reality,* 74 Or. L. Rev. 643 (1995); Ralph James Mooney, *The New Conceptualism in Contract Law,* 74 Or. L. Rev. 1131, 1159–71 (1995).
5. Of course, if one party can prove that *both* parties shared his or her idiosyncratic understanding of a contractual term, courts will enforce the term according to that understanding.
6. This assumes that contractors always prefer to maximize the joint value of their contracts ex ante and that their most preferred terms correspond to the most efficient terms. Of

course, the former does not entail the latter. Contractors might mistakenly believe their most preferred terms will maximize the joint value of their contract ex ante. But the economic analysis of contract presumes that the parties' preferences provide the best method of approximating the most efficient terms for contracts. The plausibility of this claim stems from the claim that the market will select against parties who include inefficient terms in their contracts, and will favor the evolution of commercial norms that will guide contracting preference formation.

7. Again, the "all else equal" proviso holds the costs of administering an interpretive regime constant across all regimes. See n. 3 supra.
8. Specification costs provide the upper bound of the aggregate costs attributable to inefficient contractual terms: The loss in the expected joint value of a contract due to a failure to specify the most efficient terms cannot exceed the costs of specifying the most efficient terms. Otherwise, rational parties would incur the costs of specifying the most efficient terms rather than incur the larger loss in the expected joint value of their contract. Note that under the hypothetical interpretive regime in the text, the costs of securing the most desired terms will be infinite when the parties desire a term not contained in the judicially specified menu. In that case, the upper bound of the aggregate costs attributable to inefficient contractual terms is the entire expected joint value of the contract: Some contracts will have a positive expected joint value only if they contain a term not contained in the judicial menu.
9. See Richard A. Epstein, *The Path to* The T.J. Hooper*: The Theory and History of Custom in the Law of Tort,* 21 J. Legal Stud. 1, 9–11 (1992).
10. Richard Craswell makes this point when he states that "the bulk of what is conveyed by most utterances lies in the context-dependent pragmatic implications, not in the bare semantic meaning." *Trade Customs,* supra n. 2, at 26. Craswell notes, however, that even though the interpretation of custom is necessarily context-sensitive, "merchants may still be able to . . . reach decisions in particular cases, and there may even be a large degree of uniformity in the decisions that various merchants reach – but this will be because each is exercising his or her judgment in a similar way." Ibid. at 28. For an extended analogy of the necessarily contextual and judgment-based nature of interpretation of customs to the interpretation of language, see ibid. at 18–28.
11. The empirical claim is illustrated by Lisa Bernstein's empirical study of the codification efforts by merchant associations around the turn of the century and merchant responses to the proposed Article 2. See *Questionable Empirical Basis,* supra n. 2. The a priori claim is illustrated by Richard Craswell's argument that trade practices might not exist because of their ineliminably contextual nature. See *Trade Customs,* supra n. 2.
12. *Questionable Empirical Basis,* supra n. 2, at 717.
13. Ibid., supra n. 2, at 760.
14. Ibid., supra n. 2, at 717.
15. Ibid., supra n. 2, at 717.
16. Ibid., supra n. 2, at 760.
17. Ibid., supra n. 2, at 761.
18. UCC § 1-205, com. 4 (emphasis added). See Joseph H. Levie, *Trade Usage and Custom under the Common Law and the Uniform Commercial Code,* N. Y. U. Law. Rev. 1101, 1107 (1965).
19. The evidence on which Bernstein principally relies for the claim that no uniform industrywide practices existed often provides equally strong support for the existence of

relatively clear local customs. Consider the evidence Bernstein culls from the National Hay Association debates. Bernstein quotes members of the National Hay Association Meetings to support her claim that there was no uniform customary understanding of the size of a bale of No.1 hay. For example, Bernstein quotes a member attending the Fourth Annual National Hay Association meeting as stating that if one were to "[p]ut twenty bales of different grade hay along that room, . . . there will not be five men among you who will agree" on whether each bale contains no. 1 hay. *Questionable Empirical Basis,* supra n. 2, at 720. But Bernstein also quotes another member as stating that "[b]ales are not governed by size so much as by weight in the Northwest. In Chicago, I know, they like light bales, weighing from eighty-five to ninety-five pounds; and in the East they like heavier bales. In Wisconsin they will put in 125 to 135 pounds." Ibid. at 721, n. 34 quoting NHA, Report of the Tenth Annual Convention 80 (1903). Unlike the first quotation, the second supports the claim that nationally uniform customs did not exist by evidence that local customary understandings of the term *bale* did exist. Indeed, many of the quotations Bernstein cites assert the existence of relatively precise local customs in the course of denying the existence of a uniform national custom: "What is considered as No. 1 timothy, for example, in one producing section may be considered as No. 2 timothy in another producing section, and still of another grade in the consuming section to which it may be shipped." Ibid., supra n. 2, 721, n. 35, citing NHA, Report of the Fourth Annual Meeting 40 (1920); "[S]eedsmen handle large quantities of . . . seeds . . . for few of which legal weights per bushel have been established. They have, therefore, to arrive at customary weights only, which vary in the different States." Ibid., supra n. 2, at 721, n. 36, quoting the *American Silk Throwers Association Yearbook* 59 (1914); "(. . . noting that many local rules relating to shipping time contradicted the Grain Dealers National Rules)," Ibid. at 724, n. 50, summarizing 17 *Who is Who in the Grain Trade* 31, 33 (Jan. 5, 1927–28); "[W]e are old fashioned folks at Boston, and this Association must not forget one thing, that what is applicable to one section of the country is not applicable to another." Ibid. at 724, n. 51, quoting NHA, Report of the Fourth Annual Convention 24–5 (1897); "([C]ontaining a debate over grades that emphasizes the existence of regional differences)." Ibid. at 724, n. 51, summarizing NHA, Report of the Twenty-Eighth Annual Convention 68–72 (1921).

Bernstein does claim, at one point, to have evidence that even local (uniform) customs did not exist in the grain and feed industry, but the only evidence she cites is from the Minutes of Meetings, Secretary's Book, Nov. 9, 1896 (an unpublished book of clippings on file with Bernstein), in which the secretary apparently reports that the Illinois Grain Dealers' Association created trade rules, to, among other things, "establish and maintain uniformity in commercial usages as far as the grain trade is concerned." Ibid. at 726, n. 59. At best this evidence establishes that not all customs were uniform within the grain and feed industry in Illinois. But this claim is consistent with the existence of many important local customs in different geographic areas within the Illinois grain and feed industry, as well as with the existence of many uniform grain and feed customs within the state of Illinois. In sum, the same evidence that supports Bernstein's conclusion that no uniform industrywide standard for grades of hay existed also supports the existence of relatively clear local customary understandings.

On the other hand, Bernstein's evidence might be thought to be insufficiently representative even to ground the conclusion that local customs existed. Bernstein suggests as much when she notes that "there are also reasons to be skeptical about strong statements suggesting that local customs exist. If, for example, a transactor is arguing for adoption of a particular rule (especially one that is favorable to his locality rather than simply to a subset of firms in it), he might invoke the alleged universality of the practice in his locality to give his argument legitimacy and persuasive force." Ibid. at 719, n. 28. The problem is that Bernstein's evidence typically consists of the representations of only one merchant in each of various locales. If these representations cannot be taken at face value, then perhaps, as Bernstein argues here, they provide poor positive evidence of the existence of uniform local customs. But if this is so, statements indicating conflicting customs among different locales are poor evidence that national customs did not exist. Bernstein doubts the reliability of individual statements concerning the existence of local customs when such statements are invoked in support of the claim that local customs did exist. But to establish the nonexistence of nationally uniform customs, she relies almost entirely on individual reports of local customs to argue that customs varied among different locales. Bernstein cannot have it both ways.

20. See Clayton P. Gillette, *Harmony and Stasis in Trade Usages for International Sales,* 39 Va. J. Int'l L. 707, 710 n. 10 (1999).
21. See Samuel P. Hays, *The Response to Industrialism: 1885–1914* 10, 13 (2d ed. 1995); Robert H. Wiebe, *The Search for Order: 1877–1920* (1967); Robert William Fogel, *Railroads and American Economic Growth: Essays in Econometric History* 17–9 (1964) (patterns of agricultural distribution); Glenn Porter and Harold C. Livesay, *Merchants and Manufacturers* 154–65 (1971) (consumer goods markets).
22. See Harold Barger, *The Transportation Industries: 1889–1946,* 46–8 (1951).
23. For the oligopolistic motives for forming trade associations, see William H. Becker, *American Wholesale Hardware Trade Associations, 1870–1900,* 45 Bus. Hist. Rev. 179 (1971); Lance E. Davis, Jonathan R. T. Hughes and Duncan M. McDougall, *American Economic History* 289 (3d ed. 1969).

    Bernstein correctly notes that the codification efforts do not demonstrate the paucity of uniform national customs. There are a variety of important reasons for codifying even relatively clear and uniform customs. See *Questionable Empirical Basis,* supra n. 2, at 740, 742, n. 139.
24. Ibid., supra n. 2, at 12, n. 48.
25. Bernstein's extended discussion of the meaning of critical terms in hay contracts provides another illustration. She asserts that "[t]he debates surrounding the adoption and amendment of the hay rules also suggest that there were no agreed-upon usages in relation to some of the precise aspects of a standard transaction that the Code and its Official Comments explicitly direct courts to discern by reference to usage of trade or commercial standards." *Questionable Empirical Basis,* supra n. 2, at 721. Her first example is the Code rule providing that sellers have a "reasonable time" to deliver goods to the buyer in the absence of a contractual provision specifying otherwise. UCC § 2-309. The Code directs courts to consult usage of trade to determine what a reasonable time for delivery would be under a particular contract. Bernstein claims that the debates in the hay industry surrounding the adoption of a proposed rule specifying when certain freight charges had to be requested "reveals that there was no agreement as to what a reasonable time might be." Ibid. at 722.

    But Bernstein's evidence only weakly supports the claim that usages of trade did not exist to significantly constrain the allowable time for delivery even in hay contracts in the early part of the twentieth century, let alone in most current industries in contemporary times. First, she cites the NHA Report of the Sixteenth Annual Convention 220 (1909) to quote an individual who states the "word 'ample' [as used in a rule requiring 'ample margin'] may not have the same meaning in the minds of different people." Ibid. at 722, n. 39. But even if "ample margin" has "different meanings in the minds of different people," there may be significant overlap on clearly acceptable and clearly unacceptable cases outside of a grey area of disagreement. Usages of trade that delimit this range are useful for interpretive disputes that fall within the range of clear cases, even when they cannot resolve disputes within the grey area. Second, Bernstein quotes participants at the same convention reacting to a proposed rule that provides "[w]here sales are made on destination terms any claims that may arise, including those for shortage, damage, demurrage or over-charges in freight, must be made within ten day [sic] after arrival of property at point of final destination." NHA Report of the Sixteenth Annual Convention 214. After one participant proposes to replace the phrase "ten day" with "a reasonable time," another individual responds, that "that 'reasonable time' business will not [tell] anything. You might as well leave it out." Ibid. at 223. Bernstein quotes this participant's comment and also states that another "transactor proposed 'nine months,' another 'fifteen days,' and still another, 'within ten days after the freight bills have been paid.'" *Questionable Empirical Basis,* supra n. 2, at 722. But in fact the same participant who proposed the "nine month" amendment seconds later proposed the "fifteen day" amendment, after being accused, by the author of the "reasonable time" amendment, of not proposing the "nine month" amendment in good faith. NHA Report of the Sixteenth Annual Convention 223. Bernstein's description of the debate creates the misleading impression that two different participants proposed rules that differed by eight and one-half months, rather than a mere five days, and obscures the apparent underlying consensus that claims should be made within ten to fifteen days after the freight bills have been paid.

Third, and most important, the participants in the debates Bernstein cites were not directly addressing the question of whether customs for paying freight charges such as shortages existed in their states. Instead, they were proposing and reacting to proposed rules governing the payment of these charges. Their reactions reflected the different commercial realities in their locales that would affect the feasibility of meeting the proposed time deadline in each proposed rule (such as the amount of time between delivery and receipt of corrected freight charges in various locations). See ibid. at 221. Proposals for different rules need not reflect different local customs. Indeed, because one of the objectives of codification efforts is not only to codify but to change existing commercial practice, an inference from proposed rules to existing customs is particularly unwarranted.

Bernstein also quotes a participant at the NHA Report of the Twenty-Eighth Annual Convention 68 (1921) who states that "the words 'good color' might be stricken out and insert something which the inspector or shipper or buyer will know what it means." But Bernstein fails to note that the same individual goes on to propose in the place of "good color" the rule that "it shall be hay that shall contain not an undue amount of brown heads." Ibid. Thus, the same individual who thought the words "good color" were too indefinite apparently believed the words "undue amount" were not. Moreover, even when it is clear that the individuals speaking at this convention believed crucial terms in their industry, such as "well baled" and "good color," were vague, usage of trade might establish fairly clear ranges of acceptability and unacceptability under these terms.

Industry members, for example, might have been able to agree on many cases as either well baled or not well baled, or of good color or not, even if a significant range of disagreement over intermediate cases existed. In fact, after agreeing that the term "well baled" should be eliminated from the proposal at issue, one individual reasoned that the term could be eliminated on the ground that "[i]f the customer is not satisfied with the baling he need not buy." Ibid. If the range of reasonable disagreement over the quality of baling were not fairly narrow, a practice of allowing buyers unilaterally to reject delivered hay by claiming dissatisfaction with the baling would not be tolerable to sellers.

26. The title of Craswell's piece, "Do Trade Customs Exist?," suggests that he shares Bernstein's radical scepticism about the existence of what she calls "strong form" or "Hayekian" customs. But as Craswell notes in his opening line, he intends his title to be "semifacetious." *Trade Customs,* supra n. 2, at 1. Craswell's argument acknowledges the existence of custom but questions its utility for the purposes of contractual interpretation and gap-filling.
27. Ibid., supra n. 2, at 4. The bracketed words in the quoted passage reflect Craswell's analogous discussion of Barnett's fairness-based justification for incorporation. See ibid. 5–6.
28. Craswell claims that efficiency and fairness theorists share "the premise that customs can serve as a guide to something that courts would face great difficulty identifying on their own. But this argument has force only to the extent that the identification of customs places demands on courts that are less stringent than, or at least are different from, the demands courts would face if they tried to allocate risks based on their own nonlocalized judgments of fairness or efficiency." Ibid, supra n. 2, at 6.
29. As Craswell puts it:

> [I]f individual witnesses must draw on their own analysis of particular contexts, then they are providing an assessment that is not entirely different from what would be provided by any other expert whom a court might consult, such as an economist or a philosopher. The judgment of the industry expert might of course be either wiser or less wise than that of the outside economist or philosopher – but the comparison is still between two forms of individualized, case-by-case judgments. . . . Outside experts such as economists or philosophers will usually have a relatively explicit normative framework that enables them to recommend one outcome over another. By contrast, while industry experts may be *implicitly* making large numbers of trade-offs . . . , they often do so on an intuitive basis without any explicit normative framework.

Ibid., at 29.

Craswell continues: "[T]he view I advance here suggests that the choice is often between individual judgments that are made analytically, by outside experts; and individual judgments that are made instinctively, by industry practitioners." Ibid. at 31. Finally, in comparing the judgments of industry participants and experts, Craswell worries that, "[w]hen beliefs and values are allowed to remain intuitive, rather than being made explicit (and therefore subject to scrutiny), there is always a danger that the lack of explicit scrutiny will permit the survival of assessments that truly ought to become defunct." Ibid. at 31–32.

30. Ibid., at 29.

31. For a general discussion of how legal theorists must select the data to constrain their theories, see Jody S. Kraus, *Legal Theory and Contract Law, Philosophical Issues, Nous* (forthcoming).
32. See John Rawls, *Two Concepts of Rules,* 64 Phil. Rev. 3 (1955).
33. Bernstein calls these "relationship-preserving norms." See *Merchant Law,* supra n. 2, at 1796; See also Edward B. Rock and Michael L. Wachter, *The Enforceability of Norms and the Employment Relationship,* 144 U. Pa. L. Rev. 1913 (1996).
34. Bernstein calls these "end-game norms." See *Merchant Law,* supra n. 2, at 1796–7.
35. A usage of trade is "any practice or method of dealing having such regularity of observance . . . as to justify an expectation that it will be observed with respect to the transaction in question." UCC § 1-205(2). Section 1-205(2) requires that "[t]he existence and scope of such a usage are to be proved as facts." The Code commentary emphasizes that "[a] usage of trade . . . must have the 'regularity of observance' specified," and provides that "full recognition is thus available for new usages and for usages currently observed by the great majority of decent dealers." UCC § 1-205, com. 5.
36. "A course of dealing is a *sequence* of previous conduct between the parties to a particular transaction. . . ." UCC § 1-205(1) (emphasis added). "Course of dealing under subsection (1) is restricted, literally, to a *sequence* of conduct between the parties previous to the agreement." UCC § 1-205, com. 2 (emphasis added). "Where the contract for sale involves *repeated* occasions for performance by either party . . . any course of performance accepted or acquiesced in without objection shall be relevant to determine the meaning of the agreement." UCC § 2-208(1) (emphasis added). "A single occasion of conduct does not fall within the language of [the section defining course of performance]." UCC § 2-208, com. 4.
37. It is worth noting that the mere existence of a regularity of commercial behavior at odds with the plain meaning of a contractual term alone is no evidence of the existence of an informal norm. The behavior is equally consistent with the parties intending that the contract term be interpreted by their behavior under the contract, not by plain meaning. For instance, suppose the sales contract calls for delivery of "10 bushels of No. 1 wheat per month." Seller, having difficulty fulfilling all its orders, delivers eight bushels every previous month. Buyer does not complain. The question is whether the contract calls for delivery of ten bushels in a subsequent month. Delivery of eight bushels previously is equally consistent with the following two interpretations of the contract's quantity term: (1) "10 bushels" (which Buyer can insist on but has not to date); or (2) "10 bushels or 8 bushels when Seller has difficulty fulfilling its orders." Behavior inconsistent with the plain meaning of the quantity term does not show that an informal norm is operating.
38. See Larry E. Ribstein and Bruce H. Kobayashi, *An Economic Analysis of Uniform State Laws,* 25 J. Leg. Stud. 131, 150 (1998).
39. In some cases, it is difficult to conceive of a term's meaning without taking commercial context into account. For example, the term specifying the required weight of a good to be delivered pursuant to a sales of goods contract is unlikely to have a plain meaning precise enough to determine whether a tender must fall within grams, ounces, pounds, or tons of the stated weight. In such cases, the best method available to the contractors for determining the meaning of contract terms is to incorporate commercial practice. For example, we presume that in gold contracts, the gold delivered must fall within a much smaller range of the stated weight (e.g., within one gram) than coal delivered under a coal contract (e.g., within one ton). It may be plain to the contracting parties, as well as to any

reasonable third party, that a coal contract stating weight requirements in tons, and a gold contract stating weight requirements in grams, contemplate permissible weight tolerances in terms of tons and grams, respectively. But this is plain not because the meaning of these terms corresponds to a context-independent plain meaning, but rather because the meaning of these terms is made plain by the commercial context in which they are invoked. Indeed, we suspect that very few terms have a precise and unambiguous "plain meaning." When meaning seems clear, it is usually because context makes it so.

40. This is not to deny that courts sometimes must interpret contracts without the benefit of plain meaning or commercial practice. Our point is simply that parties would never plan, as their first-best option, to create express terms that cannot be interpreted in light of either plain meaning or commercial practice. If they intend to create a dual regime, they would utilize express terms with relatively clear and unambiguous plain meaning. Otherwise, they would utilize express terms interpreted in light of commercial practice. Because of its relative unpredictability, bare judicial construction would never be the preferred method of interpretation for rational contractors.

41. UCC § 2-208 provides some evidence that the Code in fact presumes regularities of conduct to evidence formal rather than informal norms. That provision directs courts to interpret the meaning of contract terms in light of certain regularities of conduct during the course of the contract's performance: "Where the contract for sale involves repeated occasions for performance by either party with knowledge of the nature of the performance and opportunity for objection to it by the other, any course of performance accepted or acquiesced in without objection shall be relevant to determine the meaning of agreement." UCC § 2-208(1). Comment 1 to UCC § 2-208 underscores this presumption: "The parties themselves know best what they have meant by their words of agreement and their action under that agreement is the best indication of what that meaning was." UCC § 2-208, comment 1. UCC § 2-208, comment 3 states that "[w]here it is difficult to determine whether a particular act merely sheds light on the meaning of the agreement or represents a waiver of a term of the agreement, the preference is in favor of 'waiver' whenever such construction . . . is needed to preserve the flexible character of commercial contracts and to prevent surprise and other hardship." One might argue that this comment suggests the Code presumes that regularities in conduct probably constitute informal, rather than formal, norms. However, the comment refers only to a single act, rather than a series of acts constituting a regularity of behavior.

42. Of course, it bears repeating that this conclusion is merely our speculation. The best evidence of the ratio of observable regularities of commercial behavior evidencing informal norms to those evidencing informal norms would be a direct empirical study. By providing evidence of this ratio, such a study would illuminate one of the most significant factors in determining the likelihood of erroneous incorporation of informal norms under the incorporation strategy.

43. Of course, the failure of a majority of contractors to create an alternative interpretive regime would not constitute evidence that such a regime is less efficient than the prevailing regime. Transition costs, network externalities, learning costs, and structural obstacles to collective action could explain why contractors might continue to utilize a less efficient regime even when the aggregate costs of creating and utilizing a more efficient regime would be exceeded by the benefits of such a regime. In contrast, overcoming these obstacles to create and utilize an alternative regime is fairly strong evidence that the regime is more efficient than the one it replaces.

44. See *Merchant Law,* supra n. 2.
45. Ibid. at 1766.
46. As Bernstein acknowledges, the NGFA system is narrowly tailored to the uniform and idiosyncratic needs of its members. For example, it is suitable only for transactions in which most significant contingencies are well known in advance, most contractual arrangements are simple, the benefits of national uniformity outweigh any advantages of local variance, and mitigation is typically simple and universally available. In addition, its trade rules and term definitions are custom-tailored for grain and feed transactions.
47. The classic encrustation critique is presented in Charles Goetz and Robert E. Scott, *The Limits of Expanded Choice: An Analysis of the Interaction between Express and Implied Contract Terms,* 73 Cal. L. Rev. 261 (1985). Encrustation describes two phenomena. The first is a status quo bias in favor of default terms. The status quo bias weights default terms by resolving ambiguities in the meaning of express terms to preserve the continued application of default terms to the contract. See Russell Korobkin, *The Status Quo Bias and Contract Default Rules,* 83 Cornell L. Rev. 608 (1998); Marcel Kahan and Michael Klausner, *Path Dependence in Corporate Contracting: Increasing Returns, Herd Behavior and Cognitive Bias,* 74 Wash. U. L. Q. 347, 359–62 (1996). The second is the reliance on precedent to determine the customary meaning of contract terms. This interpretive practice results in a failure to recognize changes in customary meaning. Because a decisionmaker can interpret express terms without consulting default rules while also not recognizing changes in commercial practice, this second kind of encrustation can occur without the first. Both kinds of encrustration lead to a failure to acknowledge clear efforts by contractors to opt out of default rules or (stale) custom.
48. See *Rethinking Uniformity,* supra n. 2.
49. Scott cites the rejection of Llewellyn's proposal to have merchant juries decide Article 2 disputes as a "drafting disaster," and identifies the requirement that Code sections be interpreted in light of the purposes underlying the Code itself as the principal source of interpretive error in Article 2. Ibid., at 40–1.
50. See UCC §§ 1-205(1) (course of dealing), 1-205(2) (usage of trade), and 2-208(1) (course of performance). The proposed revision of Article 2 increases the extent of incorporation by repealing current Article 2's interpretation of shipment terms. Proposed UCC § 2-319 instead requires that shipment terms be "interpreted in light of applicable usage of trade, or any course of performance or course of dealing between the parties." Revision of Uniform Commercial Code Article 2 – Sales § 2-319 (November 1999).
51. See UCC § 1-205 com. 1.
52. See UCC § 2-202 com. 2.
53. See UCC § 2-202. Section 1-205(2) requires the court to interpret written trade codes when they are established to embody relevant trade usage.
54. See, e.g., UCC § 1-205(2) (the allocation of issues of course of dealing and course of performance to the trier of fact is implicit).
55. See UCC § 1-205, com. 5.
56. See, e.g., UCC § 2-607(4) (accepting buyer has the burden of proving nonconformity in goods tendered), and UCC § 1-201(8) (defining "burden of establishing").
57. For instance, the UNIDROIT Principles for International Commercial Contracts includes trade usage as part of the parties' agreement, except when the usage is "unreasonable." See International Institute for the Unification of Private Law, UNIDROIT Principles for International Commercial Contracts art. 1.8(2) (1994). The exception in effect restricts

the sort of extrinsic evidence relevant to interpreting the express terms of the parties' agreement. And, of course, the restriction is itself vague and therefore potentially increases the rate of legal error in interpretation. This might make UNIDROIT's implementation of the incorporation strategy a bad one. But this fact does not undermine the incorporation strategy generally.

58. See Rochelle C. Dreyfuss, *Forums of the Future: The Role of Specialized Courts in Resolving Business Disputes,* 61 Brook L. Rev. 1 (1995); cf. Richard L. Revesz, *Specialized Courts and the Lawmaking System,* 138 U. Pa. L. Rev. 1111 (1990).
59. See Allen R. Kamp, *Uptown Act: A History of the Uniform Commercial Code: 1940–49,* 51 S. M. U. L. Rev. 275, 292–93 (1998); James Q. Whitman, *Commercial Law and the American Vol.: A Note on Llewellyn's German Sources for the Uniform Commercial Code,* 97 Yale L. J. 156 (1987); Zipporah Batshaw Wiseman, *The Limits of Vision: Karl Llewellyn and the Merchant Rules,* 100 Harv. L. Rev. 520 (1987).
60. See, e.g., Julia A. Martin, *Arbitrating in the Alps Rather Than Litigating in Los Angeles: International Intellectual Property-Specific Alternative Dispute Resolution,* 49 Stan. L. Rev. 917, 926 n. 45 (1997); A. W. B. Simpson, *The Origins of Futures Trading in the Liverpool Cotton Market,* in *Essays for Patrick Atiyah* 179, 183 (P. Cane and J. Stapleton, eds., 1991).
61. Although Article 2 in principle allows for expert testimony to establish the existence and content of commercial norms, it is surprisingly rare. See Imad D. Abyad, *Commercial Reasonableness in Karl Llewellyn's Uniform Commercial Code Jurisprudence,* 83 Va. L. Rev. 429 (1997); compare Conference of Commissioners on Uniform State Laws, Report on the Second Draft of the Revised Uniform Sales Act, 1 *Uniform Commercial Code Drafts* 281, 335 (E. S. Kelly, ed., 1984) (comment to section 1-D considering whether formal statements of usage by merchant organizations should create a presumption of the background understanding of terms).
62. The restriction risks error when the forms do not reflect changes in trade usage. Standard forms in the grain trade apparently are slow to react to changes in shipping practices; see Albert Slabotzky, *Grain Contracts and Arbitration* 15–6 (1984); cf. Raj Bhala, *Self-Regulation in Global Electronic Markets through Reinvigorated Trade Usages,* 31 Idaho L. Rev. 863, 907–8 (1995) (same for currency "switches").
63. See UCC § 1-205, com. 5; cf. Levie, supra n. 18.
64. See *Rethinking Uniformity,* supra n. 2. An alternative speculation is that encrustation is the result of doctrinal devices such as precedent or the taking of judicial notice about commercial practice. Encrustation may have no statutory genesis. For the operation of judicial notice of trade usage under pre-Code law, see Note, *Custom and Trade Usage: Its Application to Commercial Dealings and the Common Law,* 55 Colum. L. Rev. 1192, 1201, 1203 (1955); cf. *Stoltz, Wagner and Brown v. Duncan,* 417 F. Supp. 552, 559 (W.D. Okl. 1976).
65. See, e.g., Convention on Contracts for the International Sale of Goods, art. 7(2), supra n. 1; UNCITRAL Model Law on Electronic Commerce, art. 3(2) (1997), U.N. Doc. A/51/628 (1996); Draft Uniform Rules on Assignment of Receivables Financing, art. 8, U.N. Doc. A/CN.9/WG.II/Wp.9323 (1997); Model Law on Legal Aspects of Electronic Data Interchange and Related Means of Communication, art. 3(2), U.N. Doc. A/CN.9/426 (1996); UNIDROIT, UNIDROIT Convention on International Financial Leasing, art. 6 (1988); 27 Int'l Legal Mat. 931 (1988); UNIDROIT Convention on

International Factoring, art. 4, 27 Int'l Legal Mat. 943 (1988), Proposed UNIDROIT Convention on International Interests in Mobile Equipment (tent. draft, Nov. 1997).

66. See Robert D. Cooter, *Decentralized Law for a Complex Economy: The Structural Approach to Adjudicating the New Law Merchant,* 144 U. Pa. L. Rev. 1643 (1996); Robert D. Cooter, *Structural Adjudication and the New Law Merchant: A Model of Decentralized Law,* 14 Int'l Rev. L. and Econ. 215 (1994).
67. See Robert Sugden, *A Theory of Focal Points,* 105 Econ. J. 533 (1995); Michael Bacharach, *Variable Universe Games* 255, in *Frontiers of Game Theory* (K. Binmore et al., eds., 1993).
68. Cf. UCC § 2-316(2) (statutorily described warranty disclaimer language is sufficient to disclaim implied warranties of merchantability); Robert K. Rasmussen, *Debtor's Choice: A Menu Approach to Corporate Bankruptcy,* 71 Texas L. Rev. 51 (1992).

Index

For EU product safety concerns, contact us at Calle de José Abascal, 56–1°, 28003 Madrid, Spain or eugpsr@cambridge.org.

www.ingramcontent.com/pod-product-compliance
Lightning Source LLC
LaVergne TN
LVHW090320210926
848480LV00001B/303
* 9 7 8 0 5 2 1 0 3 8 7 6 8 *